ESSENTIAL
WHOLENESS

*Integral Psychotherapy, Spiritual
Awakening, and the Enneagram*

ERIC LYLESON

BALBOA.
PRESS
A DIVISION OF HAY HOUSE

Balboa Press books may be ordered through booksellers or by contacting:

Balboa Press
A Division of Hay House
1663 Liberty Drive
Bloomington, IN 47403
www.balboapress.com
1 (877) 407-4847

Because of the dynamic nature of the Internet, any web addresses or links contained in this book may have changed since publication and may no longer be valid. The views expressed in this work are solely those of the author and do not necessarily reflect the views of the publisher, and the publisher hereby disclaims any responsibility for them.

The author of this book does not dispense medical advice or prescribe the use of any technique as a form of treatment for physical, emotional, or medical problems without the advice of a physician, either directly or indirectly. The intent of the author is only to offer information of a general nature to help you in your quest for emotional and spiritual well-being. In the event you use any of the information in this book for yourself, which is your constitutional right, the author and the publisher assume no responsibility for your actions.

Any people depicted in stock imagery provided by Thinkstock are models, and such images are being used for illustrative purposes only.
Certain stock imagery © Thinkstock.

Print information available on the last page.

ISBN: 978-1-4525-2820-5 (sc)
ISBN: 978-1-4525-2821-2 (e)

Balboa Press rev. date: 05/06/2015

CONTENTS

Acknowledgements.. vii

Preface ix

Chapter 1   Being and Becoming... 1
Chapter 2   Mapping Evolution 27
Chapter 3   How Living Systems Evolve 47
Chapter 4   The Birth to Infancy Developmental Cycle 77
Chapter 5   Network of PsychoLogical Domains............................... 103
Chapter 6   Essential Qualities 139
Chapter 7   The Systemic Change Cycle 183
Chapter 8   The Hero's Journey and Buddha's Awakening 237
Chapter 9   Compulsions of Personality... 279

      • Personality Type NINE 289
      • Personality Type ONE.. 300
      • Personality Type TWO...310
      • Personality Type THREE 320
      • Personality Type FOUR..331
      • Personality Type FIVE... 343
      • Personality Type SIX..353
      • Personality Type SEVEN 365
      • Personality Type EIGHT 375

References 389

Acknowledgements

I would like to thank all the people that inspired this book and helped bring it to print. Many thanks to Lisa Peers, Shelley Kenigsberg, Anasaskia Elsom and Richard Chambers for your assistance with the editing and your uplifting encouragement. Thanks Eva Kiss for your assistance with the diagrams.

I feel deep appreciation for all the psychotherapists that have been inspired by Milton Erickson, MD with whom I have been fortunate to train with: Stephen Gilligan, Ernest Rossi, John Grinder, Bill O'Hanlon, Jeff Zeig and John Weakland. Each in their own way instilled in me a curiosity about the patterns that underlie effective psychotherapy and how people change.

It was in a class with Enneagram teacher Lawrence Graziose that I had my first insight into this new understanding of the Enneagram. I am grateful to all the great contributors to the Enneagram community whom I have trained with and/or studied their work in depth: Helen Palmer, Russ Hudson, Don Riso, Tom Condon, David Daniels, A. H. Almaas, and Eli Jaxon Bear. I want to give special thanks to Eli and his wife Gangaji for also being directly instrumental in my spiritual awakening.

I am eternally grateful for my other primary spiritual teachers Tash Tachibana, Marianne Williamson, Lama Ole Nydahl, Lama Lobsang Tendar and Adyashanti for helping me to awaken to my essential wholeness.

A special thanks to my friends and colleagues Rick Hanson, Peter Chown and Lionel Davis for giving me the respected feedback needed to keep me going in times of uncertainty.

PREFACE

Astrophysicists tell us the universe has been expanding at an accelerating pace ever since the Big Bang. Biologists tell a long and convoluted story of the evolution of life in which humans finally enter the scene on the last page of the last chapter. Buddhists say that although our essential nature is eternal, our relative nature is impermanent. Change in modern society is faster than ever before and it is accelerating. Never before has it been so imperative for people to know how to ride the waves of change.

As a psychotherapist, I see my role as an agent of change, as much of human suffering comes from the inability to cope with change. My aim is to help those suffering to cope with change and proactively make the changes they are ready for. When I began teaching psychotherapy a little over twenty years ago, I sensed that in order for psychotherapists to be effective agents of transformation, it was vital to be able to describe how people change. Yet what were the steps those wanting help needed to take to achieve change, and how could we guide people through those steps?

My initial strategies included a four-phase model, but it became obvious it was inadequate; that is, until I went to a weekend seminar on a modality called the Enneagram. The teacher was giving a brief overview of the nine personality types, elaborating number by number around a circle, when I realized the essential qualities of each type were the qualities universally utilized in nine phases of a cycle of change.

Since humanity is a mere thread in the web of life, the validity of this pattern depends on it accurately describing not only how humans change, but all living systems. I had some background in living systems models from my training in family therapy and Systems Theory. However, these new insights led to more extensive research into the theories of evolutionary biology. In addition to the modern powerful scientific stories of evolution and development, it struck me that people have been telling stories of transformation since the advent of language.

The renowned mythologist Joseph Campbell collated many myths from cultures around the globe in his seminal work, *The Hero with a Thousand Faces*. I knew I was on to something big when the phases of personal transformation that he refers to as the Hero's Journey had a direct correlation with how biologists describe the evolution of life from the most simple to the most complex organisms.

Essential Wholeness offers a unique perspective on the Enneagram. I present the Enneagram symbol as a model of the underlying patterns that connect our knowledge of psychology, biology, physics, mythology and spirituality. Unlike other books that show the Enneagram in a static two-dimensional way, this book will broaden your perspective into an expanding multidimensional model, much like a three-dimensional spiral. With the right mathematics, it might be represented as a fractal.

This new perspective starts with an explanation of my understanding of what it is to be a healthy, whole human being; a being with a full spectrum of resources to draw upon. It shows how our personal experiences are inextricably woven into the evolving web of life. I illuminate how the compulsions of personality, those areas where we get stuck in maladaptive patterns, occur simply when we aren't embracing our essentially whole true nature.

The life of a psychologically healthy person can be seen as a journey down a river from the headwaters to the sea. Getting caught in the compulsions of a personality type is like being stuck in an eddy—even a whirlpool—somewhere along the way. For whatever reasons, people get stuck in vicious cycles that keep them from the natural flow of growth and change.

I don't spend much time describing the whirlpool-like compulsions of personality, covered eloquently in other books; rather, I describe the universal patterns of the river of life and provide strategies and guides for how to honor them more fully.

"Science without religion is lame," said Albert Einstein. And then added, "Religion without science is blind." This book draws together several major disciplines and articulates the nine developmental phases that all living systems go through. It draws on cutting-edge insights from evolutionary biology, as well as chaos, self-organization and living systems theories, whilst interweaving them with modern psychology and non-dualistic spirituality, such as Buddhism.

Like ecology in the natural world, which recognizes the value of diversity within a cooperative system, this new psychological paradigm helps us integrate the vast inner diversity of perspectives and motivations that make us human. We learn to appreciate not only the deep ecology of nature to which we belong, but also how the threads of understanding from various perspectives weave together in an evolving deep ecological tapestry of human consciousness. With the massive environmental challenges that face us, such as climate change and mass extinction of species, we can't afford to ignore the inter-connected circular laws of cause and effect.

The cyclical model of the Enneagram described in this book helps us realize the environmental, sociological, psychological and spiritual ramifications of our decisions and actions. The clear guidelines can help people from many different walks of life learn how to live more harmoniously with one another, themselves, and all creatures.

Essential Wholeness explores human development from biological, psychological, sociological, narrative, mythological and spiritual perspectives and reveals the deep underlying patterns that connect these diverse disciplines. My approach draws on the method illuminated in the classic Indian fable of six blind men and an elephant. When each blind man is asked to describe a different part of the object they are near, they have only their sense of touch with which to paint a picture. As each describes accurately what they are feeling: a tree trunk, a rope, and so on, we gain a fuller understanding of the 'elephant' from the composite picture. Similarly, as we describe the process of life and what it is to be human from these various perspectives, we can gain a fuller understanding of the process of being human.

To the untrained eye, computer generated pictures may look like one-dimensional images. However, when we focus on these images differently, they expand into three-dimensional landscapes. If we look at the Enneagram as a map of evolution, it allows us to see both the ecological niche of each personality type within humanity, as well as understanding our ego-identity and other aspects of our psyche within the wholeness of our Being.

The qualities that describe each of the personality types explained in the Enneagram are not just the domain of individual type, or the types that are related in some way, but together describe what it is to be a whole person. We will discover that it is through embracing our *essential wholeness*, that we embrace our *holiness* and more fully experience our oneness with all of creation.

Currently the Enneagram has yet to be accepted by the academic establishment. However, there are some eminent scholars who have been integral to my understanding and fascination with the system. Professor David Daniels, MD Clinical Professor at Stanford Medical School, has spent much of his career studying and teaching it, and more recently Daniel Siegel the renowned Clinical Professor of Psychiatry at UCLA has been pressing for more research to be done on what millions of readers of the popular literature have been benefitting from since the 1960s. I hope this book can help bring the Enneagram more into the mainstream of psychology.

I am confident that after reading this book, you will gain a deeper trust in your essential wholeness and your natural inclination to evolve over time.

CHAPTER ONE

Being and Becoming

Whether prompted by marveling at a photograph of earth from space, or reading theories of modern physics, or even coming to understand the wisdom of ancient traditions, more and more people are recognizing the innate interconnectedness of all things.

Essential Wholeness presents a psychology that reflects the interdependent nature of life. Do you wonder if humanity will survive the suicidal-like destruction of ecosystems, or the threats posed by weapons of mass destruction and terrorism? Western civilization has proven its cleverness to maximize materialistic prosperity in the short-term. However, faced with mass extinctions, erosion and degradation of the soil that feeds us, and a society that is increasingly violent, depressed and addicted, this way of life would appear not to be sustainable, let alone fulfilling.

If we are to create a healthier ecological, sustainable and fulfilling future, it's imperative we discover how to change the ways of thinking that perpetuate problems.

We are rapidly moving from the technological/information age to the biological age. We are learning that to survive and thrive we must honor and harness nature's wisdom and ability to evolve in the face of challenging and diverse circumstances. Should we fail in learning to live harmoniously with nature, we may very well follow in the footsteps of dinosaurs.

To live in harmony with nature, we must live in harmony with our own true natures. If we are to live in peace with one another, we must be at peace within ourselves. It is the role of psychotherapy to help people

1

find this harmony and peace so we can transform our relationships with ourselves, one another and nature.

'You are perfect as you are and you will never be perfect.' Being at peace with now and always becoming more into our full potential. Reality is as it is now and it can never be any different than it is now, yet concurrently everything is always evolving and changing. This paradox is one of the cornerstones of psychotherapy and spiritual development. Some approaches emphasize the ability to change and others emphasize the acceptance of what is; however, they are inextricably linked to one another. The more you accept yourself exactly as you are the more you recognize the ever-changing nature of life. The more you recognize and accept the impermanent nature of existence, the more you become aware of the changeless awareness of *being* within which everything is experienced. With the recent emphasis on evidence-based psychotherapy, discussions on the role of spirituality within mainstream psychotherapy have been relatively quiet compared to the human potential movement of the sixties and seventies. This is changing with the blossoming of mindfulness-based therapies and Acceptance and Commitment Therapy (ACT),[1] which draw heavily on Buddhist teachings. Psychology has strived to treat people's suffering by merely treating their symptoms. Whilst this is very important, in the process of doing so it has identified with an allopathic medicine paradigm. As a result, therapists are implored to do whatever is necessary to help a person return to functioning in their life as quickly as possible. A more wholistic approach would help people question the basic assumptions and lifestyles that perpetuate psychological suffering, and then explore an approach to life that is more in harmony with their true nature.

Our true nature may not be suited to the type of life we have been attempting to fit into. Our suffering is a wakeup call on a heroic journey to a more meaningful life, and the life that is trying to emerge will somehow contribute to a better life for others.

An Integration of Approaches

The new wave of approaches integrating mindfulness with proven therapeutic methods has begun to address this inadequacy. There are additional therapeutic methods that can deepen and broaden this integration and help people connect with the essential qualities of *being*, while trusting more fully in people's ability to change and grow.

There are four basic paths to psychotherapeutic integration. A *common factors* approach emphasizes therapeutic actions that have been demonstrated to be effective, yet are presented in slightly differently ways in different models[2]. *Technical eclecticism* looks "to improve our ability to select the best treatment for the person and the problem...guided primarily by data on what has worked best for others in the past".[3] A third model of *theoretical integration* focuses on combining and synthesizing a small number of theories at a deep level, whereas others describe the relationship between several therapeutic modalities.[4] With *assimilative integration*, the clinician has a firm grounding in one system of psychotherapy, yet is willing to incorporate or assimilate perspectives or practices from other schools of thought.[5]

Ken Wilber, in his comprehensive attempt to define an integral psychology, starts with one major rule:

> Everybody is right. More specifically, everybody—including me—has some important pieces of truth, and all of those pieces need to be honored, cherished, and included in a more gracious, spacious, and compassionate embrace... But every approach, I honestly believe, is essentially true but partial, true but partial, true but partial.[6]

In studying and applying spiritual teachings and psychotherapeutic methods to my own life and through assisting my clients, I have sought to understand what works best with whom and why.

As psychotherapy has evolved, the gap between the field of spiritual enquiry and psychotherapy has narrowed. I feel the gaps exists due to major differences in the contexts in which spiritual enquiry and psychotherapy are set and in the jargon each uses. This book is the result of following the four paths of integration through the learning and application of various psychotherapeutic orientations including: Ericksonian Hypnosis and Psychotherapy, Neurolinguistic Programming (NLP), Acceptance and Commitment Therapy (ACT), Self Relations Therapy, Solution

Focused Therapy, Systemic Family Therapy, Narrative Therapy, Gestalt Therapy, Cognitive Behavioral Therapy (CBT), Somatic Psychotherapies, Emotional Freedom Technique (EFT), Thought Field Therapy(TFT), NeuroSemantics and Jungian Psychotherapy.

My exploration in the field of psychotherapy has coincided with my journeying through the three schools of Buddhism: Hinayana, Mahayana and Vajrayana. I've been an avid student of *A Course in Miracles*, been touched deeply by the teachings of Carlos Castaneda, Osho, Adyashanti and, in the Advaita Vedanta tradition, Ramana Maharshi, Gangaji and Eli Jaxon Bear. In addition, when I was young, I was confirmed within the Lutheran Church and served as an altar boy.

Most teachings on the Enneagram do their best to describe a coherent integration of modern psychology with traditional spiritual teachings, usually from mystical Christian, Sufi and/or Buddhist perspectives. Like Wilbur, in this book I build on the foundations of all of these spiritual and psychotherapeutic traditions, and try to articulate what the common factors are, the most accurate descriptions and useful methods, and how they all fit into an integrated model.

In my study of Buddhism, I noted that Buddha, like a skilled psychotherapist, understood that different people require different teachings and methods to free themselves from suffering and realize their potential.

While the three major vehicles for realization are Hinayana, Mahayana and Vajrayana, most Buddhist and Western psychotherapy integrations appear to be drawn primarily from the Hinayana and Mahayana traditions. However, the deeper teachings of the Vajrayana school provide an opportunity to help people realize the fullness of their deeper nature by directing their attention, not only to the objects of mindfulness (breath, body sensations, emotions, thoughts and external sensory perceptions), but also towards *that* which is noticing all those things.

As Lama Ole Nydahl says, "The radiance of mind itself is much richer than the conditioned experiences of joy we all strive for. The best moments in life are actually gifts and appear when beings forget themselves. There are situations where feelings of separation disappear, like being in the arms of our loved ones; the timeless moment of 'being one'."[7] As Sogyal Rinpoche says, "Meditation is the mind turned inward, resting in its own true nature."[8] Or, as Ramana Maharshi said when speaking on working with the mind, "Let what comes come, let what goes go; find out what remains." I like to add, "And rest as that."

In his explorations into the nature of consciousness, psychiatrist Milton Erickson discovered for himself and passed on to his clients the experience of "being nobody, doing nothing, in the middle of nowhere." This is the experience of what Almaas refers to as the void, or the Buddhists refer to as Nirvana. It occurs when you go into deep sleep, but you're not awake to notice. It is what Ken Wilber refers to as the *causal realm* or the *One Taste*. That formless space of awareness is always present whether we are awake, asleep, dreaming, aware of our senses or engaged in thinking. In mindfulness approaches, it is what we are learning to perceive from when we allow everything to be as it is.

In searching for what relieves suffering and what helps people realize their potential, many therapists have recognized the importance of helping people access the essential ground of *being*. Neurolinguistic Programming (NLP) is an integration of approaches, which grew from modeling the work of psychotherapists Milton Erickson, Fritz Perls, Virginia Satir and linguist Noam Chomsky. NLP-trained Brandon Bays[9] has created a therapy known as *The Journey*, which guides people to the qualities of *being* through the direct experience of emptiness, using what NLP calls *Drop Through Technique*.[10] Very similar work is described in The Void, by A.H. Almaas.[11] Connie Ray Andreas[12] developed an NLP technique of accessing core states of *being* by dialoging with alienated parts of one's psyche.

Spirit and Matter

There is form and there is formlessness, otherwise known as matter and spirit. We call ourselves human beings. Our humanity is the world of form, of things coming into existence and going out of existence. Our body comes and goes, our activities come and go and our thoughts and feelings come and go. All the comings and goings of our lives happen in the pregnant space of existence, sometimes referred to as emptiness. In Sanskrit, it is called Shunyata and in other traditions Presence, Spirit or Being. It is the ground of awareness. It is not personal; it is universal.

Gregory Bateson described Mind as being immanent, not located in individual; rather, individual consciousness is located in an intelligent self-organizing field.[13] In Buddhism, emptiness is not a void in the sense of being nothingness. It is the infinite; it is the field of infinite possibilities out of which all form arises and dissolves into. Just as the outer world has arisen out of emptiness with the Big Bang, so also do our inner worlds of thoughts, feelings, imaginings, and so forth, arise out of and dissolve back into the empty space of *being*. There is no essential difference between inner space and outer space. It is all the same *beingness*. If the wholeness of *being* is like the ocean, then the waves of our separate sense of self arise on the surface of the ocean before dissolving back into the ocean, yet at no time are they separate from the ocean.

Human beings, like all other forms of the universe, are constantly coming into form. We play around for a while before dissolving, dying or disintegrating. All forms are impermanent and always changing, evolving or falling into decay, whereas the space in which all this occurs remains unchanged. We have a sense of this on a personal level when we open our eyes in the morning. There is a sense that whatever is looking out through our eyes, listening through our ears and sensing through all our senses is the same as when we were young, even if the eyes or ears, for example, aren't as effective as they once were, or the world we see all around us has changed. In ACT, this is referred to as 'self-as-context' or 'transcendent sense of self'.[14] Psychiatrist and interpersonal neurobiologist, Dan Siegel refers to it as 'the hub of mind, which offers a ground of *being*'.[15]

It would appear that the essence of the emptiness of being in human form and the essence of the universe as a whole have inherent qualities. As the great Tibetan Buddhist lama, the late 16th Karmapa said, "Every atom vibrates with joy and is held together by love."[16] The universe has a self-organizing wisdom that is inherently playful and caring. It looks after itself in ways that are loving, lovely and wondrous. In Christian terms, this same statement would be that God is love, and is everywhere and in everything.

Body, Mind, Soul and Spirit

Essential wholeness is the sum total of what it is to be a human being. We are human and we are *being*. Our essential wholeness includes body, mind, soul and spirit, what is changing and what is unchanging. What is changing is like an ecosystem. As human animals we are imbedded in and dependent on the rest of nature. Our wellbeing as humans is dependent on living in harmony with our own nature, which is at one with all of nature. We are also Being. Our deepest nature is spirit or pure awareness. There is only one spirit, which is the unified field of energy and information out of which all of creation arises and disappears back into.

The bridge between spirit and body is soul. Soul allows us to experience the connection to spirit and the rest of creation. It is soul that awakens to its true spiritual nature while manifesting full creative potential through the human mind and body.

Mahayana Buddhism refers to these three aspects. Dharmakaya or spirit is the Absolute, the unified and unmanifested essence of the universe. Sambhogakaya or soul is what is in the process of realising enlightenment through spiritual practice. In Eastern traditions, it is what reincarnates for lifetime to lifetime. Nirmanakaya is the body that appears in the world. Dharmakaya, spirit, is like the atmosphere; sambhogakaya, soul, is like clouds; and nirmanakaya, body, is like rain. Clouds are a manifestation of atmosphere that enables rain. These dimensions are sometimes referred to as causal, subtle and gross. They are present in deep, dreamless sleep and silent meditation (dharmakaya); dreaming, imagination and trance (sambhokaya); and ordinary waking consciousness (nirmanakaya). The unified field of these dimensions is referred to as Svabhavikakaya. I like to refer to that as *essential wholeness*.

The self-concept or ego is identified with the body and its primary focus is on our survival by satisfying our instinctual drives. The Enneagram system traditionally recognizes three basic human instincts: self-preservation, social and sexual. In other words, focusing on survival of the body with food, shelter, and so forth; survival of and within society; and survival of the species through procreation.

The ego is a collection of habitual beliefs and behaviors that dictate how one survives by acquiring things, our place in the group and sex.

Healthy egos, thanks to prompting from the soul, evolve over time and coincide with changes in how we relate to our survival. A healthy ego is going to have different concerns at eighty years old than it did at fifteen.

The development of healthy egos has historically been the focus of most psychotherapy. Symptoms usually arise in our lives when our egoic self-concept is more concerned about its own survival, even than the survival and wellbeing of the body. For example, if I identify with being the kind of person that thinks my career and money are the most important things for my survival, and consequently use most of my social relationships merely to further my career, I may find myself in the therapist's office wondering why I'm depressed. In the process of therapy, I will understand that I've been ignoring my developmental needs for friendship and sexual fulfilment.

The soul is the realm of the unconscious and what Jung referred to as the *collective unconscious*. It is the realm of archetypes and myths that inform and organize our human existence. At the most basic level we can think of soul as the universal laws that govern a self-organising universe.

Biochemist Rupert Sheldrake coined the term 'morphic field' as that which organizes the characteristic structure and pattern of activity in systems and their members. Soul manifests at different levels. There is the individual soul, the soul of a family, a soul of an organization, a soul of a nation and the soul of the planet. There are individual souls nested in collective souls. This mirrors the way life is organised, with cells within bodies, bodies within communities, within ecosystems, and so on.

Tibetan Buddhism urges us to take refuge in the Buddhas of the three times and ten directions. I believe this most aptly refers to accessing resources in the sambhogakaya or the dimension of soul. Buddha, in this content, refers to the mind's full potential. The three times are past, present and future. The ten directions refer to all of space. In other words, it is the ability to realize our full potential in infinite time and space. In the dimension of soul, which we experience through imagination, memory and our sensing of now, the past, present and future all exist simultaneously. This is why we can be feeling emotions in this present time and location in reference to a past event in a particular place, while planning for a future when we'll be in another place experiencing something completely different. Effective psychotherapy helps people travel to other times and places, whilst utilizing different archetypal intelligences to live a healthier or more soulful life now and in the future.

Demons Becoming Allies

It is also suggested we take refuge in the dharma, the realized sangha, the yidams and the wisdom protectors. Dharma translates as 'the way things are' or the truth. In other words, to let go of any concepts that would blind us to the way things actually are. The realized sangha is like the collective unconscious wisdom that has been realized by those who have come before us. Yidams are archetypal images that represent essential qualities of soul like compassion, wisdom, healing, and so forth. Wisdom protectors are those wrathful looking deities; it is my understanding that they were once demons that became enlightened and serve to protect the truth. We can think of them as the wisdom of the soul that presents itself as demons, creating problems and challenges that force us to more fully realize our essential wholeness, or else suffer. Milton Erickson, M.D., who became a prolific writer and master communicator, was so dyslexic that he didn't realize the dictionary was alphabeticalized until he was fifteen. This meant that whenever looking for a word, he began at the beginning or end of the dictionary and continued reading until he found the word. When it finally dawned on him, Milton thanked his subconscious that had tricked him into studying so thoroughly. In some Native American philosophy, this aspect of the soul is referred to as the trickster coyote. Illness serves the soul's agenda.

Effective psychotherapy helps people to be honest with themselves, to tune into their unconscious wisdom, or even read wisdom books. It utilizes and helps people access states and meta-states (how we feel about how we feel) that transform their perceptions and deconstruct problematic repeating patterns, allowing them to learn the lessons their soul is trying to teach them. An Ericksonian therapist will even set up ordeals to help their clients grow.

A healthy ego serves soul, which in turn serves spirit. Opening to soul is often experienced as a loss of identity for the ego. Opening to spirit is often experienced as a loss of the sense of individual identity for the soul.

In our essential wholeness, we are spirit experiencing soulful existence in human form.

Most often in life, the soul looks after the body; however, there are times when the soul may demand that the body be sacrificed for a greater purpose. Martin Luther King, Jesus, Amelia Earhart, or a mother sacrificing her own life to save her child's, could be examples of this. A healthy ego listens to the body as a way of staying in touch with the soul.

Separation and Identity

Anxieties, frustrations, insecurities, resentments, or even the simple discontent that drives most people's lives, are caused by the separation from our essential nature that occurs by the holding onto a solid, permanent sense of self.

This sense of an isolated 'me' is created and maintained by beliefs and consequent perceptions that leave 'me' feeling incomplete and the world, not as it should be. There seems to be a separation from one's essential wholeness and the rest of reality. To cope with this sense of incompleteness, we identify with a particular set of internal and external conditions. For example, if I identify myself as a confident, successful businessman and happily married husband then as long as business is good and the marriage appears good enough, everything seems okay. However, seeing myself as confident and successful can have the tendency to blind me to my weaknesses and failings. The same occurs in my marriage; to maintain a fixed notion of myself as a happily married husband, I need to ignore any signs of unhappiness in my marriage.

Having to hold onto and try to validate a positive self-concept is only necessary if we have a negative self-concept. When resting in the ground of being, there is an unconditional acceptance of the way things are. There is no need to define oneself in a static way, rather we are free to respond to life in whatever way is most useful. With no self-concept we are free. Negative concepts of one's self appear to be part of living in a world that believes that love and happiness are things that are earned rather than what we are.

Developing a self-concept is a normal part of human development. As children we are taught that we should know who we are. Given that most people are acting like they know who they are, we seek to define ourselves in specific ways. However, when we look within to find ourselves, there is nothing permanent there. In the backdrop of ever-changing thoughts and images is the silent emptiness of *being*. To a mind looking for some permanent sense of self, this emptiness is frightening and becomes the basis of thinking, 'I'm nothing and nobody.' Within the frame of mind that believes, 'I have to earn love and happiness', the sense of nothingness is interpreted as not being deserving of love and happiness. This drives one to try and create a self-image that one thinks is deserving of love and happiness.

As Dan Siegel says, "People do have neural propensities––called temperament––that may be somewhat but not fully changeable."[17] He goes onto to say, "No system of adult personality description that exists (except the Enneagram popular version) has an internally focused organization–– that is, a view of how the internal architecture of mental functioning, not just behavior, is organized across developmental periods."[18]

Let's look at some ways this architecture is organized in the Enneagram of personality types. It describes nine basic ways (temperaments) people try to create and hold onto a sense of self that is deserving of love and happiness. This begins early in childhood.

Type ONEs try to prove what perfect and responsible people they are.
Type TWOs try to prove what indispensible and caring people they are.
Type THREEs try to prove what capable and charming people they are.
Type FOURs try to prove what unique and deep feeling people they are.
Type FIVEs try to prove what intelligent and self-sufficient people they are.
Type SIXes try to prove what loyal and nonthreatening people they are.
Type SEVENs try to prove what happy and positive people they are.
Type EIGHTs try to prove what powerful and masterful people they are.
Type NINEs try to prove what peaceful and selfless people they are.

Essential Qualities of Being

People only need to prove themselves when they lose touch with their Essential Wholeness. The ground of our Essential Wholeness is what Buddhism refers to as emptiness. The emptiness of *being* is not nothing; it is just *not* a *thing*. All things come and go. *Being* is the ground within which

11

all objects of perception, including states of mind, come and go. It only seems like nothingness when our consciousness has separated itself from *being* and is trapped in the conceptual mind, emotional states or fixation with the objects of our senses. That emptiness is actually fullness of *being*, which is essentially loving and wise.

Tibetan Buddhist art visually represents the qualities of *being* with an array of Buddha and other deity images, be they peaceful, wrathful or compassionate. In Buddhist terms, Buddha is another name for our true nature. The arrays of Buddhist deities are symbolic representations of how our true nature can manifest. Many meditations in the various Buddhist traditions involve visualizing the deity and either receiving blessing of these qualities or becoming the deity for a period of time. However, in the completion phase, the meditator and the visualization all dissolve into the infinite emptiness that contains everything.

The Enneagram figure can also be thought of as a representation of the way things are. The circle represents wholeness and it is essentially empty or can be called clear light. The wholeness is then divided into nine aspects. If the whole of *being* is clear light, when form manifests out of emptiness, it can be seen in nine different hues. This is similar to white light being divided up along a continuum into seven colors after passing through a prism.

In his book *Pearl Beyond Price*, an integration of spirituality and psychotherapy, A.H. Almaas[19] delineates nine essential qualities of *being*: Consciousness, Compassion, Strength, Forgiveness, Space, Acceptance, Joy, Will, and Peace. These qualities are merely different faces of love and what are sometimes referred to as qualities of soul. Although not spoken about anywhere in the Enneagram literature, these qualities correlate with the Enneagram personality types. Each type favors and overly identifies with an idea of the essential quality, which separates them from the actual experience of the wholeness and emptiness of *being*. Only our ego, with its concepts of itself as separate from the wholeness of *being*, needs to search for or grasp at that which we are imagining ourselves separate from.

People with type ONE personality identify with consciousness. To prove they are conscious, this type develops a super ego that is overly self-conscious and critical. They try too hard to do things right and, in that effort, lose touch with the wholeness that can do things more effortlessly in flow.

People with type TWO personality identify with compassion. To prove they are compassionate, Type TWO people take pride in thinking they know what others need better than others know for themselves. They lose touch with the oneness that connects us all.

People with type THREE personality identify with strength. To prove they are strong they constantly try to achieve things that exhibit their strengths, not recognizing that the unconditional strength of *being* needs no proving.

People with type FOUR personality identify with forgiveness. Instead of being forgiving, they attempt to prove they are forgivable by reliving past wounding and so justifying why their inadequacies should be forgiven. *Being* is eternal and unchanging and cannot be hurt. True forgiveness is the realization that there is nothing to forgive.

People with type FIVE personality identify with space or wisdom. To prove how wise they are and to protect their personal space, they withdraw physically and emotionally from life and study it from a distance. The space-like nature of consciousness is inherently wise, as it contains everything, and we are spontaneously guided when fully immersed in the present moment.

People with type SIX personality identify with acceptance. To try and prove they are acceptable they attempt to guess what is expected of them. They either conform in search of approval or rebel to prove they don't need approval. Unconditional acceptance needs no approval and recognition from others.

People with type SEVEN personality identify with joy. To prove they are joyful they constantly seek out enjoyable experiences, not realizing that the seeking can never really make them completely happy. Essential joy loves everything and doesn't get lost in seeking.

People with type EIGHT personality identify with will. To prove the power of their will, they try to shape their world to meet their desires. Essential will, which is that worth striving for, is the willingness to surrender one's personal agenda to serve love and live in harmony.

People with type NINE personality identify with peace. To prove they are peaceful, they compromise their own preferences to keep a façade of peace at any price to maintain the status quo. Essential peace accepts the diverse and ever-changing nature of creation; things must die or be destroyed, so what is new can emerge.

The Illusion of a Separate Self

The attempt to maintain a permanent sense of self is empty of substance and is merely a habitual pattern of thinking, feeling and acting in predictable ways. It exists only in our mind. It is, in a sense, a hallucination or a dream-like trance. The reality of our own body–mind and the world around us is constantly changing. The problem is this dreamed up sense of self is living in a separate reality from what is actually happening. This separation is described in Buddhism as a type of affliction. There are three afflictions that perpetuate this separation and cause suffering: ignorance, attachment and aversion.

Ignorance is another way of describing the failure to recognize things as they are. We are ignorant because we ignore reality. We ignore reality in favor of believing in myths. The myths are encoded in trance-like internal processes. It is the way we maintain our subjective reality. These myths are the maps we follow hoping to find happiness and protect us from misery. We believe if we can hold onto the things that bring us pleasure and avoid those things that bring us pain, we will be happy. Difficulty arises, however, when pleasurable and painful things come and go, whether we want them to or not.

Trying to be the kind of person that can keep the good, while avoiding the bad, requires that we ignore the truth of how things actually are. Instead of managing the pleasurable and painful things of life skillfully, we resist letting go of the pleasure and indulge in or become addicted to them. At the same time, we avoid painful things, which invariably mean they build up and become unmanageable.

> Judgment and love are opposites. From one comes all the sorrows of the world. From the other comes the peace of God. Judgment will bind my eyes and make me blind. The ego cannot survive without judgment. *A Course in Miracles*[20]

The myth of a separate self starts with judgments of what is good and bad. This leads to feelings of anger about what is judged as bad in the world, or guilt about what is judged as bad in us. If we believe anger is bad, we end up feeling guilty about that too. With guilt there is a sense of indebtedness, usually towards our parents, and we begin trying to earn love and happiness. If we don't feel our parents love us the way we are, we often try and to create an image of what we think will be loved. As we inherently know we are presenting a false front, we feel inadequate and try to find something in our story, or the way we present it, that makes it seem more unique and authentic.

Feeling inadequate and separate from our true nature is painful; therefore, we dissociate from our feelings. We create beliefs and concepts to explain different aspects of ourselves that allows us to compartmentalize our experiences. In the attempt to find some sense of certainty, we begin following a set of rules based on our beliefs and assumptions. Disconnected from direct experience, we feel uncertain and begin looking for others to validate our beliefs. Based on those assumptions, we then seek what we think will make us happy and avoid what we think will make us unhappy.

This endless seeking and avoiding leaves us feeling empty, and consquently we become more determined to attain and protect what we desire, and defend against whatever threatens our fragile veneer of happiness. To whatever degree we succeed, we do our best to identify with what we have been able to manifest and dis-identify with whatever we have been able to avoid. At this point, we have become asleep to our true nature and tend to go into an automatic set of routines that minimize our chances of noticing how false, empty and meaningless our lives have become. We fall asleep; we fall into the dream of who we think we are within a world that we are convinced is predictable and under our control.

Coincidently, people with the different Enneagram personality types tend to identify more strongly with the associated steps leading into this sense of a solid separate self, unconscious of its true nature.

People with type ONE personality identify with judging that leads to feeling anger or guilt.

People with type TWO personality identify with feeling guilty and the sense of indebtedness, which leads to trying to earn love and happiness.

People with type THREE personality identify with 'never good enough' and the self-created image of what they think will be admired and loved.

People with type FOUR personality identify with feeling inauthentic and inadequate and thus try to present themselves in a more unique and authentic manner.

People with type FIVE personality identify with dissociation from whatever might cause pain and the beliefs and concepts that keep their experience of life compartmentalized.

People with type SIX personality identify with seeking a sense of certainty by following a set of rules and looking for others to validate their beliefs.

People with type SEVEN personality identify with seeking for what they think will make them happy and avoiding what they perceive will make them unhappy.

People with type EIGHT personality identify with being determined to attain and protect what they desire to possess.

People with type NINE personality identify with the automatic routines that minimize their awareness of how empty and meaningless their lives are and the false security of thinking life is predictable and under their control.

Waking Up

The various ways we identify ourselves create a trance-like state that leads to repetitive patterns of thinking, feeling and acting that maintain dissatisfaction and suffering. Freud called it the repetition compulsion and in Buddhism this is referred to as samsara. To be free from repetition of suffering, it is necessary to awaken from who we think we are and discover our true nature.

Life is all around us and living through us; it is ever changing, mysterious and amazing. It is what is real, and consequently, it is always trying to reveal itself to us and wake us from our trance. Every time life doesn't live up to our expectations, it is reality saying, "Wake up! This is reality." The more entranced we are by our self-made reality, the more we would rather be right about how we think life should be, rather than be appreciative or accepting of the way life is. Suffering is what happens when we argue with reality.

Unself-consciousness vs Self-consciousness

The more separate we perceive ourselves to be from the wholeness of existence, the more self-conscious we are and the more we have concern for those sets of conditions that we think define who we are. The more surrendered we are to the wholeness of the way things are, the more unself-conscious we are and hence free to authentically relate to life.

There are two aspects of unself-consciousness. First, the sense of a separate self dissolves. We have no need for a self-concept; we just are. Second, we become aware of our *Unself,* the clear light of *being.*

The clear light of *being* is inherently pleasant. *Being* is inherently peaceful, conscious, compassionate, strong, forgiving, wise, accepting, joyful and powerful. *Being* isn't personal; it is universal. Ultimately, a personal *beingness* doesn't exist. There is *being* manifesting in different forms. *Being* is that which allows everything to come and go, into and out of existence. *Being* could be thought of as the mind of God, the self-organizing intelligence of the universe. This is why in Buddhism it is said, "Cast off pretense and self-deception and see yourself as you really are. Despite all appearances, no one is really evil. They are led astray by ignorance. If you ponder this truth always you will tend to offer more light, rather than blame and condemnation. You, no less than all beings, have Buddha Nature within. Your essential Mind is pure."[21]

Having concepts isn't inherently a problem. Those concepts are maps that help us to navigate our way through life. They are what have enabled human beings to evolve to the top of the food chain and organize into complex societies. However, when we confuse the map with the territory, and when our maps blind us from seeing reality as it actually is, this becomes a problem. Insanity has been defined as the tendency to believe our thoughts over reality.

Our mental ability to map out the world in order to survive and thrive becomes a survival strategy for protecting and maintaining a separate sense of self, which in turn begins to threaten or compromise our actual well-being. If we look honestly at many of the choices we make from our false sense of self, it would appear we would rather be right about our beliefs about ourselves and the world than be happy, peaceful, loving or healthy. We interpret situations in ways that make us feel angry, guilty, sad, jealous or anxious; we attack or withdraw from others to prove ourselves right and them wrong; and we continue to consume things in an addictive manner that not only harms us but, in the process, damages the environments on which we depend for our survival.

In contrast to other creatures, human beings evolved the ability to step out of the *here and now* and of being at one with creation in order to perceive patterns that could be used for our advantage. We became identified with the mechanism of the mind we used to survive, and in doing so lost touch with our natural, essential wholeness. Adam and Eve ate the apple of knowledge of 'right and wrong' and lost touch with their innocence, which is free from moral concepts. It is in our innocence of not knowing how things should be that we remain curious about how things can evolve through the way we relate with them.

Stages of Development

A fundamental idea about evolution, which was only really recognised upon the publication of Darwin's theory, is that not only is life always changing, change itself has a direction. Creation evolves towards greater diversity and complexity.

In his book *Spiral Dynamics,* Clare Graves described eight stages of human development, beginning at the earliest stages of the human beings emerging as a species through to modern times. These stages can still be witnessed in various cultures and subcultures around the globe, and are characterised by values, beliefs, practices. In brief, these stages[22] are:

- Instinctive—Based on biological urges/drives; physical senses dictate the state of being.
- Animistic—The world is threatening and full of mysterious powers; spirit beings must be placated and appeased.

- Absolutistic—The world is like a jungle where the tough and strong prevail, while the weak serve; nature is an adversary.
- Multiplistic—The world is controlled by a higher power that punishes evil and eventually rewards good works and *right* living.
- Relativistic—The world is full of resources to develop and opportunities to make things better and more prosperous.
- Systemic—The world is the habitat wherein humanity can find love and purposes through affiliation and sharing.
- Holistic —The world is a chaotic organism where change is the norm and uncertainty is a usual state of being.
- Integral—A delicately balanced system of interlocking forces, in jeopardy if in human hands.

The stages alternate between people being individualistic or *me focused* (odd numbers), and collective or *we focused* (even numbers). This mirrors the tendency for all of life to exist on the boundary of order and chaos. People in social systems focused on promoting the individual tend to become more chaotic, as everyone does their own thing. To manage the chaos, the focus of people within social systems turns to the collective, which leads to more order. Too much order leads to stagnation and individuals begin reasserting themselves. In systems psychology, this development through balancing the twin drives for autonomy and belonging is referred to as *differentiation*.

Erik Erikson described eight stages of human development determined by the interaction of biological, mental and cultural factors extending from birth to death which, to a degree, correspond with spiral dynamics. The successes or failures at each stage affect the success or failure at later stages. Psychological health is essentially determined by how well each stage is navigated. Psychological problems are essentially a case of arrested development. According to Erikson, people have difficulty managing their life challenges because they lack access to the internal resources needed to do so, as they weren't adequately developed during early stages. Psychotherapy is a process of helping people access and develop those resources and apply them to their current situation.

Don Riso and Richard Hudson define nine stages of psychological health that apply to all nine of the Enneagram personality types, ranging from personality disorders at the bottom end to self-realization at the top. The nine stages are Pathological Destructiveness, Obsession and Compulsion, Violation, Overcompensation, Interpersonal Control, Imbalance/ Social Role, Social Value, Psychological Capacity and Liberation.[23] At each stage of development, each personality type tends to manifest different ways of functioning.

The more evolved a person is, the more free they are from recreating patterns of suffering. They are more consciously present in the *here and now*, less caught up in their concepts, and more able to respond with love, intelligence, creativity and other qualities of wholeness. The lower levels are characterized by doing too much of whatever their personality type is most identified with, which simply recreates suffering for themselves and others.

Even if people are generally evolving in their lives they will, at times, temporarily devolve or regress to lower levels of functioning. Regressions and progressions may occur at differing rates in the various areas of one's life. Ken Wilber speaks of this in his integral psychology. For example, a person may be highly evolved artistically, but not able to maintain intimate relationships at all; or someone is highly evolved professionally, but struggles in family life.

Phases of Developmental Cycles

As with most things, some change happens in dramatic ways and some in more gentle ways. At times, people will make quantum leaps to different levels, yet generally people will go through a gradual process of learning, healing or awakening. It is my belief that this cycle is universal and applies not only to human functioning, but also to all facets of life itself, as it continues its evolution from the primordial 'soup' to where we are today, and onwards into the future.

The Enneagram can be used as a way of mapping these spiraling cycles of change. We will look at this in detail in Chapter Three. Each cycle leads to greater complexity and consciousness, whether it is the evolution of species, societies, human psychosocial development, or the awakening of a Buddha.

Enneagram of the Developmental Cycle

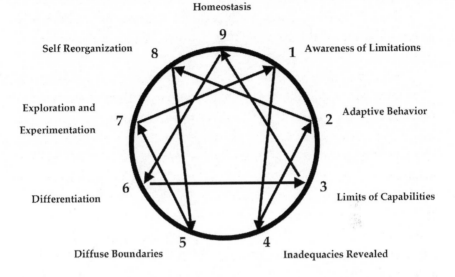

There are nine phases of the Enneagram Developmental Cycle. Here, they start at phase NINE and finish at a higher-level phase NINE:

NINE—The system organizes itself at the edge of chaos with self-maintaining feedback loops (homeostasis). It regulates predictability and equilibrium by the consolidation of emergent relationship patterns into a more robust system, which in turn will effect adjustments in larger systems to which it belongs. *Primary Concern*—How to maintain stability?

ONE—There is a growing awareness in the system of the limitations of relating to life within the parameters defined by the existing structure, which initiates the destabilization of the homeostatic functioning. *Primary concern*—What's the problem? What's the ideal?

TWO—The system attempts to adapt to the increased demands of the emergent properties of self within the parameters of the existing structure by relating to the environment more effectively. This leads to an amplification of self-reinforcing feedback loops. *Primary concern* —How to adapt to problems?

THREE—By moving toward peak fitness, the system (attempting to reestablish homeostasis) reaches the limits of its existing structure. At the boundary of its current range of functioning, the system's efforts spill over into a higher dimension of opportunity. *Primary concern*—How to promote success within the status quo?

FOUR—The inadequacies of the system become more apparent as boundaries begin breaking down, opening the system to untapped creative potentials. *Primary concern*—What are the inadequacies?

FIVE—Boundaries become more diffuse, allowing a greater flow of information into the system. A sorting of what is vitally essential for survival is initiated. *Primary concern*—Why is this happening?

SIX—The system maintains its integrity around essential structures or patterns, while others disintegrate and may be eliminated. Balance shifts away from the previous level of organization towards chaos. *Primary concern*—What to hold onto and what to let go of?

SEVEN—At the boundary of order and chaos, the system seeks out new couplings and internal patterns of organization. Exploring various ways of relating to changes in the environment creates possibilities to be discovered and experimented with. *Primary concern*—What's next? How to approach things differently?

EIGHT—Certain new couplings are selected, organized and integrated into existing essential structures, creating a more complex and robust order, and a new sense of self. *Primary concern*—How to gain control?

NINE—The system organizes itself at this new level with self-maintaining feedback loops (homeostasis). It regulates predictability and equilibrium by consolidating emergent relationship patterns into a more robust system. This in turn will effect adjustments in the larger system to which it belongs. *Primary concern*—How to regain stability?

PsychoLogical Domains

Each phase demonstrates a tendency to frame attention within a particular psychological domain, so that in any given *context or environment, ideals* emerge into consciousness that inspire us to reach beyond the status quo. To move towards those possibilities, we must exercise certain *behaviors*. To behave in a particular way, we must have certain *capabilities*, which we develop as a result of we *value*. What we value is based on what we *believe*, which is refined over time by our ability to *question* our assumptions and open ourselves up to *new perceptions and ideas*. The kind of person we *identify* ourselves to be tends to determine what ideas we entertain, which beliefs we are willing to question and that which we hold as true. Therefore, according to what we value, we develop certain capabilities to behave in ways that move us towards our ideals in a given *context*. Who we identify ourselves as is defined, and so defines the sort of *communities* to which we belong.

The primary concern of each phase is the same primary concern or perceptual bias of people caught in the compulsion of their Enneagram personality type. Each of the nine personality types overly identifies with one phase of the evolutionary process and the PsychoLogical Domain (explained in depth in Chapter 5), and so resists the next phase. They fear losing the ground they have gained and hence cling to what they are familiar with and do best. Compulsions of personality, in this light, are merely vicious cycles that keep us locked into a fraction of our wholeness, while resisting the natural tendency to evolve over time.

Enneagram of PsychoLogical Domains

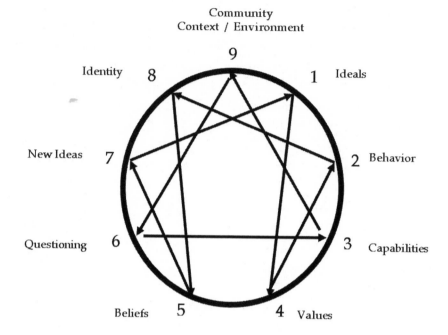

People with type NINE personality become preoccupied with maintaining stability by surrendering their own agenda, and ignore what is problematic for them and others. They tend to be overly identified with their environment or community.

People with type ONE personality become preoccupied with what's problematic and resist making adaptations. They tend to be overly identified with their ideals.

People with type TWO personality become preoccupied with adapting their behavior and resist promoting their own agenda. They tend to be overly identified with their behavior.

People with type THREE personality become preoccupied with promoting their own agenda, but resist awareness of their own inadequacies. They tend to be overly identified their capabilities.

People with type FOUR personality become preoccupied with awareness of their own inadequacies and resist clarifying their assumptions. They tend to be overly identified with their values.

People with type FIVE personality become preoccupied with clarifying their assumptions and resist questioning these assumptions. They tend to be overly identified with their beliefs.

People with type SIX personality become preoccupied with questioning assumptions, but resist considering new possibilities. They tend to be overly identified with questioning.

People with type SEVEN personality become preoccupied with new possibilities, but resist reorganizing their lives. They tend to be overly identified with their new ideas.

People with type EIGHT personality become preoccupied with reorganizing circumstances and resist surrendering their personal agenda to help maintain greater stability and harmony in their relationships. They tend to be overly identified with their personal identity.

Life Brings Us to Spirit and Spirit Brings Us to Life

It is suffering that brings people to psychotherapy and spirituality. In the beginning, it is the desire to be free from suffering that drives us to look deeper within or beyond our usual sense of self.

On one hand, self-realization and psychotherapy are retrograde processes. We relax back through our layers of constructed trance-like reality and come to rest in radical acknowledgement and acceptance of where we actually are on the human level. We then take one step deeper into the ground of our *being*. On the other hand, as we realize our wholeness of b*eing*, there is a natural desire to honor the contribution we must make in the evolution of how we live together on this planet. This is why we can say, from a scientific point of view, that personality is necessary, yet it can be restrictive. Ground of *being*, the hub of the mind, is where we can find one another, and even find ourselves.

The happier, more loving and free we feel, the more we want to share our wealth of spirit. In Buddhism, this state is called the Bodhisattva promise and is the commitment to work towards the liberation of sentient beings until they are free from suffering and realize their true nature. The sharing of our gifts facilitates the realization of our full potential at whatever our level of development.

The more we realize our essential wholeness, the more possible it is for us to become all that we can be for the benefit of all beings. We can use the awakening of the Buddha as a template. The Buddha realized the emptiness that is the oneness with everything. In that wholeness of *being,* he initially could see no reason to get involved in the world; however, because there is only one wholeness of *being,* Buddha could not separate himself from the rest of humanity. Without the perception of separation there is automatically, and effortlessly, compassion for all beings and a desire to help them. In other words, the happier a person is, the more they naturally want to share that happiness with others. Every problem or wish for a better life provides opportunities to wake up to our true nature and learn how to live and love more consciously in the world.

CHAPTER TWO

Mapping Evolution

Once upon a time, if we were lucky enough to find one, we lived in a cave. To make life easier, we learned to chip rocks to make more efficient tools. If childbirth, disease or a saber tooth tiger didn't kill us, we might live to be thirty, even though we had no way of counting the years.

Today, vast numbers of us are fortunate enough to live in electricity powered homes, while silicon chips keep us online with people around the globe. We have cracked the genetic code, which may well enable us to live beyond a hundred years. However, despite all our innovations and the transformation of the world around us, humans, both rich and poor, still experience great suffering. "Life," said Mark Twain, "is one damn thing after another." Strategic therapist John Weakland also commented on the topic, stating, "Problems are the same damn things over and over." Life presents us with challenges, which are opportunities to engage with life more fully and adapt to ever-changing circumstances. Challenges continue to present themselves until we master them or die. Einstein defined insanity as repeatedly doing the same thing, expecting a different result. We tend to experience the same damn problems over and over, as many of our attempted solutions actually perpetuate the very problems we are trying to solve.

How can humans, evolution's great success story, be so oblivious to our self-made problems? The extent to which we make ourselves miserable, according to *A Course in Miracles*, is a tribute to how powerful we really are. Our minds are too powerful at making and maintaining beliefs that perpetuate suffering. We make ourselves believe that what we are doing is working. In other words, we are overly confident. Short-term gains from our attempted solutions reinforce our confidence; yet, in order to keep approaching the problems in the same old way, we remain ignorant of the long-term consequences of our actions.

Over 2000 years ago, Jesus said, "Blessed are the meek for they shall inherit the Earth" (Matthew 5:5). By meek, was he referring to people who are uncertain about their way of doing things: People with humility? People who most readily try to solve their problems with acts of brutality are generally convinced they are in the right. Jesus didn't teach that certainty and brutality were the path of human development. The Buddha, 2500 years ago, commented that we tend to resist our evolving nature. He talked about it in terms of two processes: 'grasping', the attempt to hold on to the way things are; and 'aversion', the attempt to avoid what is perceived as undesirable. Grasping and aversion, he tells us, are the causes of suffering.

The use of violence to solve social problems generally follows the same pattern. Hurting, killing or intimidating a person or group will, most likely, temporarily stop them doing what you don't want. However, as the reasons they were behaving in undesirable ways haven't been addressed and they feel even more persecuted by the ensuing violence, inevitably they will attempt to reassert their agenda, usually with increasing levels of force. Violence leads to the perceived need for more violence.

Most people have a strong ability to 'make believe', a strategy that has us ingeniously inventing three categories that we blame for any lack of success: badness, madness and sickness. Note that these are forces outside of ourselves. Madness and sickness are generally labeled as 'bad'. What is bad is considered evil and therefore to be resisted and/or eliminated. The message that is conveyed is that anxiety is bad, so resist or try to get rid of it. Terrorism is evil, so kill terrorists. Drugs are bad, so go to war on drugs. Disobedience is bad, so punish those who would disobey. When we accept these labels, we stop being curious about how these problems have come to be. In particular, we don't examine how we have contributed to the creation or perpetuation of these problems.

If we are to learn from our biological heritage, we might realize that instead of 'problems' merely being bad and something to control or get rid of, they are nature's way of giving us feedback about the usefulness of our choices. We can either listen to the feedback and make adjustments that bring us back into greater harmony with life, or continue to have more and more of the 'same damn problems' with ever-increasing intensity and frequency.

Evolution is the story of how humans have successfully learned from feedback. In fact all of life is propelled by feedback. By getting a better grasp of the principles of how life evolves, we not only learn how to more effectively solve problems, but also how to realize our full potential.

What is the Use of Believing?

Believing is a process of mapmaking. Based on feedback we get from interacting with the world, we construct maps that categorize our experience into a body of knowledge. We use them to navigate our way through the terrain of our lives more effectively. However, if instead of making progress easier, our maps guide us around in vicious circles, we must reevaluate our maps.

In *Essential Wholeness*, we will draw from the wisdom of several established disciplines in an attempt to make better maps, which will guide us more effectively to our desired outcomes with less suffering. The Enneagram will be used to map both the spiral dynamics of evolutionary change and the multifaceted gem of our essential wholeness. The synthesis of science and spirituality will reveal what each of us has in common with life evolving from the primordial soup into our current complex biosphere, as well as what we have in common with pioneering scientists, mythic heroes and spiritual teachers throughout the ages.

Whether inspired by a photograph of Earth from space, theories of modern physics, or the wisdom of ancient traditions, people are recognizing the innate interconnectedness of all things. We are rapidly moving from the Technological/Information Age to the Biological Age. To better survive and thrive with less suffering, we must optimize how we relate to one another and the world around us. The way we relate to other people, other species, and the world as a whole, reflects the way we relate to the diverse aspects and wholeness of our individual psyches. To live in harmony with nature, we must live in harmony with our own true natures. If we are to live in peace with one another, we must be at peace within ourselves.

The Evolutionary Paradigm

Evolution involves not only survival, but also innovation. Nature has provided an extraordinary example of this in the Wollemi Pine, recently discovered in Australia, which appears to be a true 'living fossil'. It is most closely related to extinct species of Araucariaceae in the fossil record of southern Australia about 50 million years ago, and as a species it had worldwide distribution in the Jurassic and Cretaceous periods 200 to 65 million years ago. Since that time, trees have evolved through many variations before arriving at their current forms. These trees, in their isolated niche, have survived with little innovation for millions of years. In comparison, humans have been around a mere 100,000 years; a mere 'second' in Earth time. Over that period, biological evolution has been minimal. However, culturally, we have evolved from sophisticated primates who lived in small bands of hunters and gatherers to a global society.

In today's world, four-year old children communicate on the worldwide web, people regularly fly beyond the Earth's atmosphere, athletes compete internationally, and there are five major religious traditions along with numerous others existing alongside one another in our multicultural society. We in the West, especially, have a tremendous array of choices in all the varied contexts of our lives, most of which weren't even dreamt of a mere hundred (or less) years ago. Possibly never before have the choices we make had such impact on our future and the course of history.

Questions that are vital to consider include our response to nature: do we seek alternatives to fossil fuels or do we take our chances with global warming? Do we continue to generate nuclear waste, which we have no way of recycling? Do I drive my car to the store, do I order my groceries over the internet or do I ride my bicycle to the store? Do we, in the developed nations, continue to exploit people in less developed nations? Do I choose to think of people I don't understand as enemies or do I build better relationships with them in which greater mutual understanding and cooperation may be possible? Do we take our spouses for granted and refuse to learn better ways of relating until our marriages fall apart and our children are forced to live in two separate homes? There are so many choices we must make day-to-day, month-to-month and year-to-year that will shape the course of our individual and collective evolution. The quality of ours lives depends on the quality of the choices we make.

Albert Einstein said, "You can't solve a problem using the type of thinking that caused the problem in the first place." When merely focused on our short-term survival in crisis situations we tend to make fight or flight responses. Fight or flight, along with basic feeding and sexual behavior, are primarily regulated by the basal ganglia or 'reptilian brain.' When our choices are primarily determined by these reactions, we are operating in survival mode. Survival is important; however, operating out of our reptilian brain is not what has promoted human beings to the top of the food chain. When we are merely reacting to maintain our survival or sense of security, we are not using our greatest evolutionary assets, the cerebral cortex and the complex organization of our cognitive capabilities.

In our modern world, workers unable to adapt to the evolving workplace find themselves without a job. Spouses unable to embrace the evolving nature of marriage find themselves divorced. Companies unable to adapt to the changing marketplace find themselves filing for bankruptcy. Since the beginnings of life on our planet, between 99 and 99.95 percent of all species that ever existed are now extinct. In other words, it is easy to fail to learn how to adapt to a changing world. If we are unable to evolve how we relate to one another and the ecosystems of which we are a part, we human beings may very well find ourselves in nature's museum of extinct species.

Although humans have become the most proficient species at fighting and fleeing, that is not what has allowed us to dominate the landscape. Human evolution has been driven by our ability to respond creatively and cooperatively to challenges, as well as our ability to envision a better future and devise the means to achieve it. If we evaluate our reptilian predecessors, who once dominated this planet, we find that they were very good at the four Fs: fighting, fleeing, feeding and 'procreating', but had little ability to learn how to creatively and cooperatively relate to their world. Tyrannosaurus Rex, the creature at the top of the food chain, was the pinnacle of brutish reptilian power.

Forward-looking author and designer, William McDonough, commenting on society, said if the Industrial Age we are emerging from had a motto it would be, "If brute force doesn't work, you're not using enough of it." For example, we use pesticides and chemical fertilizers to force soil to yield more bountiful crops. As the soil becomes degraded, we add more fertilizer. As insects become resistant to our chemicals, we use stronger poisons, and in the process destroy the ecosystems that naturally replenish soil and keep various insects in a healthy balance with other living things in the environment. What are the effects of this brutal approach? Most dramatically, is the mass extinction of our planet's species at an unprecedented pace, even compared to the disappearance of the dinosaurs, and it's accelerating. What sort of mentality brutishly destroys the community of life upon which it depends?

Control or Cooperation?

For decades most Americans have believed their children's lives would be better than their own. However, as the conditions for life on Earth worsen, it's hardly surprising that a recent survey revealed only 45 percent of men and 24 percent of women think their children will have a better life than them.

The Journal of the American Medical Association estimates that 14 million Americans annually suffer major depression, 23 million suffer anxiety disorders and 40 percent of Americans suffer from chronic health disorders. And the numbers are climbing.

Cognitive psychology has revealed that at the heart of most anxiety and depression there are usually self-condemning and defeating beliefs such as, 'I'm useless', 'I'm worthless', or 'I'll only make things worse'. Not only have we been brutal in our efforts to dominate and control nature, we have also turned the same approach upon our own minds and bodies. Adding insult to injury, the most common treatments for these conditions involve bombarding ourselves with medication, prescriptive or otherwise. As former President George W. Bush said, "No one is going to make Americans change their way of life."

Most people who are caught illegally medicating themselves are thrown into brutal prisons as an attempted solution; yet, has this 'War on Drugs' decreased drug use? There has been an escalation of military interventions around the globe; yet, has the 'War on Terror' led to less terrorism? Has the rampant prescribing of antidepressants (for the supposed war on depression) led to less depression?

What are the paradoxes of these 'fixes' for these problems? People who use illegal drugs are often trying to escape a sense of inadequacy or frustration about living in a system of social inequality. Sending them to prison only exacerbates this. Killing tens of thousands of Iraqis (fighting) only breeds more contempt for the US and turns more young Muslims towards acts of terror. Using chemicals to override someone's unhappiness doesn't liberate people from the values, beliefs and social conditions that oppress them. At best, medications enable people to mechanically function better so as to work and shop. Could it be that unbridled consumerism and too many hours spent working lacks meaning and doesn't lead to fulfillment? Maybe Americans consuming more than their fair share of the world's natural resources breeds contempt with those whose environment and workforce are exploited?

Trying to hold on to what we make believe is best for us and avoiding what we believe is unpleasant (flight) perpetuates our suffering. Instead of brutishly trying to dominate and control (fight) those aspects of nature, society and ourselves that aren't happy and thriving, we must listen to them and learn how to live in greater harmony.

How has Culture Evolved?

In comparison to biological evolution, the evolution of human culture, especially in the realms of technology and social organization, has been very swift within a comparatively short time. Human beings are an infant species when compared with all the species that have inhabited this planet. Yet the complexity, sophistication and expansiveness of our inhabitation is unrivaled by any species before us. This is partly due to the biological evolution of our brains, but also to the evolution of how, individually and collectively, we continue to develop and utilize this biological advantage.

The evolution of language, and all forms of communication, has been instrumental in the evolution of culture. Communication is the process by which we create and maintain cooperation with one another. Cooperation and the sharing of ideas propel learning. Dialogues between theorists, researchers and mathematicians have led to many of the greatest discoveries of the last century. Deeper spiritual understandings are being realized, as people in Western religious traditions embrace Eastern traditions, and vice versa. In addition, the communication and cross-pollination of ideas between different disciplines has led to expanded understanding in each respective field: physicists communicating with philosophers communicating with athletes communicating with psychologists communicating with doctors communicating with artists, and so on.

The internet's web of communication makes a wide array of information only a keystroke away from anyone with access to a computer and will certainly play a major role in our emerging phase of evolution. Mass media has the capacity to *feed* us mind-numbing entertaining *flights* from reality, violent *fight* promoting propaganda and pornographic *sexualization* of our minds, but it can also promote channels of communication for fostering the evolution of human consciousness and cooperation.

For other species, intergenerational knowledge is communicated genetically through instincts, whereas humans communicate through language and by example to children. The accumulation of human skills and understanding has meant a larger body of knowledge can be acquired and built upon in each generation. This accumulation of skills and knowledge is compounded by our increasing ability to study and communicate the process of learning itself. This facilitates an evolution in our ability to learn new things more quickly and effortlessly.

Not only do our children more easily learn the things discovered in previous generations, they more easily make new discoveries, and synthesize those discoveries into knowledge that can be utilized by society as a whole. If our cultural evolution is recognized by the complexity of organization, autonomy of individuals, ability to convey information, and greater awareness of the way things are, we could also say there is an evolution in the way we learn how to evolve.

We Are Not Alone

As a species, we are not alone in the process of evolution; we are still interdependent with the biosphere. Nonetheless, cultural evolution has accelerated beyond the speed at which biological systems change. When considering thermodynamic systems—systems that generate and regulate heat, such as the Earth or our bodies—biological theorist, Stuart Kauffman, describes three levels of evolution.

> The first level is that of community, or an ecosystem, in which species assemble and make their living in niches each provides for the other. The second level, often occurring on a longer time scale than community assembly and ecological change, is that of coevolution...But there is yet a third, still higher level, presumably occurring on a still longer time scale than coevolutionary processes. The coevolution of organisms alters both the organisms themselves and the ways organisms interact. Over time, the ruggedness of the fitness landscapes changes, as does their resiliency—how easily each landscape is reformed by the adaptive moves of the players. The very process of coevolution itself evolves![24]

Within the ecosystem of human culture, individuals assemble and make their living in niches each provides for one another. Theorists, for example, create niches for researchers, who create niches for mathematicians, all of whom create niches for engineers and manufacturers, who create niches for consumers to incorporate new technology into their life. New technology creates new niches for teachers and experimenters who discover novel ways to use the new technology, and so on. With technological advances, more people are freed from poverty and primary production. The growth of an educated middle class means more people have had access to mystical and spiritual teachings and practices.

Throughout the world, there are communities of people engaged in a cornucopia of spiritual study, ritualized practices, yoga and meditation. This is an advantage afforded by the times we live in. Historically, access to these teachings and the time available to practice them was available only to an elite few. As the different groupings of people from the various disciplines each evolve new understandings and capabilities, there is a collective coevolution of what is possible for humanity. And at a higher level, the processes by which we coevolve: discovery, learning and communication, also evolve. In other words, we learn to learn more effectively.

Evolutionary biologist, Lynn Margulis, reminds us of our biological heritage in this process of coevolution in her description of the Earth's first living cells.

> In details of cell structure and metabolic behavior they very much resembled us. Their material constituents continuously exchanged themselves with the external environment. They vented waste as they acquired food and energy. Their patterns persisted as they replenished their innards with the chemicals taken from the surroundings. Indeed, metabolizing ancient bacteria were so effective at remaking themselves when threatened with disintegration and thermodynamic demise that the insides of our bodies today are chemically more akin to the external environment of the early Earth, in which life originated, than they are like our present oxygen-rich world.[25]

Even as human culture reaches new levels of complexity and diversity, it is the coevolution of the most simple and ancient building blocks of life within our human bodies that keeps us immersed in the primordial soup of life. Could it be that as we learn to experience and honor our place within the whole of creation, we will experience the wholeness of our being and vice versa?

A Course in Miracles teaches that there is only one Son of God and that we are all him. Buddhists dedicate their spiritual practice to the benefit of all sentient beings, vowing to continue to do their spiritual work until all beings are liberated from suffering and realize the enlightenment of their wise and compassionate natures. From the smallest microbe to our worst enemy, from our individual selves to humanity and the biosphere, we are in this together. As Zen Master Hakuin put it, "This very Earth is the Lotus Land of purity, and this body is the Body of Buddha."

By examining our evolutionary history, not only from a human perspective but also more broadly from a living systems perspective, we discover a clearer understanding of the phases, principles and dimensions of change. As we each individually evolve spiritually, emotionally and psychologically, we collectively evolve as a culture. One person's radical discoveries eventually become society's collective norm. One generation's social upheaval becomes the next generation's status quo and their stable platform for venturing into new frontiers. All of life follows this pattern of development. How can we understand this pattern better and utilize it for our own benefit?

How have we have gone from a pantheistic relationship to nature to a pan-atheistic relationship: from a world in which everything was sacred to one in which nothing is? How have we managed, in our perception, to divorce spirit from matter, mind from body, and view ourselves as separate from the rest of creation? In reality, this separation is impossible, but we make believe it is true. Could it be that this has merely been a stage of our development and that we are now coming full circle back to a spiritual reunification with nature?

Evolving Models

Psychology and the practice of psychotherapy have developed out of the need and desire to make sense of the workings of our minds. At its best, this practice is an example of how our ability to evolve has evolved. At its worst, it is an attempted solution that perpetuates suffering. Danger arises when we try to make sense of life, to bring order, within too narrow or rigidly defined boundaries, and suffer from the mind's 'make-believe' interpretations. Most psychological problems could be understood as resulting from the inability to adapt successfully to one's family and/ or society, which are themselves mired in self-perpetuating patterns of suffering.

The Enneagram has traditionally described how the more a person limits their perception of the world to the rigidities of their personality type, the more they are inclined to suffer from a personality or psychiatric disorder. In other words, the more one tries to narrowly impose order on the vast complexities of life, the more disordered one's mind becomes. This understanding compels us to open our minds to the vast complexity and ever-changing nature of life.

The evolution of human consciousness is reflected in the paradigms that frame our experience of ourselves and the world in which we live. Evolutionary shifts in human consciousness could be thought of as paradigm shifts. "Changes of paradigms", according to Kuhn, "occur in discontinuous, revolutionary breaks called 'paradigm shifts' ... a social paradigm, which I define as 'a constellation of concepts, values, perceptions and practices shared by a community, which forms a particular vision of reality that is the basis of the way the community organizes itself.'" [26] The paradigm within which we operate determines how we perceive, interpret and respond to life's events, and therefore the quality of our choices and resulting outcomes.

Social paradigms define trends in the collective consciousness of societies. Societies are collections of different communities of people, each informing one another with their own perspectives. The scientific community has been very powerful in influencing not only psychology, but also the general social paradigms of recent generations. Since psychology is the study of how our minds work, we in the field must also examine the social and scientific paradigms that inform the practice of psychotherapy. We must realize there is no correct paradigm, rather evolving paradigms that reflect the evolution of human consciousness. If psychotherapy is to promote personal evolution, it must be regularly reframed within new paradigms as they emerge.

Paradigms can be thought of as theories nested within particular metaphors. For example, Newton's descriptions of the universe were mechanical; the universe was thought of as a giant machine whose movements, once understood, would be as predictable as clockwork. This paradigm has been very useful in explaining the nature of the universe, learning to control some of its elements, and has led to the invention of tools (machines), and the lifestyles made possible by them.

Since the universe was like a giant machine, and people were part of the universe, people could also be thought of as machines. This framework has been useful, especially in understanding the bio*mechanics* of the human body. Organ transplants are a good example of treating the body as a machine. If something is broken and you can't fix it, replace it with a new part. Psychotherapy has been greatly influenced by this metaphor, and the jargon used to describe the workings of the human being reflects this. Terms like psycho*dynamic,* instinctual *drives,* unconscious *forces, reaction formation, projection, resistance, transference* and *motivations* are all borrowed from physics and could equally be used to describe a steam engine or a person.

The classical treatment under this model is to analyze the contents of the patient's mind and categorize them according to various structures, mechanisms and forces. Chains of historical events stored as memories in the unconscious are examined to see where the breakdown in the mental mechanisms originated. Operating within this paradigm has lead to many discoveries and useful understandings. However, any paradigm within which we operate will limit our perceptions and conceptualizations of whatever we are trying to understand. Although working within this paradigm has no doubt been of use for many people, it has come under scrutiny in recent years. The length of treatment is considered, by some, to be excessive; the effectiveness at helping people make necessary practical changes has also been questioned. Some psychoanalysts describe the purpose of therapy as helping people to cope better with life's suffering, as opposed to facilitating lasting change by healing what is wounded and learning how to relate to life more effectively or meaningfully. In the former paradigm, therapy can become a part of the patient's life, like addictive dependency on a drug, rather than an intervention that promotes change, or a medicine that aids healing.

Susan's Story

Let's look at the case of Susan, who had been in psychoanalysis and taking antidepressants for several years when she was recommended to me. Her stated reason for psychotherapy was to help her cope better with depression. Previous therapy had been focused on helping her to understand and live with depression, rather than listen to what the symptoms were trying to teach her. She believed the best she could hope for was more of the same type of coping therapy, only more effective.

Framing our lives in a chemical paradigm has been useful for developing a wide variety of chemicals to affect our moods. However, because these drugs are designed within a nonliving paradigm, they are designed to help people cope with the status quo, rather than to promote healing or growth. As Susan embraced her emerging sense of self and began relating to the world around her in more meaningful ways, she soon no longer needed the medication. A few months later, she had better things to do than to spend her time and money on therapy and medication.

In Search of the New

The development of science and technology has been an important part of our cultural evolution. Our ability to understand and manipulate the natural world has enabled us to thrive like no other complex living organism. As a species, we have used our ability to understand the ways of the world to survive in every environmental condition on Earth, including under water, and even in space. Only the organisms that cohabitate within us, such as bacteria and viruses, can survive in such diverse habitats. Human beings' ability to populate the planet has grown in direct relation to our ability to manipulate the natural environment and to construct shelters that protect us from the natural environment.

Rather than acting instinctively and reacting to each circumstance individually, we have increasingly developed the capacity to step out of the immediacy of experience. By mentally positioning ourselves where we can see the pattern of past events, theories have been generated that have made it possible to make predictions about the future based on the presence or absence of particular variables. Science has taught us not to simply trust what our immediate perceptual intuition tells us, rather to seek a more accurate and useful description of the universe.

Contrary to our immediate perception, we now know the Earth is not flat, nor the center of the universe. Matter is not solid. Great strides in the evolution of human consciousness are made when we realize the universe and all that is in it, including ourselves, is not what we thought it was. No matter how clever we might be, learning something new requires thinking outside the confines of our usual logic. As fellow physicist Neils Bohr reminded Albert Einstein in one of their mind-stretching conversations, "You are not thinking. You are merely being logical." Discovering new paradigms requires thinking outside the logical frameworks defined by our existing paradigms. To do this we must have the awareness that all paradigms are 'make believe' and can never capture the true nature of reality.

The Newtonian paradigm has facilitated great technological advances. However, we don't seem to have developed the emotional, spiritual and interpersonal capabilities needed to manage these technologies. We have pushed our ecosystems to their limits with pollutants, extinctions and human-made structures. The lack of respect for both the ecology of the planet and for the ecology of the human community is a reflection of the lack of personal ecology within each of our psyches. What are the conditions that support the evolution of robust ecosystems, whether biological or cultural?

A New Approach to Ecology

The old paradigm has been based on our ability to objectify nature. Collectively, as a society, we have come to think of the natural environment and less technologically advanced societies as dangerous and hostile, something to protect ourselves from, as well as the source of raw materials to exploit for our consumption: farm and grazing land, timber, fishing waters and labor source. Modern buildings are built like fortresses to protect us from the natural world. Windows are often designed not to be opened. The air we breathe is filtered, warmed or cooled. People spend most of their time inside buildings and vehicles. Many of us go for long periods without touching soil or water in its natural environment. Who is even concerned that there are so few rivers and streams we can safely drink from?

If we want our planet to be more hospitable, we need to show more hospitality to other species and elements of the biosphere. We need to treat them as friends and family, not enemies. The way the modern western world relates to the natural world is similar to the way imperialist nations have plundered the nations they have conquered. We have taken all we can, while contributing as little as possible. We have maintained rigid hierarchical control. The greatest power is at the top and the weakest power is at the bottom.

Our basic attitude toward the natural environment has been domination and control. As a result of how we treat or disregard the health of much of the natural world, few rivers and streams are safe for us to drink from. It is only most recently that we have begun to remember we are not separate from the natural world and we cannot escape the consequences of how we treat the rest of creation. In the process of relating to the environment as an enemy, dangerous and to be feared, we have created a more toxic and dangerous world.

The more we have mistreated nature, the more inhospitable it has become. We keep thinking the answer to many of our environmental problems is to develop better technology to dominate and control the problems that have been created by our abuse, instead of learning the most basic lesson nature has to teach us: cooperation and competition, not domination (of the environment), is what drives evolutionary success.

This preoccupation with domination and control is mirrored in how industrialized nations, using their technological might, have dominated less developed nations, exploiting labor and natural resources. We can also see it in our hierarchical/ mechanistic view of the psyche.

Dominant-submissive vs. Ecological Cooperation

Those who adopt psychoanalytic theory contend that it is important for the socially constructed ego to maintain control over the emotional impulses of the id and other emotional impulses stored in the unconscious mind. When drawing connections from the personal to the larger environmental and social spheres, the ego can be allied to Western European culture and the id and other unconscious processes to the less technological cultures living closer to their primal or mystical origins. Depression and other modern psychological ailments are signals from neglected, oppressed and abused parts of our mind-bodies that our way of life is not fulfilling, just or sustainable.

In an ecological psychology, the conscious mind and rational thinking do not have a dominant-submissive relationship with the unconscious and emotional intelligence any more than the sky does with the clouds, fungi with insects, or men with women. Rather, it is in the delicately orchestrated interplay and servitude of the various elements of our psyche, like the rich, biodiverse symphony of life on our planet, that our essential wholeness thrives.

As true democracy and other nonhierarchical forms of government, along with economies, become more globalized, it will become increasingly difficult for so-called 'first world' nations to exploit the labor of developing nations. It is becoming increasingly imperative that we do not exploit people of other nations, or our natural world. The whole ecological and environmental movement is built on our understanding that all of life's relationships are essentially circular and must be treated so if they are to flourish. The illusion that people can do what they want with the natural environment or other people without concern about how it affects them just doesn't hold up anymore.

Humans have been caught in the belief that somehow we exist separately from nature, from one another, and ourselves. The mistaken perception that we are separate is what supports treating nature or other humans as the enemy, or as something to be exploited. Within our own psyche, this sense of separation leads us to neglect, abuse and exploit natural aspects of the essential wholeness of our own psyches. Consider this quote from Albert Einstein:

A human being is part of the whole, called by us the universe. A part limited in time and space. He experiences himself, his thoughts and feelings, as something separate from the rest, a kind of optical delusion of his consciousness. This delusion is a kind of prison for us, restricting us to our personal desires and to affection for a few persons nearest to us. Our task must be to free ourselves from this prison by widening our circle of compassion to embrace all living creatures.[27]

To play its part, psychology today must embrace the full diversity of human nature and the community of parts, our essential wholeness.

A new paradigm is emerging in which the observer cannot be separated from the observed; the doer cannot be separated from the 'done to.' Rather than the Earth being something that we have to do with as we wish, we belong to the Earth and we must also honor the Earth's wishes. We humans are simply a part of the biosphere and our wellbeing is dependent on the wellbeing of the entire planet. There is no break in the circle of life, just an interconnected web of relationships between earth, air, water, radiation from space, the heat of the Earth's core, the cold of the polar icecaps, gravity, a vast diversity of flora and fauna (including humans), the microscopic and the macroscopic, birth, life and death, oceanic currents and the changing of the seasons.

The entire planet and all life are mutually dependent on one another. The wellbeing of the whole is dependent on a harmonious balance of all the parts of creation relating in mutually supportive ways. It is a circular process by which, as we learn to live in greater harmony within our individual selves, especially with the parts of us that suffer, we learn to live in greater harmony with others. Finding greater harmony with other people and the rest of nature also helps us to experience greater inner harmony.

We are realizing the limitations and fallacies of thinking about the universe, let alone our minds, in objectified mechanical terms. Gregory Bateson, one of the seminal contributors to General Systems Theory (GST), presented a very simple example to demonstrate a change of thinking. Think about kicking a ball and kicking a dog. If we kick a ball with an exact amount of force and that force is directed in a specific direction, we can predict with great accuracy in what direction and how far that ball will roll. It is also fairly easy to replicate the results, especially if the kicker is a machine rather than a person.

However, when kicking a dog, there are probably an infinite number of possibilities of how the dog will respond. In addition, balls don't learn; dogs do. The way the ball relates to the kicker would not change over time, whereas the way the dog relates to the kicker would. Living systems aren't as easily described in mechanical, or chemical, terms. Advances in physics, most notably quantum theory, have also shown us the limitations of the GST model, even in the realm of inanimate objects. What metaphorical context can best support the healing of suffering and evolution of consciousness?

The social scientists have been looking more to discoveries made in the life sciences, in particular biology, to better understand what it means to be human. The field of family therapy was one of the first embrace this new paradigm. Early on, theorists considered the structure and functioning of a cell a useful metaphor for understanding the structure and functioning of a family system. This metaphorical context has been expanded to describe human communities as similar to ecosystems, with different individuals and organizations engaged in interdependent relationships with one another.

Enneagram as Map

The Enneagram is a symbolic map of how living systems evolve. The circle represents the global/circular/inclusive nature of our whole being. The numbers around the circle represent the phases of the progressive, cyclical process of evolution. Each phase is regulated by its respective part or aspect of the psyche. The internal lines represent the interconnected web of mutually interdependent relationships between different parts of the whole self. Each point encodes the dimensions of the developmental task, basic function, neurological network and essential quality that engage in each phase. The nine parts are, in a sense, sub-personalities, or different sub-systems of the ecology of our essential whole self. Instead of thinking of the various aspects of our psyche in a hierarchical manner, in which one part needs to gain dominion over the others, we see that all parts support a circular, evolving sense of self.

It is when one part of us starts to dominate over the others that we become compulsively trapped by the rigidities of a personality type. Taken to extremes, this leads to personality and other severe psychological disorders. With a better understanding of our essential wholeness and the evolution of consciousness, we can more ably free ourselves from unnecessary suffering and manifest our greatest potential.

CHAPTER THREE

How Living Systems Evolve

To understand the whole, it is necessary to understand the parts.
To understand the parts, it is necessary to understand the whole.
Such is the circle of understanding.[28] *Ken Wilber*

It is with a solid understanding of the nature of living systems that we can generate a useful map for guiding ourselves though life's evolutionary challenges while, at the same time, honoring our deepest nature. It is by familiarizing ourselves with the attributes of the various elements of a landscape and how they relate to one another that we can create more useful maps. Evolutionary biology, ecology, chaos and systems theories provide us with key landmarks that define how living systems develop and evolve.

We will see how the essential processes described by these various theoretical perspectives can be combined in a nine-phase model mapped onto the Enneagram. My guidelines in creating this model are that a good theory must be complex enough to describe the nature of its subject, yet simple enough to implement. Overly simplistic descriptions use lineal causality. In human affairs, simplistic descriptions tend to appropriate blame and guilt, rather than recognizing the circular nature of relationships. Simplistic explanations lead to simplistic solutions. Violence and exploitation are common examples of the types of brutal solutions that arise out of overly simplistic descriptions, such as other people being inherently bad or inferior. On the other hand, theory that is too complex is difficult to put into practice and loses its aesthetic elegance. Therefore, as Albert Einstein stated, a theory should be as simple as possible, but no simpler. In psychotherapy, it is imperative that the theories we use to guide us follow these criteria.

Recently, a woman with an anxiety disorder was referred to me. She had seen a psychologist several years before who was unsuccessful in treating her. The psychologist worked very strictly within a Cognitive Behavioral Therapy (CBT) theoretical model. When the therapy was not successful, the conclusion she drew from his comments was that she was untreatable — his methods had failed because she had an organic brain disorder. Rather than realizing the limitations of his approach, the psychologist condemned her to believing she was untreatable.

An essential wholeness integrated approach adapts the therapy to meet the client's needs, which are better understood within a more complex model. On the other hand, some models like psychoanalysis can be so complex in theory that the change process can get bogged down in theoretical explanations about the condition with few avenues for strategic intervention.

Systems Theory

Systems Theory is at the hub of the essential wholeness approach, as it helps us understand the complex and circular nature of living things. Systems Theory gave birth to the ecology movement and recognition of the importance of respecting nature's complex network of relationships. Systems Theory recognizes the whole is greater than the sum of its parts.

In the social sciences, Systems Theory has shown us the circular (self-perpetuating) nature of interpersonal relationships embedded within the fabric of family, culture and society. Mapping the circular nature of the wholeness of living systems onto the Enneagram figure give us some not too simple and not too complex guidelines to work cooperatively with our psychobiological nature.

Living systems are open systems, meaning they have a give and take relationship with their environment. They take in forms of energy, matter and information, through processes like digestion, respiration and perception, and put out different forms of energy, matter and information through complementary processes. Living systems operate and maintain themselves in a state away from equilibrium. Although not in equilibrium, a living system will always evolve towards a stationary state (homeostasis), minimizing the distance from equilibrium by minimizing the fluctuations in its internal and external functions. Self-balancing mechanisms minimize entropy (disorder), making relative stability possible over long periods of time. The living system, at times of homeostasis, resembles a whirlpool (non-living open system), in which the basic overall structure is maintained within certain parameters, in spite of the ongoing flow and change of components.

Near a state of equilibrium, we find repetitive phenomenon and universal laws, which make the system relatively predictable. As the system is pushed further from equilibrium, by either internal and/or external stimuli, the fluctuations in the responses to stimuli get stronger, and entropy increases. At the point Ilya Prigogine referred to as a 'bifurcation point', the existing structure of the system reaches its threshold of stability. The system's structure will then either breakdown or break through to one or several new states of order. What happens then depends on external variables and how the system has used or under-used its existing capabilities and knowledge. The new order that emerges will, by necessity, be more complex, intelligent, flexible, adaptive and robust in order to thrive.

Our lives, like all living systems, have ongoing cycles of relative stability, punctuated with crisis and change. The degree of wisdom, sensitivity and creativity we employ as we live and experience determines the richness, variety and robustness of our patterns. If we stick rigidly to inadequate patterns it eventually leads to greater chaos and/or stagnation.

In periods of relative stability we live mainly in our comfort zone with minimal time challenging ourselves or being challenged by circumstances of life. In times of change, our aspirations push us into the challenge zone or life presents us with challenges we must respond to. If we cannot handle challenges well, or we simply bite off more than we can chew, we end up in overwhelm (chaos). People grow and change by learning how to have a good balance between comfort and challenge, with as little overwhelm as possible.

However, too little challenge or too much comfort leads to stagnation. Without enough challenge, our comfort zone can shrink. With a healthy balance of challenge and comfort, the comfort zone expands; what was previously a challenge becomes part of our new stability and we have a stronger foundation to stand on, as well as increased confidence in handling challenges. This process of exposing clients to increasing challenges is the basic premise of Behavior Therapy.

People generally come to therapy when the stability of their lives has been perturbed and the way they are responding is leading to escalating chaos or stagnation. A simple way I describe this to my clients is with the diagram below.

Comfort, Challenge and Overwhelm

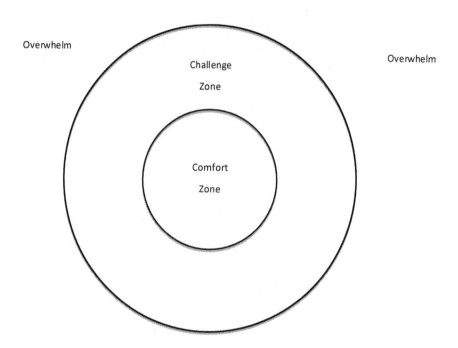

Selection and Self-Organization

For some time, life scientists have researched how and why life on Earth has evolved the way it has, from its prehistoric inorganic origins to today's complex diverse biosphere. What emerges is that the most basic key to surviving and thriving is for us to embrace cooperation at all levels: biological, social and as we will see later, psychological.

There has been ongoing debate about the two basic theories of evolution:

1. Selection — survival of the fittest
2. Self-organization — the innate tendency for the universe to organize itself into ever-increasing complexity on the edge of chaos.

Accidental or Orchestrated?

If circumstances on Earth had evolved differently through trial and error, could we be reptilian, like citizens from other planets in *Star Trek*, instead of mammalian? Or are we part of a grand design that is simply playing itself out? This question seems to be another version of the basic question, 'Are our lives determined by fate or do we have free will?'

As with most major paradoxes, the debate isn't usually resolved by 'either this or that' logic, but rather, as Gregory Bateson described, by 'both this and that' logic. There is some sort of fate, divine order or master plan, and there are individual choices and accidents that shape outcomes.

Walter Fontana, wanting to understand this question, created Artificial Life: computers with programs that are self-replicating in a way that resembles living systems. George Johnson, summarizing the findings of what became known as 'Fontana's Alchemy' states:

> Given the opportunity, Plato might have said that life arranges itself in hierarchies because of ideal form, Hierarchy, exists in a separate realm, the realm of ideas. All hierarchies in the material world are rough approximations of this idea in the mind of the gods. Aristotle might have said that the notion of hierarchy is a "final cause," immanent within all living things, compelling them to arrange themselves in these ladders of increasing complexity. In Fontana's Alchemy, the hierarchies are more Aristotelian than Platonic; they are not imposed from the top down, they bubble up from below.[29]

The process of life arranging itself in hierarchies of ever-increasing complexity is neither just Platonic — spirit creating a self-organizing world, or Aristotelian, from the father of the scientific method — a grand experiment through trial and error where the best options are repeatedly selected, creating patterns. Rather, as Stuart Kauffman asserts, "If ever we are to attain a final theory in biology, we will surely have to understand the commingling of self-organization and selection."[30]

With the quantum field of infinite possibilities, otherwise known as the universe, idyllic Platonic forms are morphic blueprints by which nature selects the best adaptations and discovers its unrevealed potentials. However, we need Aristotelian experiments to select the best options so these potentials can find their expression in the physical dimension. Idyllic structures never actually come into existence, but instead provide intricate outlines to be colored in, in infinitely creative ways. Although there is a Platonic blueprint for snowflakes, there are no two snowflakes alike. Each human soul has a Platonic blueprint that inspires us to live life in a unique way, but we only discover this by responding with Aristotelian-like rigor to the challenges that arise.

Cooperation

Self-organization is the tendency of living systems to join together with other systems to form larger or more complex systems. Organizing in this way increases the likelihood a species will be be fit enough to survive. For human beings especially, but also for other species, the level of fitness (ability to adapt) has been based on the ability to live cooperatively. Organization, at all levels, is based on distinct entities establishing patterns of cooperation with one another.

Throughout history, progress has been achieved through cooperative relationships, be it between humans and animals, such as dogs or horses, or within our bodies, for example, bacteria feeding off wastes in our intestinal tracts to keep us healthy by controlling the infestation of potentially harmful bacteria. Interestingly, if we destroy healthy bacteria, for example, with the use of antibiotics, we can get serious digestive and immune system problems.

It was not only primitive humans' ability to devise and use tools that made them better hunters, elevating them to the top of the food chain, it was also their ability to cooperate in the implementation of complex strategies with their fellow hunters.

Psychological wellbeing is largely dependent on our ability to develop cooperative relationships with others, as well as have inner cooperation between different aspects of our psyche. The relationships we have with ourselves will largely determine the quality of our relationships with others. Life is essentially patterns of relationship.

Mediating Competition

Competition for limited resources is the key dynamic of the selection process and drives innovation. However, to maximize harmony, nature creates boundaries to minimize competition by:

- separating species geographically into differing habitats
- sorting species into unique niches within habitats
- creating spatial division according to gradations of environmental factors, such as oxygen content at different levels of a body of water
- establishing territorial demarcations, such as cats using scent to mark out their territory
- establishing dominance hierarchies within social groupings of animals

Through the minimization of competition, various species, as well as individuals, fulfill their niche within the ecosystems they co-create and maintain.

Cooperation is not only a function of living together; it's also about living separately. All living things have a certain amount of individual autonomy, as well as being dependent on a larger system. Cells have boundaries that separate them from other cells, yet collectively they form an organ. Organs have boundaries that differentiate them from other body parts, yet collectively they comprise an organism. Individual organisms are separate entities, yet they join together in communities, and so on. This same pattern holds for human organizations, from economic systems to sporting leagues. For the organization to work, people must respect boundaries, play their roles and find a balance between cooperation and competition.

Our individual psyches also have boundaries and hierarchies. There are boundaries between conscious and unconscious processes, boundaries between work and family concerns, or between marital and parental concerns. There are hierarchies of values that determine how our time and energy get divided up.

Origins of Life

We are all part of the same system of life on Earth. The wellbeing of that system, and the way we collectively and individually survive and thrive, is in part determined by our ability handle evolutionary challenges. It seems to me that there is a universal pattern that is true for one-cell organisms becoming multi-cell organisms and for us as human beings. The patterns by which species organize themselves into ecosystems inform the way people organize themselves into families and larger communities. Let's explore some of the prevailing theories of how life began on Earth.

Modern versions of the origins of life tend to begin something like . . .

Once upon a time, a long time ago in the primordial soup, there had come into existence self-replicating molecules that were dependent on a particular enzyme to replicate. These molecules flourished, but eventually the replicating molecule population grew so big there wasn't enough enzyme to go around. At this point, the molecules organized into an autocatalytic web that was capable of producing its own enzyme. The individual molecules became dependent on the ongoing stability of the self-perpetuating web. Through trial and error, the web of molecules learned to maximize cooperation between its individual self-replicating molecules, creating greater stability.

Eventually, most possible niches in the environment became exploited by various versions (mutations) of the metabolisms, with each competing for whatever molecular food was available. This continued until they had no more room for further development. Maintaining stability of the metabolism eventually led to stagnation. Whereas a single molecule is free to explore vast possibilities of mutation in order to adapt to its environment, the stable network of molecules was constrained by a web of interdependent relationships, which held them together.

Since the single cell and single metabolism niches were filled, and that level of organization having been maximized, the only niches in the environment left to take advantage of required organization at a new level, with greater complexity. Alliances, or symbiotic relationships, between various combinations of metabolisms were experimented with until a new sort of stability, using the different capabilities of the cooperating metabolisms, was found. The coalition enabled each metabolism to develop their unique capabilities, with a sort of division of labor in which one metabolism's by-product is another's food. This coalition created a more robust system capable of inhabiting new territories that had previously been toxic or inhospitable to its members individually.

These super-metabolisms eventually learned to encase themselves in vesicles, which enabled them to transport themselves into and colonize new territory. In doing so, the first forms of life, bacteria or prokaryotes, were born. As stability led to stagnation, when all the niches at that level were filled, it became necessary for the simple unicellular prokaryotes to join together to form communities: more complex eukaryotic cells. These were the first cells with nuclei. Their mitochondria and other organelles had previously been independent bacterial cells before infecting one another and symbiotically linking together.

Previously independent prokaryotes, now parts of eukaryotic cell, took on the functions that their emergent capabilities could manage. One became the nucleus for managing cooperation between the parts and carrying the genetic material, another became mitochondria, with the mechanisms for burning sugars, and the chloroplasts, which handled the photosynthesis. In other words, simple bacteria, each with their own capabilities, such as swimming, metabolizing sugars and using sunlight, organized themselves into more complex one-celled organisms.

The prokaryotes (non-nucleated cells), although part of a larger cell, continued to evolve within the whole, as the cell made adaptations in how it interacted with its changing environment. What was good for an organelle was not necessarily what was good for the cell as a whole; for example, mutation that favored chloroplasts might have been detrimental to mitochondria. This competition within the cell needed to be mediated in someway for stability to be maintained. Instead of each organelle replicating independently in competition with one another, a single organelle took over the function of replication and thereby became the nucleus, specializing in harboring and activating the genetic material for replication of the cell as a whole.

In the process of stabilizing this community of previously independent bacteria, the other organelles lost their individual ability to replicate and truly became interdependent on one another for survival. Each cell integrated an 'intelligent' nucleus that helped organize the various communal parts into a more complex individual.

What are the essential elements of this self-organizing process?

- An entity does its best with what it has until the limits of this way of functioning in its environment are reached and stagnation sets in.
- To overcome the stagnation the entity seeks out more efficient ways of relating to the environment, including forming or improving coalitions with other entities.
- The entities maximize their cooperative effectiveness to exploit all the existing niches in the accessible environment.
- The entity's boundaries breakdown; what is essential is preserved, while the entities in coalition exchange information or capabilities.
- Some entities lose their ability to function individually, as various mergers are experimented with.
- The different capabilities of the previous separate entities symbiotically link to form a larger/more complex organization (organism).
- The newly formed, more complex entity has more options and opportunities in the environment. Its activities create new niches and opportunities for other entities.
- To consolidate the growth, a higher order of intelligence emerges to minimize internal competition and maximize cooperation between parts.

It's not difficult recognize the correlation of these evolutionary phases to the developmental challenges we face in personal, social and commercial contexts. Let's examine its structure more closely and articulate the discrete steps taken to get from life-threatening stagnation, while regulating potential chaos, to forming more complex and effective levels of organization.

Networks within Networks

> If people ever journey for extended periods in outer space, the endeavor will never be as machinate and barren as Star Trek. The vision of sterile engineering emancipating us from our planetmates is not only tasteless and boring, it borders on the hideous. No matter how much our species preoccupies us, life is a far wider system. Life is an incredibly complex interdependence of matter and energy among millions of species beyond (and within) our own skin. These Earth aliens are our relatives, our ancestors, and part of us. They cycle our matter and bring us water and food. Without "the other" we do not survive. Our symbiotic, interactive, interdependent past is connected through animated waters.[31] *Lynn Margulis*

Within a living system, the whole is greater than the sum of its parts. The essential qualities of a living system exist within the relationships and interactions between its parts within the context of the whole, rather than within the individual parts themselves. What makes a functioning living human body is not merely a liver, plus a brain, skin, blood and so on, but rather how all these various parts relate with one another within a system of cooperative interaction.

If we dissect a body into its parts, we will no longer have a living human; we will have a collection of dead parts. The properties of the parts are not intrinsic properties; they can be understood only within the context of the larger whole. A functioning brain, liver or eye only exists in relationship to the integrity of the whole body.

In isolation, a brain will not think, a liver won't filter blood, and an eye will not see. In isolation, we can't fully understand what role the brain, liver or eye plays in the functioning and wellbeing of the other parts and/

or the body as a whole. Just as our welfare as human beings is inexorably linked with the other organisms with which we share our ecosystems, every aspect of creation is defined by its relationships to the rest of creation. Life is relationships. The better the relationships, the better the quality of life.

People often come to psychotherapy with the idea, "I would be happy if you could just help me get rid of the part that makes me behave, think or feel in a particular way." Generally, the reason they are having the problem is their inability to include that part of them in their life. A person's psychological wellbeing, like the wellbeing of an ecosystem, is dependent on a biodiversity of participation, with each part fulfilling and finding fulfillment in its niche. As with the health of our bodies, wellbeing is dependent on all the various systems cooperating with and supporting one another. For there to be a healthy ecology of the mind, there must be cooperative and balanced relationships between the various psychological functions. For example, it is generally important to have a balance between the need to appreciate the way things are and the need to discern how things could be better: deciding to adapt to your current workplace or to look for a new job. It is in attending more adequately to the parts of us that seem to be causing problems that we gain greater inner cooperation and effectiveness in handling life's challenges.

Wisdom of Circularity

> Living systems as they exist on the earth today are characterized by exergonic metabolism, growth, and replication (and reproduction), all organized in a closed casual circular process that allows for evolutionary changes in the way the circularity is maintained, but not for loss of the circularity.[32] *Humberto Maturana*

Living systems depend on not only the internal organization and structure of relating between individual components, but also the patterns and principles of how relationships are organized within larger systems. The generative and self-maintaining patterns of relating in systems are known as feedback loops. Early systems thinkers defined two types: self-balancing feedback loops and self-reinforcing feedback loops. Self-balancing feedback loops serve to maintain stability of the status quo of a system and keep us in the comfort zone, whereas self-reinforcing patterns reinforce deviations from the status quo and take us into the challenge zone. Too much of either could be deadly.

Self-balancing patterns are essentially the habits of living that maintain safety and survival. Consider eating: our bodies need food to survive. When short-term energy reserves run low, we get a signal from our stomach that tells us we are hungry. When we eat food our stomach signals when it is full and we stop eating. This circular process continues throughout our lives and serves to maintain the overall integrity of our system.

If, for example, a person is not able to respond to the signals of hunger because of a lack of food then the self-balancing feedback loop of eating the usual amount of food is not possible. If this continues consistently for some time, the stomach will begin to shrink and the metabolism will slow down to conserve energy. This is a self-reinforcing pattern and will be perpetuated until the body reaches a point of equilibrium where the amount of food being consumed is equal to the amount of energy being expended, provided it is adequate for survival. The system then restabilizes itself within a self-balancing feedback loop that regulates food intake and energy expenditure within the parameter of sustenance available. Therefore, even if the previous amount of food became available, the person wouldn't feel hungry enough to eat the previous 'usual' amount. Since they have learned to conserve energy, they no longer require the old amount of food.

Another way one could respond to a lack of food would be to search out new food sources. The self-reinforcing pattern of exploration of new sources continues until adequate sources for acquiring food are found. Over time, these new methods are integrated into new self-balancing feedback loops that regulate stability. Challenges to self-balancing patterns become opportunities for the innovation and development of new interactional patterns.

Life Creates Opportunities for More Life

Necessity is the mother of invention and invention is the mother of necessity. Much of evolution results from species or organisms trying to adapt to new environmental demands. At the same time, when an evolutionary innovation, such as humans, arrives on the scene, other species and aspects of the ecosystem must change in order to accommodate the change. This is the necessity for the twin processes of self-organization and selection. The internet is a good example of this. Human understanding evolved to the point where the internet came into existence, and now so much of our innovation is evolving because of and in relation to it.

Systems exist in relation to other systems, within an environmental context, as parts of a larger system. Changes in the environmental system (less food available) will cause the smaller system to reorganize itself (eat less and conserve energy or discover new food sources). Likewise, changes in the smaller system will cause the larger system to reorganize itself. For example, rainforests attract rain. Too many trees cut down to graze animals for food production will, over time, lead to a decrease in rainfall, which in turn reduces available water for animals and grass, forcing a reduction in grazing.

The larger the system, or the smaller the subsystem, the more stable the self-balancing feedback loops will be. If our hungry friend (discussed above) discovers wild berries growing in the countryside near his home and picks them for himself and his family, he may also discover other natural food sources, such as wild fennel. Harvesting these for himself and his family will probably affect the community and environment he lives in very little. However, if he tells other people, or others simply begin copying him, there could be a change of eating habits for many people. If enough people do this, it may impact on the food available to wild animals that eat these foods, forcing them to find other sources. At some critical point, the larger system would reorganize itself into new self-regulating patterns in which a new stability could be maintained.

Intelligence Reigns

Living systems respond intelligently in self-regulating ways to internal and external changes in order to maintain the integrity of their wholeness and circularity. Living systems operate away from equilibrium. Living systems periodically destabilize and re-stabilize in response to internal and external events.

Non-living systems are far more stable and therefore predictable, depending on how networked they are with living systems. Tidal fluctuations of sea levels, regulated by the oceans' relationships to the sun and moon, are very stable and predictable. The water cycle on the other hand is much more linked with life on earth, which meant predicting rainfall (part of the water cycle) is more difficult unitl recently. Using chaos theory computers are able to model living systems and make weather prediction relatively reliable. Non-living systems primarily consist of self-stabilizing feedback loops, whereas living systems operate within ever-changing patterns of self-stabilizing and self-reinforcing feedback loops.

Living systems must have a constant flow of energy in order to survive. For evolution to occur, there must be fluctuations in the flow of energy to which the system must adapt. Too much fluctuation will stretch the system beyond its capacity to adapt; too little fluctuation won't provide the necessary stimulation or challenge for it to respond with innovation. The ever-increasingly complex and varied forms of energy and matter a system must respond to require the system to create increasingly complex patterns of behavior.

When a system has little innovation and is dominated by self-stabilizing patterns, it is called a closed system. Living or open systems, says biologist Stuart Kauffman, "exist on the boundary region of order near the edge of chaos." Chaos, in this context, is defined as infinite random fluctuations of energy and matter with the absence of predictability and order.

As part of the biosphere's self-organizing process, our lives as humans are also constantly destabilizing and restabilizing on the boundary region of order, near the edge of chaos. Although the process of destabilization and restabilization is constantly approaching chaos, there is an identifiable pattern we can understand, trust and even honor.

If we ignore this natural process, we relegate our lives to repetitive whirlpool-like vicious cycles. The more overly predictable and stable (compulsive) we try to keep our lives over long periods, the more we objectify our lives and are most likely to use brute force to maintain the status quo. However, since the balance between stability and change must be maintained, the greater the stability, the greater the potential for change and vice versa. Therefore, no matter how much we try to ignore the challenges that present themselves, the universal laws of self-organization will come to our rescue by increasing entropy and chaos to a point at which we need to recognize our true nature and change, or suffer!

Echoing Ericksonian psychologist, Ernie Rossi in *The Symptom Path to Enlightenment*, problems or symptoms that perturb the stability of our lives are simply an opportunity to wake up to a more expanded and evolving sense of who we are. The more we embrace our ability to change, the more relatively stable our lives become. The more we are able to maintain relative stability, the more resources we develop to respond innovatively.

Self-Organization Cycle

Systems regularly evolve new patterns of perception, cognition and action that regulate the flow of energy, matter and information, and require adjustments until new self-maintaining patterns are found. Once established, these homeostatic patterns ensure a system continues what is needed for it to survive until the next developmental challenge.

Homeostasis

As we adapt to change, our internal systems reorganize themselves. Homeostasis is maintained by learning how to relate to people and other members of our environment in ways that invoke predictable responses. The more we achieve predictability, the more predictable we become ourselves. Established patterns of interaction become habitual and automatic. Even when novel events enter into the picture, we will respond by bringing the system into familiar homeostatic patterns.

Destabilization and Reorganization

As the patterns reach their limit of being able to mediate our internal and/or external relationships, life gets more chaotic. When usual patterns don't bring the desired outcome, or if a previously acceptable outcome no longer feels adequate, the chaos can be perceived as external, internal or both. If we try to use the same old inadequate patterns, there will be an increase in the experience of chaos. This is a signal that the 'chaos' needs to be embraced in some way, so that new ways of relating more cooperatively can, out of necessity, be discovered and experimented with. The possibilities found to be most useful are then organized into new homeostatic patterns in which stability can be maintained.

The process of approaching equilibrium — destabilization — approaching chaos — reorganization — approaching equilibrium occurs with mathematical regularity. These developmental cycles can be represented mathematically as waves. (See diagram 3b.)

Self-Organization Cycle

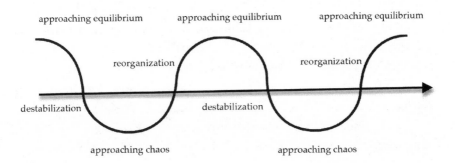

The Flexibility to Adapt

> Poised systems will therefore typically adapt to a changing environment gradually, but if necessary, they can occasionally change rapidly.[33] *Stuart Kauffman*

On one hand, surviving and thriving in the increasing complexity of life is dependent on our evolving ability to understand the underlying patterns in what can seem like the random chaos of life. On the other hand, being able to discover the unknown variables (potentially better choices) in what appears to be a predictable and uncooperative world is equally important. We experience life as being less chaotic and more cooperative the more we learn to adapt and cooperate with it. To do this, we must let go of our fixed notions of the way things are, while embracing what appears chaotic.

Leaps of Faith

The region between order and chaos is what Dan Siegel refers to as the *River of Integration* (2010). It is where leaps of faith are taken. We use what is known as a platform to leap into the unknown, trusting we will find new footholds of understanding as we become grounded in our experience of the new territory. Approaching order is more or less within the boundaries of what is known; approaching chaos is crossing the boundary into the unknown.

The river of integration fluctuates between a sense of *knowing* and a sense of *not knowing*. As we come to know more, we also come to know that there is more that we don't know, and we become more curious about what we don't know. A moment of recognition occurs. "Of course," we say. The 'penny drops', a veil falls away, and we see what was there all along. Our Aristotelian mind realizes what our Platonic mind has known all along.

Albert Einstein said, "The intuitive mind is a sacred gift and the rational mind is a faithful servant." We are always being invited into a deeper experience of our true nature and the true nature of the world around us, with its infinite possibilities. Too often, as Einstein goes onto to say, "We have created a society that honors the servant and has forgotten the gift." When people have lost their trust in the self-organizing guidance of their intuitive mind (soul), they will find themselves stuck in symptomatic, self-repeating vicious circles. It is the job of psychotherapy to help people open to the gift, learn how to serve the true nature of things (dharma), and get themselves back into the flow of the *river of integration*.

When orienting a client to the *river of integration*, Milton Erickson suggested, "Hypnosis is the ceasing to use your conscious awareness; in hypnosis you begin to use your unconscious awareness. Because unconsciously you know as much and a lot more than you do consciously. The conscious mind understands the logic of it, and the unconscious mind understands the reality." To embrace the evolving nature of life, we must learn to surrender what we know, so we can open to what we know that we didn't know we knew, and allow ourselves to know what we knew, but in a new way and to explore the unknown that is revealing itself to us in a new way.

Our Expanding World

The larger and more complex the system, the larger the field of evolutionary possibilities for the members of that system. For example, the societies that have been the quickest to evolve culturally and technologically have resided within the landmass of Asia and Europe. Contrast them with the Aboriginal people of Tasmania, who less than two hundred years ago were still using Stone Age tools and living in a hunter-gatherer society. There has been an ongoing exchange of information regarding language, writing, agriculture, art and all sorts of technological developments between the cultures of Europe and Asia, whereas the Aboriginal Tasmanians lived for tens of thousands of years in isolation.

For a system to evolve, boundaries must be strong enough to minimize conflict and competition, yet permeable enough to allow for an exchange of energy, materials and information. Being more complex does not equal being better. I'm not saying it is better to be European than Aboriginal; rather, I refer to a pattern in the way things evolve. When modern and primitive cultures meet, they do learn from one another; however, the overall trend is always towards modernization, even though many useful capacities may be lost along the way.

This trend is this same in our individual lives. The more we are involved in life, the more opportunities we are exposed to. The more we take advantage of those opportunities, the more we must learn to integrate them into our lives. With greater or deeper involvement in life and the knowledge that comes with that, we become more aware of things we don't know, yet are drawn to know more about. Innovations create new opportunities and challenges. In addition, each generation tends to build on the order of the previous generation.

As a global society, with even greater capacity to exchange information between various subsystems (countries, cultures, disciplines), cultural evolution has accelerated to the point where most of us feel like it is hard to keep up with a changing world that consistently brings us to the brink of chaos. This process seems to be accelerating; therefore, our ability to continually surrender to the unknown and find effective ways of managing the changes seems more imperative than ever.

It's not hard to feel like life is a bit like being a nuclear reactor. It is our developmental challenge to keep up with the emerging changes, while slowing some of the chain reactions, so our lives can thrive on the boundary region of order, near the edge of chaos; not to be out of control like a nuclear explosion (chaos), or just stagnant like a lump of uranium (order).

The most common problems individuals seek therapy for are depression (clinging to order) and anxiety (resisting chaos). The two most common problems couples seek therapy for are too much arguing (chaos) or not enough passion from playing it too safe (too much order).

Siegel uses the acronym FACES: Flexible, Adaptive, Coherent, Energized, and Stable, to describe the qualities needed to maintain the balance between these polarities and stay in the self-organizing cycle of the *River of Integration*.

Attractors of Self-Organization

In Chaos Theory, *strange attractors* are processes that are stable, confined, and yet never do the same thing twice: living or life-like systems. Computer generated fractal patterns are simulations of strange attractors generated from three non-linear equation solutions. Each solution curve generated by the equations tends to occur in a particular area (the attractor area), cycling around randomly, no set number of times, never crossing itself, staying in the same phase space, and displaying similarity at any scale.

Given these qualities, fractals are of the one the best models available to us as simulations of living systems. Fractals demonstrate clearly how attractors act on the system by collecting the responses systems make to internal and external events (trajectories of perturbation) within a pattern with boundaries. Attractors act as the determinants of patterns of self-organization. A gene is an example of an attractor that determines patterns of how an organism self-organizes. The social sciences recognize that certain ideas or beliefs serve as attractors around which society organizes, which are referred to as memes.

Attractors are themes the universe self-organizes itself around and within; they are another name for Platonic forms or morphic fields. These themes operate in same the way jazz musicians begin with a particular chord progression combined with melody and rhythm. Once the groove is set, the musicians are then free, within inter-woven and overlapping musical patterns, to improvise upon those themes. Nations are organized within and around attractors defined by their unique environmental context, sets of ideals, principles, values, beliefs and capability to relate to one another and other things in the environment in a way that reflects a national and/or cultural identity. Individual human beings, as subsystems within the larger cultural or familial systems, are self-organized in the same way. Systems, regardless of their size, can organize themselves around attractors that naturally promote growth and evolution, or around attractors that simply lock a system into vicious cycles and entropy.

> Attractors describe the long-term behavior of dynamically changing systems in biology and the depths of the human psyche as well as social and cultural institutions.[34] *Ernest Rossi*

To promote healthy systems it is helpful to understand the different types of attractors. Periodic regimes are characterized by fixed-point attractors, which at least for a while regulate a steady state or limited cycle of interaction within a larger system. Chaotic regimes (evolving systems) are characterized by strange attractors, which typically demonstrate a high dimension of complexity. Strange attractors are self-generative and are calculated by using the output of the initial step as the input for the following step. They also have a self-reflective quality in which patterns form on infinitely large and small scales.

The macrocosm reflects the microcosm; organizational patterns of family systems are similar to the organizational patterns of one-celled organisms, which have similarities to the organizational patterns of ecosystems. To maintain homeostasis, a system will organize itself for a period of time around a fixed-point attractor. The longer a system remains organized around a fixed-point attractor, the more it will resemble a nonliving system, such as our solar system or a whirlpool. Non-living systems will remain in stable patterns for relatively long periods of time with relatively little change, whereas living systems are characterized by ongoing cycles of change punctuated by periods of relative stability. To be most alive and healthy, we need regular periods of stability punctuated with breakdowns in the stability that lead to breakthroughs into more evolved patterns of organization.

Evolution is the process by which a system develops within the basin of one attractor, until it has more or less exhausted the creative range of possibilities of that region of perception and capability. The system, having reached the peak of fitness at the boundary of that attractor, spills over into a higher dimensional phase space: the basin of a higher-dimensional attractor. Ernest Rossi describes this as, "a process that gives evolutionary significance to the phrase *out of the frying pan and into the fire!*" When our level of frustration reaches breaking point and we must make a change, we must leap out of our realm of known possibilities into the chaotic fire of infinite possibilities, before finding a frying pan of higher dimension to accustom ourselves to.

Our lives are most likely to resemble a nonliving system when operating from ideas that tend to concretize our perceptions of life. When our lives are organized too long around a fixed-point attractor, symptoms will arise that make it increasingly difficult to continue to act in predictable ways. Rigid beliefs (fixed-point attractors) tend to nominalize the evolving processes of life into static objects. Our patterns of language reflect this when we speak of a 'relationship' (concrete and static) instead of ways of 'relating'. Rigid beliefs keep us locked into a world we think we know and blind us to the creative potential of the unknown.

We could say that an unhealthy self-concept (ego) is where a fixed-point attractor has enough gravity to overcome the influence of strange attractors (our soul's agenda). Our lives then become more similar to nonliving systems: repetitive and predictable, thereby increasing the likelihood of psychological and physical disease, premature aging, and even death.

Nine Phases of the Developmental Cycle

Drawing on these theories enables us to expand our understanding of the four phases of the self-organization cycle (approaching order, destabilization, approaching chaos, re-organization) into nine:

- In homeostasis, the system operates in relative stability and approximates a non-living system.
- Perturbation of the homeostasis raises awareness of the limitations of the current level of organization (attractor basin).
- The system attempts to make the necessary adaptations by doing more or different combinations of what it already is doing.
- The system climbs to the rim (fitness peak) of the basin of that particular attractor, pushing the current mode of functioning to the limit.
- At this point it moves into the transitional phase, between levels of organization, in which the inadequacies of the system's ability to relate become more apparent and boundaries begin breaking down, opening the system to creative potentials.
- Boundaries become increasingly diffuse, allowing a greater flow of information into the system, and it sorts for what is vital for survival.
- The system maintains its integrity around essential structures or patterns, while others disintegrate and are eliminated.
- Balance shifts away from the previous level of organization towards chaos.
- On the boundary of order and chaos, the system seeks out possible new attractors to organize itself around.
- New attractors are selected, organized and integrated with existing essential structures.
- The changes become consolidated into a new level of homeostatic functioning.

The Enneagram as a Map of Growth and Change

Upon completion of every developmental cycle, the system does not return to the same homeostasis, but to a higher level of organization. A spiral is likely the best geometric representation, though some view cycles as a wave or a circle (see diagram 3c). With each complete cycle, the circle goes higher and wider.

Each phase correlates with core attributes of each of the Enneagram's nine personality types. Although the creators of the Enneagram didn't have the theoretical constructs available today, I believe they had an intuition about this pattern. Perhaps the Enneagram was their attempt, with the mathematics available at that time, to construct, like fractals, a model of living systems.

The Enneagram is a geometric structure consisting of three geometric forms: the circle, the inner butterfly-like shape and the equilateral triangle. Traditionally, these geometric figures are said to represent various metaphysical principles.

Change Cycle

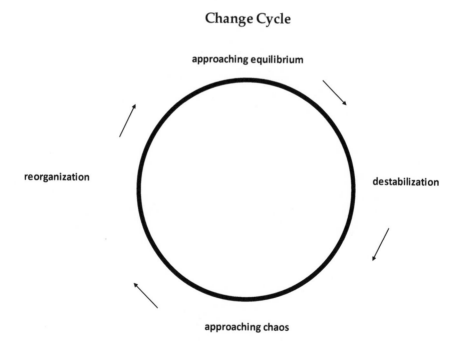

approaching equilibrium

reorganization

destabilization

approaching chaos

The circle represents the whole of creation. It can also represent the circular nature of creation and the cycles of life.

The equilateral triangle represents the tendency for the oneness of creation to be perceived in divisions of three:

- gas, liquid and solid
- proton, electron and neutron
- strong force, weak force and electromagnetism
- greater, lesser and equal
- height, depth and breadth
- past, present and future
- birth, life and death
- beginning, middle and end
- inner, outer and membrane
- three primary colors (blue, yellow and red)
- thought, feeling and action
- towards, away and stationary
- self-preservation, social instincts and sexual instincts
- This is echoed in the way the great religions perceive spiritual reality
- Christianity: Father (God), Soul (Holy Spirit), Jesus (Human Son)
- Buddhism: dharmakaya, sambhogakaya and nirmanakaya
- Hinduism: Brahma, Vishnu, Shiva
- Taoism: The Three Pure Ones

The butterfly-like form figure connects the repeating numbers *1, 4, 2, 8, 5, 7,* and is generated by the mathematical equation $1 \div 7 = 0.142857142857\ldots$ It is symbolic of the oneness of creation perceived in divisions of seven. This is recognized in schema that are counted in sevens:

- colors of visible spectrum of light
- physiological systems (respiratory, immune, endocrine, digestive, nervous, circulatory, reproductive)
- energy levels of the periodic table
- basic measurements: meter, kilogram, second, ampere, kelvin, mole, candela

- notes of the musical scale
- chakras of the human energetic system
- continents and oceans of Earth
- days of the week

How the Enneagram symbol was discovered is unknown, but its ability to represent the nature of creation is elegant and simple. The integration of the three mathematical principles — wholeness, and wholeness divided by three and by seven, like the integration of three mathematical formulas to create a fractal — has created a framework for profound understanding of the basic patterns by which life self-organizes. Combining the three principles produces an image of a circle (cycle) divided into nine phases (see diagram 3d).

Enneagram of the Developmental Cycle

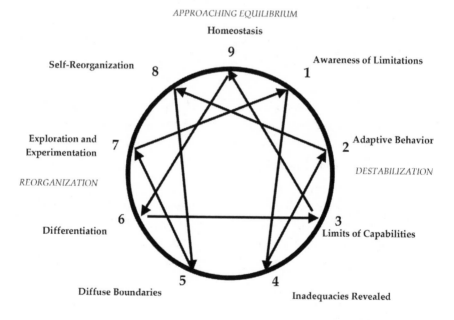

At the top of the circle is NINE, which represents homeostasis and the system approaching equilibrium. Going clockwise around the circle, as the system moves towards destabilization, ONE represents awareness of limitations, TWO, adaptive behavior. At THREE the system reaches the limits of its current structure. At FOUR the system disintegrates further as it approaches chaos, highlighting the inadequacies of the system. FIVE represents boundaries becoming increasingly diffuse and sorts for what is, and isn't, vital for survival. SIX represents the system maintaining its integrity around essential structures or patterns, while others disintegrate or are eliminated. On the boundary of chaos, moving toward reorganization, SEVEN represents the system seeking new attractors to organize itself around. EIGHT represents the selection of new attractor(s) and beginning the self-reorganization process, returning to NINE and the consolidation of new ways of organizing life into self-maintaining homeostatic patterns.

It is possible to think of the movement around the circle as a step-by-step process, though living systems are more complex than this. Some parts of the system are more active in relationship to one another at any time. If we were in phase TWO, we would also draw on the qualities associated with EIGHT and FOUR. In addition, remnants of phase ONE and preludes of phase THREE would play a part. However, because we are discovering essential wholeness as a web of relationships between all its parts, all aspects of our wholeness are always presents and accessible. To help us understand the complex relationships of a system, we have dissected it; however when a living organism is dissected, what is destroyed is the pattern of life itself. This is why we need an approach that addresses wholeness.

Although essential to the structure of the Enneagram, we will not be discussing the inner network of relationships represented by the internal connecting lines until a later chapter. Remember, however, that the design of the Enneagram, and therefore its integrity as a system, is based on these internal structures and how they support the cyclic process of change.

Phases of the Enneagram Developmental Cycle

NINE —Homeostasis

The system organizes itself at the edge of chaos with self-maintaining feedback loops (homeostasis). It regulates predictability and equilibrium by the consolidation of emergent relationship patterns into a more robust system, which in turn will effect adjustments in the larger system to which it belongs.

Primary concern: How to maintain stability?

ONE — Awareness of Limitations

There is a growing awareness in the system of the limitations of relating to life within the parameters defined by the existing structure, which initiates the destabilization of homeostasis.

Primary concern: What's the problem?

TWO — Adaptive Behavior

The system attempts to adapt to the increased demands of the emergent properties within the parameters of the existing structure by relating to circumstances more effectively. This leads to an amplification of self-reinforcing feedback loops.

Primary concern: How to adapt to problems?

THREE — Limits of Capabilities

By climbing fitness peaks the system (attempting to reestablish homeostasis) reaches the limits of its existing structure. At the boundary of its current attractor basin, the systems efforts spill over into a higher dimension of opportunity.

Primary concern: How to promote success within the status quo?

FOUR — Inadequacies Revealed

The inadequacies of the system become more apparent as boundaries begin breaking down, opening the system to untapped creative potentials.

Primary concern: What are the inadequacies?

FIVE — *Diffuse Boundaries*

Boundaries become more diffuse, which allows a greater flow of information into the system and initiates a sorting of what is vitally essential for survival.

Primary concern: Why is this happening?

SIX — *Differentiation*

The system maintains its integrity around essential structures or patterns, while others disintegrate and may be eliminated. Balance shifts away from the previous level of organization towards chaos.

Primary concern: What to hold onto and what to let go of?

SEVEN — *Exploration and Experimentation*

At the boundary of order and chaos the system seeks out new couplings and internal patterns of organization. Exploring various ways of relating to changes in the environment creates possibilities to be discovered and experimented with.

Primary concern: What's next? What else is possible?

EIGHT — *Self Reorganization*

Certain new couplings are selected, organized and integrated with existing essential structures into a more complex and robust order and a new sense of self.

Primary concern: How to gain control?

NINE — *Consolidation and Re-stabilization*

The system organizes itself with self-maintaining feedback loops (homeostasis). It regulates predictability and equilibrium by consolidating emergent relationship patterns into a more robust system. This in turn will effect adjustments in the larger system to which it belongs.

Primary concern: How to regain stability?

Spirals of Change

With each complete cycle there is a shift to a new level of organization. If we turn the Enneagram on its side, we see that it is a spiral with one level of growth leading to another, in a fractal-like pattern.

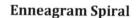

Enneagram Spiral

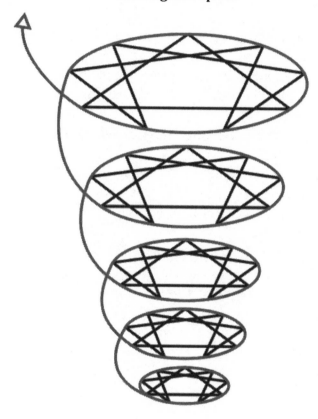

CHAPTER FOUR

The Birth to Infancy
Developmental Cycle

Life is a series of developmental cycles. These cycles occur in a variety
of interwoven streams, including physiological, physical coordination,
communication, intellectual, psychosexual, social, creative and spiritual.
Some of these develop relatively independently from others, while others
seem to be quite interdependent. For example, we could be advanced
in analytic thinking, but have poorly developed verbal communication
or emotional empathy skills. However, to develop through different
psychosexual stages, it is imperative to develop verbally, emotionally,
sexually and socially. In order to thrive in life and handle its full spectrum
of challenges, we need a robust ecology of psychological, emotional,
physical and spiritual capabilities.

Blueprint for Life's Transitions

Aside from conception, we could say our first major developmental
transition is from the prenatal life of the womb, through birth, and into
infancy. It is a radical transition in how we experience who we are and the
world we live in. Psychological theorists who have differing orientations,
from Otto Rank and Margaret Mahler to John Bowlby and Stanislav Grof,
have explored ideas about how this initial transition may affect the way
an individual handles many of the other transitions in life. This initial

transition serves as a sort of blueprint of how we will experience later developmental crises.

An interesting question is whether the sort of birth we have defines our personality characteristics, or do prenatal personality characteristics determine the way we respond to the birthing process? As we discussed with evolution, it is likely to be both (selection and self-organization) at the same time. In *The Brain that Changes Itself*, Norman Doidge, MD describes how the thoughts we think can switch our genes on and off, thereby altering our brain anatomy. The anatomy then affects the kind of world we perceive. We are able to think about the world as we would like it to be. In the process of doing this, our brain begins to rewire itself by turning on and off the relevant genes. The new brain structure begins perceiving a different world; it is able to conceive of a world that is different from the one we live in. The process of imagining it switches on genes required to activate the brain structure needed to bring that reality into existence. This seems to point towards consciousness that transcends the brain: a consciousness that can shape a brain the way it prefers, rather than merely a brain that shapes consciousness.

While examining the birth to infancy developmental cycle, we might ask how experiencing difficulties or trauma in one phase or another could shape a person's perceptions of the process of change and the personality characteristics that encode those assumptions.

As we examine how the developmental transition of birth to infancy follows the phases mapped by the Enneagram Developmental Cycle, it is important to remember that life processes do not occur in simple, discrete steps; rather, there is an ebb and flow. It is most likely a two-steps-forward-one-step-back progression, with more than one context of development actively changing at any one time. There are, however, distinct and recognizable phases that living systems, human beings included, pass through in the processes of growing, learning and evolving at every stage of life. Although the contexts, agendas and relationships may change throughout our lives, we can recognize that the essential qualities that inform the processes, albeit with ever-changing faces and circumstances, remain consistent.

There is anecdotal evidence that the type of birth experience a person has seems to have an impact on that person's basic orientation to life.

William Emerson, PhD, in his article the Vulnerable Prenate[35], reported his discussions with R. D. Laing, Frank Lake, Stan Grof, and other prominent psychotherapists, revealing common threads that emerged during psychotherapy with patients with violent and aggressive tendencies:

- Multiple prenatal traumas are more likely to result in violence and aggression than single traumas
- The greater the degree of bonding deficits, the greater the likelihood of violence and aggression in adulthood
- Prenatal traumas that involve loss, abandonment, or rejection are more likely to impact bonding than other traumatic themes
- Direct exposure to aggression and violence during the prenatal period is highly predictive of violence and aggression during adulthood

There is a different orientation to life for those babies who have a pleasant time in the womb and a gentler transition out of the womb and into the larger world.

Therapist as Midwife

I like the notion of the role of the psychotherapist being like a midwife to the aspects of a client that are trying to emerge into life. The role of a midwife is to first and foremost help the mother to trust in the birthing process and know what to expect. The skilled midwife only intervenes if the mother and/or baby are stuck in a particular phase of the birthing process; otherwise, she holds the space to allow nature to take its course. In order to help his patients trust in their ability to change and grow, Milton Erickson, MD was known for telling stories to his clients about the different learning and developmental processes they have gone through quite naturally, like learning to walk, talk, read or write. Making the transition from the womb to living in the world is one of the most radical changes in circumstances that people experience in life. A skilled therapist will help their clients trust in their innate ability to make the transition from one stage of life to the next. Any skilled therapist, like Erickson, intervenes by helping the client

Eric Lyleson

find the resources to release their inhibitions to the natural process and to make the next most obvious step in their life's journey.

Mapping the Birth Process onto the Enneagram Developmental Cycle

I will examine the developmental process of moving from life in the womb to infancy and how it maps onto the Enneagram Developmental Cycle. By examining the key characteristics of each phase of development, we will not only understand this primary stage of development, but also see how it is a template for all of life's transitions. The universal patterns that inform the evolution of life at the most primordial level are the same that inform human birth and all developmental processes.

NINE — Homeostasis

The system organizes itself at the edge of chaos with self-maintaining feedback loops (homeostasis).

Some key characteristics of phase NINE are:

- undifferentiated and merged relationships
- effortless automatic relating
- maintaining harmony
- minimizing conflict
- maximizing stability and comfort
- appreciation and contentment with the status quo
- germination of potential capabilities

Phase NINE — Fetus at about 30–36 Weeks

A fetus is from about twenty-four weeks old may survive birth, but chances for survival greatly increase after thirty-six weeks. It is generally best that the baby continues to mature in the safety and security of her mother's womb for a full nine months. Stanislav Grof describes the fetus' experience of the womb as "an 'oceanic' state without any boundaries where we do not differentiate between ourselves and the maternal organism or ourselves and the external world." There is little, if any, differentiation between the individual self and the maternal-infant system. In a Japanese study, researchers found clear evidence that babies are profoundly affected by their mother's emotional state.[36] It appears that if the mother generally feels happy, the fetus will generally feel happy, and if the mother feels distressed, the baby will also feel distressed.

The emphasis at this phase of development is on maintaining harmony within the parameters of the current system, which allows the momentum of development to be sufficiently nurtured. With homeostasis, there is a tendency towards individual components of a larger system (in this case the mother–fetus) merging into an undifferentiated relationship with one another, which minimizes conflict and maximizes stability.

In the intrauterine environment, the fetus automatically makes the necessary ongoing homeostatic adjustments to maintain stability and equilibrium. Everything may not be perfect, but they automatically find ways to be content with the status quo of their womb world, including adapting to adverse conditions. For example, the fetus of a woman who smokes will adapt to the poorer health conditions inside the womb and be born weighing less than a child of a nonsmoker. At this early phase of life, we really have little option other than to take what it brings us, and adjust our needs and potentials for development within the parameters of what is available.

There is slow, steady growth within the stability and confines of the womb. Seeds of potential capabilities begin germinating, although they won't become actualized until later developmental stages. For example, the prenate uses its lungs to practice breathing by inhaling amniotic fluid. They also drink about a pint of amniotic fluid a day and urinate the same amount. Early in the third trimester, the limbs and sense organs are fairly functional, but will not be used or developed much until after being born. Studies have shown that prenates who are spoken or read to while in the womb tend to develop verbal skills more readily later in life. The richer and more stable life is for the fetus, the more they will have to draw upon during future windows of opportunity to learn.

Babies in utero sleep a lot in their early weeks and months and, judging by the frequency of their REM sleep, have active dream lives. This happens despite their waking lives being confined by the limits of the uterine environment, which it can be assumed is relatively unstimulating. Dreams activate neuro-circuits in the brain that may later be needed in their waking life.

Although the child begins moving fairly early and continues to kick, poke and prod their mother's abdominal wall, it is important, especially in the last few weeks before birth, that she doesn't 'rock the boat' too much and trigger contractions before it is ready to be born. This need for stability is a very common one and is necessary at stages throughout our lives. We will all need periods where we avoid rocking the boat: at work, with our spouses, or even with friends, by not being too assertive with our personal agendas. During these periods, there is an appreciation of life as it is and development tends to continue in an effortless, automatic way. There can be a sense that everything will take care of itself. We may sense this when our jobs, living situations and relationships feel 'good enough' and have settled into comfortable routines.

Because we live in a world where change is the only constant, it is important that we rest every now and then. To rest we must be comfortable. Since this is the phase in the developmental cycle where we get to have a rest, comfort and stability are what are most important. However, like a duck that is paddling crazily, while seeming to calmly glide across the surface of a pond, the unconscious mind is processing information and preparing for change through dreams and fantasies, even if these dreams never make it into consciousness.

Core questions

How can I continue to feel content and live harmoniously in the world as I know it? How do I maintain stability?

ONE — *Awareness of Limitations*

There is a growing awareness of the limitations, which initiates the destabilization of the homeostatic functioning.

Some key characteristics of phase ONE are:

- experiencing the limitations of the systemic context
- frustration with the status quo
- perturbation of undifferentiated relationships
- need for greater self-direction and independence
- intention to move onto to the next stage of life.

Phase ONE — Fetus at about 34 - 37 Weeks

At about thirty-four weeks the baby begins to experience the limitations of the environment they live in. They have a very good chance of surviving if born from this point on. This gives them a type of independence should the womb environment cease to be nurturing or safe. Their eyes tend to be open when awake and closed when asleep, and their waking state gains a greater level of awareness.

The womb is progressively less sufficient for ongoing development. The bigger they grow, the greater their capabilities for movement become. However, due to the limitations of the womb, they are less able to exercise these emerging capabilities; therefore, the mother experiences the kicks as less forceful. The flow of nutrients through the umbilical cord is becoming increasingly insufficient for continued growth. The maturing digestive and respiratory systems are nearly developed and need a different environmental context to be of use to the infant. There is growing frustration with the limitations of the intrauterine environment.

This pattern continues throughout the lifespan. At any stage of life, as the limitations of our habitual patterns of maintaining comfort and stability become increasingly apparent, we inherently begin to feel a growing sense of dissatisfaction, annoyance, or anger. This could happen in relation to work, socializing, and many other contexts. We naturally ask ourselves, "What's wrong?" or "What is limiting my growth?", and then "How could or should things be better?"

For the child almost ready to be born, there are more ideal circumstances suited to their emergent needs and capabilities. They need air to breathe, milk to drink, space to move in, and things to hear, see, feel, taste and smell. There are people, places and things to make contact with and relate to. And there is an ever-smaller, increasingly constrictive womb to escape from. The undifferentiated relationship with the mother is perturbed by the awareness of increasingly apparent limitations of space and nutrients needed to grow. By noticing the negative elements of womb life, the prenate is beginning the process of separating from the existing type of relationship they have with their mother.

At any stage of life, the frustration of limitations wakes people from the dreamy inertia of operating on the automatic pilot of dependency on a larger system. The need to become more self-directed and independent intensifies as the once comfortable and supportive womb-like structures of our lives become untenable for our continued growth.

There are other dimensions of experience that our emergent self will need to expand into. In a sense, there is a biological realization that the purpose of being in the womb is not to stay there comfortably forever, but to be born. The organism's intention is to be born and move on to the next stage of life. The ending of life in the womb is necessary for the reformation of life as an infant in the world. We have life beyond the boundaries of the womb and that transition is critical for our survival.

The baby's intention has changed from maintaining stability to being born, but there are still many smaller steps to take before that goal realized.

Core questions

What are the limitations of my circumstances? How could life be better?

TWO — Adaptive Behavior

The system attempts to adapt to the increased demands within the parameters of the existing structure by relating to the environment more effectively.

Some key characteristics of phase TWO are:

- the rise of a sense of two aspects of self
- making accommodations to optimize survival
- awareness of who in the system holds power
- focusing on the needs of emergent self
- desire to engage in more enriching ways
- manipulating circumstances to achieve the most advantageous position

Phase TWO –– Fetus at about 36 - 39 Weeks

As further development becomes increasingly constrained toward the end of the third trimester, the unborn child's emerging needs for space outside the womb, greater nourishment, and so on, become more imperative. Frustration about the status quo, in comparison to what could be, gives rise to two separate agendas. One part of the child is committed to maintaining comfort and stability within the status quo and the other knows something else is not only possible, but also necessary, to survive and thrive. They are totally dependent on their mother's womb and the mother has the power to determine the baby's quality of life. They contort physically; even their growth is limited to accommodate to the limitations of the womb and not overly stress the mother.

At this phase, we are focused not only on who has the power to dictate the quality of our lives, but even our survival. The potential danger of being overly accommodating to the powerful other is that our emergent self is compromised, like in codependent relationships. This affects us later in life because at any age there are certain people or systems with whom we are in dependent or interdependent relationships. The child naturally begins to redirect the focus of empathic accommodation away from the 'significant other' towards the needs of their emergent self.

The current relationship to mother is no longer adequate as the emergent self has needs that will require different ways of relating, other than simply being in the womb, absorbing nutrients from the placenta. There is an increasing desire to engage with the mother in a fuller and more enriching way, thereby enabling the prenate to get more of what they need to grow. For example, the prenate generally rotates at about thirty-six weeks from being upright to placing their head (or buttocks for a breech birth) at the mother's cervix. This serves to achieve the most advantageous position for the birthing process. These manipulations also increase the mother's awareness of her relationship with her unborn child and her own need to prepare for the birth. It is not insignificant that many mothers take on some sort of last-minute home improvement project, such as painting the nursery or reorganizing the kitchen cupboards, to prepare their 'nest' (functional aspects of the emergent environmental system).

The awareness of the prenate's growing needs, and the need to grow, increases until they reach the threshold of knowing they can't continue accommodating the womb. This is basically an amplification of a self-reinforcing feedback loop. The bigger, more mature and uncomfortable the fetus becomes, the more uncomfortable the mother becomes, and therefore she prepares for birth and her pelvis opens to accommodate her growing baby. The more the mother's hips open, the further down the prenate can rest, putting more pressure on the cervix, abdomen and pelvis. As these structures adjust to accommodate the child, the prenate drops further into position, and so on. In preparation for birth, the mother's uterus begins having increasingly frequent, irregular contractions (Braxton Hicks). These contractions may serve as signals to the prenate to prepare for birth, and they also amplify the already growing discomfort for both prenate and mother. As the mother and prenate continue to accommodate the escalating changes in preparation for birth, the more intolerable the existing relationship becomes.

Core questions

How do I get my desired response? What do I need, not just to maintain my current circumstances, but also to grow and thrive, to get ahead? How do I get myself out of this escalating predicament?

THREE — *Limits of Capabilities*

By climbing fitness peaks, the system (attempting to reestablish homeostasis) reaches the limits of its existing structure. At the boundary of its current attractor basin, the systems efforts spill over into a higher dimension of opportunity.

Some key characteristics of phase THREE are:

- developing and utilizing capabilities
- promoting one's agenda
- molding self to promote success
- assuming responsibility for evolving needs

Phase THREE — Fetus at about 38 - 41 Weeks (Full-term)

With development complete, during week 38 healthy babies gain about an ounce (28 grams) of fat per day, which helps regulate body temperature after birth. There is little room to move. The prenate knows they must develop and utilize new capabilities if they are going to continue their growth as a human being. The efforts they invest to get the process moving demonstrate their commitment to their own development. It is their responsibility, in preparation for birth, to move further down into their mother's pelvis and engage with the top of the cervix. This action impresses upon the mother her intention to do whatever is needed to promote the goal of being born.

In promoting her birthing agenda, the mother activates her adrenals in order to maximize her energy level. The cortisol circulates through her body and then is expelled via the prenate's urine into the amniotic sac. It stimulates the placenta and uterine membranes, communicating the message to alter their function from holding and containing to contracting and expelling the baby. The contractions are the mother's response to the fetus' efforts to meet the needs of its emergent self. As the baby's head engages further into the pelvis, it is pliable enough to be molded into the

87

streamlined shape needed to promote successful passage through the birth canal.

At any developmental life cycle stage, our intention to change is marked by taking steps in the desired direction that take us to the limits of our capabilities within that context. We make a commitment and assume responsibility for meeting our evolving needs by reaching beyond the comfort zone of our previous accomplishments.

Core questions

How do I begin getting what I need? How can I best promote my agenda?

FOUR — Inadequacies Revealed

The inadequacies of the system become more apparent as boundaries begin breaking down, opening the system to untapped creative potentials. Some key characteristics of phase FOUR are:

- realizing previously unused abilities or talents
- longing for what we most deeply want and need
- experiencing the humility of being stuck in circumstances beyond our control
- defying convention
- making our unique presence seen, heard and felt

Phase FOUR — Entering the Birth Canal

The maternal contractions initiated by the baby loosen the mucus plug in the cervix. Small capillaries in the cervix break and mucus and blood are discharged from the vagina and signal the onset of labor. In the uterus, the fetus has been encased in a membrane (amniotic sac) floating in fluid. Once the amniotic sac—the boundary that defines the womb—has ruptured, the fluid begins to leak and labor usually progresses more rapidly.

During birth, the fetus is expelled from the mother's uterus by the force of strong, rhythmic muscle contractions lasting anywhere from one to forty-eight hours. If the prenatal child thought the uterus was uncomfortable, they discover the birth canal to be even more limiting and painful. The baby descends into the birth canal and rotates its head and body to find its way through the constrictions of the pelvis. Under the pressure of uterine contractions and the narrow passageway of the birth canal, they realize previously unused abilities to squirm and withstand discomfort. Who hasn't experienced the frustration that comes with starting something new (to improve our circumstances) only to find we are worse off than before? This great sense of discomfort and disappointment can trigger an intense longing for what we most deeply want and need. This compelling desire keeps us moving towards a possibility of 'greener pastures'.

While at phase THREE the child has the power to initiate the birthing process, at FOUR they suddenly find themselves at the mercy of that process. How effective their mother's contractions are and how wide the birth canal opens is out of their control. The support available for their mother and the degree to which she is emotionally prepared are also beyond their influence. These factors are all part of a larger story, of which the baby is only a small part. Except for a bit of squirming, all they can do is surrender to the process that has begun.

Very few, if any, of the rules of the womb apply here. Most of the things the fetus did to maximize their well being in the womb are of little or no use. However, necessity is the mother of invention. To relate creatively to the unique circumstances, they are required to defy convention and have an attitude of, "I'll do what I want, when and how I want to." Any creative process entails allowing us to be affected by the creative forces of the universe, while adding our own unique way of relating to and expressing that process. In this way, we make our unique presence seen, heard and felt. Just as no two infants are alike, no two births or lives are exactly alike.

As adults entering into a creative change, we become aware of the pain of restricting patterns. Repressed memories and emotions often emerge that reinforce our need to change patterns of the past. Regression-based therapies are based on the premise that difficulties we have with life's transitions will reflect the difficulties we had at birth, or other early traumas. Quite often, what gets in our way most is our expectation that what has happened in the past is going to happen again. When making any transition, it is important to let go of any limiting perceptions based on past experience so that we may fully embrace new experiences as they present themselves. We can really squirm emotionally at this phase.

Core questions

What is getting in my way? What am I experiencing? What are my authentic desires?

FIVE — Diffuse Boundaries

Boundaries become increasingly diffuse, allowing a greater flow of information into the system. A sorting of what is essential for survival begins.

Some key characteristics of phase FIVE are:

- conserving energy for essential functions
- immersing oneself in observations
- dissociating from pain
- preparing for survival in new circumstances
- gathering information
- gaining insights from broader perspective

Phase FIVE — Descent into the Birth Canal

The passage through the birth canal signifies the dissolution of the boundary that has defined the fetus's life support system for nine months. As the child makes their way through the birth canal to the vaginal opening, endorphins released into the blood stream allow for some dissociation from the pain. As with any painful or traumatic effect, after an initial period of discomfort, the body goes into survival mode.

Although the uterine contractions continue to push down, once the baby is up against the vaginal opening, it must wait for the mother's vagina to open. Depending on how many babies the mother has birthed, her anatomy and her emotional state, the time in this position can last from minutes to twenty-hours or more. Physiological systems shut down whatever functions are not necessary for survival, conserving energy for those functions that are essential. After spending hours in a tight, periodically contracting birth canal, they are confronted with the limitations of their circumstances. The longer the birth takes, the more need there is to conserve energy. This concern can magnify the further the baby goes into the birth canal, as increased pressure on the umbilical cord can restrict the amount of blood reaching them. The wisdom of their body must decide what is essential to survive the transition to the external world.

Given that the birth canal is overwhelmingly confining, it's easy to imagine that finding more personal space would be of utmost importance. We can also imagine that being stuck in such a tight spot for hours could leave one feeling inadequate; many mothers in labor express their own self-doubts at this phase. Essentially, all the prenate can do is immerse themselves in their perceptions. In a sense, they are gathering information that might help them eventually escape this overwhelmingly intense relationship with the mother, and gain some sense of separation and independence outside of the womb. The learning process of this struggle prepares them for survival in the entirely different circumstances that await them. The necessity of the struggle is sometimes misunderstood. A story that is useful here is that of the young boy who, in seeing a butterfly trying to free itself from its cocoon, decides to help by opening the cocoon. The butterfly having not struggled to free itself didn't have the experience it needed to prepare itself for flight. When it tried to fly it couldn't.

Sensing the way ahead opening up, or seeing the light at the end of the proverbial tunnel, illuminates this as a process of transition, rather than just a painful dead-end. As adults, it's often when we feel we have hit rock bottom that a natural dissociation occurs and insights about the 'bigger picture' effortlessly arise in our consciousness. At the depths of catharsis, we can have spontaneous insight into our life situation from a broader, more universal perspective. FIVE represents this detached perspective of seeing where we are coming from and where we might be headed.

Core questions

Why is this happening? What is, and is not, essential? What do I need to know to get through this?

SIX — Integrity and Disintegration

The system maintains its integrity around essential structures or patterns, while others disintegrate and may be eliminated. Balance shifts away from the previous level of organization towards chaos.

Some key characteristics of phase SIX are:

- transition from what is known to what is unknown
- differentiation
- dissolving of psychosocial structures
- separating from dependent relationships
- becoming available to new ways of relating
- assuming greater personal authority

Phase SIX – Crowning, Extension and Birth

This is the final stage of transition from the known environment of the mother's womb to the unknown outside world. At this point, the baby begins to crown. Although they are trying to extend their head into the opening, they must wait for their mother to relax and allow her vagina to open. The mother is usually coached at this time to stop pushing, breathe, relax, and allow their vagina to open in its own time. The baby is totally dependent on the mother's ability to let go and trust in the natural forces of birth.

Shortly after leaving the womb, they must let go of total dependence on the umbilical cord and womb environment and begin depending on their own respiratory and digestive systems. Once the baby begins breathing, the umbilical cord can be cut, signaling the transition to the next level of differentiation. The baby's world is not totally chaotic, yet in comparison to the ordered structure of the womb, there are unknown variables to contend with. In making this transition, they do not lose anything that is essentially part of them; they simply shed the structures they have outgrown. After gaining a sort of independence from the mother, the baby quickly establishes a new relationship structure and set of interpersonal parameters. They achieve a greater level of differentiation between their sense of self and the self-mother system they have been enmeshed in — a process that will continue with each developmental crisis throughout their life.

Differentiation is the developmental process of balancing the drive for autonomy and the drive for relationship. To be human is to continually evolve in the way we experience ourselves as separate individuals, while evolving the ways we relate to and interdepend upon others. Giving up our individuality to be together with someone in a particular way is as defeating, in the long run, as giving up a relationship to maintain our sense of individuality. While not fully formed until much later, at birth a baby begins to develop an independent sense of who they are, separate from their mother, and straightaway begins exploring new ways of relating and depending on the mother and significant others.

When a baby is placed on their mother's chest immediately after being born, this transition, this separation, is likely to be made easier. With their head near their mother's heart, they can hear the sound that was familiar in the womb. At the same time, they are close to the breasts, the new source of nourishment and nurturing. The neonate who began sucking their thumb in the womb (an essential structure in their life up until this point) is ready to begin suckling their mother's breast, although they are entirely dependent on the mother placing the nipple in their mouth. Thumb sucking, like other important behaviors, will normally fall away at later developmental stages when it is no longer needed.

At any time in life, we arrive at SIX having gained insight into our old patterns and our need to move on. We ask ourselves whether we will remain faithful to our old ways or whether we are willing to have faith in the unknown possibilities before and within us. This usually means a deconstruction of inherited psychosocial structures (cultural memes) and opening to a greater inherent sense of personal responsibility. It is the sense of personal authority or power that makes re-authoring the emergent stories of our lives possible.

Core questions

What will I remain faithful to, and what will I begin to have faith in? What am I leaving behind and what am I opening up to? What if I do this, or what if I do that?

SEVEN — Exploration and Experimentation

At the boundary of order and chaos, the system seeks out new couplings and internal patterns of organization. Exploring various ways of relating to changes in the environment create possibilities to be discovered and experimented with.

Some key characteristics of phase SEVEN are:

- processing a large amount of information and sensory experience
- making new connections
- coupling new activities with existing capabilities and resources
- experimentation and exploration
- craving stimulation
- learning through trial and error
- spontaneous self-expression

Phase SEVEN — Post-birth to Age 7–8 Months

At birth, a baby's brain contains 100 billion neurons, roughly as many as there are stars in the Milky Way. In addition, there are a trillion glial cells, which form a kind of honeycomb that protects and nourishes the neurons. However, only a rudimentary pattern of wiring between these neurons is needed for them to function in the world. In the womb, the brain has laid out circuits that are, in a sense, its best guess about what will be required for vision, hearing, movement, language, and so forth. This is the result of a complex interplay of genes and environmental stimulation. Entering the world where so much more of the brain is put to use, it is up to neural activity driven by a flood of sensory experiences to take this rough blueprint and progressively refine it.

To accomplish this, the brain produces trillions more connections between neurons. The number of synapses in one layer of the visual cortex, for example, rises from around 2,500 per neuron at birth to as many as 18,000 about six months later. The brain is wide open for taking in masses of information and making incalculable new connections.

The infant, with a mind eager to learn, enters into an expanded world that has almost infinite possibilities. There are existing capabilities that are coupled to new activities; for example, sucking is now for nipples instead of only thumbs, as in the womb. In the first weeks of life, they are exposed to a new set of experiences rich in sounds, images, colors, textures, tastes and smells never perceived before. They begin mimicking and experimenting with which sounds and facial gestures get what sort of reaction. Every waking hour they are enthusiastically taking in all they can. That excitement and enthusiasm, which grows exponentially each day as the brain generates new connections, spreads to most people they come in contact with. It seems that everywhere they go they are the center of attention. People find them stimulating and they crave stimulation.

Sucking is a reflex and happens automatically. Nursing, however, is a skill to be learned. The baby needs its mother's assistance to learn about how to nurse properly. When their cheek is stroked the newborn will turn their head in that direction and suckle the breast presented. After a few days, the breast against the cheek will be enough. Initially they need help burping. Eventually, through trial and error, they will learn to swallow less air and develop the skill to burp themselves. They learn so much simply by doing whatever brings pleasure or avoids pain.

Babies are the ultimate consumers of sensory information and experience. Their attention quickly jumps from one stimulus to another, being drawn to whatever they find most attractive or appealing. Having an innate curiosity about faces and other complicated shapes and patterns other than their primary caregivers, babies are relatively unbiased in finding delight with whoever's face is most interesting at the time. They haven't learned object permanence, so when someone or something leaves their perceptual field, it as if it no longer exists, enabling them to find great enjoyment in playing peak-a-boo. They will visually track a moving object or person with curiosity. It can take about three of four months before they show consistent preference or attachment for Mom, Dad or 'significant others' over other people.

At any stage of life, having left behind old limiting concepts and behaviors (SIX), we discover a new sense of freedom. We're able to entertain new ideas, new perceptions, and new experiences. We sample the new range of possibilities that have opened up to us, dabbling in different areas, to experiment with what brings us pleasure and what doesn't. It can be a time of inspiration, when untapped potentials must be nurtured and experimented with.

Core questions

The basic questions asked at this phase are: What's new or next? What is attractive? What else is possible?

EIGHT — Self Reorganization

Certain new couplings are selected, organized and integrated with existing essential structures into a more complex and robust order, forming a new sense of self.

Some key characteristics of phase EIGHT are:

- gaining mastery
- exercising willpower to manifest one's wishes
- influencing the behavior of others
- uninhibited and impulsive
- pushing boundaries
- seeking a clear set of rules
- eliminating the uncertainty of unknown factors
- giving activities full attention.
- responding to the distress of significant others

Phase EIGHT — Age 5–11 Months

By eight months, the first teeth appear. They can reach for a cup or spoon when being fed and drink from a cup with help. There is an increasing need to feel in control and do things for themselves, in their own way. They are learning to more clearly communicate 'no' and close their mouth firmly or turn their head when no longer hungry.

They need structure and are developing a rhythm for feeding, eliminating, sleeping, and being awake. Since being able to crawl is a skill that belongs to the next cycle of development, they are beginning to develop the preliminary capabilities and understandings required for this. They seek to master rolling from back to stomach and stomach to back, sitting alone without support, and holding their head erect. They may even raise themselves up on their arms and knees into a crawling position and rock back and forth, but are not yet ready to move forward.

Throughout this period, the infant is learning to use their will. They act deliberately to realize their preferences. They practice manipulating things of the world by using finger and thumb to pick up objects and transfer them from one hand to the other. The baby learns which sounds get the desired reactions and how to most effectively suck the nipple to obtain milk. They practice these and other activities until they master them and can more effectively manifest their wishes. Everything is a challenge, and they exercise their willpower to master them. There is increasing ability to mobilize energy for the satisfaction of needs. They are able to more effectively influence their parents' behavior by crying in different ways, to communicate whether they are hurt, wet, hungry, or lonely, or vocalizing sounds of pleasure.

Babies are not born understanding the basic laws of physics such as gravity. However, they soon get an intuitive sense of this by dropping objects over the edge of their chair or crib. They love to push the boundary of how far they can take this game or any other enterprise, yet they also want a clear set of rules, not just about physics, but about the dynamics of social interaction. Understanding the rules and how to use them helps to eliminate the uncertainty and anxiety of unknown factors.

They now understand the rule of object permanence and will look for a ball that has rolled out of sight or will search for toys hidden under a blanket or other object. They have an all-or-nothing style of attention, focused on getting what they desire. Giving an activity their full attention, while being oblivious to the background or periphery, helps them quickly gain mastery over that activity. Their intensely focused attention also allows them to spend a great deal of time watching and observing what others do and how they do it. They differentiate between strangers and close family members and clearly demonstrate whom they like best and are most attached to. They will even respond to the distress of people they are close to by crying or showing distress in some way.

Babies at this phase take up a lot of space. In their innocence, they are completely uninhibited and simply follow their impulses. If babies are hungry they cry. If they want to throw food on the floor they will. They are totally honest and explicit about what they want and how they feel. The more they make their presence felt, the more people must adapt in order to incorporate them into the family system. This can cause existing problems, which have been hidden, to become more apparent. Many couples will say their marriage problems began at some point after the birth of a child.

As adults, in this phase, we choose the activities or avenues of thought we believe will be most fulfilling and dedicate ourselves to those endeavors, mastering them and calling them our own. We discover our calling in life: a role that will not only be most fulfilling for us, but which will naturally fulfill a niche in the ecology of the greater community.

Core questions

The core questions are: What am I mastering or manifesting? How can I take control?

NINE — Consolidation and Re-stabilization

The system stabilizes once again with-newly formed, more complex patterns of self-maintaining feedback loops (homeostasis), regulating predictability and stability within ever-evolving structures.

Some key characteristics of phase NINE are:

- minimizing effort
- establishing predictable routines and habits
- consolidating growth
- reaping the benefits of one's efforts

Phase NINE — Age 9–12 Months

Over time, newly acquired skills become second nature for the infant. They are able to relax into an easier, more comfortable state and enjoy their abilities in a familiar environment. They don't need to put so much effort into their newly mastered abilities any more. They have developed unconscious competence in various domains. They know by rote how to live in stable equilibrium with their environment. Activities that took their full attention now can be accomplished out of habit, thereby freeing their attention to roam to other things. They can suck at the breast while playing with the other breast with their hand. Things like eating, eliminating, sleeping and waking have become fairly predictable routines.

Each of their newly acquired abilities, and the understandings that go with them, define the new relationships they have with different aspects of the world. These relationships are defined by the repeating patterns of interaction that have been established by having found what works best. At the same time, new cycles of change come quickly at this time in life, and the skills they have developed are the foundations on which more complex relationships will be built in future developmental cycles. Their ability to push themselves up on to hands and knees will soon evolve into crawling. The sounds they make are the seeds of words yet to come. There are many different contexts of learning happening at the same time, each with their own timeframe for development. A plateau of competence is reached, where consolidation occurs. However, the process of development already begins preparing for the next cycle of change.

No matter how old we are, we need these phases of stability. To consolidate our growth, we make what we have learned so habitual that we can do it without thinking. Once functions are taken over by unconscious processes, our conscious mind is free to focus on new developmental tasks. As adults, we find ourselves settling into the harmonious routines of our ecological niche and reaping the fruits of our labor.

Core questions

We are back to the phase represented by NINE on the Enneagram where we ask the question: How do I consolidate the changes and maintain stability?

Realizing our Potential

We each go through many cycles of change in our lives, starting with birth and infancy. How freely and effectively we make our way through these transitions determines how well we are able to deal with the challenges of our lives. Articulating the various phases of these cycles gives us a map of understanding that can help us open more fully to the capabilities and qualities that assist us in realizing our full potential for learning and growth.

In the following chapters we will refine and flesh out these patterns and see how they apply to the process of psychotherapy. In the final chapter we will explore how people's different personality types tend to inhibit the developmental cycle, as parts of themselves become stuck in earlier stages of development.

Dimensions of Self-Organization

At each of the nine phases of the developmental cycle, there are four key dimensions within our essential wholeness that we systemically organize ourselves around:

- PsychoLogical domains
- Essential qualities
- Primary developmental tasks
- Basic functions

In the next three chapters we will see how these dimensions (attractors) of self-organization guide human development and the evolution of consciousness.

The majority of qualities traditionally attributed to each of the Enneagram personality types fall under these subheadings. Most good therapies will touch on aspects from each dimension; however, I don't know of any system that is as comprehensive as the essential wholeness model. To my knowledge, the system that comes closest is Acceptance and Commitment Therapy (ACT)[37]. ACT uses a hexagram model of psychological flexibility that defines the six core therapeutic processes: Contacting the Present Moment, Diffusion, Acceptance, Self as Context, Values, and Committed Action.

The key aspects of psychological flexibility and their associated core processes, along with what I would consider missing links, are layered onto the nine aspects of the Enneagram symbol. These dimensions of self-organization, on one hand, define psychological health, and on the other, help us diagnose peoples' temperamental tendencies to get stuck in their ability to evolve in response to life's demands.

CHAPTER FIVE

Network of PsychoLogical Domains

The notion of a network of PsychoLogical domains has evolved out of the concept of 'logical levels' as used in NLP and originates from the work of Gregory Bateson. Bateson's ideas were inspired by philosopher Bertrand Russell's work on logic.

Bateson defines mind as processes of transformation that disclose a hierarchy of logical types immanent in the phenomena. To understand how something works or what purpose it serves requires making distinctions within the wholeness of our experience. If we are simply immersed in our senses, in the present passing moment, we aren't sorting for patterns. By framing our attention in various ways we are able to make distinctions not otherwise available. For example, viewing events over an extended timeframe enables us to see the self-perpetuating nature of particular behaviors. Or by observing a situation, while framing it in comparison to how we would ideally like it to be, we highlight what could be done differently to improve it. There are many perceptual frameworks that, for the most part unconsciously, shape the way we perceive, give meaning to and relate to life.

Levels of Learning

Theoretical biologist Stuart Kauffman's[38] proposed three levels of evolution, with evolution being synonymous with learning. If we add 'not evolving' or 'not learning' we have four levels of learning. This latter level is what he referred to as 'rule-based behavior', in which there is no trial and error and therefore no learning; we simply maintain the status quo within that environment. This level of relating to the environment approximates nonliving systems.

In the first level of evolution, we learn from trial and error to improve the way we relate to other elements in our environment. This necessitates and also precipitates other people evolving the way they relate to us. It is coevolution. These types of changes often create new niches that invite innovation. This coevolution evolves further when we learn how to learn better. To examine how we learn requires a much different way of framing our perception than acting by rote, or even learning through trial and error.

The next level of learning is that of epistemology, which basically means the study of 'how' we know what (we think) we know. In other words, how we learn to learn what we learn. Each level is a further abstraction from the physicality of our experience until we are actually examining the nature of perception. In meditation, we see a similar pattern in observing the nature of mind, as contrasted with observing the objects of our perception, the objects of our thinking, or the interaction of the objects of our thinking.

An example of these four levels of learning can be seen in marriage. A couple in homeostasis are basically behaving by rote. They have developed automatic behaviorial patterns and, with a certain feeling of, 'This is as good as it gets', neither party is thinking about how they can learn from their experience to improve their marriage. If, however, one or both of them begins to feel dissatisfied, for whatever reason, then they begin to pay attention to what is causing the problems. They might even experiment with ways of approaching things differently. This might lead to new ways of communicating, in particular talking about ways to improve their relationship. It may include not just talking about what they can change, but discussing how they can improve they way they address problems and look for solutions. In the process of trying to improve the way they go about solving problems, they become even more aware of how they each perceive and think about things very differently. Some of these ways of thinking seem to help them solve problems; others keep them going in circles.

A very sophisticated couple might be able to help one another to explore how they know what they think they know, or this might be when they approach a therapist. To observe the way the mind thinks means being able to observe these processes from a perspective outside of the processes that make the perceptions in the first place. A skilled therapist can show a person how to observe the workings of their mind well enough to identify the processes of making the meanings and beliefs that shape perception and behavior. Therapy with mindfulness meditation methods could help them develop awareness of how their minds manufacture perception and beliefs.

Behavior, Capabilities, Beliefs and Values, and Identity

Bateson described four levels of learning in terms of 'behavior', 'capabilities', 'beliefs and values', and 'identity'. At the first level, we can simply behave without learning. At the second level, through trial and error, we more fully use our capabilities to improve the quality of our behavior. At the third level, we can ask what is the purpose of using particular capabilities to behave in a particular way. How we learn and what we choose to learn is determined by what we value and believe. At the fourth level, the way we decide what to value and believe and to maintain those values and beliefs is often thought of as being simply who we are. Our style of thinking and feeling defines our personality, which is why when someone is first asked how they know what they know or how they know what they want, they say, "It's just who I am."

NLP innovator, Robert Dilts, refined Bateson's model by adding 'spiritual' and 'environmental' levels. All behavior happens in an environment, and the different environments will determine what will or won't occur. Having a transpersonal perspective of oneself is often thought of as a 'spiritual' experience. Dilts' model has proven useful in facilitating change, yet it is flawed, theoretically. I will attempt to address the flaws within the essential wholeness model.

First of all, Dilts describes these definitional categories in a hierarchy, one stacked upon the other, with 'environment' at the bottom and 'spirituality' at the top. Each category is supposedly a member of the categories above it. However, 'environment' is not a member of the category of 'behavior'. 'Behavior' is a subset of capabilities, but it is not a 'value' or 'belief'. The

105

problem occurs from trying to place these useful distinctions into a linear hierarchical model, when life is better understood, as Fritjof Capra described it, as "networks nesting within other networks". Since application of these principles requires some linear sequence of behavior, the hierarchical model can be useful, yet we must not confuse the map with the territory.

Transferring the model to the circular representation of the Enneagram with its internal lines of connection creates a model that more closely resembles the network-like structure of a living system. At each phase in the developmental cycle, there is a tendency for us to organize or frame our cognitions into one of these categories. However, since they are merely artificial distinctions within the wholeness of our experience, all levels are always available for us to frame our experience. It is also important to remember that words such as 'behavior', 'values', 'beliefs' and 'identity' are nominalizations; that is, concepts created from verbs or actions. They are not actually things; rather they are processes (behaving, valuing, believing, identifying), ways of constructing perception, which are, by nature, fluid and changing. For these reasons, we will refer to the categories as 'PsychoLogical networks'.

Each number on the Enneagram, in conjunction with representing a phase in the process of change, also represents a corresponding PsychoLogical network. Dilts' list of logical levels is expanded to nine domains (including community) mapped out around the circle. The Spiritual or Being level is represented by the Enneagram symbol as a whole. According to Bateson's model of logical types, it would appear that ideals should be part of the category including beliefs and values.

Differentiating Types of Knowing

The Enneagram helps us differentiate beliefs and values into five categories ranging from values at FOUR, beliefs at FIVE, new ideas at SEVEN, identity at EIGHT and ideals at ONE. The model shows us that at ONE, Ideals, is connected to FOUR, Values, and SEVEN, new ideas. FIVE, beliefs, is connected to EIGHT, identity, and SEVEN, new ideas.

It is important to understand how values inform ideals. Ideals are organized by and help organize new ideas. In addition, personal identity and the beliefs and values one identifies with are largely shaped and informed by the communities to which we belong or are born into. We could think of community in a sense as a cultural context or environment. That is why these two distinctions are both located at NINE on the Enneagram.

An overview of this expanded model shows us that our evolving life occurs in a particular *environment,* and we have a network of associations that define what happens in that environment. Whether we are conscious of them or not, there is a network of *ideals* (platonic ideas) that define the optimal events in that environment. To move in the direction of those ideals, specific *behaviors* must be performed. To behave in those specific ways, we must have specific *capabilities* that we engage. Whether we use those capabilities depends on what we *value.* What we value is organized by what we most deeply *believe.* What we believe has been organized by our *questioning* of what is true, important and useful. We question what we believe because of the *new ideas* and perceptions we become aware of. The structure of our personal *identity* organizes our awareness of ideas, how we question, believe, value, and are capable of behaving in moving towards an ideal in any environmental context. The *communities* to which we belong tend to organize the way we identify ourselves.

Each PsychoLogical domain acts as an attractor basin of possible ways of framing our experience. The smaller the volume of the basin, the more limited our perception. As consciousness evolves, the volume of the basins expands to more global or universal frameworks. The perceptual framework of each psychological domain facilitates the achievement of the developmental task of the corresponding phase in the developmental cycle. For a complete cycle of change to occur, there must be potential for something new to emerge at each level. New growth and learning are informed by self-organizing morphic fields; however, they must be implemented in ways that allows the best options to be selected and evolve towards their potential.

For our homeostatic patterns in any *environment or context* to be perturbed enough to break habitual patterns, there must be a compelling *ideal* to motivate one to attempt new *behaviors*, which require developing latent or emerging *capabilities.* These capabilities are in part supported by existing *values* and *beliefs*, yet also restrained by them. To evolve to a higher or more complex order, existing *values* and *beliefs* must be *questioned* and, at least in part, let go of in order for *new ideas* to emerge and be appreciated. Putting new ideas into practice allows a new sense of *identity* to be recognized. That identity will then seek to see how it fits within existing communities, or become part of, or even create, a new sense of *community*.

David's Story

Let's consider this process by examining David's crisis. For whatever reasons, David believes that he's the kind of person that people dislike. He thinks that whatever he does in relation to others will be unappreciated and disapproved. He also feels unable to cope with this disapproval and, after even the briefest interactions, usually feels rejected and hurt. To cope with this, he tries to convince himself that he doesn't care what others think and that he doesn't need people in his life. He works as a bookkeeper for a warehousing and distribution company. For the most part, he can avoid contact with people by staying in his isolated office and keeping his nose in the books and computer. Everyone who has contact with him has largely given up trying to talk with him. They rarely converse beyond the minimum exchange needed to conduct business. As David's discomfort with personal contact is so apparent and he is so awkward to deal with, most people communicate through notes and email. On one hand David likes the space, but interprets people avoiding him as evidence that people don't want to have anything to do with him.

David lives by himself and has set routines of where he shops for food and other activities, which also minimizes his contact with others. He has learned, increasingly over time, to disregard and repress any internal thoughts or feelings that would challenge this pattern of thinking and relating. Day-to-day, month-to-month, year-to-year, his life has little change. However, recently his employer has been finding more simple mistakes in his bookkeeping. David interprets this as his boss just not liking him and being out to get him.

Out of a growing sense of resentment towards the company, David begins to feel justified in stealing small amounts of petty cash. He knows he is jeopardizing his job and security, but can't help himself. As he's afraid to raise suspicion, he truncates any contact with fellow employees. His behavior, however, has the opposite effect, as his boss notices this change and suggests that he talk to the employee assistance counselor. David denies any problem and argues he is doing his job well and should be left alone. This isn't good enough for the boss, who tells him if things don't change, he will be forced to consider laying David off. This sends David into a crisis.

David's job has been the main focus of his life. He feels overwhelmed by the idea of being unemployed or having to look for a new job. He decides his only option is to see the counselor. Out of desperation, he continues to see the counselor long enough to establish the kind of rapport that means he can begin freeing himself from the rigid ideas and perceptions that have controlled his life.

The therapist helps David not only to question his old belief about being disliked by others, but also to entertain and experiment with the idea that there are people who will like him, once given the chance to get to know him. Instead of becoming more limited and lifeless, the pattern of his life reverses and begins to open up to wider circles of interaction. He starts to think he is the kind of person people can get along with, as he feels more a part of the workplace community, and eventually even makes some friends outside work.

What sort of questions might the therapist have asked in each domain, to facilitate this change?

NINE — Context/Environment

Heredity is nothing but stored environment. *Luther Burbank*

Any systemic process of living happens in an environment. The environment, in part, defines the contextual framework in which certain categories of events are likely to occur. For example, different sorts of things occur within a 'home' context, as contrasted with a 'work' context, just as different sorts of things happen at a baseball park, as opposed to a rainforest. Different sorts of things occur for a baby within their mother's womb as contrasted with at their mother's breast. Ecosystems will organize themselves differently in the arctic than in the tropics.

The environments of living systems are living and growing ecosystems. An individual person or organism lives and grows in relationship to an evolving community, which co-inhabits, co-creates and maintains the environment. When planning any new activity or change, we must consider the environmental factors that we encounter. Gravity, for example, is a part of life on earth, yet if we were planning an activity in a space station orbiting earth, we would have to factor in the absence of gravity.

Environmental factors include variables and constants. Some factors, like the weather, may vary, yet we have no control over them. Many environments contain or are a part of living systems, and can always be in a state of flux.

Modern human-made structures try to minimize the fluctuations that would be experienced in natural settings so people using those structures can come as close as possible to achieving their ideal outcomes. Air conditioning of buildings helps to maximize people's ability to work or to relax and have a pleasurable experience.

Environments evolve when individuals evolve the way they relate to optimize the chances of more closely approaching ideal outcomes in that environment. We ask questions, such as, 'Where?' 'When?' 'In relation to whom or what?', to help us determine environment or context.

David's therapist asked David, the troubled bookkeeper, about the environments of his life (work, home, neighborhood) and the community of people with whom he shared those environments. The therapist then asked what changes David wanted: in what context and with whom he was having problems that he might want resolved. David responded that it was work and work colleagues that were his major concern.

In Essence at NINE

By organizing our cognitive framework within the psychological domain of the environment, we can attend to what is needed to maintain homeostasis.

ONE — *Ideals*

Ideals are like stars. We never reach them but, like the mariners
on the sea, we chart our course by them. *Carl Schurz*

Ideals are imaginary standards of excellence that serve as models or
templates for creating designs. Imagination and dreaming are the stuff of
what Carl Jung called the 'archetypal realm'. Funk and Wagnall's Dictionary
defines an ideal as, "A concept or standard of supreme perfection; a thing
conceived as an ultimate object of attainment." Ideals are like archetypal
structures that energize a context with a set of organizing possibilities
or purposes, and differentiate it from other environmental contexts.
People hold ideals for every environmental context. Ideals define how an
environment might best be used, or in what directions life might evolve.
In a self-organizing universe, ideals begin to organize our thinking in the
direction of yet-to-be manifested emergent possibilities. The internal ideal
images serve as beacons that we consciously, or unconsciously, set our
sights on. We are drawn to them because they represent the life we are
growing into.

On one hand, the images of our ideals inspire us to begin moving
in that direction, and on the other hand, they highlight the limitations
of our current level of functioning and magnify our frustration with the
status quo. In George Bernard Shaw's understanding, "Reasonable people
try to adapt themselves to the world. Unreasonable people try to adapt
the world to themselves. That's why all progress depends on unreasonable
people." Inspiration and/or frustration motivate the destabilization of the
homeostatic equilibrium of our lives. Ideals are unreasonable expectations
of how things can be.

Gregory Bateson said, "The individual mind is immanent but not
only in the body. It is immanent also in pathways and messages outside
the body; and there is a larger Mind of which the individual mind is
only a sub-system." Ideals are hints from the larger Universal Mind, the
intelligence of a self-organizing universe, that point to what is possible
outside the limits of our smaller minds. Ideals are the archetypal patterns
emerging from what Jung referred to as the collective unconscious, the
larger mind, that precipitate life's continual creative reorganization.

"The ideal," according to *Webster's Dictionary*, "is to be attained by selecting and assembling in one whole the beauties and perfections which are usually seen in different individuals, excluding everything defective or unseemly, so as to form a type or model of the species. Thus, the Apollo Belvedere is the ideal of the beauty and proportion of the human frame."[39] Although everyone has individual preferences, there do seem to be some universal standards, some things that people agree upon universally. This agreement may be explained by idealistic structures in the collective mind.

The contexts of human endeavor are often more defined by purpose than by specific environmental factors alone. For example, a room with a table could be used for playing cards, for reading poetry, or for a meeting of a board of directors. The people involved, however, would have images of what an ideal card game, poetry reading or board meeting looks like. Ideals help define the purpose of particular environmental contexts.

Objects that symbolize ideals are often placed in an environment to help define what the place will be used for. A room decorated with portraits of famous poets would more easily host a poetry reading than one whose walls were adorned with sales graphs and prospective marketing charts. Environments designed with particular purposes in mind are often described as 'being ideal' for whatever it is that people want to experience in that context. There are very different factors that define an ideal womb, the environmental context for a fetus, compared to the factors that would define an ideal environmental context for a newborn baby.

Ideals evolve by working towards them. As certain milestones are reached, we are better able to assess how useful or even desirable an ideal might be. Ideals can modify or even deconstruct under closer scrutiny, creating space for new ideals to take shape in our mind's eye. Ideals are images of perfection and therefore rarely, if ever, match up with reality, yet they give us something to strive for. As parents, for example, we may have an ideal of how we would like to parent, although we may not have been parented that way or even seen someone parenting in that way. As we attempt to parent in that way, we see the benefits and detriments of trying to parent with a new method. Our ideals of what good parenting is will evolve and mature as we do.

Parents often talk about the difference between their ideals at the birth of their first child and their ideals after the birth of their subsequent children. Ideals serve as a representation of what is our current highest truth and serve as a reference for discerning what is needed to live with the greatest amount of integrity and impeccability. If we don't live our current truth, we never get to find out how useful those ideals are or aren't, and what the self-organizing intelligence of the universe has in store for us.

Ideals inspire to go beyond what is familiar and known, yet what we eventually accomplish or realize is never exactly what our ideals inspired us seek. Spiritual teacher, Adyashanti[40], speaking on the realization of enlightenment, reminds us that our idealized ideas about enlightenment are not enlightenment; however, without any wish to realize this idyllic experience, one would never do the necessary inquiry to realize it.

Phase ONE is the beginning of the creative or reformative process and ideals give us clues about which fundamental foundations we want to build upon. Ideals can provide guidelines that keep us moving in the right direction. Danger can arise when we interpret our ideals as being the truth, rather than our best representation of the truth. When we focus on one set of ideals as being the one true way of being, we are in danger of becoming fundamentalist and no longer open to how reality is so much more complex than any single description. We should remember that ideals are essentially metaphors or dreamlike images, and like dreams, they are constantly changing and our interpretation of them may change each time they are reviewed.

To determine ideals we can ask, "What is my ideal outcome in this specific context?" "If a miracle were to happen, how would things be different in this situation?" or, "If I were guaranteed success, how would things be?"

When his therapist asked him how his situation would be different if a miracle was to occur, David responded by saying he would be able to keep his job and his boss would appreciate what he did for the company. When probed further, he said he would be more comfortable with his fellow employees.

In Essence at ONE

Organizing our cognitive framework within the psychological domain of ideals helps us to separate ourselves from the context and discern what is limiting or wrong with the status quo.

TWO — *Behavior*

The test of one's behavior pattern is in their relationship to society, relationship to work and relationship to sex. *Alfred Adler*

Behavior or action is the doing of something in relation to someone or something else. It is the exertion of energy or force of one body upon another, and it is the resulting effect of the energy exerted on one body by another. In other words, behavior is both cause and effect. Fritjof Capra informs us that, "A living system interacts with its environment through 'structural coupling', i.e. through recurrent interactions, each of which triggers structural changes in the system. The environment only triggers the structural changes; it does not specify or direct them."[41]

All behaviors occur in relationship to something or someone else, and the patterns of recurrent behaviors form the network that gives life structure. We initiate behaviors to achieve particular outcomes and we respond to others' behaviors in hope of achieving particular results that approximate our ideals for that situation. How well we do what it takes to reach our ideal outcome is determined by how capable we are, how much value we place on it, what we believe is possible, whether it fits into our self-concept (identity) and how well it is received by the communities to which we belong.

In a given context, there are specific ways to relate to the various components of an environment in order to reach towards our ideals. At home there is cooking, eating, sleeping, conversing, and so on. At work there are specific tasks defined by the type of workplace. Whilst people might talk about personal matters, just as at home they might talk about how work is going, conversations generally have an emphasis on the production of goods or the providing of services. The fetus has a very different set of behaviors in relation to the womb environment than those outside of the womb.

Behaviors evolve by exploring the limits of our *capabilities* in striving towards corresponding *ideals*. People have many capabilities they never use and therefore never have the opportunity to behave in particular ways. For example, not everyone plays music, but that is not to say they are not capable. A person's ability to play music will evolve as the boundaries of their musical capabilities are explored.

Behavior, in my use of the term, refers to external actions, even though we could say that thinking, believing, valuing, and so on, is as much of a behavior as digestion, telling a lie or climbing a mountain. Most behaviors are actually a complex set of behaviors. For example, in order to tell a lie, various cognitive analyses and decision making processes occur before the breath moves through the vocal cords and is articulated by the lips, tongue and teeth into words. Most behavior is unconsciously autonomous either because it is instinctual or conditioned. This doesn't prevent it from evolving, as conscious awareness or control is not a prerequisite for change.

To determine behavior in a context of interest, we ask, "How specifically did (does, will, can) that happen?" or "What specific action was (is) needed?" Following up on the miracle question, the therapist asks David specifically what he would be doing differently should the miracle outcome have occurred. David responds by saying he would be engaging in more verbal communication with others. When pressed for what the quality of this interaction would be, David replies, "Business-like, but friendly and enjoyable at times." Clarifying further, the therapist inquires as to how specifically he would be acting that would let people know he was feeling friendly and enjoying himself. David says he would be genuinely smiling at times and making comfortable eye contact.

In Essence at TWO

Organizing our cognitive framework within the psychological domain of behavior helps us to identify how we need to relate better in order to adapt to the circumstances that we face.

THREE — Capabilities

Practice rather than preach. Make of your life an affirmation, defined by your ideals, not the negation of others. Dare to the level of your capability then go beyond to a higher level.
Alexander Haig

Capabilities are the capacity to perform particular behaviors. To be capable is to have the know-how to do what is needed to move towards one's ideals in a given context. How we behave, in any given context, is determined and limited by the capabilities we possess or have developed. If someone is paralyzed and cannot walk, what they do in a rainforest or a baseball field is going to be different from someone who can walk. A herbalist is going behave differently than someone who has trained as a lumberjack. Someone who is capable in accounting and economics is going to be doing something different in a workplace than someone who doesn't know how to multiple and divide numbers. A newborn baby uses a different set of capabilities to relate to their world outside of the womb than they did inside the womb. On one hand, the capabilities we choose to develop are determined by environmental demands and opportunities, and the ideals that guide our actions, and on the other, by what we actually discover works best in improving the quality of our lives. The quality of our life is a subjective experience based on what value we perceive something has. Only a person who has found playing music a rewarding experience will explore the limits of his musical capabilities.

Stuart Kaufffman says that as a living system develops, its structure reaches a threshold of stability where it will either break down and/or break through to new states of order.

> What exactly happens at this crisis depends on the system's history of utilization and under-utilization of capabilities and other potential capabilities, coupled with the nature of the external conditions. The new order that emerges will, by necessity, be more complex, intelligent, flexible, adaptive and robust in order to thrive even further from equilibrium.[42]

The capabilities we develop, and how fully we develop them, will determine future opportunities available to us. Those individuals who optimally use their capabilities will have higher level of fitness to face the inevitable crises that arise in life. In addition, the capabilities that have been most developed are also the ones that will most likely continue to survive and thrive through the crises. Highly skilled people are more likely to thrive through crises, and their most perfected skills are most likely to continue to be used and evolve through crises. The most accomplished hunters were the most likely to survive through a shortage in game, just as the best computer programmers are likely to survive a company's downsizing.

"I'm a great believer in luck," said Thomas Jefferson, "and I find the harder I work the more I have of it." Exercising our capabilities to the full, we tend to create opportunities for other elements in our communities and environments to co-evolve and respond more robustly. Luck is not something that happens when we are sitting around waiting. Rather, we get lucky (the self-organizing universe supports us) when we are 'out there' and making things happen.

Capabilities are internal resources we draw upon to relate to our environment and other members of the environment (community) in order to live and prosper. Capabilities evolve when doing what we know how to do to the best of our ability still isn't good enough. For example, when spoken language was no longer adequate for all of human communication, writing evolved. When crawling is no longer adequate for getting where we want to go, we learn to walk. The capability that makes all other capabilities possible is the ability to learn, however it is obvious that certain capabilities are easier for certain people to learn than others.

We ask questions to determine capabilities. They include, "Are you capable of _____?" "How do you know you can do _____?" and "What makes it possible for you to do _____?" The therapist clarified David's capabilities by asking if he is capable of conversing in a friendly manner and smiling. David says he's not sure. The therapist asks if he thinks he has been friendly and ever smiled in their conversations. David says yes. When the therapist asks if he thinks he has exercised these capabilities to his fullest, David replies no, but says he would like to explore how he might.

In Essence at THREE

Organizing our cognitive framework within the psychological domain of capabilities helps us to initiate the promotion of our emerging agenda.

FOUR — *Values*

> The best and most beautiful things in the world cannot be seen
> or even touched. They must be felt with the heart. *Helen Keller*

The values we hold represent the emotional investment we have in our experience in relation to the people and things in our environment. Values are defined by what we consider is most important; what we want most. Values give our life direction and purpose. They can be personal or collective. Social groups are often organized around particular values and corresponding beliefs, although individuals in those groups may have varying degrees of investment in those values.

Which capabilities we use to work towards our ideals in an environment are determined by what we value. The experience of what we value is what we perceive maximizes the quality of our lives. Values determine what we want and don't want, what we move towards and what we move away from. Values are what motivate us to use or develop particular capabilities in order to behave in specific ways. Someone who values financial security and sees little value in creative expression is unlikely to have been developing the capabilities of self-reflection and creative writing so that they can write poetry. Conversely, the person who highly values self-reflection and creative expression, but doesn't place a high value on financial security isn't going to develop a high level of accounting skills. Of course, most people tend not to be black and white in their values, but instead have some sort of hierarchy of values.

All organisms learn to value what supports not only their individual prosperity, but maximizes the quality of the ecosystem upon which they depend. The healthier the ecosystem, the healthier the members of the ecosystem (community) will be. The more robust and prosperous a community is as a whole, the more supportive and enriching it can be for its individual members.

Values determine which capabilities are developed, but the way specific behaviors will be shaped is determined by what people believe is the best way.

Values also determine the way we choose to demonstrate what is valued. One person who values creative expression might write poetry, while another might choreograph modern dance. One person who values financial gain may invest in the stock market, while another may work long hours in a corporation. There are different ways people demonstrate how they value what they value.

A fetus values having the space it needs to grow. When there is no longer space to grow, they use their untapped capability to initiate the birthing process. Once born there are new sets of values, such as mother's milk, physical contact, warmth, which they will discover through their interaction with the world. Values do not exist outside the process of valuing. Fully valuing our experience is to open to it as fully as possible. It is through opening to our experience of life that we gain appreciation for what enriches the quality of our lives. Most of us value what we perceive enables us to feel most alive as a contributing and supported participant of a community, while honoring our unique individuality. Our perception of any situation is largely determined by what we believe.

Values determine the meaning we place on other people's behavior. If a person who highly values creative expression and poetry (John, a freelance writer) is married to a person who values financial security (Mary, an accountant) they will relate and interpret the other's behaviors according to their individual values. If each of them values generosity then John might write poetry for Mary, and Mary might pay the bills and keep the checkbook balanced. John might complain that Mary doesn't do enough for him, because she never writes him poetry. Mary might complain that John doesn't do enough because he doesn't help enough with the finances. Or, if the both valued diversity and specialization, they might both appreciate what the other brings to their relationship.

Asking John, "What is important about writing poetry for Mary?" John responds, "It is how I show that I love her." "What is important about showing her that you love her?" "It is important to be generous with the people you love." "How might Mary show her generosity with you?" John, "By handling the finances." "What might be important about you contributing poetry and Mary contributing her financial skills to your relationship?" John, "We are good at different things (specialization) and that diversity makes for a more enriching relationship." People can often disagree about how values are best expressed, yet agree upon what they intrinsically believe is most important.

This has been explored by Dr. Gary Chapman[43] who, in the *Five Love Languages*, defines the ways people most value having the value of love demonstrated in an intimate relationship: Words of Affirmation, Quality Time, Receiving Gifts, Acts of Service, and Physical Touch.

There are hierarchies of values that determine most interpretations of situations and motivations for decision-making processes. In determining the hierarchy of values we can ask questions like, "What is important about _____?" or "What is the purpose of _____?" "What are you hoping to experience by exercising that capability?" "What experiences in life have been most meaningful for you and what made that meaningful?" To access deeper values, it can be beneficial to keep repeating the questions above and asking, "What is important about what you just said was important?"

Consider the idea of having free time, for example. Why might it be important? One person might say it gives them time to relax and another might say it gives them time to exercise. What is important about exercise? One person might say feeling good and another might say looking good. What is important about looking good? To be attractive. What is important about being attractive? To be desirable. What is important about being desirable? Feeling lovable. What is important about being loved? To feel loved. What is important about feeling loved? To feel love.

Inquiry into the deepest levels eventually leads to the kinds of core values that include contentment, love, acceptance, serenity, happiness or peace. Often, we have made these qualities of being conditional upon achieving other valued things. However, love, for example, is a quality of being that we have often lost touch with by pursuing the other things we think will make us happy. The core values that connect us to essential qualities of being also connect us with the innate inner resources needed to help us realize the external things we value.

Using the example above, we could start a series of questioning:

As you allow yourself to feel love, would that make it easy or harder to feel loved? Easier.
As you are feeling more loved, would that make it easier or harder to feel lovable? Easier.

As you are feeling loveable would that make it easier or harder to feel desirable? Easier.
As you are feeling desireable would that make it easier or harder to feel attractive? Easier.
As you are feeling attractive would that make it easier or harder to look good? Easier.
As you are feeling good would that make it easier or harder to exercise? Easier.

When David's therapist asks him what is important about conversing in a more friendly way, he responds that his job is important to him and his boss expects him to get along better with others or he might lose the job. The therapist continues by asking what his boss thinks is important about him learning to get along better with others. David repies that it helps things get done more easily and in a more enjoyable manner. When asked if he thinks finding easier and more enjoyable ways of doing things is important to him, David says yes.

In Essence at FOUR

Organizing our cognitive framework within the psychological domain of values helps us tune into our personal experience of what really works for us.

FIVE — Beliefs

Each problem that I solved became a rule, which served afterwards to solve other problems. *Rene Descartes*

Believing is a process of mapmaking. We use the maps to navigate our way through life. Beliefs encode the controlling, organizing, governing and evaluating principles by which we live. We can have beliefs that are answers to where, when, how, what, who, with whom, and why. We have beliefs about all the PsychoLogical domains, including beliefs about beliefs.

Beliefs are our attempt to articulate our understanding of the patterns of life. Our minds categorize experiences into patterns. By knowing the patterns for how things work, we hope to be able to determine the outcome of our actions, others' actions (people and other forms of life), and the activity of the universe. Each of us is personally affected by our various experiences, which we perceive to varying degrees as positive, negative or neutral. Our beliefs about these patterns, and the patterns of our subjective experience, form the assumptions or presuppositions that define what is most important for us and how we relate to those aspects of life.

When we are able to extrapolate the pattern of action needed to solve a problem, we create a map that we can follow to replicate success. The successful management of life on one level inevitably leads us to new problems on the next level and therefore new challenges for understanding the nature of things. Beliefs define what we value and hence inform what capabilities we develop to assist the pursuit of our ideals in any context.

Beliefs must evolve when they no longer describe the territory of our lives as accurately as is needed for us to navigate our way towards what we want and need and away from what we don't want and need. In questioning our existing beliefs, new ideas can arise, leading to new theories that eventually form beliefs.

David, having discovered that his counselor was someone he could trust, begins exploring different ways of relating to other people at his workplace. He begins to discover a new pattern of people being helpful and pleasurable to interact with. As he comes to believe more fully in the benefits of relating with others, he is then faced with the problems of learning how to manage the new set of challenges that come with being more involved with others.

Beliefs are mental representations of reality that are constructed with internal visual, auditory and kinesthetic components. To uncover someone's beliefs we ask 'Why' or 'What causes' questions. To understand the structure of the belief we can ask, "How do you know that?" Just asking this question tends to remind one of the belief-making process. Helping David to clarify his beliefs, the therapist asks him to say why it is important for him, besides keeping his job, to find easier and more enjoyable ways of doing things, particularly communicating with others. David says because life is too short to waste time and not enjoy oneself.

In Essence at FIVE

Organizing our cognitive framework within the psychological domain of 'beliefs' helps us investigate life more deeply in order to deepen and expand our understanding.

SIX — Questioning

> All truth passes through three stages. First, it is ridiculed. Second, it is violently opposed. Third, it is accepted as being self-evident. *Arthur Schopenhauer*

Beliefs are not things, so much as they are mental constructions that maintain their form through the action of believing. The more useful a belief appears to be, the more solid it becomes in our minds. The more it seems set in stone, the less the process of believing is apparent. There is the danger of confusing the map with the territory the map is attempting to describe. Imagination is referred to as 'make-believe', and said to be not real, yet all of what we believe is 'made-beliefs'. It is often our imaginations that reveal deeper understanding of the nature of things, rather than our understandings that appear to be set in stone.

When we know we are using our imaginations, we recognize the living-breathing nature of our process of making beliefs, allowing us to at least map the process of mapmaking more accurately. Being able to imagine a different way of going about life leads us to question our beliefs and to wonder, what if this or that type of experience were possible? What other ways might there be of explaining what has been happening?

Questioning and doubting arise out of uncertainty. In turn, new understandings arise out of the ability to doubt the validity or usefulness of our existing beliefs. English writer Charles Caleb Colton expresses that thought well: "Doubt is the vestibule through which all must pass before they can enter into the temple of wisdom." The Webster Dictionary defines doubt as, 'To waver in opinion or judgment; to be in uncertainty as to belief respecting anything; to hesitate in belief; to be undecided as to the truth of the negative or the affirmative proposition; to be undetermined.'[44]

To question our beliefs is to set aside the map we are following and open our awareness to the territory we are navigating. We ask if we can be sure if what we thought is actually true, let alone useful. Claude Levi-Strauss reminds us, "The wise man doesn't give the right answers, he poses the right questions." In order to embrace our inherent genius and expand our understanding, we must accept how ignorant we really are. Albert Einstein said, "Only two things are infinite, the universe and human stupidity, and I'm not sure about the former." All further learning will illuminate inadequacies in our ways of thinking and lead to more sophisticated understandings.

Beliefs arise in the first place out of the ability to question the nature of our experience and hypothesize why things are the way they are. This hypothesizing is also a way of simultaneously exploring the usefulness of alternative perspectives and questioning existing beliefs, of viewing subjects from certain premises (given or assumed) and inferring conclusions. It is a way to try to answer 'what if' or 'what will happen if' questions. What if the Earth is round, how do we explain why it appears to be flat? What happens if the earth isn't flat and we sail our ships toward the horizon?

We question beliefs by asking, "How do you know that?", "Is it helpful believing that?", "What evidence do you have of that?", or "What evidence do you have that might not be true?", "What doubts do you have about that?", "What other explanations can you come up with about why that might be?", or "How might someone else explain that situation?"

Hypotheses can lead to new theories which, when tested and found true or useful, become beliefs. To test our new theory of the flat earth, we get in our ship and sail west, hoping to get to India. As new and more useful ways of understanding a situation arise, previously held beliefs are disempowered and relegated to the status of old notions or superstitions, irrational beliefs resulting from ignorance or fear of the unknown.

Humans are capable of abstract beliefs. Religion and culture often ask us to believe things when we have had no direct experience of the patterns they describe. Often, we merely take other people's words as truths. Therefore, it is liberating to think about beliefs more as hypotheses and then to regularly assess their usefulness. Our ability to question and hypothesize evolves as the way we make sense of the world expands and deepens.

Beliefs are encoded in the mind using various combinations of visual, auditory, kinesthetic, and to a lesser degree gustatory and olfactory representations: the cinema of our minds. Most of these processes generally happen outside of conscious awareness, although people tend to be more aware of one sensory input than the others. When we believe in our beliefs it is like we are hypnotized, entranced by our own assumptions. Simply examining the structure of beliefs tends to deconstruct them, just as dissecting the production elements of a movie as you watch it will mean you just don't get caught up in the story. Beliefs encode the story of our lives; if you want to change the script, you need to step out of the movie.

Mindfulness

Mindfulness practice, the conscious attending to our moment to moment experience, opens our awareness to the activity of mind and the automatic thoughts, emotions, imagery and body sensations that are encoded in our beliefs. By resting as awareness, we can observe the play of mind without buying into the meanings being conveyed. Thoughts are viewed as clouds in the sky. Thoughts and all phenomena of the mind are merely the free play of consciousness.

Using this practice, we exit the meaning and evaluating mind, and let thoughts and feelings pass without evaluation. This allows for a sense of freedom from the usual frames of reference and life at that moment can be accepted for what it is. In an open mind, information previously screened out can be perceived; new ideas can arise.

To help David articulate self-limiting beliefs, the therapist asked him what he thinks has held him back from finding easier and more enjoyable ways of relating to people. David says he has always thought that he wasn't very likable. "And because you think in that way you have tended to relate in what way?" the therapist inquires.

David: "I have tended to hold back and not let people get to know me."

Therapist: "Which would have made you come across in what way?"

David: "Either as boring, not interested in them, or both."

Therapist: "Are you boring and not interested in them?"

David: "Sometimes."

Therapist: "Not all the time?"

David: "No."

Therapist: "What evidence do you have that the idea about you not being likeable isn't true?"

David: "I had a good friend when I was a kid, I got along well with my brother, and you seem interested in me."

In Essence at SIX

Organizing our cognitive framework within the psychological domain of questioning helps us to differentiate fact from fiction and better anticipate the consequences of our actions.

SEVEN — New Ideas

Every really new idea looks crazy at first. *Alfred North Whitehead*

Ideas are the seminal cognitions of the objects of our perception: essentially, untried concepts. All creativity begins with the possibility of something new being conceived. New ideas that are inspiring lead to the birth of new hypotheses, beliefs, values, capabilities, behaviors and ideals of what can be created and changed, both within ourselves and our environments. The more we learn, the more new possibilities arise, which fuels greater curiosity.

Ideas, made of the same stuff as ideals, exist in the immanent mind of our self-organizing universe all the time. When appropriate conditions arise, new ways of thinking (ideas) about the nature of the objects of our perception can take hold and be conceived in the fertile womb of our mind. An idea, as defined by the Webster Dictionary, is, "A fiction object or picture created by the imagination; the same when proposed as a pattern to be copied, or a standard to be reached; one of the archetypes or patterns of created things, conceived by the Platonists to have excited objectively from eternity in the mind of the Deity." A mind able to question existing beliefs is an open mind. In open minds — not predetermined minds — new ideas can be conceived, developed and evaluated for their usefulness.

Out of trial and error, new hypotheses generate which, in turn, eventually mature into useful beliefs.

Lama Ole Nydahl says the brain is like a television and mind is space, inherently wise and full of potential; the more open our minds are, the more information our receivers can pick up. Gregory Bateson also had the notion of the mind as immanent, and the mind we think of as being our own simply a fragmented part of a larger mind field. This might explain the phenomenon of the simultaneous discovery of new theories from separate individuals working in physical isolation from one another. Our thinking and perceiving are all part of the self-organizing nature of the universe in which new structures, including ideas, emerge out of the universal field of possibilities. Certain people just happen to be the most fertile soil for these ideas to germinate and take root. New ideas about future possibilities are, in essence, fragments of ideals yet to be acknowledged. New ideas also help clarify and refine existing ideals.

Realization is the process of coming to know what is real. What is real becomes more apparent when we have seen past the myths and superstitions that have obscured our perception. It is by examining phenomena of life from alternative perspectives that we begin to be cognizant of elements of our experience not previously noticed. This leaves us open to receiving new information that can also stimulate new ideas. Curiosity is driven by new ideas and information, and the desire to more fully discover the nature of existence.

Curiosity is lost when we hold our beliefs with such certainty that we accept them as reality and, in the process, censor or distort other ideas or perceptions that don't fit with the existing patterns. Having a curiosity to learn more leads us to learn enough to know how little we know and how much more there always is to discover. Many advances in understanding the world have come when a person from one culture or discipline entertains a perspective from a different culture or discipline.

Since the universe is infinite, there are infinite points of perspective by which to view anything. "One's mind," said Oliver Wendell Holmes, "once stretched by a new idea, never regains its original dimensions." Rather than being trapped by the stupidity and ignorance of any one limited perspective, our curiosity keeps us open to discovering and realizing more about the nature of things. The evolution of human consciousness is dependent on regularly entertaining new ideas and discovering how they may be useful in gaining greater mastery in the process of learning to relate more respectfully and harmoniously with the rest of creation.

New ideas are articulated by asking, "How else are you thinking about this?", "What other ways are there to think about this?", "What else is possible, or a possible explanation?", "When you let go of how you have been thinking about this, what comes to you?", "What would you rather believe?" Brainstorming sessions in which the mind is free to throw out uncensored ideas can lead to useful new ideas.

David's therapist asks him what he would be thinking about being likeable, after the miracle. He answers:, "I'd be thinking I'm likeable when I give people a chance to get to know me."

Therapist: "Any other new ideas come to you when you imagine yourself thinking you are likeable?"

David: "The more I show interest in other people, the more likely they are to show interest in me."

In Essence at SEVEN

Organizing our cognitive framework within the psychological domain of new ideas helps us discover new possibilities and begin planning for new outcomes.

EIGHT — Identity

What you are now is what you have been, what you will be is what you do now. *Buddha*

We are not who we think we are. Identity is a conceptualization that attempts to define what it is about how we are in the world that specifically pertains to us as individuals. Webster defines identity as, "The state or quality of being identical, or the same; sameness." [45] Identity is who we believe we are. Like other beliefs, identity attempts to predict how similar (sameness) we will be in the future based on how we have been in the past. A clear sense of identity creates a sense of certainty that helps us to act in a world in which everything is always changing. In order to contend with the vast array of variables in life, it is nice to think there is something about ourselves we can count on.

Identity is not a single idea about our selves; rather, it is a system of beliefs about who we are based on what we believe, what we value, our capabilities, how we behave, our ideals, the environments we inhabit and the communities to which we belong. Once an identity is well formed, it can be impervious to change. A healthy identity, however, is always evolving and hence is inclusive of whatever experiences we have. An evolving sense of self is consistently being reshaped and reformed by life experiences. The more rigid the sense of an identity, the more information and ideas that don't fit within its boundaries are deleted or distorted. In order to maintain its sameness, it is selective about what we take notice of, recognize, value, pay attention to, think about and act upon. Who we identify ourselves as determines who we think we are and who we think we aren't, as well as where we go and who we associate with.

Externally, we can think of this in terms of us as having clear boundaries between self and others. Observing in others those characteristics we don't identify with, we say, "That way of acting, dressing, talking, thinking is not me." We say the same sort of thing when we observe ourselves thinking, feeling or acting in ways that we don't identify with. We say things like, "I don't know what made me say (or do) that." "I'm not feeling myself today." Or when we decline to do something outside of our identity, we'll say things like, "That's just not me."

If I identify myself as being a left-wing activist, I will make sense of the world with a whole different set of constructs than if I identify myself as a right-wing capitalist. Encoded within our personal identity are our most basic — and most unquestioned — assumptions or beliefs about life. Usually, we don't consider the process of how we identify ourselves; rather, we assume it is simply our nature. This is why when our identity is evolving from one to another, it can feel like we are dying.

Arguments about politics, religion, parenting or anything that people are very identified with can become quite heated because people feel that who they are (identity) is being threatened when their core beliefs, values or practices are being attacked or invalidated. They feel it as an attack on or invalidation of themselves. Although much of who we think of ourselves as is not verbally articulated, we tend to reveal aspects of our identities with statements that begin with "I am a…" For example, "I am a loner… a father… a happy person."

People have various sub-identities that, in conglomeration, become one's identity. These sub-identities are often associated with different psychological network domains. For example, an identity associated with the *environment* domain could be, "I'm a city person." An identity associated with the *ideals* domain could be, "I'm a good person." In the *behavior* domain could be, "I'm a psychotherapist." In the domain of *capabilities*, "I'm a communicator." In the domain of *values*, "I'm a choosy person." In the domain of *beliefs*, "I'm a Creationist." In the domain of *questioning*, "I'm a skeptic." In the domain of *new ideas*, "I'm a curious person." At the level of *identity*, "I'm a character, or I'm no one." In the domain of *community*, "I'm a New Yorker." Words that define our identity tend to follow "I am".

There are qualities we all possess, yet are less identified with. Compare "I live in New York" or "I like living in New York" with "I'm a New Yorker". Similarly, compare "I'm a Buddhist" with "I believe in Buddhism" or "I am practicing Buddhism". We can imagine the statement of identity "I am a Buddhist" most likely includes believing and practicing, as well as holding Buddhist values, aspiring to Buddhist ideals and participating in a Buddhist community, in environments that are designated for Buddhist purposes. Identity establishes personal boundaries. If I'm a Buddhist then I'm not a Moslem. If I'm a New Yorker, I'm not an Alaskan. It defines who I am and who I am not.

Who we identify ourselves as is a reflection of the world we see. Consider the difference between someone who thinks of himself as the Son of God or Buddha, as compared to someone who has come to identify himself as a worthless nobody or a misfit. The world that each one of these people perceives will be quite different, not to mention the sorts of hypotheses they generate, the beliefs and values they hold, and the capabilities they develop to relate to the world. What we do tends flow from what we believe.

Once formed, identities and the constellation of beliefs, questions, values, capabilities, behaviors, ideals and the environments we live in take on a life of their own that creates a sense of certainty about who we are.

This certainty, at various times of our lives, is very useful in helping us make the most of the life we have created for ourselves.

The danger of becoming trapped arises for us when we forget that our identity is not who we are, rather it is who we think we are. If the identity that has served a purpose at one stage of our lives doesn't change, it will keep us locked into old ways of thinking, perceiving and acting. If, for example, a person who has grown up in an abusive family has learnt to survive by thinking and acting tough and always being ready for a fight, he has become identified as an intimidating kind of person that will use whatever violence is needed to protect against possible threats. The problem is that all of his posturing, threats and violent attacks antagonize and provoke others to be critical, defensive and attacking. His actions and attitudes end up creating and perpetuating the very attacks he is trying to prevent. The self-fulfilling prophecy keeps him locked in his identity, unable explore alternative and more fulfilling ways of relating.

What you really are is the radiant emptiness of Being. You are that which can conceive of a self, can have ideas, beliefs, values, emotions, capabilities, behaviors and a body. By dis-identifying with all the objects of awareness, we can rest as awareness itself. When resting in the essential wholeness of being, there is no separate self, only a unified field.

We can help articulate the identities we hold by asking, "Who are you?","What kind of person are you?", "Who would you be, if you couldn't believe those old beliefs any longer?"

David's therapist continues by exploring with him what kind of person he would he be, once he believes people will like him when they get a chance to get to know him. What kind of person would he be discovering and allowing to be discovered as the more he shows interest and takes pleasure in others, the more they are likely to show interest and take pleasure in him? Who would he sense himself to be when he was consistently finding easier and more enjoyable ways of doing things? David replied by saying he would be a friendly person. He added that he would still be the kind of person who needed his own space and time to himself. The evolution of identity is a process of becoming more inclusive of ways of being in the world and integrating them into how we think of ourselves.

In Essence at EIGHT

Organizing our cognitive framework within the domain of identity helps implement the ideas, beliefs, values and capabilities needed to master they challenges we take on. It can be like a vessel that allows us to cross a river, yet once we get to the other side we need to be able to leave it behind, rather than trying to travel overland in a boat.

NINE — Community

A proper community, we should remember also, is a commonwealth: a place, a resource, an economy. It answers the needs, practical as well as social and spiritual, of its members — among them the need to need one another. *Wendell Berry*

In biology, we think of communities as groups of plants and animals living and interacting with one another in an environment. We think of human communities as groups of people that share in some common personal identities, beliefs, values, capabilities, behaviors, ideals and environments.

Communities exist at neighborhood, city, state, national, multinational and global levels. Community and context, as the model demonstrates, overlap. For example, for some people, the sexual context of their life will define membership to a particular community. For others, the work context of their life will determine what community they identify with. Most of us would recognize ourselves belonging to and participating to varying degrees in a multiplicity of communities that coincide with the various contexts of our lives. Context, environment and community are nearly synonymous with one another.

Like personal identities, human communities are defined by shared themes of the various psychological domains. Some communities are primarily defined by environment, others by ideals, behavior, values, beliefs or the personal identities the members hold in common. For a community to be viable over time, there needs to be some degree of congruency in all the domains for most of the members. Congruency does not exclude diversity. In fact, robust communities, while being quite congruent about particular individual identities, beliefs, values, capabilities, behaviors, ideals and contexts, will allow for a diversity of ways these aspects are conceived of and expressed.

One can be a member of the psychotherapy community, yet identify as a Jungian, Behaviorist or Humanist, holding to any number of theories and value systems, and performing psychotherapy in any number of ways, working towards diverse ideals, in a variety of environments. This community maintains itself through the relating of its members through books, periodicals, seminars, conferences and professional associations. The psychotherapy community is a good example of how most communities are made up of many interwoven and overlapping smaller communities. The interweaving and overlapping of communities, human and otherwise, forms a biological, cultural and economic ecosystem that is self-supporting and evolving.

The type of person we identify ourselves as is largely determined by the type of communities we belong to or, in many cases, are born into. A person born into an Afro-American household in an inner-city community will identify differently from a person born into a Hindu rice-growing family in rural Bali. Human communities are, for the most part, determined by environment, yet also by social or cultural context.

A fetus would primarily experience themselves as a member of the mother–child community. After birth, infants almost immediately find themselves developing relationships with their father, siblings, or other people who they might be in regular contact with, along with a new sort of relationship with their mother. Evolving personal identities need to be supported by evolving communities, in which each individual must find and fulfill a niche. A baby quickly becomes a member of their family. Incorporating the baby into the family changes the family and will precipitate developmental challenges for the other family members.

As we mature, our various sub-personalities evolve and, in addition, newly emergent identities must be incorporated into the organization of our whole sense of self. Each of us is, in a sense, a community of sub-identities that are organized into a network of self-maintaining relationships with one another. Any new (or newly evolved) identity must be incorporated into my community of identities, which include father, son, husband, friend, therapist, writer, adventurer, ecologist, activist, spiritual seeker, and so on.

The word community is a nominalization; it codifies a system of organisms communing with one another. Communing is defined as 'to be in a state of intimate, heightened sensitivity and receptivity, as with one's surroundings: hikers communing with nature.'[46] In addition, it shares the same root as *common* and *communicate*. To commune is to be in an intimate heightened state of communication with what all beings share in common: our unity with all creation.

Different contexts define different patterns of interaction that, in turn, are based on different sets of beliefs, values, capabilities and ideals. When consolidating and stabilizing our developments in any particular context, we often become more identified with the organization than with our individual sense of self. Maintaining a harmonious environment is of the highest importance during this phase. We know there is little difference between what is good for us as individuals and what is good for us as a whole.

Community evolves as individuals realize their potential in cooperation with others. To help articulate the communities to which we belong, we can ask questions like, "With whom do you belong?", "What group might best support the kind of person you are becoming?", "Who are the people you support and who supports you?", and "Who are your people?"

The therapist asks David, "Who are the people you can imagine supporting and having them support you, as you grow more fully into that friendly kind of person that is easy to get along with and takes pleasure in others' company?"

David replies, "Probably most people at work, and who knows where that might lead? I'd probably end up making friends elsewhere too."

The therapist first vivified the experience described in the community domain and backtracked through the previous domains. He then asked David if he would like to explore this future scenario more fully.

David: "Okay."

Therapist: "Since our focus started with work matters, let's stay focused on that context. Let's just assume elsewhere in your life you have ended up making some friends, but for now you are at work. Tell me how you imagine you are experiencing being more supported by others?"

David: "Because I'm talking more with others, they keep me more informed about things that I'm not directly aware of, and instead of having to do everything myself, because I'm on good terms, I feel more comfortable asking people for help."

In Essence at NINE

Organizing our cognitive framework within the psychological domain of community helps us develop the cooperation with others needed to consolidate the changes we have manifested.

Evolving Individuals — Evolving Communities

Working through the psychological domains can be done in a systematic way by asking simple questions leading to framing ones, as a way of approaching a given context that is congruent at each level. When there is congruency, it is more likely a person will take the steps needed to evolve through that cycle of change.

While working at a college, I had an opportunity to work with many graduate students who wanted to learn psychotherapy and become licensed clinicians in the community. Although all were interested in therapy, each of them organized themselves at the different psychological domains in their own unique way. Psychotherapy is what this group was attracted to (an attractor), however the same process of self-organization applies to whatever people may be drawn to, whether it be architecture, nursing, driving race-cars, and so on. To help prepare them for the process of becoming practicing clinicians, I asked each of them clarify to the best of their ability their perceptions and understandings in each domain.

Insights and characteristics

NINE — Each student was attracted to a particular therapeutic context, whether it was private practice in a downtown office, or in their home, at substance abuse rehabilitation center, or an adolescent treatment facility.

ONE — Each student had ideal images of what working in that context could be like.

TWO — There were particular behaviors they needed to perform in order to be working towards those ideals.

THREE — In order to perform those behaviors they needed develop certain capabilities.

FOUR — Each student had their own set of values that motivated them to develop those capabilities.

FIVE — Each student had underlying beliefs that supported those values.

SIX — Each student eventually needed to let go of limiting ideas about themselves and the profession to work towards what they truly believed in and valued.

SEVEN — Each student accumulated many new ideas about themselves that deepened and clarified the functioning and understanding of their beliefs, values, capabilities, behaviors, ideals and therapeutic contexts.

EIGHT — Each successful student's identity eventually evolved from being a student of psychotherapy to being a psychotherapist. Quite often in our development we don't give up old identities; we simply take on new ones. A good psychotherapist, for example, is most likely a student of psychotherapy for as long as they are psychotherapist. I can be a son, husband, father and grandfather all at the same time. However, just as the identity of son will evolve when one becomes a husband or father, so too will the identity of 'student of psychotherapy' evolve when one become a psychotherapist.

NINE — As those therapists became more established, they not only contributed and made a difference in the communities that they worked, but also became part of a professional community of other therapists that supported them in their identity and work as a therapist.

Taking the time in their training to articulate each one of these domains formed a sense of congruity and clarity of purpose that, many reported, supported them through the process of evolving into the types of professionals they wanted to become.

To facilitate change in any area of life we can explore each psychological domain, as well as the network formed as an ecosystem of cognition. To facilitate this exploration we can ask:

NINE — In what environment or context are you wanting to make a change?

ONE — What is your ideal in that context?

TWO — How would you be behaving in order to be moving towards that ideal?

THREE — What capabilities would you be exercising in order to take action in that way?

FOUR — What values motivate you to develop those capabilities?

FIVE — What beliefs do you already hold that support those values?

SIX — What limiting ideas would you come to question in order to honor those beliefs?

SEVEN — What new ideas are coming to you that support those doubts and enable you to invest in what you value most?

EIGHT — What sort of person would you be? Who, in that environment, is working towards those ideals, by behaving in those specific ways, utilizing those capabilities, because you hold those values, which are supported by those beliefs, which you were able to honor because you began to doubt those old limiting ideas, which enabled you to realize those new ideas?

NINE — What sort of community would you eventually be a part of that supports you in being that kind of person?

People tend to think of their essential wholeness as something they will realize in the future, or something they had in the past and lost. In hypnotherapeutic processes, we use this tendency to help them access these resources by associating into a time in the past, or an imagined future, where they can experience being more resourceful.

In doing this exercise, we aren't just interested in a hypothetical intellectual exercise; rather, we are genuinely getting a sense of what the future as that sort of person in that sort of community supports. In this way, the person doing this PsychoLogical Domains exercise can get a sense of seeing the world through the eyes, hearing with the ears, moving and feeling with the body of that kind of person, supported by that sort of community, as if it was happening now.

We can then associate back through the other logical dimensions. For example, how does this kind of person that you are with the support of this sort of community, who sees, hears and feels in those types of ways, embrace these new ideas and possibilities? And how do you, as that sort of person, question old beliefs, and remain true to the beliefs that support your deeper values? How do you, as a person like that, live those deeper values by developing and exercising your capabilities? What specific actions are you taking to move towards those ideals which represent what matters most to you in that particular context of your life?

In this manner, we are to identify with aspects of ourselves that we project into the future and anchor them in the environments and communities that present us with challenges to evolve more fully in the way we play our part.

CHAPTER SIX

Essential Qualities

The Essential Qualities of Being are the ways the soul enlightens our day-to-day challenges and the opportunities to realize our essential wholeness.

> When an object moves through space relative to us, its clock runs slow compared to ours. That is, the speed of its motion through time slows down. Here's the leap: Einstein proclaimed that all objects in the universe are always traveling through space-time at one fixed speed — that of light.
>
> Something traveling at light speed through space will have no speed left for motion through time. Thus light does not get old; a photon that emerged from the big bang is the same age today as it was then. There is no passage of time at light speed.[47]
> *Brian Green*

Have you ever noticed that when you open your eyes in the morning, the consciousness that looks out through your eyes never changes? When some of us look in the mirror, we're shocked to see someone that looks more like our mother or father than the person we sense ourselves to be. Yet no matter what we see reflected, there is a sense of being that supersedes our physicality.

When describing being or true nature, Buddhists sometimes referred to it as timeless light or luminescent spaciousness. This idea of our selves as light is not uncommon. Often, people's presence is described as radiant, or bright; we say, she was absolutely beaming, he is glowing, she has an aura of kindness, he is very clear, she has a luminescent presence. We use light as the metaphor when we are talking about essential qualities of being: he has a peaceful glow, it's an illuminating state of consciousness, her eyes sparkle with joy, she's blessed by the light of forgiveness, she has an aura of acceptance. We also call people who excel 'stars'.

The references to light to go hand-in-hand with the way we describe hearing something true: that was very enlightening, I feel clearer about that, that's illuminating, it was a brilliant insight, the truth came shining through, the truth was brought to light.

Similarly, when we hear the terms dull, dark mood, gloomy, in the dark, dim-witted, has a dark cloud hanging over her, shady character, murky past, foggy headed and the future looks bleak, we identify this with various states of psychological unwellness. When trapped in suffering we are out of touch with the light of being and overly preoccupied with the gross physical level of existence.

People tend to get overly preoccupied with any one of the three basic instincts: self-preservation (survival of the body), social (survival of the group) and sexual (survival of the gene pool). Out of touch with their essential peaceful loving nature, they go searching for fulfillment in temporary fixes that, as it is not what we really need, leave us always needing more. When this happens, simple survival needs get exaggerated, with people needing too much food and material stuff, sacrificing too much of their time and individuality to belong, and being preoccupied with sex, romance and altered states; in other words, all the ways people get addicted or give their power away, trying to find happiness and safety. These addictions are fed and maintained by what the Enneagram literature refers to as the vices: anger, pride, deceit, envy, avarice, fear, gluttony, lust and sloth. These are all versions or manifestations of what Buddhism calls the Three Poisons: ignorance, attachment and aversion.

At the physical level, our consciousness is preoccupied with survival; not just survival of body, community and gene pool, but also survival of egoic identity and our attachment, aversion and ignorance in the way we relate to the three instincts. People can get so identified with their ego and their attachments that it can even override their need to survive physically. At the extreme end of this reaction, some people choose suicide. This may be a response to losing their standing in the community, losing their security or money, or being rejected by their sexual partner. These processes of getting caught in cycles of suffering will be covered in depth in Chapter Nine — Compulsions of Personality.

Spiritual Impulse

In addition to the three mammalian instinctual drives, people are also motivated by what could be called the spiritual impulse: what Buddhism would describe as the impulse towards enlightenment, or what Adyashanti refers to as, "Existence becoming conscious of itself through the human experience." This impulse towards a more soulful life, the spiritual impulse, is the movement towards what is unborn, unchanging undying –– the clear light of being. For those who can be completely absorbed in this, as many spiritual leaders can, the ability comes to sit in a cave for years, like Ramana Maharshi or Milarepa, with almost no concern for their human life. Shaktamuni Buddha had this impulse, but then was moved by compassion to return home and to teach what he had learned.

It is the work of the soul to bring spirit to our human life and bring our human life to spirit. At the level of soul we are not just interested in survival; in fact, we may be willing to sacrifice our life for a greater cause. At the level of soul, we are interested in the quality of life. Soul is interested in making life beautiful, joyous, loving and meaningful. Soul wants to make love, not just have sex. Soul wants to play, dance, create art, tell stories, joke around, laugh and sing. Soul needs vehicles like ceremony, ritual, trance and psychotherapy to find expression, create a sense of sacredness, and be irreverent. Soul speaks through the imagination; it is expressed through intuitive phenomena like gut feelings and creativity. In bringing spirit to the physical world, we co-create the world and bring the unconditional love of our spirit into life.

When we shift our awareness from the gross realm of the survival of the body, community and gene pool to the subtle and causal realms, we begin to experience the essential qualities of our light-like nature. The more soulful our engagement in life, the more fully the essential qualities of consciousness, compassion, strength, forgiveness, spaciousness, acceptance, joy, will and peace inform our experience.

With those qualities evident, we begin living with the spiritual attitude of: "Be in the world, but not of it." It's what can be thought of as spirit realizing itself as a soul in human form. We realize our essential wholeness when there is congruency within the human, soul and spiritual spectrums of experience, coinciding with an ecological balance in the way the spectrum of essential qualities informs our lives.

Essential Qualities

The circle of the Enneagram represents the unified field of creation. Just as white light, when filtered through a prism, separates into the colors of the rainbow, this unified field can be divided into its essential qualities. Each segment on the continuum around the circle represents an essential quality. These qualities are essential for a soulful life and, like a light shining through a stained-glass window, they bring beauty and meaning to the undifferentiated white light shining into the lives of humans.

The interconnectedness of these essential qualities forms an ecosystem of human consciousness and informs the way we relate to our emerging experience. Neuroscientist Francisco Varela describes mental states as transitory, with a feeling tone that colors the experience. Each cognitive experience is a unified, transient and yet coherent ensemble of oscillating neurons related to sensory perception, emotions, memory, bodily movements, and so on. Varela states, "The primary conscious experience, common to all higher vertebrates, is not located in a specific part of the brain, nor can it be identified in terms of specific neural structures. It is the manifestation of a particular cognitive process –– a transient synchronization of diverse, rhythmically oscillating neural circuits." [48]

The Enneagram provides us with a visual representation of the 'diverse oscillating neural circuits' upon which we can map our cognitive processes. Each number represents the frequency band of the specific neural circuitry our consciousness is attuning itself to at any given time. All our learning to survive and thrive is an interplay between our humanness struggling to learn from experience at the gross level (selection), and essential qualities at the subtle level (self-organization) informing how we develop emergent capabilities.

The frequency bands of essential qualities blend from one to the other, just as in a rainbow there is a continuum of color in which each color blends into the next; consciousness blends into compassion, which blends into strength, and so on. Just as the full spectrum of colors reflected by the vast diversity of creation enables us to visually experience the world, the full spectrum of essential qualities brings richness to how we experience day-to-day existence.

Our essential qualities are not transient, however, our awareness of them is, just as red light is always present within white light, but is only reflected by particular objects. Essential qualities are not dependent on conditions, yet conditions call them forth. For example, the essential quality of forgiveness is not dependent on conditions of our life going a particular way; however, difficult life experiences that lead us to feeling resentful call forth the need for forgiveness. Connecting or reconnecting to essential qualities brings us back to our essential wholeness when our gross humanness has become dissociated from the white light of our spiritual nature.

Essential Qualities and Cycle of Change

Each essential quality is like a' basin of attraction' that we become attuned to, depending on what phase of a change cycle we are passing through. Like other attractors, our perception organizes itself according to qualities of the attractor. The developmental challenges of each phase are naturally supported by the associated essential quality.

Enneagram of Essential Qualities

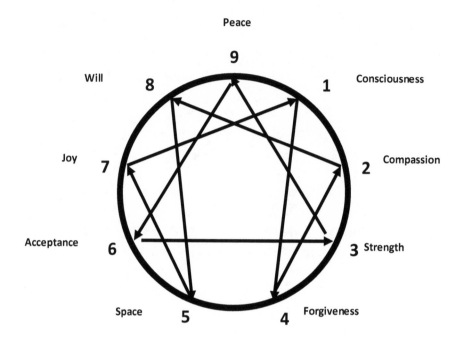

Peace

9

Will 8 1 Consciousness

Joy 7 2 Compassion

Acceptance 6 3 Strength

Space 5 4 Forgiveness

NINE — Peace

Peace is the quality that holds not only our lives in harmony and cooperation with others, but the entire universe in eternal harmony. At phase NINE our tendency to regulate internal and external harmony and stability within any given context arises out of our essential quality of peace. Essential peace is not merely the absence of conflict; it is the fabric of universal wholeness and unity.

ONE — Consciousness

To be conscious is to be awake and aware. At phase ONE, as our self-regulating patterns eventually become inadequate to support our ongoing development, the spotlight of consciousness highlights the limitations inherent in stabilizing homeostatic patterns. Consciousness is synonymous with mindfulness. To be mindful is to pay attention to how things really are, rather than assuming they are how we *think* they are. To be mindful is to remember to be present with what is.

Consciousness is always guiding us to more fully remember what is true in reality. Consciousness allows us to be discerning of what supports us and what doesn't. Consciousness keeps of us mindful of our emergent potential, as opposed to getting entranced in the autopilot complacency of homeostatic feedback loops.

TWO — Compassion

Compassion comes from the recognition that everything is part of the whole and has a place and a function. At phase TWO, the quality of our lives depends on attending to the needs of our emergent selves. Compassion holds everything with love. When we become conscious of emerging needs for healing or growth, our compassionate nature attends to those needs. Compassion can be fierce or gentle, yet it is always attending our deepest needs, while tapping into the capabilities needed to relate more fully to life.

THREE — Strength

Essential strength gives us the backbone to remain upright and resilient when we are being pushed to the limits of our capabilities. At phase THREE, essential strength carries us to the boundaries of our current level of development. It is our strength of character that commits to going to the limits of our capabilities to do what is needed.

Strength keeps us honest when it would be easier to believe our own lies and not be true to our deeper purpose. Essential strength is always there, just like gravity holding planets in solar systems, but it also initiates novas when a star has reached its limit.

FOUR — Forgiveness

Forgiveness is the ability to let go of the past and the old ways of thinking, perceiving and behaving. At phase FOUR, the inadequacies of our way of life become more apparent, as we are pushed beyond the limits of our normal patterns. Forgiveness frees us from the judgments of how we thought the universe was supposed to unfold. It allows us to rest in a sense of innocence, free from guilt and blame, and recognize that we are all doing the best we can, given what we know at any given time.

Instead of dwelling on what could or should have been, we are open to learning from our mistakes and how we can do better next time. Forgiveness allows us to return to loving our whole selves, especially those parts that have failed or been inadequate in some way.

FIVE — Space

It is our experience of essential space that puts our petty attachments and self-imposed limitations into perspective, just as the vastness of outer space reminds us that Earth is but a speck of dust in a universe of billions of galaxies. At phase FIVE, the old boundaries of the way we have thought about and interacted with the world continue to dissolve or fall away.

It is in space that our mental activity of generating images, sounds, words and sensations occurs. Thoughts manifest into space and dissipate back into space. A narrow mind has a very limited perspective on life and is confined by mental frameworks that we can become attached to and identified with. A spacious mind is open to seeing how things really are. Space holds the awareness in which thoughts and perception come and go, and frees us from the thoughts and perceptions we have become identified with. Rather than being caught up in the activity of our minds, by resting in essential space we are able to experience depths of our being. In spacious awareness, we are able to determine what is and what isn't essential to our wellbeing.

SIX — Acceptance

Acceptance ends our arguments with the way things are and allows us perceive the world and ourselves more realistically. At phase SIX, it is the acceptance of our true nature that allows us to surrender to the processes of evolution that are beyond our control and limited perception. With acceptance, there is a shift from 'either or' thinking to both, and from exclusive to inclusive.

This shift in perception allows paradigm shifts to occur that make sense of what previously seemed irreconcilable. Acceptance, for example, embraces and listens to those aspects of ourselves we have rejected, denied and ignored. When given a voice, these parts of us will question the authority of limiting beliefs and help open us to new ways of perceiving.

SEVEN — Joy

To be joyous is to feel expansive and free. At phase SEVEN, we dance on the boundary of order and chaos or, as Deepak Chopra refers to it, "The field of infinite possibilities." We follow our blissful curiosity into exploration and experimentation, and play with the possibilities available to us. The things that bring us into the most contact with joy become the areas we want to invest more fully in. What we are best at is what brings us joy and what makes for our greatest contribution to the wholeness of creation. Joy is the experience of being in the flow of the ever expanding and changing creative process of the universe. It is essential joy the enables us to fall in love with life over and over again.

EIGHT — Will

Through willful determination and constancy, practice leads to mastery. At phase EIGHT, we choose which possibilities are worth committing to and willfully begin organizing them into new patterns. We know we have truly mastered something when we no longer have to think about what we are doing and effortlessly participate fully in whatever it is we are doing. Giving ourselves fully to manifesting our gifts in the world arises out of divine will or what the buddhists might call 'dharma'. Divine will guides us in playing our part in the evolution of humanity and the co-creation of the world we live in. In the manifesting our creative impulses, with become more identified with the creator.

The *will* to creatively manifest is not something we control with our egos, rather it is the divine role that we surrender to. Will allows divinity to act through us, guiding our thoughts, words and deeds.

NINE — Peace

Peace mediates and minimizes conflict in order to maintain relative stability and order (homeostasis). At phase NINE, we consolidate our newly mastered skills into habits — self-perpetuating patterns of interaction — within the larger systems to which we belong: family, community, and so on. Peace allows for harmonious diversity, but also encourages us to sacrifice individual concerns for the greater good. Peace allows our lives, internally and externally, to be organized with increasing complexity and cooperation, in which all the parts of us have a sense of belonging.

Full Spectrum

In summary, *peace* seeks to cooperate more fully with life as it is emerging within and around us. This inspires greater *mindfulness* of our internal and external experience. This leads us to a greater sense of *compassion* in the way we relate to ourselves and the rest of creation. Out of *compassion* we find the *strength* to promote life's emerging agendas and address our inadequacies and past mistakes with *forgiveness*. Through *forgiveness* we are able to experience the present moment as it is, which in turn opens up the *space* in our consciousness to investigate the nature of reality more fully. *Spacious* awareness just *accepts* everything as it is, helping us to differentiate fact from fiction. *Acceptance* of everything opens us to appreciation of everything and the *joyously* blissful nature of consciousness. It is when we follow our deepest bliss that we are in alignment with divine *will* (dharma). In surrendering to divine *will*, we manifest our part to play in *peaceful* harmony with the rest of creation.

Seeking and Being

Jesus said, "But seek ye first the Kingdom of God and His righteousness, and all these things shall be added unto you" (Matthew 6:33). The suggestion is that only when we reconnect with our essential wholeness and discerning wisdom will we be able to attain what we truly need and want. When we aren't living in our essential wholeness, we are doing the opposite; we are trying to get what we think we want and need, believing that then we will be joyful, peaceful, forgiving, and so on. We tend to dissociate from our essential wholeness and then project out into the world, and into either the past or the future. If forgiveness, acceptance, and so on, are in the past, we feel hopeless, which presents as depression; if the 'Kingdom' and its essential qualities are in the future, there is hope, yet no guarantees, which leaves us feeling anxious.

We mistakenly think by fulfilling our conditions we will find joy, peace, acceptance or forgiveness. By constantly trying to improve our situation first, we are endlessly chasing those qualities. The basic belief is that these qualities are somehow separate from what we are. We believe that we must earn, achieve or acquire these ways of being. When we come up short, it reinforces the idea that most of us have — the reason we aren't fulfilled is because we're not good enough. However, consider the opposite. First of all, when we are in touch with our essential wholeness (Kingdom of God) and its essential qualities, a lot of our craving falls away. Additionally, those qualities are very attractive and have a lot of creative potential. Joyful people create more joy. People, who are compassionate with themselves and others, attract people who are compassionate.

A Gambler's Story

A gambler I was working with felt the amount of money he had lost was unforgiveable; he had to get back the money he lost so he could forgive himself and be free. Of course, the way he tried to get the money back was by gambling. Yet, once he was able to forgive his past mistakes and make peace with himself, the gambling became pointless. Looking at what people want, and identifying the underlying elements, invariably leads to an answer in the form of an essential quality.

Our essential qualities are the spiritual fabric of our relationship to life. However, many of us make our happiness dependent on something happening in the future: once we find our romantic partner then we'll be happy, once some other event happens, we'll be successful. What generally happens though, when we're not happy, is that those attracted to us are other desperate souls; whereas, when we are in touch with joy, compassion, acceptance, and so on, not only are we more attractive, we also have a lot to offer.

Call for Help

When we lose touch with our essential qualities, we get caught in vicious cycles of negative emotions and self-defeating behaviors. These psychological symptoms are a sort of call for help — a way of reminding us to come back home to our essential wholeness. At the source of this plea, an essential quality is waiting to be experienced. One way to answer the plea and uncover the essential quality is to inquire into what our pain or dysfunctional behavior is seeking.

A way to identify it is to create a dialogue with a symptomatic part, for example, by using the Core Transformation Process.[49] First, ask what that part is trying to experience, then project into the future when this quality has been realized so the person is experiencing now what they had relegated to the future. We then explore how that essential quality would handle current circumstances, bearing in mind, that our essential qualities are unconditional and ever present.

An example of this inquiry might be to work with a person stuck in resentment. We could ask the part of them that is holding onto the resentment what they are hoping to experience by doing so. Their inner response might be, "To punish that person for what they have done." We then inquire as to what does that part hopes to experience by punishing them. The part answers, "Teach them a lesson." And once that part has been taught a lesson? "See that they are remorseful and won't do that behavior again."

And what would that allow you to experience? "Then I could forgive them and begin to trust again." What would that feel like? "A deep sense of forgiveness and trust." If that sense of forgiveness and trust had a color what color would it be? "Pink" And when you open up to that pink sense of forgiveness and trust, where do you feel it most strongly in your body? "In my chest." Does that feel good? "Yes." Would you be willing to allow yourself to experience that sense of forgiveness and trust more fully and deeply now? "Yes." If your inner soul or higher self could help you to open more fully to that sense of forgiveness, could you close your eyes, as you relax into and open more fully to that pink glow of universal forgiveness and trust?

We might see the client's eyes closing and notice a shift in breathing, as they appear to relax and soften. We could continue: As you enjoy that sense of forgiveness and trust and you bring that person you were resentful of closer to you, how does that affect your perception of them and what they have done? "I can see they are in pain and were taking it out on me. I don't need to take it personally and feel bad." What can you imagine saying to them now? "I can see you are having a hard time, but I really don't like you taking your pain out on me. If you are having a hard time, just talk to me please."

Enlightening Ourselves

Spiritual seekers, such as those practising Vajrayana or Tantrayana Buddhism use the tendencies of the seeking mind to bring what is being sought into the here and now. Like other seekers, they do the same thing of putting their realization of enlightenment or of their essential qualities in the future. In meditation, it is common to use colored lights to experience these qualities. The meditator will visualise an image of a highly realized lama or a Buddha image shining light into their body.

The name 'Buddha' is synonymous with one's unconditioned fully realized mind. Archetypical images of various Buddhas referred to as 'yidams', symbolic representations of aspects of our essential wholeness or Buddha-nature, are invoked as a way of experiencing different essential qualities. With some meditations, the meditator becomes the Buddha image. Lama Yeshe, referring to meditating with the deity or yidam of Heruuka, states, "Tantra says essentially every human being is divine and pure. This is why it is important to identify yourself so strongly as being a deity, to regard yourself as perfectly developed. Instead of seeing yourself as something miserable, transform it into a radiant blue light-body."[50] He suggests we identify with the deity we resonate most with, as, "The more strongly you identify with the deity, the more transformation you achieve and the more fear and uncontrolled emotion you eliminate".[51]

In therapy, it can be very powerful for a client to invoke these qualities from a third person perspective. For example, a client is having difficulties with his boss. I'll ask them to imagine a dialogue with their boss, often done in Gestalt Therapy two-chair work. Instead of just staying in their own first person perspective or taking the second person perspective, it can be useful to step out of the dyad into the perspective of a third person. It's what I like to refer to as the co-therapist position. From this perspective, the therapist can ask the client/co-therapist what essential quality or state of mind the client would need to be in touch with in order to handle that situation better.

Let's say the client says they would need confidence and inner strength, the therapist can then ask the client to dive into the inquiry, "If inner strength and confidence had a color what color would it be?" The client would be encouraged to imagine that light shining down from above filling them with inner strength and confidence and asked to experience that affecting their posture, facial expression and voice tone. Once they have an empowered image of themselves, you can ask them how they could see themselves handling the interaction with their boss. If it isn't quite enough to alleviate the problem they are having, you may need to access other essential qualities in the same way. Once their image of themselves handling the situation is robust and effective, you then have the person step into their empowered self— they will have the first person embodied experience of that way of being.

I suggest that whenever they need to tap into those qualities of being, they can feel the light filling them up and radiating out to everyone around them. It can be helpful to have the image of carrying that into a number of contexts.

Essential Qualities and the Meditative Mind

Meditation is a context in which we use methods that help us experience our essential wholeness at all three levels of body, soul and spirit. Meditation reawakens our awareness of the infinitely changing nature of experience, or what Buddhists call impermanence. In meditation, as we let our awareness open, we realize the thing we call 'I', our personal identity, is not really a thing at all, but rather a network of processes that are constantly evolving and changing. In meditation, we learn to rest as the still, silent presence of being. As Sogyal Rinpoche says:

> To meditate is to make a complete break with how we normally operate, for it is a state free of all cares and concerns, in which there is no competition, no desire to possess or grasp at anything,

no intense and anxious struggle, and no hunger to achieve: an ambitionless state where there is neither acceptance nor rejection, neither hope nor fear, a state in which we slowly begin to release all those emotions and concepts that have imprisoned us, into the space of natural simplicity. [52]

This experience of resting in the *natural simplicity* of essential wholeness is paradoxically not so easy for most of us to access. Recognizing and opening to the essential qualities of the different stages of meditation can help with this realization. The goal of meditation isn't to make it necessary to formally meditate for the rest of our lives in order to experience the simplicity our true nature; rather, it is to live in the simplicity of a meditative mind, in which we can be aware of emotions and concepts and appreciate and/or use them when appropriate, instead of letting them unconsciously shape our perceptions and define who we are. The Enneagram provides us with a useful map of the essential qualities of meditation.

Trust and Permission

Meditation and psychotherapy are contexts in which we learn to access and trust in our essential qualities of being. Giving our selves permission to trust and experience these qualities is often the first step to harmonious living. Often, these qualities have gone unacknowledged.

A therapist can ask the simple question, "Can you give yourself permission to experience inner peace? Or be mindful? Or compassionate?" The act of giving oneself permission is a process of claiming our authority and trusting our essential goodness. When we become disconnected from the essential qualities of our innate goodness, we lose touch with the spontaneous intuition of how to authentically respond in any situation. We begin acting how we think we should, or sometimes we rebel and do quite the opposite. We end up living out of a set of socially constructed concepts that obscure our essential wholeness. At its essence, meditation and psychotherapy give us permission and, through practice, enable us to trust more fully in our essential wholeness.

ONE — *Mindfulness (Consciousness)*

Meditation is bringing the mind back home, and this is first
achieved through the practice of mindfulness.[53] *Sogyal Rinpoche*

Mindfulness is the essential quality represented by ONE in the
Enneagram. In some books, the higher virtue of ONE is described as seeing
the perfection in things as they are. This is mindfulness. Mindfulness has
the quality of being awake to one's experience, in contrast to being in a
trance or oblivious to what is happening. Common everyday trances can
happen when we are on automatic pilot, doing things without really paying
attention. Trance can be thought of as an altered state of consciousness.
Being in a trance is not inherently problematic; some trances are useful,
meaningful, or even healing. Sometimes, when we know the task we are
doing well, our minds are free to wander.

Problems (suffering) persist when we are on automatic pilot,
thinking and perceiving in habitual ways without paying attention
to the consequences of our thoughts and actions, or to the alternative
choices available to us at any given moment. We form habits, generally
with the hope of maintaining the most pleasure and least pain. Many of
these habitual ways of living, however, end up creating and perpetuating
suffering. Mindfulness awakens us to the self-perpetuating nature of our
suffering and the recurring problems of our daily routines.

Our Natural Way of Being

Enlightenment is our natural way of being; mindfulness reveals how
we un-enlighten ourselves. If we want to make the most of any situation,
we need to be as fully aware as possible. In meditation, we discover how
difficult it is to be fully aware, moment-to-moment. How difficult it is to
be aware of all of the sights, sounds, smells, tastes, sensations and emotions
of being in a loving sexual embrace, body surfing a wave, eating a meal,
walking through the woods, singing songs with our children, or whatever
is happening in any given moment. Meditation is a process by which we
can learn to more deeply appreciate the gift of life in all its many facets, and
it begins with learning to appreciate the simple act of sitting and breathing.

Trance can be useful as a narrowing of attention and in this sense it is called tunnel vision. It is a quality of vision in which we see what is within a narrow range of vision: nothing above, below, to the left or to the right. This is a very useful skill; in fact, in meditation mindfulness is often referred to as one-pointedness. However, in order to distinguish this one-pointedness from narrow-minded obsessive-compulsivity, we need to understand the differences. The differences originate from where we are in our consciousness, and what our intention is.

In meditation, our intention is to awaken more fully to experiencing our true nature and the nature of the universe. There is the intention to discover the nature of our experience when we let the world and ourselves be. With some meditation methods, we are instructed to let our awareness rest in our center point below the navel. When our awareness is centered here, we can experience ourselves at one with all things.

In the day-to-day tunnel vision trances, our minds are being driven by fear. Our focus is usually on how to maintain control of our circumstances, and rather than opening to a greater awareness and acceptance of how things are. We are trying to keep our consciousness and our movements through the world within the narrow boundaries we have come to perceive as safe. In the habitual problematic states of mind, we pay attention to an isolated fearful part of us usually located in the head; whereas, with meditation, we are interested in becoming mindful of what is happening from the perspective of our essential wholeness.

Beginner meditators often make the mistake of taking an obsessive-compulsive tunnel vision approach to meditation. They are, for example, so determined to keep their attention on their breath and to keep out any thoughts, that they enter into a rigid state of vigilance, in which, instead of becoming more relaxed and comfortable with themselves, they merely continue the tendency to rigidly control themselves.

In meditation, as in therapeutic hypnosis, narrowing one's attention can be a useful starting point, in which we actively choose to tune out distraction. However, as the Buddha said, we must tune our minds like the string of the lute: not too tight and not too loose. Trying too hard to be mindful, rather than resting in mindfulness, can lead to holding too rigidly onto an object of concentration and/or trying to block out anything we consider undesirable. In the process, we end up resisting the heart of compassion taking us deeper into communion with essential wholeness. Let mindfulness be effortless.

To experience life deeply we need to be fully present and aware in the moment, rather than distracted by fears, disappointments, resentments, or whatever mental phenomena may pull our attention into the future or past. This is most obvious in our intimate relationships. The quality of the connection and the interaction between two people is directly proportional to how fully present the two people are with one another. Meditation is an exercise in becoming more intimate with our essential being. With meditation, as with relationships, sometimes we can simply let go of the distractions, and sometimes it is in the process of acknowledging the distractions that we find a way to connect more deeply.

You Are and You Aren't What You Think

We are not generally aware of the thoughts and emotions that determine what we do. This is made apparent over and over again in my psychotherapy practice when I ask people to describe what they were thinking or feeling just prior to behaving in a particular (problematic) way. Most commonly, I hear, "I don't know," or "Nothing". The dissociation from these processes is so profound that most of us don't even recognize how we come to feel the way we do, or why we do what we do. Since how we feel and what we do are largely determined by how and what we think, it is in our own best interests to be aware of the thoughts that drive us. Once aware, we can decide whether those thoughts are useful or if there is a better way of thinking.

Robert, a therapy client, complained of depression. However, after some discussion, it became apparent that his biggest problem was not being able to enjoy the company of others (social phobia). When I asked him what is going on inside when he realizes he is not as outgoing and friendly as he would like, he said, "I don't know, *something* just stops me from getting involved." That *something* turned out to be, with more mindful recollection, particular internal dialogues, images and sensations. These internal processes were part of what had become his habitual way of coping with social situations. Robert didn't like the pattern, but it had repeated itself so many times that he identified himself as a shy person.

Generally, people don't ask for help with problems they attribute to their identity; it's more often the resulting depression, relationship difficulties, or prompting from others, that leads some people to get help. In Robert's case, it was depression; he didn't feel his shyness was something that could change. Initially, he just wanted help coping better with his circumstances so he wouldn't feel so depressed.

To be unconscious of what we do habitually is a perfectly normal part of functioning in the world. When we have learned something, it becomes automatic. Once a behavior has become automatic, our consciousness is free to focus on other elements of our experiences, or move on to learning something else. Problems arise, however, when the unconscious automatic processes are limited solely to coping strategies to the exclusion of learning strategies. When we perceive there is nothing we can do to relieve our suffering and we need to learn to cope with it, we develop coping strategies. Robert had learned to cope by avoiding social situations. He told himself he didn't need people, he was okay keeping to himself and if he were meant to meet someone, it would happen. It was, as it seemed, not meant to happen.

To cope is to live with a certain amount of suffering, rather than to either learn how to change our external circumstances, or change our perception of the situation that causes us suffering. Coping involves trying to avoid or minimize that which troubles us. However, the way we do this tends to perpetuate the problem. Robert's habit of isolating himself, for example, kept him from learning how to relate better to people.

The tendency is for us to assume that the patterns of what we think, feel and do are who we are, and who we are is fixed and unchanging. However, in reality, whatever we can observe and have choices about is not us. Mindfulness enables us to realize that we have thoughts, feelings, impulses and behaviors, rather than them having us. Rather than unconsciously thinking we are our habits, we rest as the consciousness that can choose how we think, perceive and act.

Intention

To be mindful is to be conscious of the intention or the purpose of our actions. Sogyal Rinpoche talks of three powerful and enlightening principles that can be applied to any action, but especially to meditation. The **Three Noble Principles** are:

- Good in the Beginning — establishing motivation
- Good in the Middle — non-grasping attitude that anchors the action
- Good in the End — dedication of merit that seals the action

The depth and breadth of the motivation (intention) will determine the depth and breadth of the practice of meditation, or anything we do for that matter. In *Diamond Way Buddhism*[54] there are four basic thoughts that define a meditator's intentions:

- These methods of meditation are precious and by practicing them we benefit many beings, including ourselves, by finding freedom from the causes of suffering and opening to unconditional happiness.
- The relative world is impermanent; only our true nature is lasting, and we can't know for sure how long we will have the opportunity to fully realize this.
- We are always creating our world through what we believe and how we act, therefore let us choose wisely.
- Enlightenment is timeless, highest bliss and we can only help others to the degree we realize this.

Is there any reason why these shouldn't be the intentions behind all we do? Having this intention is the opposite of having the intention of simply being able to cope with suffering and survive another day. To be free to be ourselves is to be happy and free of suffering; anything less is a compromise and denial of our true nature. By doing what we do for all sentient beings, we are identifying with our wholeness, which is at one with all of creation. A commitment of being mindful of the wellbeing of all beings naturally points us towards compassion.

TWO — *Compassion*

When we let ourselves just be, we rest as the awareness of the eternal now. When we realize ourselves as awareness, there is nothing outside of us. This includes other people, animals, trees, stars, mountains, everything. As Albert Einstein said so clearly;

> A human being is part of a whole, called by us the "Universe", a part limited in time and space. He experiences himself, his thoughts and feelings, as something separated from the rest — a kind of optical delusion of his consciousness. This delusion is a kind of prison for us, restricting us to our personal desires and to affection for a few persons nearest us. Our task must be to free ourselves from this prison by widening our circles of compassion to embrace all living creatures and the whole of nature in its beauty.[55]

Compassion, in its deepest sense, is the experience of no separation between our awareness and whatever is arising in awareness, inside and out. Compassion allows us to deeply listen, with warmth and a generous heart, to whatever arises. Listening and attending with compassion to a fellow human being tends to encourage that person to open up more deeply to the source of their suffering and reveal more to us. The same can happen in the initial stages of meditation.

Due to the oppressive nature of our coping mechanisms, we aren't aware of the extent of our suffering, or the lack of the happiness and freedom. Only to the extent that we are aware of our suffering will we be able to liberate ourselves from the habits of mind and body that imprison us. Compassion guides us to love and work with what we perceive as painful, rather than struggling against it. Compassion teaches us to make friends with what or whom we perceive as our enemies, rather than rejecting, or even merely tolerating them.

Saying, "I can't stand you, but I'll try to put up with you the best I can," imposes a guilt trip on the person in question. Merely coping with what we perceive as causing us suffering perpetuates the perception of separateness from the rest of the universe. Coping is essentially a form of blaming someone or something for making us suffer, and being unwilling to take responsibility for our own wellbeing; it encourages us to think some aspects of creation are good (deserving of love) and some bad (undeserving of love).

Mindfulness and compassion lead us to greater awareness of the nature of our suffering. We can become aware of aches and tensions on the body, and disturbing, anxious thoughts related to painful events of the past or feared events of the future, which distract us from experiencing the fullness of the present moment. Meditation techniques serve as a vehicle to carry us through these difficulties on the path to experiencing our wholeness. Through the practice of meditation we can redirect the energy invested in automatic coping mechanisms into self-supporting processes of learning, evolution and resting in our essential wholeness.

We use our conscious intention to focus and then soften focus of mindfulness enough to embrace our arising experience with compassion and love. In doing so, we discover that disturbing thoughts and emotions, like disturbing people or occurrences in our lives, are not inherently bad. Rather, when they are acting in problematic ways, they are merely acting out their own sense of fear or lovelessness.

Fear or a sense of lovelessness arises when we are out of touch with our wholeness. The book *A Course in Miracles* describes just two basic human communications: expressions of love or calls for love (requests for help). When we react to others or to our own internal experiences out of fear, either by trying to fight them off or run from them, we are perpetuating the myth that the world (other people, ourselves or our thoughts) is inherently bad. Whatever is labeled bad is therefore not to be accepted and embraced with love, but rather is denied, rejected, ignored or disowned. The basic structure of coping mechanisms (ego defenses) is to maintain the limited perception of ourselves, which we do at the cost of the ecology of our essential wholeness.

Trying too hard to be compassionate, rather than resting in compassion, can lead to ruminating about how to help others or ourselves by improving something outward. Denying our innate strength can mean an indulgence in our emotions and lead us to self-pity. Let compassion be effortless.

By simply resting in loving compassion and embracing whatever disturbances arise, the fears of judgment or rejection are calmed, and we may have the realization that there isn't anything to fear. Just as a parent's loving arms and calm presence are able to help their frightened child to realize their nightmare was only a dream and there is nothing to be frightened of, sitting compassionately with someone (including ourselves) sends the implicit reminder that this too will pass, and in the meantime, we know that we are loved and appreciated no matter what happens.

THREE — *Strength*

We need skillful means, or techniques, that bring forth underdeveloped capabilities. By having a structured process, we can move through the obstacles that block us from experiencing calm. We must honor the mind's natural way of bringing itself home. The Enneagram offers a map of that natural process. Just as an engineer will use scientific theories (maps of the physical universe) to build a bridge, a meditation practitioner can use maps of consciousness to create techniques for bringing the mind home to rest in its true nature. However, as Sogyal Rinpoche says, "The vast majority of us find it difficult to arrive at that state straight away. We simply do not know how to awaken it, and our minds are so wild and so distracted that we need a skillful means, a method to evoke it."[56]

Images that Inspire

Even more important than any method for meditating is the attitude we embody as we sit. Our attitude is not simply something in the mind; it is something that informs our body and senses.

At THREE we can be inspired and empowered by identifying with powerful images. Contrary to the ego's images of status and materialistic success, we can identify with the vast equanimous image of a mountain. Unperturbed by the changes of weather, seasons and centuries passing, a mountain sits in the vastness of sky that surrounds it. We connect with qualities we associate with being mountain-like; our view stretches out in all directions. We sit solidly on the earth, with our head reaching towards heaven. Although we exist in time, the events that transpire, such as storms, droughts, landslides, and so on, leave us relatively unmoved.

The technique while meditating is to not put too much effort into staying with the image of the mountain, but rather using it to establish a sense of equanimity and stability, and then relaxing and opening to the qualities the mountain invokes. Rather than *trying* to be mindful, compassionate and spacious, we need to relax into our essential capability to be mountain-like and weather the storms of distractions or obstacles to experiencing abiding calm. The mountain, a symbol of strength, endurance and equanimity, represents the qualities of THREE and NINE.

For those practicing Buddhism for centuries in Tibet, a land locked country situated amongst the highest mountains of the world; there are readily available natural metaphors for the meditative state. However, features of other landscapes can also be used to inspire our meditation.

While on retreat, I found the expansive view of a lake to be very useful for developing a sense of spacious serenity. Half-way between my home and office is a beautiful headland overlooking the Pacific Ocean. I find identifying with the depth and breadth of the ocean with its ever-changing faces helps me to open more deeply to the ever-changing impermanent nature of my human condition. Opening even wider, I become aware of the coastline, where the water meets the land, and the horizon, where the sky meets the sea. Though my feet are on the land, my consciousness is open and spacious like the sky; I open to the depths of my being, like the depths of the sea. Being aware of the curvature of the earth, I can, at times, have a sense of identifying with the entire earth in a sort of global consciousness. As the earth, I am a heavenly body teaming with life, while traveling through the infinite spaciousness of the universe.

Posture

The word 'backbone' is often used to refer to people who display or have inner strength. A powerful posture of meditation is conveyed as gold coins stacked one upon the other. When coins are balanced properly, they can sit indefinitely.

If we are exhibiting or experiencing essential strength, our shoulders can easily be held in a strong poise, not compromised by self-deprecation (tension rounding the shoulders inward in fear or guilt) or self-inflation (tension holding the shoulders back in defiance or pride). Tension, the result of pushing and pulling ourselves out of shape, shows us how we are in conflict with our natural way of being.

With rounded shoulders, we have lost touch with the strength needed to live with an open heart; we perceive ourselves as weak and not capable of being ourselves in the world. Without this connection to our strength, we collapse in on ourselves. With our shoulders pulled back, we have become overly identified with our need to be strong. We have identified with an image of appearing strong, but which needs a constant effort of holding ourselves upright and pushing ourselves forward into the world.

Be ready for anything

An Aikido precept, 'Expect nothing, but be ready for anything,' is particularly useful to consider right now. When our shoulders and upper torso are poised in effortless strength, we are not expecting good or bad. We're not on the attack or the defense. We are simply present with whatever arises and, with an open heart, can respond with compassion, generosity, appreciation and wisdom. A metaphor of our essential wholeness commonly used in Buddhism is that of being like the ocean, while our ego mind is like a wave. We can use this image to evoke the strength of being as vast, deep and all encompassing as the ocean.

Compassion helps us to establish the mountain-like posture. The meditative posture or poise is not something we can impose on ourselves. It evolves through a compassionate sensing of one's body, which enables us to stack the coins of our spine, one by one, on top of one another with mindfulness and care, rather than tension and holding. Mindfulness naturally leads to compassion, which in turn leads us into strength, and so on.

Vajrayana Buddhism uses a plethora of symbolic Buddha images that represent different aspects of essential wholeness. By invoking these images, we tap into the inherent strengths and capabilities of our true nature. Since we generally see these qualities outside of ourselves, the meditations often brgin with a sense of receiving a blessing of some sort from the Buddha images, yet sometimes we imagine ourselves as that Buddha form.

Playfully imitating a Buddha is to make-believe you are a Buddha. Just as you can make-believe you are a mountain, you can concentrate on an image of a Buddha in your mind's eye, then merge with that image. This process of identifying with an image of success comes quite naturally to people with a type THREE personality. It is a way of accessing collective unconscious capabilities associated with the desired outcome.

The image of Buddha archetypally embodies certain qualities and understandings that have been associated with the historical Buddha and other enlightened men and women. These images represent the essential qualities these beings have realized. Associating with these images builds unconscious associations with those Buddha-like qualities. As children we learn how to behave the adult world by playing make-believe 'mommies and daddies'. Playing make-believe that we are a Buddha, helps us realize the essential wholeness of our buddha nature. Similarly, if we were to meditate upon an image of Jesus, we can invoke the qualities of Christ consciousness. Naturally, we can use the image of anyone who inspires us as a spiritual role model.

Embracing essential strength is not a matter of trying to be strong. Indeed, trying can lead to a rigid numbness and a false sense of realization, and would involve denying our unwanted, unhealed or unforgiven parts. These aspects then remain in the shadows of our subconscious mind and are projected on others. A version of ego develops that leads us to see ourselves as superior to others. Let strength be effortless.

When truly awakened, we know that all beings are Buddhas, whether they realize it or not. Seeing everyone in this way from our essential strength is to see with forgiving eyes.

FOUR — Forgiveness

You leave all your senses — hearing, seeing, feeling — just open, naturally, as they are, without grasping after their perceptions.[57]
Sogyal Rinpoche

To be *forgiving* is to be willing to let things be as they are. To perceive without prejudice based on past experiences. That which isn't judged is innocent. To see things as they are is to view an innocent universe through innocent eyes. Forgiveness and innocence go hand in hand. By not using concepts or judgments based on past perceptions to interpret our experiences in the present moment, we are able to experience each arising moment as unique.

Beginner's Mind

Forgiveness allows us to experience what is referred to in Zen as 'beginner's mind': a mind that is free of judgment about what things mean. Each arising moment is unique and therefore should not be categorized and judged according to concepts we have formed through past events. As soon as we say to ourselves, "This is just like 'so and so" (something I have experienced in the past), or, "This means something and so forth" (an interpretation that through our self talk creates an imaginary story), we limit our experience of the uniqueness of that moment.

A Course in Miracles reminds us, "In my defenselessness, my safety lies". If we grasp at or try to avoid what is happening in the present moment, we stop being open to the uniqueness of the ever-changing present.

Grasping and avoidance are based on our desires or fears — prejudice of what is good or bad. We have separated ourselves from experience and are interpreting life with prejudice through the stories we tell ourselves. It is only our ego that can be afraid. Essential wholeness cannot be hurt or destroyed. Once we are conceptualizing about something, we no longer experience it innocently. What is not innocent is, by implication, guilty.

A very common response to something undesirable happening is, "What have I done to deserve this?" It assumes guilt and that this sort of thing happens because we are bad and deserve it. When we perceive something as bad, wrong or dangerous, we close off our appreciation of that awareness as essential part of the wholeness of all creation.

Forgiveness

Forgiveness is remembering the innocence of all creation in each unfolding moment. All forgiveness is essentially self-forgiveness. No one, including ourselves, deserves to suffer; painful things are merely part of life. Forgiveness allows whatever arises in our senses to come and go without attaching a story to it and then getting lost in the story. Suffering is created and maintained when we get lost in the stories, especially those of guilt and blame.

To forgive is to let go of our attachments (grasping) to how we think anything or anyone is — even God. We become attached to the notion that if we experience life in a particular way, according to a particular storyline, then we will be happy. If ourselves or others do things in a particular way then we are lovable, otherwise we're not. Attachments are the conditions we place on love and happiness. The more we hold on to our attachments, the more we suffer. Forgiveness leads us to enlightenment, as we awaken from the dream of separation from our essential infinite and eternal wholeness, which is our natural inheritance. Jesus prayed on the cross, "Father, forgive them, for they know not what they do" (Luke 23: 34). To forgive is to realize that we are all doing the best we can, given what we know and where we are coming from.

Hold Opinions Lightly

The Third Zen Patriarch, says, "Do not seek the truth. Only cease to cherish opinions." Our opinions (how we think things should be) are forgiving up. It is not that we shouldn't have opinions or life stories, only that we could cease to cherish them as reality. We all formulate opinions and live out different stories; however, when they cause us to suffer, we must be willing to relinquish those opinions and stories. We remember that we are consciousness aware of the opinions that maintain a story, rather than a person who is captured and enslaved by opinions and their stories. We can be sure that whatever opinions we form will eventually be disproved in the course of living. When we hold onto our opinions in the face of evidence to the contrary, we suffer. To hold religiously onto our opinions is to believe that the nature of life, the universe and God can be accurately defined within the limited awareness of our opinionated mind.

Doing this would be like taking a photograph of a section of a river at on point in time and then saying that photo is the way all rivers are and will always be. All we ever get in life are snapshots or video-clips from our own limited perspective within the minuscule timeframe that is our life. Our opinions, and the stories we tell ourselves serve as maps. However, maps are not the territories they describe.

Loving and Being Loved

For many people feeling loved has felt conditional. Children grow up feeling that they must behave in a particular way in order to be loved. The parents of these children convey these ideas to their children directly or indirectly based on how they were raised. Parenting, like life, is an ongoing process of discovery; however, many parents think in order to be a 'good' parent they must act like they know what they are doing with their children. If a child is behaving in a way the parents don't know how to handle, instead of embracing their own ignorance and innocence, they rely on acting in the ways they have learned. They end up doing much the same to their children as has been done to them.

If a parent acts as if they know what they are doing and their opinions are right, and yet the child isn't happy, that child assumes, 'There must be something wrong with me.' To be forgiving is to realize we know not what to do. With forgiveness, we innocently embrace each situation as unique by realizing our opinions are just our opinions and not something to be cherished. In so doing, we are free to choose a path of love and wholeness in place of one that perpetuates guilt, fear, isolation and suffering.

Trying too hard to be forgiving can leave us searching for forgiveness, rather than resting as forgiveness. We can end up trying to convince ourselves why we should be more forgiving. Instead of giving up all hope of a better past, we may seek justifications for our actions or rationalize others' behavior by continuing to blame ourselves. Meditation can become a sort of penance, a way to earn forgiveness. Let forgiveness be effortless.

In meditation, forgiveness allows us to witness all that arises in our awareness like innocent child, even though many of those aspects of our mind would appear to have lost their way. By being willing to give up our stories and judgments, our minds become more spacious.

FIVE — Space

It is common in meditation practice for thoughts and emotions to consume our attention. By trying to avoid or push away the thought, they tend to only consume our attention more. When we cease to struggle with or indulge them they tend to dissolve back into the spaciousness of mind.

Space is empty of meaning or concepts, yet is full of infinite potential. Out of space, all objects of our perception arise then play around, before dissolving back into it. It is our concepts that organize the essential spacious wholeness of the universe into form or matter. As Einstein said, 'There is no place in this new kind of physics both for the field and matter, for the field is the only reality."

When lost in our concepts, we are not directly experiencing the nature of things. We have separated ourselves from experience and are thinking about it to understand what is happening so we can better learn how to survive. Thinking about life is essentially a defense mechanism against the conditions that could cause us pain and ultimately death.

Scientific understanding of the world has enabled technologies to be created that have generally enabled us to live longer and safer lives. There is nothing wrong with this; however, while we are engaged in this process we are identified with matter, rather than the field (space). We are identified with relative truth about various particulars, rather than the wholeness of our being. Scientific thinking has tended to see nature and the universe as something separate from us. We have become preoccupied doing things for survival of the world, rather than experiencing being with the wholeness of creation. Many of us, even with all the affluence we have, spend a vast majority of our time struggling, or recovering from the struggle to survive. We allow little space in our lives to just be.

A spacious mind is an open mind, in which new ideas and understandings can be formed. Space allows us to see more clearly the patterns of evolution over time. As astronomers gaze into the vastness of space, they are able to see events that happened seconds ago in our own solar system, right back to events that may have occurred shortly after the Big Bang in distant parts of the universe. Taking the space to stand outside time enables us to better understand the patterns of the universe, the world we live in, as well as our individual lives. By taking space from the activity of our lives, we can reflect upon the outcomes of the decisions we have made, as well as why we made them.

Within essential space we can transcend time and experience the eternal now.

In meditation, we take *space* from doing what we need to do to survive, or escaping into entertainment, and open ourselves to the experience of being alive. By embracing our experience of space, we begin to realize we are the unified field within which the activities of our minds give rise to the perception of matter. And what we think matters. We are wholeness and therefore there is nothing we need to do; we can just be. We also begin to realize that the sense of struggling with or against life is our doing.

Emptiness

Emptiness is not a vacuum; it is the unified field — unconditioned, undefined. My experience of this is best described as infinite loving light beyond time and space, at one with the universe. Emptiness is another name for essential space. To perceive the empty spaciousness of the objects of our attention, we must allow ourselves space.

In his poem On Trust in the Mind, Seng-ts'an, the third Zen Patriarch, describes the space-like nature of mind.

> The Way is perfect like vast space, where there's no lack and no excess.
> Our choice to choose and to reject prevents our seeing this simple truth.
> Both striving for the outer world as well as for the inner void condemn us to entangled lives.
> Just calmly see that all is One, and by themselves false views will go.[58]

In meditation, we can become aware of the emptiness or the space into which our perceptions emerge. If thoughts are like clouds, space is the sky in which the clouds form and where they dissipate. As we identify more with the sky nature of our mind, we are better able to observe thoughts without getting cloudy and being carried off by them. We only experience our thoughts or other objects of our attention as separate entities because we experience ourselves as solid discrete objects.

Trying too hard to get space from thoughts and feelings can lead to a detachment or dissociation from our experience; it can make everything seem like nothing. We can get stuck in witnessing reality, rather than surrendering to the nothingness that accepts everything as it is. Let spaciousness be effortless.

As we open to spaciousness, we are able to perceive the emptiness of the objects of our attention and our objective sense of 'self' and 'other' fades back into the essential wholeness of being. It is only in our subconscious habit of perceiving ourselves as separate that we feel we are lacking in any way. As we embrace our spaciousness, there can be no lack because we are at one with all things and what is there not to accept?

SIX — Acceptance

Third Zen Patriarch continues:

Using mind to stir up more mind —
What grosser error than this?
Delusion breed concepts as "tranquil" or "disordered";
Enlightenment tells you there is no good or bad.[59]

Accepting reality as it is, without judgment, without trying to make it better, more tranquil, more blissful, less painful, means we are not projecting our concepts onto to reality. 'Samsara' is the cycle of existences imprisoned by a mind conditioned by hatred, craving and delusion; it is the mind turned outward but lost in its own projections. Enlightenment is the mind turned inward, resting in essential wholeness.

When we stop trying to make reality fit into how we think it should be, we just let it be, and we let ourselves be. In meditation, if we think of our mind being like a pond, and our judgments and other thoughts like silt, if we stop stirring things up with our efforts to make it right and just let the pond be as it is, the water will become still and the silt will settle to the bottom. As the silt settles, the water becomes calm, and the clear spaciousness of the water in which particles can arise and settle become more apparent. This tranquil clarity (spacious emptiness) is the nature of our being, which we experience when we let ourselves be. As long as we use our minds to manipulate experience, our awareness will continue to be muddled by our projections (the muck we stir up), rather than clear to perceive unpolluted awareness of true nature.

Approval or Acceptance

Trying too hard to be accepting can be confusing; often we equate acceptance with agreement. The illusions of the mind seem valid — equally valid as reality — and we lose our ability to be discerning. We end up being loyal to illusion, rather than opening to the joy that comes with the new eyes of a beginner's mind. With acceptance, there is nothing to get right, to prove or disprove. To accept everything is to let everything be. To accept ourselves is to let ourselves be. When we are simply being, the illusionary dreams that perpetuate our suffering are put to rest as we experience our true nature. Let acceptance be effortless.

Acceptance and approval are contradictory. Seeking approval is a process of trying to prove we are good (innocent, deserving, lovable, and so on). We seek approval by obeying rules: those we believe determine what is right or wrong. In order to let ourselves be (loved, we must be good and not bad. If we need to prove we are good enough for God's love or accumulate enough merit to earn enlightenment, we are obviously not experiencing unity with the wholeness of Being. We seek approval by trying to act or think in a ways that will be rewarded with what we think we are missing.

The more effort we put into trying to prove our goodness, the more we are invested in the idea that we are not complete as we are. As a child, I was led to believe that if I was a good boy and obeyed the Ten Commandments, and the rules of my parents, I would go to heaven when I died. If I didn't, I would burn in Hell for eternity. I was born a sinner (original sin) and needed to prove my worthiness of heaven. God was a judge who would either reward or punish me based on my ability to follow the rules, whereas unconditional acceptance requires no proof. When accepting our essential wholeness, what we consider right or wrong are relatively minor aspects within the field of our awareness. As we open wider and deeper to the essential wholeness of being, the less separation we experience from the rest of the universe.

Buddhism describes samadhi is a nondualistic state of consciousness in which the consciousness of the experiencing 'subject' becomes one with the experienced 'object'.[60] As the subject, we become one with the object, the universe. We are not separate from the whole, needing to prove we should be included in the wholeness. We experience ourselves as whole and an integral part of the wholeness of creation. We are wholeness. We are holiness.

The more separate we feel from everything, the more desperate our need is to regain our sense of wholeness or belonging. Desperate people tend to do desperate things. This is when we do things to get what we need to feel whole. Endless consumption, or even stealing (both forms of greed), could be thought of as attempts to get what we think we need to be whole. Alternatively, we may behave in certain ways try to win the approval of whoever we think has the power to give us what we need to feel whole. Following the rules of a dictator would allow us to gain a sense of belonging to a larger group. However, being part of that group is predicated on the belief that this group is the one true group and other groups founded on other beliefs are false and therefore bad. Violence against the 'other' is a sanctioned way of maintaining a sense of belonging. Unapproved parts of society need to be tightly controlled, or preferably eliminated.

When we rest in our essential wholeness as part of creation, we don't really need the Ten Commandments to tell us what is right and wrong. There is no difference between subject and object, between you and me, us and them. I am you and you are me. We are you and you are us. What I do to you, I am doing to myself. Within the experience of wholeness, there is nothing to get and nothing to prove. There is acceptance of the universe and myself (one and the same) as we are, and the universe accepts me as I am.

Feeling at one with all of creation is a conscious, compassionate, empowered, forgiving, spacious, accepting, joyful, loving, peaceful experience. Experiencing ourselves in this way leads us to think and act in ways that embody these essential qualities. The self-righteous person makes people feel judged, whereas the truly righteous person makes people feel accepted.

This Is as Good as It Gets

You are never going to get it all together; neither will the world. This is as good as it gets, and it's getting better and worse all the time. *Krishnamurti*

Long ago there lived a man named Jacob who was considered very fortunate by those who knew him because he owned a fine mare. The horse made tending his fields and transporting his goods to the market much easier. One day, however, the horse wandered off and was nowhere to be found. The people of the village lamented Jacob's plight, "What a horrible curse to lose your horse."

Jacob responded to their concern by saying, "Maybe it is and maybe it isn't."

A week later the mare returned and in its company was a fine young wild stallion. The people rejoiced, "Oh Jacob, what a wonderful blessing; now you have two horses and you can breed them."

Jacob responded to their jubilation by again saying, "Maybe it is and maybe it isn't."

When Jacob's eighteen-year-old son was breaking in the wild horse, he was thrown off and severely broke his leg, which meant he would be off his feet for some time and unable to help around the farm. Again, the people of the village lamented his plight saying, "Oh Jacob what a horrible curse for you and your son."

Again Jacob responded by simply saying, "Maybe it is and maybe it isn't."

A week later word was sent out from the king that war had been declared and that all young men were required to join the army. The people of the village declared, "Oh Jacob, what a blessing it was that your son's leg was broken. Now he doesn't have to go off and fight in that awful war."

Jacob responded, "Maybe it is and maybe it isn't..."

With acceptance, we let things be as they are. We rest in the essential wholeness of life, within which all relative experiences come and go. We do not think of ourselves as people who deserve 'good' or 'bad' things to happen. We are human beings who experience a whole spectrum of events within the wholeness of life. Our mind's true nature, like the water in a pond, even when muddied with fear, polluted with judgments or stirred up with anger, remains unchanged and will return to a state of clarity when not manipulated.

We can identify with the circumstances of our lives and interpret whatever happens in terms of good and bad, just like the villagers, or, like Jacob, simply allow ourselves accept life as it unfolds. As acceptance deepens, we can really begin enjoying life on its own terms.

SEVEN — Joy

> But because you have let yourself be inspired by a joyful trust
> in your own true Buddha nature, you can accept your negative
> aspects more easily and deal with them more kindly and with
> more humor.[61] *Sogyal Rinpoche*

Recognizing and accepting our relative condition — the positive and
the negative, pleasure and pain, useful and useless, essential and non-
essential — we flow into and are supported by joyful trust and related
humor, the essential quality of joy.

To take joy in someone's company is an expression of love. If being
with someone is merely a duty or a chore, we may also experience guilt
and resentment in their presence, as well as not wanting to be where we
are. What allows us to fully *be here now* is to enjoy now. Meditation is a
way to take time to enjoy the now, even with the confusion, disturbing
thoughts and emotions that arise.

Trying Too Hard Means Missing Unity

If we can become aware of it, there is an unconditioned bliss of reality
at its most basic level. Trying too hard to be joyful can leave us seeking
spiritual highs that come and go, rather than simply experiencing. This
can lead to a sort of spiritual bypass of what is perceived as negative or
unpleasant. From this dualistic perspective we miss out on experiencing
unity and oneness. Let joy be unconditional and effortless.

Being joyful is the opposite of being serious. There are things in life
that need to be taken seriously; and there are things that need to be laughed
off. By not taking the habits of mind seriously, we don't give them power
to effect us. It's only when we cling to pleasant thoughts or try to fight off
unpleasant thoughts that we give them power to control us.

The more we invest in our thoughts, the less we are free to just be.
Thoughts we invest energy into are the ideas (rules) that 'rule' our lives.
Rules define boundaries, make distinctions and create separation. Anything
that is made up by our minds is imaginary and what is imaginary should
be held lightly and enjoyed, not taken too seriously. Joy helps us see life

more like a game, albeit with rules. With games, we make up rules to create imaginary circumstances so that we can have fun playing within that structure.

Humor is a natural consequence of being joyful, and enables us to dance around and beyond the limitations of our prejudices and preoccupations.

When we see ads on television for things we know we don't need, we laugh at how ridiculous it is that someone is trying to sell us rubbish. The same is true with our minds. Joy enables us to observe with humor the workings of our minds and not to buy into our projections or take our precious opinions so seriously.

Curiosity and Boredom

Meditation is not easy or a natural fit for all people. For some who have tried it but not gotten very far with it, meditating can seem boring. Experiencing boredom is an indication that we have lost curiosity. Boredom is a pessimistic attitude; there is nothing else in a given experience to discover. As meditation deepens, we penetrate the nature of consciousness more deeply, and become more aware of the impermanent nature of everything.

Those who have meditated for some time know that each time we sit with ourselves, our ongoing experience of the human condition is different. Every moment as we sit, there are subtle movements in mind and body. The more we open to new levels of awareness, the more previously unnoticed dimensions of experience become available. The process of opening to wholeness is only boring when we have a limited idea of how that awakening is supposed to happen.

As we follow our curiosity into an ever expanding and deepening experience of our infinite wholeness, boredom is impossible. We can even be curious about how boredom has a place within the wholeness of our experience. Boredom is the sense that we could be missing out on something more enjoyable. However, when experiencing essential wholeness, there is no sense of missing out. The experience of boredom is hence a cue to become more curious about how we are limiting our perception.

According to Thomas Aquinas, contemplation is the "simple enjoyment of the truth." Any experience of our self as unwholesome is mistaken. The truth of our wholeness is that it is joyful. Our true nature is found, as the 16th Karmapa reminds us, when "disturbing feelings and stiff ideas dissolve, (and) our mind becomes spontaneous joy. It is space and bliss inseparable."[62]

Joy reminds us of the impermanence of life; we may be experiencing the last day we have to live in this human body. This is the first, last and only moment we can experience what is happening. Joy allows us to experience it to the fullest. Small children and babies help us to open to joy. While standing in line at the bank, a one-year-old boy in a stroller caught my eye. I could have looked away, but the joyful openness of his gaze held me. Smiles came to both of our faces. The intimacy was instantly profound. I began a game of peek-a-boo. Our eye contact felt like a mutual recognition of our belonging to the family of humanity. The peek-a-boo was not necessary, but fun. Our connection was essence to essence. It was wordless and non-conceptual. His eyes drew me into a vast spacious emptiness that was totally accepting and joyous. I expected nothing of him and he seemed to have no expectations of me; the issue of expectations was not relevant. We were simply being together. Opening to a child in this way is the same process as opening to our true 'child of God' nature.

As we sit in meditation we have the opportunity of gazing into to the spacious acceptance of our own true nature, in which we are filled with joy. Following our joyful bliss is divine will.

EIGHT — *Will*

To be steadfast is to be willful. Steadfastness is said to be one of the keys to a rewarding meditation practice. We can think of steadfastness as a combination of patience and determination. Divine will is eternal and timeless. In meditation we are determined to wake up now, yet give ourselves eternity to fully realize our true nature. By placing timeframes on enlightenment, we keep our consciousness in the relative world and separate from the infinite nature of our essential wholeness. We also realize that awakening awakens us; divinity has its own curriculum that we surrender to. Infinite patience calls upon infinite love. When we forget that it is surrender to divine will that awakens us to the truth, we lose our determination to reach enlightenment, and instead impose ideas of how enlightenment should happen on ourselves. It is by surrendering that we open to the peace of essential wholeness.

> Rather than "watching" the breath, let yourself gradually identify with it, as if you were becoming it. Slowly the breath, the breather, and the breathing become one; duality and separation dissolve.[63]

Identifying with the breath, in which duality and separation disappear, is to become at one with experience. We are no longer observing the in and the out, the expansion and contraction, the Yin and the Yang, the ever changing experience of life; we are the in and the out, the contraction and expansion, the Yin and Yang. We are not observing the way of things, the Tao; we are the way of things, we are the Tao. We are no longer separate from the Will of God; we are the Will of God.

In the New Testament, Matthew says, "Our Father who art in heaven hallowed be thy name. Thy kingdom come, thy will be done. On earth as it is in heaven" (the Lord's Prayer — 6:9-13). Embracing our essential Will dissolves the duality of heaven and earth. When we are at one with our breath, mind and body are one; the spirit (heaven) is united with the body (earth). To fully experience ourselves at one with any part of creation is to experience atonement (at-one-ment with all of creation). We identify with our essential nature as a child of God or spirit in human form. The Buddhist term for Essential Will or the Will of God is 'dharma', the nature of reality.

We suffer when we think we need to make ourselves into someone other than who we really are. If I am a river, it is my nature to flow down hill. I will suffer if I think I should flow uphill, or if I try to make other rivers flow uphill. To know dharma, is to surrender to what is and how life is unfolding in the moment. In the deepest meditation we let go of the meditator who has ideas of how meditation should go. We rest as the sea of awareness and allow it to reveal to us what it will. In life, we let go of the personal will that thinks it knows how life should go and surrender to the way life is unfolding through us, moment to moment. Surrendering to divine will is unconditional cooperation with the truth of this moment. It is giving up all resistance to what is emerging now. Let will be effortless.

At EIGHT our experience tends to congeal into an identity. By identifying with the ever-changing experience of our breath, instead of congealing into a static notion of ourselves, we open to the impermanent empty nature of experience. We identify with the vast joyful spaciousness similar the consciousness naturally experienced by small children. We remember we are not our petty concerns or the day-to-day roles we may play. We are children of God, we are Godliness, and our Joyful Spaciousness is infinite.

The native Mexican shaman Don Juan spoke to Carlos Castaneda about his two very different teachers:

> They were empty. The nagual Elias was a collection of astounding, haunting stories of regions unknown. The nagual Julian was a collection of stories that would have anyone in stitches, sprawled on the ground laughing. Whenever I tried to pin down the man in them, the real man, the way I could with my father, the man in everybody I knew, I found nothing. Instead of a real person, there was a collection of stories about persons unknown. Each of the two men had his own flair, but the end result was just the same: emptiness, an emptiness that reflected not the world, but infinity.
>
> ...Infinity is all that surrounds us. The sorcerers of my lineage call it *infinity*, the spirit, the *dark sea of awareness*, and say that it is exists out there and rules our lives.[64]

What we are is the infinite spacious sea of awareness. To identify with anything less is to deny our true nature. Essential wholeness has no beginning and no end. When we are everything and everything is us, nothing can be done to us, and nothing can be taken from us. When we are out of touch with infinity, we experience ourselves as a separate entity, not whole, and vulnerable to being hurt. Essential wholeness is always calling us back. All suffering or experiences of lack are evidence that we have mis-identified ourselves as something less than essential wholeness. When we surrender to divine will we end our argument with reality as it is emerging. Our little separate sense of self dissolves into the essential wholeness of the eternal now and we are at peace with existence.

NINE — Peace

> So take care not to impose anything on the mind, or to tax it. Don't be overly solemn or feel that you are taking part in some special ritual; let go even of the idea that you are meditating. Let your body remain as it is, and your breath as you find it.[65]

At NINE we let ourselves and all things be; there is nothing to do, nowhere to go. This is truly being at peace. Once we are in the meditative state we are to do nothing. We are not to feel special in anyway. We are at peace with our experience; therefore, there is nothing to do. To make the experience special in some way would be to say that this moment is better than others, evoking conflict or judgment of other experiences.

> Peace is the greatest love. *Dalai Lama*

At NINE we exist in harmony with creation, and there is no need to change anything. We merge and just let whatever is happening happen. This level of meditation is sometimes referred to as 'no meditation'. Having identified with the coming and going of our breath and everything else that comes and goes, the boundaries between the observed and the observer dissolve, and we merge with existence. As the Third Zen Patriarch says,

> Absolute reality is beyond time and space,
> Empty and infinite existing as one,
> opening before your eyes,
> A vast presence.[66]

> The largest is the same as the smallest;
> No boundaries are visible.
> Existence is precisely emptiness;
> Emptiness is precisely existence.[67]

We experience ourselves as the nothingness in which the many things come and go. Simultaneously, we are all the many things that are inherently no-things. Being and non-being cease to exist as separate phenomena, as there is nothing that is and nothing that is not. Everything is and everything isn't at the same time, in no time at all. This sounds like double talk; however, when we truly rest in the nondualistic experience of reality, we are moving out of the realm of conventional logic and experiences, beyond which language is very inadequate.

Sufi poet Rumi says,

Out beyond ideas of wrongdoing and rightdoing,
there is a field. I'll meet you there.
When the soul lies down in that grass,
the world is too full to talk about.
Ideas, language, even the phrase *each other*
Doesn't make any sense.[68]

Opening to our true nature, we experience a peace that is beyond understanding. We are so at peace, we are no longer even meditating. We are simply resting in the field of essential wholeness, beyond all concepts.

However, trying too hard to be peaceful can lead us into a dull complacency in which we ignore anything that might take us out of our comfort zone. Instead of being mindful, we keep ourselves mindlessly ignorant. Instead of awakening to the universal peace of unity, we stay asleep in the limited perspectives of our conditioned mind. Instead, let peace be effortless. The antidote to the dreamy dullness of lazy self-forgetting is returning to mindfulness. The circle from NINE to ONE turns once more.

There is not just one process that is enlightenment or awakening, but rather continual re-awakenings or new awakenings. The universe, through us as human beings, is continually becoming more conscious of itself. As humans living in duality, we move around the cycle of change, invoking and flowing through our essential qualities. As we open to our true nature and duality dissolves into infinite wholeness, the essential qualities blend together within the clear light of our Being, just as the colors of the rainbow come together as clear white light.

In meditation we can, through skillful means, invoke the nine essential qualities of Being, and thus come to rest more fully in the essential wholeness of Existence, from which all perceptions of separateness emerge and recede.

CHAPTER SEVEN

The Systemic Change Cycle

They must often change who would be constant in happiness or wisdom. *Confucius*

At each phase on the Systemic Change Cycle there are *developmental tasks* and *basic functions* that coincide with the *PsychoLogical domains* and *essential qualities* that facilitate new levels of organization and functioning. Since the tasks and functions are so interwoven, we will explore them in conjunction with one another. To evolve to the next level of our life, the *developmental task* of each phase is accomplished with a focus on the corresponding *psychological domain*, while drawing on and realizing the *essential quality* in order to perform the *basic function* needed to successfully address the primary concern. Once we adequately attend to our current phase, we naturally move into our next phase. Although these tasks and functions are part of both conscious and unconscious processes, when we are most in the flow, they are mostly intuitive. Embodying the various qualities — not thinking about them — is what carries us through the phases of change.

The more we stagnate, the more we need to consciously draw on our internal resources to accomplish the tasks of each phase. Most effective therapies facilitate this process, although different therapies place more emphasis on different phases, and different elements of those phases. For example, some therapies are better at helping people move from phase TWO to phase THREE, but not so good at knowing how to help people move from FOUR to FIVE. As people have different strengths and weaknesses, they need different kinds of support in accessing the appropriate resources to tackle the specific challenges associated with each phase. Different personality types tend to get stuck in the phase associated with their type and therefore need interventions that address the developmental tasks, basic functions and primary concerns of that particular phase. This will be addressed in depth in chapter nine.

Cycles of change occur naturally in every life — in every family. People come to therapy because that process has become stuck in some way and the role of a therapist is to join the person, family, couple, or organization at whatever phase they are at in the cycle of change, and help them continue to evolve. This often requires both helping them access internal/external resources and releasing constraints. Sometimes one or two sessions of solution focused therapies may be all that is needed to get people unstuck and back into the flow of life. At other times people may need to be guided through a whole cycle, or even several cycles, as they learn how to use and trust in these natural processes again.

Enneagram of

DEVELOPMENTAL TASKS

& *Basic Functions*

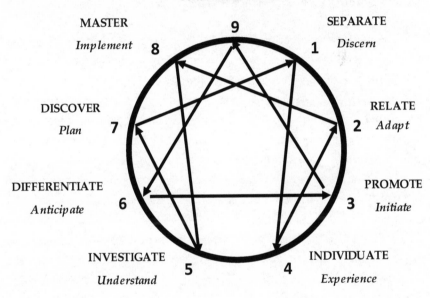

COOPERATE

Consolidate/ Mediate

MASTER   **9**   SEPARATE

Implement   **8**   **1**   *Discern*

DISCOVER   RELATE

Plan   **7**   **2**   *Adapt*

DIFFERENTIATE   PROMOTE

Anticipate   **6**   **3**   *Initiate*

INVESTIGATE   INDIVIDUATE

Understand   **5**   **4**   *Experience*

NINE — Homeostasis

- Primary Question: How to maintain stability?
- Developmental Task: Cooperate
- Basic Function: Consolidate and Mediate
- Essential Quality: Peace
- Psychological Domain: Environment/Community

Eric Lyleson

Primary Question — Maintain Stability

At any level of development, we learn to maintain stability by maximizing cooperation between different aspects of the systems to which we belong. To accomplish this developmental task, we focus primarily on the domain of *environment and/or community,* while drawing on the essential quality of *peace.* The basic function of this process is to *consolidate* the growth of the previous cycle of change and *mediate* any conflicts that could perturb the newly established *homeostasis.*

Developmental Task — Cooperate

The level of cooperation we achieve within our communities defines each new level of development. This is made possible by orchestrating greater inner cooperation between the community aspects that make up our essential wholeness. To cooperate is to work or act together in association with others for common purposes and benefits. Cooperation involves the minimizing of conflict and the maximizing of harmony. When you and I operate with common values and goals, we are cooperating.

The quality of the interaction between the parts of any system determines the quality of the homeostasis achieved. In an orchestra, for example, the quality of the cooperation between members of the orchestra largely determines the quality of the music being performed. The conductor helps to mediate a harmonic balance between the musicians. We see the same phenomena in team sports; the team that works better together will often defeat the team with individual stars who haven't learned to play cooperatively. Naturally, the best quality of any organization, organism or community will be achieved by a combination of both. Like an orchestra conductor, we achieve the developmental task of cooperation by mediating the relationships between different parts of ourselves to maintain internal and external stability and harmony.

When we view the Enneagram as a symbol of our wholeness, like an orchestra, the essence of NINE is like a very humble conductor who doesn't write the score and doesn't play an instrument; their job is to make sure the rest of the parts maximize their ability to play together in harmonious cooperation.

Basic Function — Consolidate and Mediate

> Humankind has not woven the web.
> We are but one thread within it.
> Whatever we do to the web, we do to ourselves.
> All things are bound together.
> All things connect. *Chief Seattle*

Through mediation we find agreement and cooperation. A system's developmental task of cooperation is achieved in relation to its environment and the communities within which it resides. Our basic function at this phase is to consolidate any changes made in the previous stage of growth by mediating the varied and disparate agendas of our different internal parts, and also by mediating with the other parts of the environment and larger communities. Through mediation, we administrate our lives in ways that benefit everyone we are involved with.

The ability to form and maintain complex cooperative relationships correlates with the degree of internal harmony. When we have mediated cooperation between competing agendas or conflicting emotions, we feel peaceful and at ease. Being at peace within leads us to act in a peaceful manner with others, creating harmonious relationships.

Essential Quality — Comfort and Ease

We mediate cooperation to maximize comfort and ease. After a period of facing the challenges of growth and learning, we need to rest and reap the benefits of our labor. What is comfortable is what comes easily. The more we do something, the easier it becomes, until it becomes an unconscious skill or habit.

To maximize cooperation, we adjust what we do and how we do it to fit in with the larger community. In order to help maintain stability and harmony, we tend to accept, ignore or minimize our perception of flaws or inadequacies and the problems they cause. We adjust our expectations to fit within the boundaries of what is immediately and easily available.

Focusing our attention on what is comfortable and easy means we are not focusing on what is difficult and uncomfortable. Since we are a diverse collection of various psychological, emotional, spiritual and physical needs, desires and potentials, maintaining a general sense of comfort can entail certain parts being ignored or compromised for periods of time. We think of this as 'not rocking the boat'. To mediate a peaceful atmosphere, people purposely don't raise contentious issues or criticize other's mistakes. Although most of us know the dangers of letting these annoyances build up over time, a certain amount of this in any system is natural and healthy.

When things cannot be moved aside or minimized, any good mediation process helps the various parties know where they stand. A good process will establish the minimum a party will settle for when negotiating a mutual agreement between people or parts of a system with divergent interests.

Stability

To maintain relative stability it is important to modulate our hopes, expectations, behaviors, time constraints and emotional responses. Remember that when our lives approach equilibrium they become more akin to the predictable nature of nonliving systems. Once routine is established, we tend to ignore or avoid anything that is out of the ordinary.

The more effectively we mediate life's fluctuations, the greater the stability. The longer we maintain these patterns, the more automatic and unconscious they become. Recently adopted ways of thinking, perceiving and behaving become incorporated into our way of life. They become stable structures upon which we can evolve more complexity and specialization.

Psychological Domain — Environment/Community

Each new level of homeostatic stability becomes the ground upon which the relationship systems of our lives develop. A stable network of friendships, for example, allows us to rely on people to be there when we need companionship, rather than needing to go out and meet a new friend every time we want a conversation or to share a meal. Having a support network of friends makes it easier seek out new relationships, including courting possible mates. Marriage or a stable committed relationship then becomes a foundation for creating a family (not the only way of course).

Families organize themselves into self-maintaining patterns and then mediate that stability so each family member can develop other potentials or learn to better satisfy their individual needs and contribute to the group.

Each period of stability serves as fertile ground for new seeds of growth, which will play an active part in the next developmental cycle. We bring together all we have learned from the varied sources in our lives and consolidate them. We form a synthesized amalgam that helps us articulate a new vision of an ideal life or ideal world for us to live in. Interestingly, the very act of consolidating our developments also germinates new seeds of discontent that will inevitably arise out of comparisons between these ideal visions and the stability of the new status quo.

ONE — Awareness of Limitations

* Primary Question: What is limited or flawed?
* Developmental Task: Separate
* Basic Function: Discern
* Essential Quality: Mindfulness
* Psychological Domain: Ideals

Primary Question — What is limited or flawed?

After a period of relative stability, we naturally begin to identify the limitations and flaws of our circumstances by being stand separate from the systems we belong to. To accomplish this developmental task, we focus primarily on the domain of ideals, while drawing on the essential quality of mindfulness. Being mindful of our ideals and our circumstances supports the basic function of discerning what does and does not get in the way of us realizing our emerging potential.

Developmental Task — Separate

'Separate' comes from the Latin *se* meaning 'aside' (as with sever) and *parare,* 'to make ready' (as with prepare). To prepare for a new cycle of change, we must separate ourselves from the larger system and individual parts from one another, so we can discern what supports growth, evolution and health from what doesn't. Systems and individuals do not change as a unified whole; they separate into smaller parts, so distinctions about particular relationship patterns, and the values and beliefs that inform those behaviors, can be examined with more discernment. Thomas Moore, in reference to Jung's study of alchemy, writes:

> Separatio was an operation the alchemist considered essential to the process of turning ordinary materials into gold. Jung understood imagery psychologically; to him separatio was a breaking apart of materials in the psyche that needed differentiation. They were perhaps too tightly packed and couldn't be known for what they were individually. Paracelsus understood separatio as the primary activity in the creation, both in the creation of the world and in every human creative act.[69]

The criteria we use to we separate things is primarily their differences. Gregory Bateson wrote, "A 'bit' of information is definable as a difference that makes a difference. Such a difference, as it travels and undergoes successive transformation in a circuit, is an elementary idea."[70] Consciousness allows us to be aware of the differences between the way things are and the way our ideals point towards how they could possibly be. Life is not one immutable union; it is an ever-changing ecological process in which we play a role. Being able to step back from the systems we live within allows us to perceive those differences that, if experimented with, could make a meaningful difference in our lives and to those communities to which we belong.

Basic Function — Discern

> He who knows others is clever; He who knows himself has discernment. *Lao-Tzu*
> A journey of a thousand miles begins with a single step. *Confucius*

Discernment is the process by which we determine the differences that 'make a difference'. When these different ways of thinking, perceiving or relating are put into practice they lead to changes in the larger system. Discernment is the conscious recognition of specific differences that distinguish one individual from another, useful from not useful, healthy from unhealthy, and truth from falsehoods.

Separating the whole system into individual components allows for the discernment of their specific uses and effectiveness. Making distinctions highlights the limitations of the system's current structure and the need for reform or change.

Roger Baldwin, founder of the American Civil Liberties Union, said, "So long as we have enough people in this country willing to fight for their rights, we'll be called a democracy." Countries as a whole don't initiate change; rather, it is individuals that will perturb a system's stability. The United States as a whole did not initiate the process of ensuring equal rights for people of color. It was individuals like Martin Luther King Jr., Malcolm X, Rosa Parks, and the Freedom Riders who initiated social reforms in America. In a marriage, it will be one of the partners that will begin addressing the inadequacies, often unilaterally and possibly even in the face of significant resistance from the other party. In a family, it could be a child or a parent. In our own psyche we have a chorus of internal voices, but it will generally be a dissenting inner voice that complains about the status quo or simply urges us to strive for something better. These dissenting voices raise issues that aren't easily dismissed. This is what propels us as individuals, families and societies into new cycles of change.

Principles are basic truths, rules or laws concerning the functioning of natural phenomena or mechanical processes. They help us discern what is supporting our evolution, collectively and individually, and what isn't. For example, the democratic principles set down in the U.S. Constitution and Bill of Rights were our founding father's attempt to articulate a set of guidelines that would best help American society realize their democratic ideals. If democracy is an ideal we are striving for and we find discrepancies between our behavior and the principles of democracy we hold as guidelines, we need ask how to be more true to the principles.

In the homeostatic phase we can be lulled into the trance-like, auto-pilot state of unconscious competence. As the limitations of a system become increasingly apparent, our previously ignored individual needs and new creative potentials emerge into consciousness. This prompts us to pay closer attention to what we are doing in order to avoid repeating mistakes driven by unconscious habits. In a family system, there will be one or more family members who will communicate, directly or indirectly, that their personal needs and emerging potential are not being adequately attended to. The longer these inadequacies go unattended, the greater the likelihood that the individual will escalate communication of their frustration.

For example, a child needing attention might first ask their mother to play with them. If not responded to adequately, they might keep asking for drinks and food. If not attended to adequately, they might accidentally knock over and break something. If still not attended to adequately, they might pick on a younger sibling. If they find that picking on a sibling is the only way they are guaranteed to get their mother's undivided attention, this pattern becomes part of the family homeostasis. The problematic, disruptive behavior will escalate or become more intolerable until the parents find more adequate ways of attending to the child's needs in ways that are less compromising and more affirming for everyone.

In the system of our personal psychology, certain parts of us will suffer more than others from limiting patterns. As the suffering increases, the unfulfilled part of us will increasingly make its frustration known. The severity of the problem (symptom) will generally increase until the limiting factors are adequately addressed.

Woodrow Wilson once said, "If you want to make enemies, try to change something." People become attached or identified with the status quo. They fear change, because they fear the unknown. However all growth, progress and evolution rely on moving from what we know to discovering what we don't know. The homeostatic mechanisms of any system are very powerful and the impulses for change, which often come from the weaker and more disenfranchised, or their supporters, are usually met with resistance. Those with the most power in social systems — parents, the rich and powerful, or dominant nations — have the choice of attending to inadequacies and injustices, or ignoring them. In the face of resistance from weaker parties, the dominant ones will resort to violent means to maintain the status quo. Violence and ignorance are the factors that invariably escalate problems, regardless of the size of the community.

Whilst violence can have the short-term effect of regaining stability in the larger system, the limiting patterns go unaddressed and eventually resurface and escalate. Each time we become aware of the limitations of a system, we have a new opportunity to learn how to relate more compassionately and responsibly to the people, communities, countries and compromised parts of our own psyches that raise these issues.

Autonomy

To be autonomous is to be self-governing — independent from external authority. Our degree of autonomy is defined by how self-reliant, self-sufficient and self-directed we are. To separate ourselves from the collective whole of our society, community, family, or even marriage, we must have a certain level of autonomy. We must be able to find a niche in which we can look after ourselves. The opposite of autonomy is enmeshment. With high levels of enmeshment there is so much dependence on the system that there is no space to stand apart and challenge the status quo.

As women in our society have become more self-supporting, they have become less defined by the previously male-dominated societal norms. "Unless we include a job as part of every citizen's right to autonomy and personal fulfillment," declared Gloria Steinem, "women will continue to be vulnerable to someone else's idea of what 'need' is." As women have been able to claim greater equality in our society, men have been forced to evolve in their identities, beliefs, values and behaviors correspondingly. As our society has evolved, there has been a growth in opportunities for women to become more autonomous. Systems evolve by balancing the integrity and autonomy of the individual parts with the interdependent integrated functioning of the larger system.

The purpose of the larger system is to support the individual parts, and the system is only as healthy as the collective well being of its individual parts. The evolution of human consciousness is the ongoing discovery of how to adapt to evolving collective conditions, coupled with the realization of the greatest possible freedom for individual self-determination. Likewise, our personal wellbeing is maximized when there is a balance between the autonomy of various parts and the integrity of our whole self. If our internal landscape becomes overly dominated by a particular part, other parts will be exploited or neglected and we will feel emotionally discontent. Therapies like Gestalt, Voice Dialogue, Self-Relations and Jungian Analysis recognize that each part of us needs to have a voice that is respected by the rest of us. To have integrity is be true to our deepest ideals and values in the face of resistance and difficulty. Progress requires individuals who, to maintain their integrity, stand apart from the collective consensus and act autonomously.

When our stability is being perturbed because a part of us is frustrated, we often try to ignore or suppress this part in order to regain stability. There is a growing awareness of having two (or more) selves as the voice of dissent challenges the voice of conformity and maintaining the status quo. This will be obvious to anyone who has ever tried to give up a bad habit. The voices of dissent are often resisted because we know they initially push us in the direction of chaos and disintegration, and away from our comfortable, albeit outgrown, state of homeostasis. We seem to fear that if we let the idealistic individual voices have more power, the integrity of our whole self — or of the whole society — will disintegrate into chaos forever. However, for any reformation to take place, there must be a deconstruction of the existing structure. We didn't find a healthy economy free of slavery until we destabilized the slave-based economy. It is not until the limitations of the status quo become intolerable for an individual or for enough of the population that the principles of idealistic leaders begin to be put in motion. Eventually, however, ideas that were considered extremely radical, threatening and anarchistic have become institutional norms. Once a cycle of change is completed, once-feared radical leaders like Martin Luther King Jr. come to be seen as heroic pillars of the more evolved society.

TWO — Adaptive Behavior

- Primary Question: What is needed?
- Developmental Task: Relate
- Basic Function: Adapt
- Essential Quality: Strength
- Psychological Domain: Behavior

Primary Question — What is needed?

Having identified limitations and flaws in our circumstances, we begin asking what is needed in the way we relate to life in order to move in the direction of our ideals. To accomplish this developmental task we focus primarily on the domain of behavior, while drawing on the essential quality of compassion. Being compassionate towards the parts of ourselves and other people that are stuck in limiting patterns supports the basic function of adapting our way of relating in a way that supports our emerging potential.

Developmental Task — Relate

All things appear and disappear because of the concurrence of causes and conditions. Nothing ever exists entirely alone; everything is in relation to everything else. *Buddha*

To relate is to have or establish a reciprocal interaction with someone or something else. Essential compassion compels and assists the enhancement of our relating. Biologically, we know that couplings (ways of relating) are sought within the current boundaries of the system that will maximize the ability to attend to the limitations and bring things back into equilibrium. Behavioral variables are manipulated within the status quo of the system in order to adapt to emerging needs and address problems.

The quality of our life is a reflection of the quality of our ability to relate to the various components of our moment-to-moment experience, both internally and externally. Our relationships with others are reflections of the relationship we have with ourselves. In the deepest sense, there really is no difference between inner and outer, since everything we perceive is an experience of our mind.

The quality of interaction is not necessarily determined by what happens, but by the spirit in which it is perceived or enacted. Actions taken out of anger or fear are experienced differently than those taken out of love or joy. Another person's actions perceived with eyes of love and compassion are perceived differently than those same actions perceived from an attitude of fear and judgment. Having compassion for oneself and those we are relating to helps us find the most mutually beneficial ways of relating.

Basic Function — Adapt

To adapt is to make adjustments in order to achieve more suitable conditions. Adaptation asks, "What do we need to do differently to get the world to give us what we need?" To get a sense of what is needed, we must put ourselves in the others shoes, sensing what they need in order to respond differently in relation to us. The more sensitive we can be to whomever or whatever we are relating to, the better we can manipulate the variables to get more of what we need. We realize that the more we can give the other person what they truly need, the more likely they are to give us what we truly need.

When we operate in true cooperation, with common goals, a win for our partner is a win for us also, and therefore choosing to give up something we want for the sake of our partner can benefit us through strengthening the relationship. As long as we are getting others to respond in ways that benefit us, we will continue to adapt our actions accordingly. At this phase, we are not yet ready to challenge the boundaries of the relationship system, therefore we adjust our expectations to cope with the limited responses to our efforts. As we push the limits of what the system can offer us, we are often forced to settle for less in return for our efforts. This highlights the discrepancies between our lives and the needs of our emergent self.

In cybernetic terms, negative feedback loops are those patterns of relating that return the system to homeostasis. Positive feedback loops (or amplifying feedback loops) are patterns of relating that seek to accommodate new adaptations into the system. These adaptations amplify awareness of the limitations of the homeostatic functioning even more, leading to the need for further adaptations.

As the limitations of our system of relating become more apparent, we seek out who, or what, has the power to help us meet the needs of our emerging self. The sense of having two selves — the self that has power to attend to our needs and the part that is in need — magnifies as the needs of our emergent-self demand more attention. Our needs stem from either emergent potentialities for growth or dissociated wounded parts that need healing. In therapy, this can be explored through how our compassionate adult self can relate to our wounded or neglected child self.

A major step in our evolution is learning to respond more compassionately to our needs than our parents were capable of when we were children. The more sensitive and responsive we are to the needs of our emergent self, the better we will be able to maximize the potentials for the self-organizing universe to evolve through us. Albert Einstein reminded us, "The significant problems we face cannot be solved at the same level of thinking we were at when we created them." However, before moving to the next level we usually must exhaust all possibilities within our current level of understanding.

Vulnerability

Evolution is life learning to relate in more effective ways. Over time, species have adapted by becoming more varied, intelligent, resilient, perceptive and cooperative. This has required becoming more open and responsive to the flows of information, energy and matter. In the process of becoming more responsive to changing demands, species have increasingly become less armored and brutish and more vulnerable and sensitive. Humans have evolved sensitive protuberances such as unclawed finger tips, sensitive (and sensual) lips and ears, noses that if bumped bring tears to our eyes, and eyes in the front of our head, leaving our backs vulnerable to attack. It is our sensitivity that enables us to relate more intimately with whatever or whomever we come into contact with. Standing upright has exposed our hearts and soft underbellies to the world. Women's sensitive breasts and men's penises protrude forward into the world, increasing our sense of vulnerability even more.

To deal with this vulnerability, our intellects have developed sophisticated means of manipulating the natural world. All technology is designed to help us feel safer and thrive in challenging and varied environments. All of our tools, technologies and infrastructures can be thought of as extensions of our bodies and minds. They make it easier to live, however our dependence on them makes us even more vulnerable. Not only can our bodies be damaged, if the extensions of us — shelters, vehicles, communication, water, sewage and agricultural tools — are compromised in any way, our lives come under threat. What would happen if our urban electricity or water systems were shut down for a mere month? The wider we extend our web of relating to the world, the more robust and complex is the system we create, and the more vulnerable and therefore the more sensitive we need to be in caring for ourselves.

As humans, we emotionally experience the world through our hearts and our guts. We have an amazing ability not only to emotionally interpret our own experience; standing upright with our vulnerable hearts and guts facing the world has given us the ability to feel other people's emotions. Our ability to empathize might be the most sensitive protuberance we have. On a more subtle level, we are able to project our sensitivity to another person and sense what an experience is like for them. With the people, animals and things we are most closely associated with, we tend to do this without any effort. Who hasn't felt their heart ache at someone else's misfortune? Or what parent hasn't felt their guts churn when they see their child fall and hurt themselves? Our compassion enables us to act with love.

Love is essentially remembering we are all part of the same web, and feeling our interconnectedness with it. All behaviors either enhance the quality of the connection to the web of life, or they detract from it. Our vulnerability allows us to receive more and higher quality information from the world we live in. This information feeds back to us how well we are relating to the other members of the web. It is through improving the quality of our relating that we move towards our ideals of how things can be; and we naturally take more pride in our actions, which in turn pushes us to the limits of our capabilities within the existing systemic structure of our lives.

THREE — Limits of Capabilities

- Primary Question: How to succeed?
- Developmental Task: Promote
- Basic Function: Initiate
- Essential Quality: Strength
- Psychological Domain: Capabilities

Primary Question — How to succeed?

Through the trial and error of adapting our behavior to address our problems, it becomes clearer what we need to promote the success of our emergent agenda. To accomplish this developmental task we focus primarily on the domain of capabilities, while drawing on the essential quality of strength. Inner strength allows us to exercise our capabilities to their fullest in carrying out the basic function of initiating changes that help us get more of what we need and want within the existing systemic structure.

At every level of our development, we tend to seek out the best ways to manage our lives within the boundaries defined by current homeostatic patterns of behavior. Pushing our capabilities to adapt to our circumstances in the attempt to regain homeostasis actually pushes us towards a new world of creative possibilities. It is the commitment of doing our best with the resources available to us that brings us to the boundaries of the status quo. Stuart Kauffman writes, "Adaptive walks on rugged landscapes eventually reach a local optimum, and then cease further improvement." He goes on to suggest, "Systems on the boundary between order and chaos may have the flexibility to adapt rapidly and successfully through the accumulation of useful variations. In such poised systems, most mutations have small consequences because of the 'systems' homeostatic nature. A few mutations, however, cause larger cascades of change."[71]

Many of the capabilities we develop will serve as a foundation for the next level of functioning; however, simply improving upon what we are currently doing can carry only us so far. Consider horse drawn carriage over a century ago: the wheels, bearings, suspension and steering can be of the best quality, yet there is a distinct limit to how fast you can go and how well you can maneuver with horses as your source of power. However, the improvements made to the carriage were useful in the creation of a prototype automobile.

At some point, we reach a limit regarding how far we can develop within the boundaries defined by the structure of how we do things. Achieving success in a particular context ultimately leads to an impasse. It is in the failure to find the innovations we want in the usual framework that eventually opens us to a paradigm shift. Experienced psychotherapists know that it is not until their clients reach this type of impasse, referred to in the Acceptance and Commitment Therapy (ACT) literature as 'creative hopelessness', that significant transformation can occur.

Developmental Task — Promote

To promote is to cause to move forward or upward, as toward a goal. We do what is needed bring about improvement, progress or growth. To promote a way of doing something is to contribute to the progress or growth of that enterprise. When we promote an idea, we are urging others to adopt that idea and establish it as part of the organization of that system. When successful, this leads to a promotion in status within the system, with more power and responsibilities. This is easily seen with an employee in the workplace or a teenager in a family.

In promoting the agenda of our emerging self, we foster its inclusion into our lives. Like a foster parent, we take responsibility for the development, nurturing and support of the parts that need to be adopted by us to reorganize the ecology of our lives at the next level. We get to know the wards in our care and how to attend to their specific needs. When we reach the point where a deeper structural change is necessary, rather than just more efficiency or effort, it is our responsibility to promote this change. As we reach the limits of our capabilities within a specific framework we eventually realize, 'There has got to be a better way.' It is as if we have tried every avenue to find our way to a better place and come to realize that where we need to go is not delineated on the maps we are working from.

Basic Function — Initiate

We initiate a new course of action by taking a step in the direction of what we want to promote. By taking the initiative at work, we promote our capabilities to handle more challenging roles. By initiating more honest and open conversations with our spouse, we promote a more honest and open relationship. It is our essential strength of character that allows us to take the initiative.

To be initiated, is to confer membership. In promoting our evolution, we sponsor our emergent-self into the membership of the community of our essential wholeness. A sponsor assumes responsibility for another person or a group during a period of instruction, apprenticeship or probation. It is our task to introduce this aspect of ourselves and help it through the initial birthing pains of coming into the world. With initiation comes a commitment to maximizing the opportunities for our emergent selves to discover their full potentials.

The process of adaptation can be described as a process of hill climbing. Some of the hills take us to higher mountains, or what are referred to as 'peaks of fitness on a fitness landscape'[72]. The variations in particular characteristics or capabilities that prove to be most useful are preserved as part of our way of being in the world. In Darwinian terms, this is referred to as natural selection or *survival of the fittest*. Although Darwin was referring to successive generations inheriting the characteristics that have proven to be best adapted to their respective environments, we can see with our personal evolution that it is the capabilities that have proven most useful which will be carried with us through periods of destabilization. Whatever has proven to be useful is incorporated into the new sense of ourselves, as we are reorganized at the next evolutionary level. The ways of thinking, sensing and acting that are less usefully adaptive tend to recede or fall away (die off) as the system of our lives approaches chaos (phases FOUR to SIX).

The skills developed crawling serve as the foundation of walking. The communication and organizational skills developed by a CEO to manage his company under his direct control serve as a foundation for how to reorganize the company into a more power-sharing model.

Responsibility

Taking initiative is how we take responsibility for improving our circumstances. All adaptations come in response to the demands of our life circumstances. We each must make choices and assume the responsibility of living with the consequences of those choices. Becoming more responsible is learning how to better respond to the challenges and opportunities in our lives.

It is a parent's responsibility to prepare their children to meet the challenges and inevitable crises of life. Good parents arrange opportunities that will promote the development of the capabilities needed for their children to successfully manage developmental challenges. We provide them with education, social activities, sports, and so on. As they are faced with difficulties, we help them find ways of learning how to handle these successfully, and to learn from the positive and negative consequences of their actions. Learning to be more responsible enables them to be more independent and autonomous, which in turn leads to more freedom in determining the course of their lives, and paradoxically allows for greater *inter*dependence. There is always a balance between freedom and responsibility throughout our lives. The person who has best learned to adapt to the circumstances of life responsibly will have more freedom and a higher quality of choices available to them.

Systems that can coordinate the most complex behavior (adapt most readily) are the ones that have constructed the most useful models or internal maps of their environments. In learning how to address the challenges of our lives, we naturally refine these models. From these models, strategies for achieving desired outcomes can be formulated. The better the model, the more effective the strategy. Highly effective strategies become automatic, which allows us to use multi-tracked thinking and polyphasic activity. In this way, a variety of capabilities are all coordinated towards addressing a specific problem or goal.

Reciprocal patterns of relating are essentially contracts we have with others. Most of them are unspoken; however, it is presumed that if I do what you expect, you will do what I expect. Part of being responsible is keeping contracts. At this phase, we do what we can to maximize and maintain our status or relative position within our families, communities and society by impressing upon others that we will do our best to fulfill our contracts.

Contracts, which can be explicit or implicit, are set up to achieve the best results within the bounds of the status quo, although this may not be obvious to someone outside of the system. An obvious example is the unspoken contract between a spouse who is alcohol dependent and the codependent spouse. They behave in mutually self-maintaining patterns that to an outside observer look very self-detrimental, but would, for each partner, be their best efforts to cope with circumstances within the dimension of life they function in. At this phase, we do our best to honor our commitments/contracts to the best of our current ability and knowledge.

Eventually, we reach the limit of being able to function in fulfilling ways within our existing contracts and we must initiate change by doing something different. We promote our evolution by breaking and/or renegotiating the contract. However, we may not be able to fully articulate what new contract we want to negotiate. With an alcoholic couple, for example, this quite often begins with the codependent spouse breaking the contracts of silence and cover-up, allowing the problems of addiction to be seen by others. Any move of this sort tends to lead to an escalation of the problem situation, as the relationship system destabilizes more and moves towards chaos. Doing our best and admitting failure is the gateway to the next phase in the process of change. As W.C. Fields put it, "If at first you don't succeed, try, try again. Then give up. No use being a damned fool about it."

FOUR — *Inadequacies Revealed*

- Primary Question: What is inadequate or missing?
- Developmental Task: Individuate
- Basic Function: Experience
- Essential Quality: Forgiveness
- Psychological Domain: Values

Primary Question — What is inadequate or missing?

Exercising our capabilities to the fullest highlights the inadequacies of our circumstances, even with the adaptations we have made, and awakens our need have greater individuation from the system. To accomplish the developmental task of individuation we focus primarily on the domain of values, while drawing on the essential quality of forgiveness. Forgiveness helps us to let go of what we thought was most valuable so we can open to the basic function of having the experiences needed clarify what our emergent self values at this next stage of development.

At this phase we find ourselves in uncharted territory and our perception begins to open to experiences that have been outside our old mindset. This includes the internal representations that have previously unconsciously guided our decisions. They can come to us in the form of memories, dreams, fantasies and longings, or envy, resentment and regret. At the previous phase we were full of hope and feeling capable; in this phase, hope turns into hopelessness and feeling capable turns into a sense of inadequacy and failure. Doing what we know and what has worked for us in the past no longer adequately meets the needs of our emergent self.

Developmental Task – Individuate

There is a destination, a possible goal. That is the way of individuation. Individuation means becoming an "individual", and, in so far as "individuality" embraces our inner most, last, and incomparable uniqueness, it implies becoming one's own self. We could therefore translate individuation as "coming to selfhood" or self-realization.[73] *Carl Jung*

Individuation refers to the breaking down of obligatory social contracts so that an individual is free to make new connections that are more supportive of the emergent self. It is the orientation towards greater personal choice and freedom. Individuation is the recognition that although we participate in larger systems, we are separate individuals with unique ways of experiencing and contributing to life. Many choices are about what we do, but much of our personal freedom is about how we interpret our experience, or as Nietzsche wrote, "There are no facts, only interpretations." By separating oneself from the social systems that have conditioned our perceptions, we begin interpreting life more directly through our personal experience.

Gaining freedom from the habitual group-think that maintained the homeostasis of our social systems frees us to embrace our inner-most incomparable uniqueness. At this stage, our attention is drawn inward to the subjective experience of sounds, sights and sensations of our inner world. Gaining greater awareness of our emotions, dreams and fantasies helps us become more familiar with the unconscious myths that have governed our lives and the newly emerging and/or neglected parts requesting our attention.

Not until there is enough individuation from the mind-set of the status quo is it possible to recognize our personal woundings. On many occasions early in therapy I have heard people say things like, "Of course I deserved to be hit," or "If this sort of parenting was good enough for me, it's good enough for my kids." Those who haven't opened to the personal experience of the effects of neglectful or violent parenting won't have the ability to feel into their children's experience and how their parenting methods effect them.

Carl Jung said, "Show me a sane man and I will cure him for you." Sanity is largely defined by the dominant social paradigm. Individuation is accomplished in part by embracing aspects of personal experience that we may label as 'crazy'. We can feel pretty crazy when certain archetypal myths play themselves out through the re-creation of the experiences that wounded us in the past. We feel out of control and like something or someone is causing us to reenact the patterns with our spouses, bosses and children and recreate the painful emotions. At these times, it's like we all have multiple personality disorder as our wounded and neglected selves act out, looking for attention and help.

The more pain we feel, the more the necessity for doing something about it. Necessity is the mother of invention. The more resourceful we become, the more we are able to use reenactments to experience our woundedness, find the healing needed, and learn to handle our relationships in more enlightened ways. As Aldous Huxley said, "Experience is not what happens to you; it's what you do with what happens to you."

Basic Function — Experience

What each must seek in his life never was on land or sea. It is something out of his own unique potentiality for experience, something that never has been and never could have been experienced by anyone else. *Joseph Campbell*

To intimately experience life is to participate in it fully, unmediated by concepts. Opening more fully to each moment takes us beneath surface appearances to where we can be moved, touched and undergo transformation. Relating from our concepts and preconceived notions creates filters that keep life predictable, rather than being impressed by the uniqueness of each emerging moment. The more fully we open to our direct experience, the more lasting impressions we are left with.

Having spilled over the boundaries of the attractor basin of the status quo, our consciousness is flooded with experiences that weren't previously consciously available to us. They were there all along, but our awareness was not open to them. While minimizing disturbances and maximizing equilibrium, our minds are good at ignoring things that could possibly perturb us. Indeed, one of the primary functions of the brain is to filter out information not directly relevant to our immediate survival. As social animals, we naturally tend to only want what is available within the status quo's accepted basin of possibilities. Exposure to avoided situations is the key intervention of Cognitive Behavioral Therapy (CBT). By experiencing situations that have been habitually avoided, people become more aware of the emotions and underlying beliefs that have restrained them in the past.

At this phase, we start thinking outside the box. As Frank Zappa declared, "Without deviation from the norm, progress is not possible." Great innovators like Einstein, Gandhi and Jefferson weren't satisfied with standard explanations and ways of doing things. Their dissatisfaction, driven by their longing for something better, led them to inquire deeply into the nature of experience. By following through on their desire to experience more of what the world has to offer they were able to discover their unique contribution to the evolution of human culture.

The hope we feel at phase THREE allows us to dream bigger, but when the inadequacies of our circumstances become apparent, hope turns to disappointment and despair. Sadness and disappointment highlight what is missing in our lives. Our self-confident egos suffer humiliation when our efforts have failed us in some way. The humiliation of facing the inadequacies of our previous way of living leads to the humility that allows us to be open to new ways of approaching the unfolding mystery and complex diversity of life. At phase THREE we often say, "I've tried everything." Humility leads us to say, "I don't know what it is yet, but there has got to be a better way." As poet David Whyte writes,

> Ambition takes us toward a horizon but not over it — that line would always recede before our reaching hands. But desire is a conversation between our physical bodies, our work, our imaginations, and the new world that is the territory we seek.[74]

Our essential wholeness speaks to us through imagination. Late in life, Einstein reflected, "When I examine myself and my methods of thought, I come to the conclusion that the gift of fantasy has meant more to me than my talent for absorbing positive knowledge." It is through our dreams and imagination that we can begin to experience what it might be like to live in a way that honors our ideals and deeper values. In this phase, we can be visited by forgotten memories that were 'exceptions to the rules' — the relationship that never quite happened, the trip to an exotic location, the career opportunity that slipped away.

Experiences that resonated with our deeper values recalled with grief, regret and appreciation help us remember what is most important to us. Wanting to discover how to satisfy the ache in our hearts is a compelling motivator for continuing our journey through unknown internal and external landscapes. The deep longing and associated creative impulses of individuation call upon us to relate uniquely to circumstances and break with convention.

Longing of the soul can be disguised as envy as we begin to imagine what experiences we are missing out on that others are free to enjoy. When we give ourselves permission to experience what others experience, the envy transforms into motivation.

It is important to connect with the essence of our longing, rather than just the objects we hope will give us the experience we long for. With individuation, we come to realize that love, joy, forgiveness, and other essential qualities, are within us. By following our longings to their source within, we connect more fully with the essential qualities we believe those experiences will bring us, which in turn inspires us to relate in ways that create the kind of life that embodies those qualities. For example, say you are longing for an apology from your spouse. You ask yourself, "What am

I hoping to experience by receiving that apology?" The answer could be to be acknowledged for how that person disappointed me. We keep asking what that experience would do for us until we get to an unconditioned state or essential quality.

"Having received the acknowledgement, I would hope to experience more trust that my spouse wasn't going to do that again. If I had that trust, I could forgive them. If I could forgive them, I would feel forgiveness and acceptance." We could then explore how relating from that sense of forgiveness and acceptance might make a difference with that person. This is the opposite of thinking we have to satisfy our desires before we can experience the essential qualities of our wholeness. Instead, we reconnect with our wholeness so that we can manifest a more wholesome life.

Uncharted Realms

Past disappointments often resurface when we sense the chance of finding fulfillment. We often carry previous disappointments with us like old wounds, because our families or communities weren't adequately able to help us reconcile them. Old woundings get encapsulated in emotional scar tissue and placed in an isolated place in our consciousness where we hope not to have to feel them anymore. When we reach a healthier level of functioning, the wounded parts of us, sensing they can be adequately attended to, tend to come out of hiding. The more we open to joyful, loving, successful life, the more the parts of us that have shut down out of hopelessness start to wake up.

Couples who have been distant can end up crying or having a fight after connecting more intimately than they have for years. If these emotions aren't attended to well it can send the couple back into their old patterns. In therapy this often addressed by predicting a relapse into old reactions. We can explain that if this happens, it is just showing the person that there is still a part of them that needs more healing and support. This helps people have a more forgiving attitude towards their difficulties.

Emotional wounds are healed when embraced by the essential qualities of our wholeness. In fact, they are wounds precisely because they have been dissociated from our essential wholeness. Forgotten, neglected and rejected parts of us are re-membered as contributing members of our wholeness when, through forgiveness, we recognize the innocence and intrinsic value of these parts. This inner process can be likened to a family in which, instead of trying to control or reject their difficult child, the parents forgive that child's bad behavior and explore how to meet her needs so that she can live more harmoniously in the family.

Valuing Woundedness

> When you are despairing, when you are confronted with a situation you fear will overwhelm you, don't ask God to take away the problem, but instead pray that He gives you the strength to deal with it. *Rabbi Harold Kushner*

Milton Erickson, M.D., founder of modern hypnotherapy and pioneer in brief therapy, strategic family therapy, and other revolutionary psychotherapeutic techniques, was paralyzed by polio as a child. In the many hours he was forced to sit by himself and observe his personal experience of paralysis, he began to notice the effects of his thoughts, memories and fantasies on his physiological functioning. He noticed the ever so slight movements in his fingertips when he vividly remembered picking apples. When he relived riding a horse in his imagination, the rocking chair that he was strapped into began to rock. He continued to explore his personal experience, which eventually led to the recovering of many physical capabilities, including the use of his hands and the ability to walk. He was able to use these personal experiences to develop therapeutic techniques that were highly effective for treating a wide range of problems. Moshe Feldenkreis had a similar experience with exploring a knee injury that led him to discover his therapeutic method. It is through healing our wounds that we become healers.

When an intellectually disabled child is born, a question often asked is, "Why does God let this happen?" A better question might be, "What kind of community would we need to be so that being intellectually disabled wouldn't be a barrier to honoring one's full humanity?" How can we judge how a human should be? A woman with cerebral palsy was interviewed on a television show when she protested the use of genetic testing in pregnancy. If it had been used in her case, she may have been aborted and she felt her life was one worth living. If we knew Stevie Wonder was going to be born blind, should we have had his fetus terminated? Or is it our deficits, woundings and abnormalities that make each one of us unique? Would Milton Erickson have made the discoveries he did about the nature of the mind if he hadn't been paralyzed twice in his life? Would Helen Keller have realized such a unique greatness if she had been born 'normal'?

Intrapsychically, we tend to want to abort the birth into consciousness of anything we feel is 'not good enough' or out of the ordinary. We label parts of ourselves as dysfunctional or bad and quickly abort their attempts to arise in our consciousness. Like many of society's disabled, we try is to isolate and hide them away from our mainstream consciousness. In this phase, we find the value inherent in the inadequacies we have felt hopeless about and begin listening to what they have to teach us.

FIVE — Diffusion of Boundaries

- Primary Question: Why is this happening?
- Developmental Task: Investigate
- Basic Function: Understand
- Essential Quality: Space
- Psychological Domain: Beliefs

Primary Question — Why is this happening?

With greater individuation from the existing system, with all its inadequacies, we are able to ask, 'Why is this happening?' Our failure to get what is needed drives us to investigate into the nature of our experience more fully. To accomplish the developmental task of investigation, we focus primarily on the domain of beliefs, while drawing on the essential quality of space. Space allows us to step back from subjective experience so the basic function of understanding objectively how things work or why they are not.

Developmental Task – Understand

> Minds are like parachutes. They only function when they are open.
> *Sir James Dewar*
> The wisdom of life consists in the elimination of nonessentials.
> *Lin Yutang*

To understand is to perceive and comprehend the nature and significance of something. We come to understand something thoroughly by experiencing it through a variety of perceptual positions. Understanding comes from being deeply involved and relating to something, putting ourselves into others' perspectives, and being aware of the systems we are part of as a whole. Deeper understanding ripens over time, drawing on many different experiences in various contexts.

Intense experiences and realizations occurring during phase FOUR tend to overwhelm us with a wealth of sensory and subjective information. This flood of information is like a large meal of rich food; we need time to digest it. We digest things, food or experiences, by breaking them down into smaller bits, separating what is useful from not useful, then absorbing what we can use and eliminating the rest. As we absorb new information it joins the pool of existing knowledge where new connections can be synthesized.

Deeper understanding is realized when we are able to reconcile what appear to be contradictory descriptions of what we have experienced. A husband gains fuller understanding of his marriage when he can make better sense of his own personal perspective, his wife's perspective, and an impersonal objective third person perspective. To gain understanding, the usual boundaries of our thinking must open to be inclusive of what was previously ignored and what is now emerging. Understanding comes from an open and spacious mind in which new cognitive structures can be constructed, rather than merely fitting the new information gained from experience into existing cognitive frameworks.

Basic Function — Investigate

Research is what I'm doing when I don't know what I'm doing.
Wernher Von Braun

To investigate is to observe or inquire into a subject in detail; to examine it systematically and take note of the information derived from observation. We do this to gain a greater understanding of the nature of the world and ourselves. Rather than immersing ourselves in immediate experience, as in the previous phase, we tend to stand back and observe the processes of interaction in the external world and/or the internal workings of our mind. In our attempt to gain understanding of the underlying patterns of our circumstances, we can review past events with objectivity. We all have the ability of mapmakers to dissociate out of our personal perspective, rising above the individual circumstances of our lives so we can gain a more global perspective.

Like early mapmakers who didn't have the advantage of satellite photos, we are able to synthesize information we have gathered into a comprehensive picture of how things are organized in relation to one another. As we are able to more fully articulate the various elements within the framework of the map, we are more able to see what is still missing and what doesn't make sense yet. Our need to complete the map leads us to further investigation of what is needed to complete the picture.

The more we learn, the more we realize the inadequacies of our old maps and how they limited us or led us astray. In this way, misleading beliefs begin to lose their power. Without the certainty of accurate maps to guide us, we are naturally reluctant in this phase to do any more than is absolutely necessary. We tend to be more inhibited, knowing our usual choices could bring about more of the same troublesome results. This uncertainty can help us be more open to other people's opinions. Entertaining multiple perspectives can help us generate a more comprehensive view of a situation, yet it is easy to feel overwhelmed by all the additional information and then need time out to sort out what fits for us.

To help with the sorting process, we compartmentalize and categorize our experiences. By grouping similar things together, we are better able to decipher the essential patterns they have in common. In the science of biology, to understand the patterns of life, we divide living things into categories whose members have something in common, such as kingdoms (plants, animals) and species (mammals, insects, etc.). When trying to understand personal relationships, we might sort people into friends, strangers, acquaintances, relatives, work associates, lovers. These categories might further be divided into whom or what we perceive to be helpful, cooperative, antagonistic, fun, and so on.

Bertrand Russell reminds us, "What is wanted is not the will-to-believe, but the wish to find out, which is its exact opposite." Initially, we try to fit our findings into our existing categories of understanding. However, the more information we acquire and assimilate that doesn't make sense within those frameworks, the more our minds must stretch to accommodate the incongruencies. New understanding arises out of the detection of patterns previously unrecognized.

The Realm of Art and Science

Where the world ceases to be the scene of our personal hopes and wishes, where we face it as free beings admiring, asking and observing, there we enter the realm of Art and Science.
Albert Einstein

In phase FOUR we connect most fully with our personal hopes and wishes, our unique way of connecting with the world, and open to a deeper appreciation of the nature of things. In phase FIVE the sincere appreciation of life's experiences motivates us to investigate the nature of things more deeply.

To create a more fulfilling life, we need to be both artist and scientist. All great artists, in addition to being in touch with their creative impulses, have a thorough understanding of the materials and subject matter that they work with. Through study and experience, an artist learns the properties of different paints and canvasses, as well as how colors combine and relate to one another. Studying anatomy can enhance the way an artist represents the human form. We realize the value of gaining more knowledge and know-how.

This is a phase of preparation. The more we understand about our circumstances, the more we realize even greater challenges await us. It is similar to preparing for a long journey and accumulating all the supplies, maps and information that could be needed along the way. Preparation leads to anticipation, and thoughts of what we find most frightening begin to arise, which we often try to allay with more information and storing resources we may need.

SIX — Differentiation

- Primary Question: What to remain loyal to and what to let go of?
- Developmental Task: Differentiate
- Basic Function: Anticipate
- Essential Quality: Acceptance
- Psychological Domain: Question

Primary Question — What to remain loyal to and what to let go of?

The more we investigate the nature of our experience, the more are able to differentiate fact from fiction. Unconditional acceptance of the world and ourselves helps us to see through the myths and wishful thinking that has obscured our perception of the true nature of things. Seeing how things are more clearly causes us to question our beliefs.

The more clearly we see where our past assumptions have led us, the more we are able to anticipate the problems and pitfalls if we continue to make choices based on those assumptions. This enables us to better differentiate what does not truly serve us, from what is essential to our evolution.

Developmental Task — Differentiate

To differentiate is to make distinctions about what is more useful and what is less useful. We distinguish and discriminate between the options available and determine our best course of action. Biology defines differentiation as the process by which cells or tissues undergo a change toward a more specialized form or function. A human embryo develops through cell division and by cell specialization. The more mature the evolving embryo, the more differentiation between the structure and functions of the various cells and parts of the body. Within the brain, as well as other organs, further specialization takes place; for example, there are regions of the brain that specialize in vision, hearing and speech.

The diversity of specialized parts of mind and body function interdependently. Our physical health and growth as biological creatures is dependent on the ability for each part to get what is needed to grow and perform their specific individual functions in relationship to other parts. Our psychological wellbeing is dependent on the various aspects of our psyche being able to preserve the integrity of their individual function in relation to the whole of us.

To become more differentiated as a person is to become more individually distinct, to honor our unique differences and to discover the unique contributions we can make to the larger systems within which we participate.

In *The Sexual Crucible*, marital therapist David Schnarch defines differentiation as:

- the ability to maintain one's sense of separate self in close proximity to a partner
- non-reactivity to other people's reactivity
- self-regulation of emotionality so that judgment can be used
- the ability to tolerate pain for growth[75]

It is easy for us to be absorbed by the relationship systems to which we belong and simply become part of the machinery. When we don't exercise our ability to make distinctions and act in our own best interests and in the best interests our relationships, evolution, both individually and collectively, is arrested. We perpetuate dysfunctional patterns by reacting indiscriminately to people's self-defeating behaviors. When we can regulate our emotional reactivity, we are more likely to exercise choices that support the evolution of our relationships and ourselves. Being able to anticipate the benefits of the accepting the short-term discomforts of destabilization, along with the effort needed to create something new, is the backbone of the differentiation process.

Fact and Fiction

> The Church says that the earth is flat, but I know that it is round, for I have seen the shadow on the moon, and I have more faith in a shadow than in the Church. *Ferdinand Magellan*

Questioning beliefs defined by the status quo leads us to differentiate between fact and fiction. In doing so, we risk resistance, ridicule and rejection from other members of our community, or the internal community of various sub-personalities. Differentiation is the process by which we remain true to what we perceive to be true.

It is easier to collude with the collective denial of the status quo, rather than acknowledging the shadow on the moon, or to shout out that the Emperor's has no new clothes. At this phase, we are naturally suspicious of people who would tell us what to believe, rather than encouraging us to find out for ourselves. To differentiate fact from fiction, we don't take things on faith; instead, we put our hypotheses to the test, actively seeking to reveal hidden facts and agendas.

Self-organization of a whole system requires differentiation of its parts. We must embrace the diversity of parts and accept the individual roles each part has to play. Our wellbeing as a society is dependent on a diversity of individuals each contributing in their unique way. Cooperation does not mean everyone doing the same thing, the same way, at the same time. Cooperation is everyone contributing their individual skills and understandings in their unique way, just as when we play in an orchestra we must be able to perform our part clearly, even when everyone around us is playing something different. Our internal psychology requires the same type of orchestrated differentiation. At phase SIX, we continue to allow space for the newly emerging or neglected inner voices, especially when the voices of dominant themes threaten to drown them out.

As we give emergent and dissenting voices more space on the internal and external stages of our lives, it can sound like a cacophony. The competing voices of new and old paradigms can leave us feeling confused and uncertain of who and what to listen to, and what to do. Since most of us are uncomfortable with confusion, we must be careful not to suppress the dissenting voices and attempt to return things to the previous status quo. Attempts to repress these voices, either psychologically or socially, will in the long run require force and lead to conflict and wasted energy. Resolution of conflict arises out of unconditional acceptance of the reality of the way things are and the direction life is evolving.

"The opposite of a correct statement is a false statement. But the opposite of a profound truth may well be another profound truth," writes Niels Bohr. Confusion is the initial response to paradox. Boundaries serve to differentiate one thing from another. At any stage of development, we will define ourselves as the kind of person who is this, and not that, for example, we are shy and not outgoing. As we approach this next level of differentiation, we notice we feel shy, but consider reaching out more assertively at the same time. This throws our old way of organizing reality into confusion. However, as Carl Jung explained, creativity and growth come out of the union of opposites.

By embracing opposites, we have a greater experience of wholeness. We recognize, for example, we can be both inward (shy, introspective) and outgoing at the same time by sharing our feelings of shyness with someone. By sharing our inner experience of shyness, we break out of the bonds of that shyness. Being in touch with our inner world will enrich our relating with others, and being in relation with others will enrich our inner experience. We can be simultaneously still and active, knowledgeable and ignorant, strong and weak, and so on. Differentiation involves being certain and uncertain at the same time.

There are structures of thinking and doing that are essential for our evolving existence, and at the same time there are structures that are limiting and can even lead to our own demise. As Havelock Ellis said, "All the art of living lies in a fine mingling of letting go and holding on." No other phase requires us to split our attention more, trying to see both sides of the coin at the same time as much as possible. We simultaneously pay attention to where we might be headed and where we have been. We vigilantly monitor where our significant others and ourselves are, emotionally and physically. We split our attention between desired and undesired outcomes. Being able to anticipate the best and the worst-case scenarios generates motivation to make choices. We pay attention to maintaining certain points of stability while stepping into the chaos of unknown possibilities.

Basic Function — Anticipate

There are theoretical reformers at all times, and all the world over, living on anticipation. *Henry David Thoreau*

Wisdom consists of the anticipation of consequences. *Norman Cousins*

To anticipate is to consider the possible future consequences of our or others' actions. In anticipation of possible futures, we plan and make preparations that will limit undesirable outcomes and maximize positive ones. The maps of experience we have been refining in the previous phase allow us to define patterns with greater accuracy and therefore predict what is likely to happen. Learning from experience creates wisdom. Our deepest wisdom understands the process of evolution: the deepest and most pervasive pattern of all. Every structure of our minds and bodies — with a genealogy rooted in the primordial soup of our planet — is evidence for trusting in the self-organizing nature of an evolving universe. This knowledge is very encouraging.

When asked about their acts of courage, most people respond by saying something to the effect of, "I was just doing what needed to be done at the time." Doing what is needed, rather than reacting out of fear, is the hallmark of differentiation and is based on the acceptance of cause and effect, and the responsibility that comes with that. This kind of knowing is not so much intellectual, but rather an intuition that arises out of one's life experience, combined with the information gained through the study of historical precedents.

In anticipation, we imagine outcomes ranging from the best to the worst-case scenarios. Anticipation can evoke fear and/or excitement. On one hand, we are increasingly aware of the ideas, actions and respective institutionalized relationship patterns that have been oppressive; on the other, there are visions of freedom. Freedom equals choice, and with each choice comes responsibility. To act responsibly is to make informed choices, based on understanding and anticipating what will happen. If the outcomes of our actions prove us wrong then we need to formulate alternative hypotheses.

Fritjof Capra writes, "At the bifurcation point, the system can 'choose' — the term is used metaphorically — between several possible paths, or states. Which path it will take will depend on the system's history and on various external conditions and can never be predicted. There is an irreducible random element at each bifurcation point." [76] At each bifurcation point, there is the inherent choice of either restabilizing in less evolved patterns of organization, or opening to new possibilities of functioning at more highly differentiated patterns of organization. In human terms, we either hold onto our existing identity and ways of thinking and acting, or we open to the unpredictable possibilities of what is trying to emerge into our life.

Although we make decisions based on past experiences and how they have shaped our identities, at the bifurcation point something new and unpredicted emerges. All new choices lead us beyond the territory defined by our existing maps. Our anticipation leads us to make more informed choices, yet the creative nature of our self-organizing universe is always acting through us in innovative ways that take us beyond our best predictions. This is the point of death of old paradigms and the birth of new ones. Anyone who has attended a birth knows what a miracle it is. At this phase it is helpful to anticipate a miracle.

Confusion and Courage

If stupidity got us into this mess, then why can't it get us out? *Will Rogers*

The test of a first-rate intelligence is the ability to hold two opposed ideas in mind at the same time and still retain the ability to function. *F. Scott Fitzgerald*

Our personal integrity — the ability to remain true to our wholeness — enables us to enter into confusion. Confusion is the experience of approaching chaos. To avoid the uncomfortable state of chaos and confusion, we will ignore those things that don't fit into our maps of the world, adhering to the notion that ignorance is bliss. The chaos that we fear could be defined as the phenomena that don't fit into any of our existing maps of how the universe operates. We experience what happens as random and chaotic because we have yet to discover the patterns that will organize our lives at this level of development. Experiencing confusion is the first step to greater wisdom. Those who are always certain only do what they are certain of; in other words, what they have always done. Approaching life in this way avoids confusion and the learning of anything new. Courage is acting with faith in the unknown — the self-organizing nature of the universe.

Having Our Cake and Eating It Too

Personal evolution continues when we are able to accept the agendas of seemingly contradictory voices and open to discovering structures that will support all of them. At the same time, we must free ourselves from beliefs that keep us alienated from parts of ourselves.

A common example of this is seen with couples, when one partner is more dissatisfied with the status quo of the relationship. For some time, both partners may have been relatively comfortable with the way they related to one another, but the wife has become increasingly dissatisfied and wants to have more diversity in the way she experiences intimacy. She's been unconsciously operating under two presuppositions: first, that once married she would live happily ever after, and secondly, that it is normal for a couple to settle into a less passionate, more subdued way of being together. As hard as she tries to re-convince herself of these ideas, some part of her inside continues to feel dissatisfied. She believes in monogamy, but finds herself dreaming and fantasizing of being with another man. She decides she should contact a therapist who recommends she come in with her husband. At one point in therapy, after much of this dilemma has been discussed, she is asked, "What would it be like to have the sort of passion and intimacy you have been fantasizing about (with the other man) with your husband?" In other words, how could she have long-term monogamy and fresh passionate intimacy at the same time?

Her first response to this question is to go into confusion, and say she doesn't think it is possible. It is like asking her to sail around the world, when she believes the earth is flat. However, through further enquiry she is able to generate some hypotheses of what this might be like. Her husband is uncertain about whether these ideas are something that he wants to explore. She is frightened of losing what is good about their relationship, but as she becomes stronger in her resolve to honor her emergent self, she begins relating verbally and non-verbally with her husband in ways that approximate her ideals. Her husband is initially resistant to making a change. She is frustrated, yet remains true to her twin commitments to monogamy and to getting more of what she wants.

After a period of time in which nothing changes, she decides she must make a move. She tells her husband that she is no longer willing to compromise her desire for more passionate intimacy and, unless something changes soon, she will leave the relationship and make herself available to finding it with someone else. When the reality of losing his wife hits home, he is thrown into a crisis; either he expands his ways of relating or lose his marriage. Once he makes the choice to grow, he is able to receive the assistance from his wife and therapist to free himself from the limiting beliefs that have oppressed him. Social systems, such as marriage, evolve to a higher level functioning when we take the differentiated action of remaining true to ourselves while remaining in close proximity to the ones we love.

SEVEN — Exploration and Experimentation

- Primary Question: What is next? What else is possible?
- Developmental Task: Discover
- Basic Function: Plan
- Essential Quality: Joy
- Psychological Domain: New Ideas

Primary Question — What is next? What else is possible?

Free from limiting past beliefs, we are open to new ideas. New ideas allow us to anticipate where new possibilities may lead us. Being able to imagine a richer life, we begin formulating plans of how to experiment with and explore these options. What resonates with our essential joy helps us to discover what our emergent self needs and has to offer others.

Developmental Task – Discover

> Imagination is more important than knowledge. Knowledge is limited. Imagination encircles the world. *Albert Einstein*

> A bifurcation point represents a dramatic change of the system's trajectory in phase space. A new attractor may suddenly appear, so that the system's behavior as a whole 'bifurcates', or branches off, in a new direction. *Fritjof Capra*

To discover is to notice or learn about something for the first time. The root meaning of discover is to reveal or expose. Learning emerges out of our intention to expand our understanding and ways of living. The nature of the universe is what it is; however our ability to perceive it is limited by our belief structures, our senses, and the tools we have to amplify our senses. Discovery often comes from seeing the same-old-same-old in a new light. Freeing our minds from perceptual filters allow us to make sense of things in more enlightening or useful ways, and leads to the construction of more useful maps of the territory we are exploring. Experimenting with the usefulness of our discoveries leads to inventions. Edison discovered that electricity passing through a conductor gave off light, however it wasn't until he ran thousands of experiments that he discovered the effectiveness of tungsten and the light bulb was invented.

Many discoveries are made while experimenting with one new idea, only to find something else. Columbus was trying to find a shortcut to India and ran into America. 'Post-it notes', commonplace in most offices, have a weak adhesive that allows them to be temporarily posted on various surfaces. It was discovered while researchers were looking for a strong adhesive. However, with someone's genius working, they saw the potential of this substance that failed in one context as useful for another purpose. Much of our personal evolution comes with recognizing the value of the parts of us that we have previously perceived as useless. A person who is plagued by worries of what could go wrong realizes that when these thoughts are attended to properly, they enable him to be a good trouble-shooter. The person stuck in ruminations about past disappointments discovers that when she writes about these experiences, she can transform them into soulful poetry or humorous insights.

We are able to make these discoveries when we have been able to differentiate between our maps and the actual territory they describe. Liberating our minds from limiting beliefs allows us discover the inner and outer terrains of our lives more for what they actually are and how to make the most of them.

Basic Function — Plan

> The future belongs to those who believe in the beauty of their dreams.
> *Eleanor Roosevelt*

To plan is to formulate a strategy for the accomplishment of a specific aim or purpose. The more elaborate the plan, the more the details will have been worked out. Working out detailed plans emerges out of our ability as humans to anticipate the consequences of our actions accurately. Imagination enables us to envision futures we would like to have and the steps needed to take to bring them about. The more attention we pay to detail, the clearer our imaginations paint the pictures of where we are heading. It doesn't matter whether we are trying to vivify the past or the future; the more we articulate the various components and the details that comprise those components, the more real our internal imagery appears.

As a simple example, notice the difference between, "I want to write a book and get it published," and "I want to have a book published by a well-known publisher. It will be approximately 400 pages long, with about a dozen diagrams. It will sell in bookstores around the world. I will sell it at workshops that I teach. People will contact me through my website to arrange seminars and book signings. To get it published, I will approach as many agents needed to find one who is enthusiastic about it. To complete it, I will allocate a minimum of twenty hours per week. The chapters will be titled…" The old saying, 'Seeing is believing' is very apt here. Being able to see things clearly in our imaginations helps to create the new conceptual maps needed to arrive at our chosen destinations.

We accumulate knowledge through trying to satisfy our curiosity about the nature of creation and what it has to offer. Our ability to imagine a better life ignites our curiosity to explore beyond the horizons of our known world, discovering people, places and things we never knew existed. How often do we set out on a vacation, with an itinerary all planned out, and when the trip is over, what stands out in our minds are the accidental and spontaneous experiences that we had no way of planning. As John Lennon reminds us, "Life is what happens when we are busy making plans." That said, without having plans in the first place, we never would have gone to the places where new discoveries can be made.

Imagination is the connection between what we know from our experience and our idealized future. Our imaginations elaborate on alternative destinations and ways of getting there. In this phase, our minds are often filled with a wealth of possible options and outcomes. Aristotle said, "It is the mark of an educated mind to be able to entertain a thought without accepting it." Brainstorming sessions maximize the production of creative new ideas by uncensored fantasizing and free-associating. Freedom from constraining 'logic' or 'correctness' facilitates an outpouring of options not usually considered. In the phases leading up to this point, our minds can feel like they are working hard to understand what is happening, where we might be headed and what no longer serves us. In phase SEVEN we have an effortless flood of new perceptions, ideas and options.

It's not until we break with convention that we have the opportunity to find and create new possibilities. As physicist Paul Davies commented, "Creativity happens when we are dancing on the edge of chaos." To be creative, we don't have to break all the rules or to destroy the structure of our lives. An artist doesn't need to stop using all the skills and media she has used to date. Instead, she discovers new choices of how to apply the skills she has, adds new techniques or media to her repertoire, and/or explores new subject matter. Bruce Lee had to completely master Wing Chun Kung Fu before he was able to let go of techniques and distil everything he had discovered to its essence in the creation of Jeet Kune Do.

We dance on the edge of chaos by holding on to what is essential, while letting go of unnecessary limitations, so that we can welcome and explore creative possibilities for a richer and more fulfilling life. Einstein said that theories describing the natural world should not only be the simplest ones available, they should also be beautiful. This is an important point. Useful strategies for creating a better life in the long run inherently include making it more aesthetically pleasing.

Curiosity

> The important thing is not to stop questioning. Curiosity has its own reason for existing. One cannot help but be in awe when he contemplates the mysteries of eternity, of life, of the marvelous structure of reality. It is enough if one tries merely to comprehend a little of this mystery every day. Never lose holy curiosity. *Albert Einstein*

Curiosity leads us to explore new territory, to try new ways of doing things and to put our hypotheses to the test. We learn through trial and error what works best; therefore, the only failed experiment is the one in which we fail to learn something. As with Thomas Edison, our curiosity keeps us exploring and experimenting with new possibilities. Essential joy supports playful curiosity and experimentation. There tends to be no other phase where we have more fun. Like small children who are discovering the world for the first time and never get bored, everything is new and waiting to be enjoyed.

Having freed ourselves in phase SIX from expectations of what or how things are supposed to happen, in phase SEVEN we are free to enjoy whatever is happening in the moment. Although we make plans easily, we aren't yet ready to be too committed and we keep ourselves open to better options should they arise. We are particularly sensitive to and drawn to anything out of the ordinary, as we follow our bliss.

Freely Associating

Our minds tend to make new associations, linking together understandings from one context to another. Our minds are filled with many ideas, like a windy spring day in which pollen from different plants blows around making cross pollination and new hybrids possible. When the Soviet Union collapsed, a level of economic chaos ensued. Free from the old structures, and driven by necessity, people ingeniously began experimenting with new ways of doing things. Whilst it wasn't an easy time, the economy didn't simply collapse. Instead, a new hybrid economy that combined elements of socialism, capitalism, barter and extralegal activities emerged. The people of Russia, at that time, had a certain level of excitement and enthusiasm about the opportunity to create something new — note that currently they are in a different phase.

When a relationship breaks down, we are presented with the realization that our patterns of relating with that person were problematic. Naturally, if we want to create a better relationship next time, we must consider other ways of relating. Getting curious about what works for others can provide us with useful information. The more numerous and varied the new ideas we accumulate, the greater the potential for making new associations and hybridized ways of organizing our relationships.

Margaret's story

Margaret, a client of mine, who had been divorced for two years, had gotten over her grief and was interested in getting involved with someone new. She didn't want to fall into the same patterns of relating she had with her ex-husband and began reading books on relationships. She talked to her friends and others about what they found most helpful, pleasurable and meaningful in their relationships. The more she considered the wide array of ways people organized their relationships, the freer she felt from the old patterns that had constrained her. Being able to consider how others related allowed her to vicariously experience what it would be like to adopt those styles and whether or not she would find them pleasurable. Having imagination means that we don't have to actually *do* everything just to sense if it is right for us. We can imagine it. We can place ourselves into situations and 'test' what they may be like.

Margaret came to realize there were wide variations in how much time couples spent together, how often and what kind of sex they had, the styles of interaction and communication, the level of involvement with extended family, and other aspects of relating. With these options in mind, she began to imagine what it would be like to be with someone in these ways. She was surprised by some of her fantasies. As she began making herself more available and reached out to men, she found herself drawn to different sorts of men than she had been in the past. She was able to consciously experiment with different ways of relating and at other times found that she spontaneously related in new ways.

Quantum Leaps

Networks on the boundary between order and chaos may have the flexibility to adapt rapidly and successfully through the accumulation of useful variations. In such poised systems, most mutations have small consequences because of the systems' homeostatic nature. A few mutations, however, cause larger cascades of change. Poised systems will therefore typically adapt to a changing environment gradually, but if necessary, they can occasionally change rapidly.[77] *Stuart Kaufmann*

experiences and/or ideas that come to us at this phase that can radically alter the course of our lives. Phases ONE to THREE use small variations to improve the overall functioning of our lives. At phase SEVEN, new possibilities can capture our curiosity and enthusiasm and propel us into periods of rapid change. Brandon Bays, in seeking a non-medical intervention for her basketball size tumor, discovered various psychotherapeutic processes that not only led to the elimination of the tumor, but dramatic changes in many facets of her life. She synthesized these methods into a new approach to working with chronic physical and psychological ailments that has proved very useful.

Evolution is more than just random mutations and natural selection. It is the creative process of life reorganizing itself with ever-increasing complexity and diversity. It is in opening to what seems like the chaos of the unknown that we discover the novelty needed to create new patterns of living.

EIGHT — *Self-Reorganization*

- Primary Question: How do I reorganize my life?
- Developmental Task: Mastery
- Basic Function: Implement
- Essential Quality: Will
- Psychological Domain: Identity

Primary Question — How do I reorganize my life?

Discovering what new possibilities resonate with us the most leads to wondering how we can reorganize our life through the implementation of the new ideas and emergent skills. Willful determination drives us to gain mastery of the knowledge and know how, which are gradually woven into the fabric of our emergent identity.

We begin *reorganizing* our lives around the new discoveries we decide to *implement*. Through our *willful* determination we gain *mastery* of new skills and strategies that lead us to a higher level functioning. With mastery, these skills and strategies eventually contribute to a new sense of *identity*. Through further *implementation* we find new ways to contribute and be supported by and give to the communities to which we belong.

Developmental Task — Master

> We are what we repeatedly do. Excellence, then, is not an act, but a habit. *Aristotle*

To master something is to acquire and or demonstrate facility in a specific activity. Mastery implies skill, adeptness, artistry, expertise, proficiency and technique. With mastery comes authority. We achieve command of the language, skills, knowledge and rules of our field of mastery so we can exercise control over all relevant variables. With mastery comes a sense of confidence or self-assurance only achieved through having successfully put our discoveries into practice. Authority is the power to influence others and to facilitate new patterns of organization. In phase SEVEN we visualize outcomes. In phase EIGHT we actualize them.

Through the actualization of our dreams, we master the skills needed to reorganize our lives into higher-dimensions of order. Mastery is not an imposition of something foreign upon us; rather, it is the germinated seeds of development coming to fruition.

Mastery is the integration of our emergent selves into the evolving organization of our lives. Mastery, like parenting, requires us to take responsibility for helping the emergent parts of us to mature into contributing parts of the whole. Like children, each emergent self has unique qualities and gifts that seek a context in which to be expressed. Emergent qualities, like children that challenge parents to expand their self-concept, demand that we expand our identities to include them. They call upon us to do things that we hadn't previously thought was part of our makeup, forcing us to become more of who we can possibly be. The self-organizing universe calls upon us to play our part in its evolution and, in the process, realize just how great we can be. True mastery lies in the will to become the best that we can become, to surrender to the will of what the universe wants us to become, and in the process realize they are one in the same.

Basic Function — Implement

> Do what you can, with what you have, where you are. *Theodore Roosevelt*

To implement is to put something into action or practice. To put something into practice requires practice. Through practice we achieve mastery. Albert Einstein said, "It's not that I'm so smart, it's just that I stay with problems longer." To implement a new strategy or skill we make use of our discoveries and in the process realize their true worth. As we realize the worth of what we have to offer, we realize our own personal worth, and in the process our value to society, family or whatever communities we belong to. It is through implementation that we make a contribution to the greater good. An implement is a tool or instrument used in doing work and/or achieving an objective. By implementing our ideas and talents, we become instruments for the continuing evolution of our world.

If *divine will* is another name for the self-organizing intelligence of the universe then it is in the manifestation of our God-given inspirations and talents that we play our part in the realization of our divine nature. William Jennings Bryant wrote, "Destiny is not a matter of chance, it is a matter of choice; it is not a thing to be waited for, it is a thing to be achieved." We realize our destiny — our divine potential to contribute in the co-creation of life on earth — through the implementation of what inspires us most. Inspiration is the Tao, *divine will* breathing our destinies into us.

Determination and Authority

> Concerning all acts of initiative (and creation), there is one elementary truth, the ignorance of which kills countless ideas and splendid plans: that the moment one definitely commits oneself, then providence moves too. All sorts of things occur to help one that would never otherwise have occurred. A whole stream of events ensues from the decision, raising in one's favor all manner of unforeseen incidents and meetings and material assistance, which no man could have dreamt would have come his way. *W.H. Murray*

In this phase we feel we are, at least in part, masters of our own destinies. The greater the mastery we achieve, the more power we have in shaping the world and our lives. When we are determined to implement our ideas, we do whatever it takes to succeed. It is with this sort of certainty that we solve problems and finely tune our methods. When we are committed to manifesting our dreams, every obstacle is perceived as a challenge to overcome. The more we exercise our determination to overcome obstacles, the stronger our resolve becomes. When we give our whole being to the task, the universe responds in kind and gives us all we need to play out our calling. Committing ourselves fully is an act of surrender to forces that are beyond our control. There is an all-or-nothing quality to our attention. We will give nearly all our time and energy for those things we wish to manifest and almost nothing for those things that are not immediately relevant to our cause. The more time and energy we invest, the more determined we become.

There is a charisma that comes with being so committed to a course of action, and people are naturally drawn to us. They sense the greatness of our vision and want to be a part of it. In our dedication, we walk our talk and earn respect and admiration. We lead by example and command the authority to inspire others to join our cause.

Mastery gives us the authority to instruct others in what to do and how to do it. Since very few great acts are done in isolation, we learn to delegate responsibility and build organizations that can more effectively implement our agendas. New organizations usually spring up around a single person's vision and authority, such as Bill Gates creating Microsoft, Lama Ole Nydahl creating Diamond Bay Buddhism, and Mrs. Fields making her cookies famous.

The organizations created to implement our ideas become important new entities in larger communities. To be viable, new organizations must network with existing organizations. Through the building of these new organizational networks, human culture evolves. Life is always recreating itself in news ways. Implementing what our soul calls us to do is the way me make our contribution to the collective evolution of humanity. Our personal achievements are only possible because of all that humanity has achieved. Many people in this phase have a sense of pleasure at being able to give something back to the web of life that provided a niche for them to live out their dream. Of course, there is no way of paying back our ancestors; all we can do is pay our gratitude forward. Our contributions become the foundations for others to build their dreams upon.

Survival of the Fittest

> The ultimate measure of a man is not where he stands in moments of comfort and convenience, but where he stands at times of challenge and controversy. *Martin Luther King*

Survival of the fittest is a dominant theme in phase EIGHT. The innovations that prove themselves to be more useful or desirable in some way will drive less adaptive ways of doing things into a less dominant position, if not extinction. With the advent of telephones and the Internet, the once great innovation the telegraph has gone the way of the dinosaurs. Automobiles have replaced horses, buggies and saddlery. Horses still have a niche in the world of transport, but it is a much smaller one. The advent of cars paved the way for the creation of niches in which innovations such as rubber tires, paved roads, traffic lights and drive-through restaurants appeared. Through natural selection, the stronger or smarter will survive and replace those who are less effective at adapting to the environment. The innovations themselves change the environment, creating new needs and niches that then must be filled to restabilize the larger system at a higher dimension of order.

Overcoming Inertia

> The horse is here to stay, but the automobile is only a novelty — a fad. *Bank president speaking to Henry Ford's lawyer*

In any large system, immense inertia will resist anything that would upset homeostatic stability. Innovations, once adopted, cause waves of change. At this level we push the boundaries of the status quo of larger systems until we get a reaction.

When we encounter hardships or controversy, we are tested to see how true we will be to ourselves. Some say that the truth comes out in a fight. When we are faced with people or circumstances that seem to stand in our way or defy our will, we cannot fake who we are or what we are made of. We find out if what we are attempting to implement truly stands up to the challenge or if it is simply full of false promises.

Uncovering false promises, however, doesn't mean that what we are doing has no value. It just means we must learn from our mistakes, refine what we are doing and, like Thomas Edison, keep trying to put our promising ideas into action by every possible avenue. The more we practice manipulating the variables, the more we learn to control the circumstances that lead to success.

NINE — Homeostasis (at new level of order)

- Primary Question: How to maintain stability?
- Developmental Task: Cooperate
- Basic Function: Consolidate and Mediate
- Essential Quality: Peace
- Psychological Domain: Environment/Community

Primary Question — How to maintain stability?

At any level of development we learn to maintain stability by maximizing *cooperation* between different aspects of the systems to which we belong. The cooperation needed to maintain *homeostasis* is accomplished by focusing on our relationships with the *environment* and/or *community*, while being informed by our inner *peace*. In doing so, we *consolidate* the growth of the previous change cycle and *mediate* any conflicts that could perturb the newly established *homeostasis*.

Developmental Task — Cooperate

We move from the previous phase of making things happen to letting things happen. Instead of continuing to control and dictate what happens, we learn what it takes to help all parts of the organization we have created, or recreated, to cooperate with one another as smoothly and automatically as possible. As Capra writes, "...we are now beginning to see continual cooperation and mutual dependence among all life forms as central aspects of evolution." [78]

Basic Function — Consolidate

Our institutions have a potent digestion, and may in time convert and assimilate to good all elements thrown in, however originally alien. *Herman Melville*

We consolidate our new ways of doing things by finding ways to merge with existing models or processes within the larger systems to which we belong. We adapt our ways of doing things to fit with the existing culture as much as possible to minimize conflict and maximize cooperation. A larger system's or community's culture is like a *net*work of shared beliefs, values and capabilities in which any string in the net pulls and is pulled by the others, thus perpetually changing its configuration while remaining whole. Our individual effort to implement ideas leads to creating new patterns of organization in a local subsystem. The consolidation of innovations occurs when new patterns of organization are integrated into a larger system of cooperation. The cultural web, having been stretched out of shape, must rebalance it itself to accommodate the changes our efforts have created.

Societies, families and communities, of all sizes and complexity, must evolve to stay vital and healthy. They are dependent on individuals, and the grass roots organizations that form around them, to implement change. To consolidate our efforts and have them assimilated by larger systems, we need to introduce them in ways that maximize their acceptance without compromising their integrity. We naturally tend to network with the individuals and subgroups that are most receptive to our contributions, adapt our communication style to match those we are trying to influence, respect the pace at which our innovations can be assimilated, and make minor alterations to best suit the needs of individuals or subgroups in order to consolidate the new processes into the community's way of doing things.

Bernie's story

Bernie, a college student, returned to his family home having discovered he enjoys hugging his new friends. His family never touched one another much, let alone hugged. To consolidate hugging into his life, he wanted to be able to hug his family members. He realized there was no comfortable way to just start hugging them. On one visit he began touching family members on the shoulder or hand. On his next visit he offered to rub his mother's neck and shoulders when she complained of feeling tense. This process gradually continued over the next few months until he began asking for or offering hugs. Everyone was initially awkward, especially his Dad; but over time, through his consistent efforts, the family incorporated hugging into their network of behaviors. Hugging became a ritualized part of greetings and partings. In addition, family members spread the practice to relatives and friends of the family.

In phase EIGHT we adopt certain beliefs, values and their corresponding practices into an identity related to the context we have been developing. At phase NINE, the new identity finds its place within the community to which we belong. It also finds a place within our internal community of identities, creating a greater sense of self-complexity.

The phases of the change cycle are universal and have been articulated throughout human history. Joseph Campbell's work on the great mythological stories helped to decode these phases that define the Hero's Journey to self-realization.

CHAPTER EIGHT

The Hero's Journey and Buddha's Awakening

A hero is someone who has given his or her life to something bigger than oneself. *Joseph Campbell*

Heroes start out as ordinary people who, faced with a tragedy, crisis, or an irresistible opportunity, go in search of a better life. In order to meet challenges and overcome obstacles, they must unearth qualities and abilities they didn't know they had. Anyone who has felt let down by a parent, lover, health, or any aspect of life, is a prospective hero. We can discover ways of rewriting stories of victimization into tales of transformation and self-realization that can bring greater meaning and purpose to our lives. Psychotherapy can be an invitation to and facilitator of that heroic journey.

Power of Myth and Story Telling

In *The Hero with a Thousand Faces*, Joseph Campbell reminds us of the universality and power of the great myths. His term *monomyth*, or what he calls *The Hero's Journey,* refers to a basic pattern in human consciousness expressed in both Eastern and Western religious and cultural myths. Campbell states,

Mythology is not a lie; mythology is poetry. It is metaphorical. It has been well said that mythology is the penultimate truth

— penultimate because the ultimate cannot be put into words. It is beyond words. Beyond images, beyond that bounding rim of the Buddhist Wheel of Becoming. Mythology pitches the mind beyond that rim, to what can be known but not told.[79]

Since the beginning of time storytellers have enchanted with us with both tales of transformation and enlightenment, as well as myths that urge us to protect certain traditions from change. Stories have the power to promote healing and transformation or to perpetuate ignorance and suffering. By understanding the storytelling process more fully we can not only benefit from the old stories, but also create new ones (and new ways to tell the old stories) that more meaningfully reflect back to us the evolving story of what it is to be human.

Psychotherapy more than anything is a story telling process. People come to therapy because they are caught in reruns of old stories that perpetuate the myths that define them. From the moment therapy begins we want to help people to tell their stories in new ways so that they can discover alternative pathways, rewrite their internal maps and face their demons and challenges with access to more resources. As therapists, we also tell our clients stories that allow them to experience new ideas and perspectives that may assist them in rewriting the stories of their lives. Towards the end of his career, Milton Erickson's primary therapeutic intervention style was a series metaphors and stories designed to loosen up people's rigidities and activate their creative potential.

Storytelling is an innate part of being human and of how we define ourselves. Just as media shapes public opinion and national identity, personal identity is constructed from and maintained by the types of stories we have been told and the stories we tell and retell. These stories are not just told with words, but with images, sensations, and the ways we move and hold ourselves. The language of our bodies, which directly expresses itself through posture and movement, often tells a clearer story than our verbal descriptions, which we have come to think of ourselves as. For example, shoulders held back and chest inflated in defiance, tell a much different story than shoulders rounded in shame, surrounding a chest sunken with despair. Stories that reflect and maintain our identities are expressed symbolically in the unconscious implications of our habitual ways of moving through the world. It is the subtext encoded in how we tell the stories, generally more than just the content of the stories, which reflects how we think of ourselves. One reason film has become such a powerful storytelling medium is that a picture can be worth a thousand words, and moving pictures can say even more. Facial expression, posture, movement, as well as vocal inflection, convey more to us about a character than merely the words read off a page with no dramatic effect.

As we know from coroners and forensics experts, even a corpse can tell stories of the life lived in that body. The rings of a tree and the growth pattern of its branches tell stories of droughts, floods, fires, soil quality, weather, interactions with birds and insects, disease, and other events which express that tree's unique identity. Unlike corpses and trees, however, living human beings have creative choice about how we tell our stories. We can alter the submodalities of our storytelling and in the process the meaning and identity encoded in the story will change. If we change our posture, although we may be speaking the same words, the meaning of our story will change. If we change the sequence in which we relay events or the perceptual position from which we tell the story, the meaning will change. Depending on how details are colored or what is left pale, vague or gray, the meaning will change. In the telling of our stories, components of our experiences are edited, emphasized or minimized to maintain the dominant themes that define who we think we are.

Storytelling evolves as we evolve and the style of our telling reflects the level of integration we have achieved regarding the experiences we are relaying. When describing an ordeal, the first version of our story is generally told as a tragedy, the second as a journalistic account, and in the end it is retold as a humorous tale or wise anecdote. When the same old tragic stories of victimization, subjugation and/or retribution keep showing up, even if the characters and locations change, then we know we aren't learning from those experiences. The way we tell our stories reveals how much wisdom we have or haven't gained. The purpose of therapy is to help people gain wisdom from their life experiences so they can go from being victims to heroes.

George Santayana famously said, "Those who do not remember the past are condemned to repeat it." However it is not only important that we remember the stories of our lives; it is how we remember. Stories that were punctuated at moments in time when we were experiencing ourselves as powerless, victimized or disenfranchised can become chapters of a larger journal of self-discovery. Psychotherapist George Kelly described many of the repetitive problems that people get stuck in as,"…urgent questions, behaviorally expressed, which somehow lost the threads that lead either to answers or better questions." [80] The way we tell our stories can either concretize the old dead-end self-perpetuating stories by concluding, "This is the way it is and will always be," or we can expand our storytelling to, "This is what *has* been; what can I learn and how do I make use of what I'm learning when facing the challenges of life?"

Sometimes therapy can get stuck in reliving painful memories that recreate limited or disempowered states of mind. This merely compels us to act in familiar ways that recreate familiar outcomes. Old tragic myths will continue to be reenacted as long as we remain identified with old emotions and the roles they compel us to play. By stepping back and reviewing the story from a director or author-like perspective, we are also able to re-author the stories so that we create a richer, more robust and liberated sense of self. We can use the Jungian method of *archetypal amplification* to help us reframe our suffering from merely a personal problem to a universal challenge by retelling and reimagining of our story within the framework of mythological archetypes.

Michael White, cofounder of Narrative Therapy, describes the correlations between therapeutic conversations and literature:

> There are some parallels between the skills of re-authoring conversations and the skills required to produce texts of literary merit. Amongst other things, texts of literary merit encourage, in the reader, a dramatic re-engagement with many of their own experiences of life. It is in this dramatic re-engagement that the gaps in the story line are filled, and the reader lives the story by taking it over as their own.[81]

Although the context and text of our individual stories and the heroic stories may vary, the underlying themes are universal. The way we tell our personal stories can determine how we re-author the stories of victimization, disenfranchisement and suffering into accounts of heroic journeys of transformation, healing, growth and self-realization.

Christopher Vogler's guide for screenwriter's[82] articulates twelve stages of a character arc. This, as well as Joseph Campbell's twelve stages of the Hero's Journey, can be mapped onto the Enneagram Developmental Cycle. Layering the twelve phases into the nine phases of the Enneagram Change Cycle adds richness and depth to our understanding and its practical application.

The Journey of a Hero

I have mapped the Buddha's journey to Enlightenment onto the Enneagram. So, we can take inspiration from his story of liberation from suffering, and transform our stories of suffering and the suffering of others into heroic journeys of liberation.

At the end of each phase I have included a list of re-authoring questions you can use to guide your own or other people's heroic journey. To better understand the process of change it can be helpful to review in detail the different phases you or the person you are assisting went through in a previously completed developmental cycle.

The questions can also be used for a change you may want to make, or are currently in the process of making, by answering them as if you had already completed the change cycle. At the end of the chapter, the questions are written in present tense to guide the therapeutic process that you are currently going through.

When answering the questions, take yourself back into particular times and places as vividly as possible. The more experiential the exploration is, rather than conceptual, the more useful it will be, so take your time and allow your memories and imagination to become vivid and deeply felt. The more specific you can be with your answers, the more you will connect with the strategies and states of mind that helped you to make the change. Not all questions may be relevant; however, you will benefit in trying to answer questions that at first glance don't seem relevant, as they may help you connect with something that has occurred outside of conscious awareness, or that you have forgotten. As you write an answer to one question, you may find it leads you to the answer of another question. It may be that as you recount in detail your experiences, your memory will take you through all the stages, and the questions will help to fill in more details. Since life is not necessarily a linear progression of events, you may find that your experience doesn't follow in the exact sequence as outlined. These questions serve as a map, but more importantly than following the map is finding out what is true in one's direct experience.

This outline of questions doesn't take into consideration the internal structure of the Enneagram, which supports the flow around the cycle, especially when we get stuck somewhere in the process. In recounting your own story, you may discover how qualities of these connected Enneagram points supported your journey. Some aspects of the lines of integration and disintegration will be covered in the next chapter on personality types.

Buddha's Story

The name 'Buddha' commonly refers to Siddhartha Gautama, who became enlightened and founded the tradition of philosophy and self-realization we know as Buddhism. The name 'Buddha' also refers to our essential enlightened nature. Enlightenment is the experience of the true nature of mind, which Buddha tells us is timeless, limitless, spacious, radiantly intelligent and full of potential. To follow the Buddhist path is to discover and experience the Buddha nature in everyone, starting with oneself. Taking this path is referred to as taking refuge in the Buddha: one of the Three Jewels of enlightenment. Taking refuge in the Buddha has two meanings: to be inspired by the life of the historical Buddha and to trust in our own essential Buddha-like nature.

The Buddha's story is about one man's heroic journey of self-realization, and it is also a map for all of us to follow in discovering our own Buddha Nature and essential wholeness. Another word for map is 'dharma', the second jewel, which is usually translated as the path, or teachings, to liberation and enlightenment. Learning to tell our personal stories within this heroic Buddha-like structure helps free us from the tragic myths that have dominated our lives so we can not only gain journalistic objectivity, but also discover the joyful wisdom and courageous compassion of our essential wholeness. The third jewel of enlightenment is the Sangha or the spiritual community of friends along the way that support you in realizing your Buddha-nature. It would seem that the first and foremost role of a psychotherapist is to help people to realize their essential wholeness, Buddha-nature, Christ consciousness, self-realization, or whatever name they choose for realizing their potential.

The Enneagram of the Hero's Journey
Cycle of Change
Buddha's Story

Ordinary World
Homeostasis
Secure and luxurious routines of a prince.
Returns home to share his teachings with his family.

Resurrection and Return with the Elixir
Self-Reorganization
Overcomes reluctance to teach, by realizing his oneness with all beings.

Call to Adventure
Awareness of Limitations
Increasing dissatisfaction with palace life and became disturbed when exposed to old age, sickness and death.

Reward & Road Back
Exploration and Experimentation
Explores profound meditation, comes to understand karma and realizes enlightenment.

Refusal of the Call
Adaptive Behavior
Threw himself even further into his indulgence only to become even more frustrated.

Ordeal
Differentiation
Takes his stand under the Bodhi tree. Assailed by all his attachments and fears, but finds what is true.

Meeting with the Mentor Crossing First Threshold
Limits of Capabilities
Chandaka teaches him how to be a better prince; he becomes a father, but leaves the palace to become a spiritual seeker.

Approach to the Inmost Cave
Diffuse Boundaries
Nearly starves himself to death, breaks rules by receiving food from a woman.

Tests, Allies and Enemies
Inadequacies Revealed
Every spiritual teacher failed to help him realize the truth within. In despair he is tempted to return home.

243

How They Line Up

THE HERO'S JOURNEY	ENNEAGRAM	CHARACTER ARC
1. Ordinary World	NINE	limited awareness of problem
2. Call to Adventure	ONE	increased awareness
3. Refusal of the Call	TWO	reluctance to change
4. Meeting with the Mentor	THREE	overcoming reluctance
5. Crossing the First Threshold	THREE – FOUR	committing to change
6. Tests, Allies and Enemies	FOUR	experimenting with 1st stage
7. pproach to the Inmost Cave	FIVE	preparing for the big change
8. Ordeal	SIX	attempting big change
9. Reward (Seizing the Sword)	SEVEN	consequences of the attempt
10. The Road Back	SEVEN — EIGHT	rededication to change
11. Resurrection	EIGHT	final attempt at big change
12. Return with the Elixir	EIGHT – NINE	final mastery of problem

NINE — The Ordinary World

The Ordinary World is the day-to-day world of fairly predictable routines that we are for the most part comfortable in. Our soon to be hero has not yet received her call. "The Ordinary World, in one sense, is the place you came from last. In life we pass through a succession of Special Worlds, which slowly become ordinary as we get used to them. They evolve from strange, foreign territory to familiar bases from which to launch a drive into the next Special World. [83] *Christopher Vogler*

The Buddha was born into the Gautama clan and given the name Siddhartha. His father and mother were the king and queen of the Shakyas. Brahmins told his father that his son would grow up to be a great man, either a universal monarch or a completely enlightened holy man, depending on the path he chose. His father wanted him to be his heir to the throne and to extend his rule. He did all he could to keep Siddhartha ignorant of the outside world, and surrounded him with luxuries and pleasures, hoping he would have no reason to consider the spiritual path. At sixteen, a suitable bride was chosen for him, making his life seemingly complete. Until the age of twenty-eight, he was caught up in carefree pleasures and family expectations.

Many of us grow up in families in which maintaining the status quo is what is of utmost importance. Although our parents may wish for us to have a better life than they had, their concept of a better life is bound within the paradigm in which they operate and perceive as feasible and good. It is important for parents to provide security and safety in the 'womb of childhood' to prepare us for our birth into adulthood. However, to evolve into mature human beings, we must find our own way in life. The sheltered pleasure-filled life of the palace, along with strong family ties, were the backbone of the homeostatic patterns of the family system, and Siddhartha's Ordinary World. Within this stable environment, he learned the ways of his family's world, yet, as Joseph Campbell says, "We must be willing to get rid of the life we planned, so as to have the life that is waiting for us."

Exploring Your Heroic Journey

Milton Erickson would often encourage people to remember and relive earlier learning experiences. In remembering the process of learning to walk or learning the alphabet, or any experience that led to new skills and understandings, people naturally regain their trust in their ability to learn and grow as human beings. Whenever we make a transition from the comfort zone of our ordinary world and learn new things that open new worlds of possibilities, we are engaging on a heroic journey to some extent.

The Ordinary World — How to maintain stability?

1. Describe your *ordinary world* before going through the changes or upheaval in your life.

2. How were your routines in that context or environment different before and after the changes you went through?

3. What did you feel was vital to your sense of security and stability that you eventually outgrew?

4. What relationships or activities helped you to maintain the stability of the status quo?

5. How did you limit exposure to experiences that might have been disturbing, exciting or novel?

6. What did you tend to avoid because it made you or others too stressed.

7. What did you appreciate that outweighed any frustration or dissatisfaction?

ONE — The Call to Adventure

The hero is presented with a problem, challenge, or adventure to undertake.[84] *Christopher Vogler*

When a problem disturbs the peaceful harmony of ordinary life, it demands that the hero take action outside of usual routines in order to regain stability. Problems may come in the form of a tormentor, illness, accident, or injury, escalation of conflict with someone, or mistake(s) whose consequences begin an unfamiliar chain of events. Carl Jung referred to these seemingly random events that precipitate change as *synchronicity*. Archetypal forces orchestrate circumstances to play out in a ways that appear, especially in hindsight, to be destined. In the East, this can be seen as one's karma playing itself out.

A crisis in the community, family or country could require an individual to respond in a new way. It could be an event such as a call to war, drought, famine, sickness or, death of a loved one, threat of foreclosure, loss of a job, discovery of your son's drug addiction, and so on. On the other hand, the call to adventure may present itself as an opportunity for a better life. The would-be hero may be presented with a treasure map, a trip overseas, a business opportunity, a blind date, a genie's lamp, etc. It could also be that a yearning or idyllic dream emerges from the unconscious that highlights the limitations of ordinary life and inspires or compels the hero to seek greater fulfillment. The dream could be of riches, adventure, love, spiritual enlightenment, or a creative enterprise; or it may be that one has just become fed up with one's ordinary life and out of sheer boredom or frustration steps beyond the ordinary, and in the process encounters challenges at or just beyond the boundaries of one's Ordinary World.

> Nonetheless in the course of time the spell of the palace wore thin. When the sorrows and limitations of ordinary life finally began to beat on the prince, they struck him as an insult, an insolent intrusion.[85]

No matter how pleasant our Ordinary World is, something within begins growing frustrated and discontent, and beckons us to consider what lies beyond. At ONE, frustration leads us to discern what it is we are not content with.

There were four encounters that contributed to shattering Siddhartha's contentment with his Ordinary World. Occasionally, he would have outings outside the palace with a charioteer named Chandaka as his guide. The King carefully orchestrated these outings and care was taken to remove anything from Siddhartha's sight that was unpleasant. Nonetheless, on one fateful outing, Siddhartha had his first disturbing encounter with a very old man, the second with a man suffering from disease, and the third with a corpse. These three encounters, along with Chandaka's ensuing explanation that old age, sickness and death were all unavoidable aspects of life, left the prince disturbed, and he found increasingly less enjoyment in the pleasures of the palace. On the fourth fateful outing they encountered a holy man whose serene and radiant demeanor profoundly impressed Siddhartha. Chandaka's explanation of the spiritual path of renunciation sent Siddhartha into deeper rumination.

Exploring Your Heroic Journey

The Call to Adventure — What is not right? What is the ideal?

1. What were the first signs (calls to adventure) that told you something needed to change?
2. What was frustrating or unfair about your circumstances?

3. How did you cope with those frustrations or injustices?
4. How did you try to fix what you thought was wrong?
5. How was your life at the time not matching up to how you thought it ideally should be?
6. What were you most critical of in yourself or others?
7. What mistakes were most difficult to admit to yourself?
8. What ethical considerations or dilemmas came into focus?
9. What concerns were important for you to take more seriously?
10. How did trying to do the 'right thing' help (or not help) you discover what you really needed?
11. How did focusing on certain details clarify the need for change?
12. How did expressing your anger or frustration help you to connect with your needs?

TWO — Refusal of the Call

The question now arises of how the hero will respond to the 'Call'? The initial tendency is to try to re-stabilize back into his ordinary life, and possibly make excuses why he shouldn't take up the challenge or opportunity. The hero's reluctance indirectly points out what resources are needed to answer the Call. His refusal also highlights the limiting and self-perpetuating (or addictive) nature of the patterns of his Ordinary World, and therefore the need for change. The hero's dependence on others, their dependence on him, or mutual codependency are powerful restraints. The hero's weaknesses, doubts, and attachments exposed at the beginning of the journey often foreshadow crises yet to come, when these factors must be addressed if the hero is to realize his potential.

In hoping to provide his son with a diversion from his turmoil, the king sent Siddhartha to a nearby village to observe their farming practices. However, when he saw the suffering these practices caused the oxen and the slaves, out of compassion he freed both the beasts of burden and the slaves from their bondage.

At TWO it is often easier to see what others need more clearly than our own needs. We'll even project our emergent needs on to other people and do for them what we need to do for ourselves. Siddhartha was feeling enslaved by the bonds of his life, yet was only able to make a symbolic approximation of a step toward his own freedom by freeing the oxen and slaves.

The life of a spiritual seeker called out to Siddhartha, magnifying his discontent, yet he continued his shallow decadent way of life. Finally, late one night after an evening of particularly hedonistic indulgence, he realized the futility and emptiness of these preoccupations.

We often need to go to the extreme of our habits or addictions before we realize that no matter how much we have or do, it is not what we need to be fulfilled.

Exploring Your Heroic Journey

Refusal of the Call — What's needed?

1. What was life trying to get you to embrace that you attempted to avoid?
2. What helped you to deal with your frustration and begin moving towards your ideals?
3. What self-limiting patterns were you resistant to changing?
4. Who did (and didn't) you feel you could ask for help?
5. What enabled you to overcome pride so you could admit you needed help?
6. Whose approval or disapproval did you feel you needed?
7. What helped you to separate your needs from the needs and expectations of others?
8. Who's behavior did you try to change, rather than changing your own?
9. How did your dependence on others help or hinder you take the necessary steps?
10. How did others' dependence on you, help or hinder your ability to take the necessary steps?
11. How did you begin attending to neglected aspects of your life?
12. How did the goodwill you had created with others come back to support you in making a change?
13. How did your need for independence help you to take more responsibility?

THREE — Meeting with the Mentor

Mentors prepare the hero for his journey. They help him to develop the capabilities needed for facing upcoming challenges. Mentors empower heroes with maps (made by those who have gone before), tools or weapons, instruction in specific skills or strategies, healing of old wounds, exercises to strengthen weaknesses, or the discipline needed to begin severing the ties with old attachments and habits. Mentors introduce the hero to the path he must eventually travel on his own.

The word 'mentor' comes from the Greek 'menos' that can mean intention, force, or purpose, as well as mind, spirit, or remembrance. As Christopher Vogler reminds us, "Mentors in stories act mainly on the mind of the hero, changing his consciousness or redirecting his will. Even if physical gifts are given, mentors also strengthen the hero's mind to face an ordeal with confidence."[86] Developing capabilities and confidence is represented by the transition from TWO to THREE and helps heroes find the courage needed to respond to their calling.

Heroes can get stuck at this stage by simply modeling or walking in their mentor's footsteps. Students must leave their teachers, just as children must leave their parents to discover their unique path and calling in life.

Chandaka's role with Siddhartha evolved from that of chaperone to mentor. With preparation for the journey nearly complete, he accompanied Siddhartha to the border of the First Threshold. Each threshold of the journey has room for just one person to cross at a time and mentors must be left behind if the hero is to put his learning to the test beyond the borders of the Ordinary World. Siddhartha eventually benefits from two more significant mentors further along his journey.

Crossing the First Threshold

Deciding to take action, the Hero crosses the first threshold by confronting the problem or challenge he faces. Although there is always more to be learned or training that could be done, the hero must put his emergent capabilities to the test. The real lessons in life cannot be learned in the classroom or the therapist's office; eventually our learnings must be put to the test in the world. Through experience, the hero discovers what these capabilities are really for. Initiating purposeful action commits him to the journey and makes it nearly impossible to return to his Ordinary World. For some, it seems that external circumstances compel them to take action. For others, it's as if their soul is pushing its way into consciousness, forcing the hero to ask the question, "Am I going to keep living my life in this way, or will I follow my dreams for a chance at a better life?"

At THREE the hero takes responsibility for finding what is needed to begin fulfilling his destiny and realizing his potential. Siddhartha let go of the harem girls and boozing it up and focused on being a better husband, son and prince. However, succeeding in his ordinary world was still not enough. He was plagued by dissatisfaction. It is the inherent unsatisfactoriness of the ordinary world that eventually outweighs the safety, status and pleasure. The more we succeed in that world, the more we become compelled to forge a new path.

Not long after the birth of his son, Siddhartha decided to leave his secure life and enter the path of a homeless spiritual seeker. It is said that he swore not to return until he realized enlightenment. By making this promise to himself, he was committing to doing whatever was needed to reach his goal. All great journeys begin with a single step, but the hero initiates that step. The decision can't be made for him or merely be a consequence of preceding events. If the hero hasn't really made up his mind or hasn't committed himself wholeheartedly, the tests that will beset him will cause him to turn back. Sometimes more suffering or dissatisfaction is needed, and sometimes more preparation, before the hero can make a vow to do whatever is needed to realize his aspirations.

Although we may have role models or internal images of hope, no one really knows where our heroic journey will take us. Yet, everyone must begin somewhere, and it is the hope for a better life that motivates and empowers us to get the ball rolling. The first steps towards our goals are often external or superficial, symbolic demonstrations of our commitment to change that get us moving in the right direction.

Crossing the First Threshold is represented by the movement from THREE to FOUR on the Enneagram. At FOUR the hero discovers his unique gifts. At the same time, by putting his developing capabilities to the test, he will become more aware of his inadequacies and/or woundedness.

Eric Lyleson

Exploring Your Heroic Journey

Meeting with the Mentor and Crossing the First Threshold — How to begin?

1. What did you learn from your mentors or tor-mentors?
2. How did you initiate change?
3. To whom or what did you first reach out to?
4. What step out of your usual routine helped you start something new in motion?
5. What under-utilized capability did you exercise when initiating change?
6. How did you find the strength to make the initial step?
7. What image of yourself in the future helped you to feel you could get to where you wanted to go?
8. Which role models did you emulate or were you inspired by?
9. What did you tell yourself to help motivate you?
10. Who, if anyone, did you hope would notice your efforts?
11. What did you need to ignore or disregard to get the ball rolling?
12. How did your naiveté of what you were getting yourself into help you get started?
13. What sort of promises or oaths did you make to yourself?

FOUR — Tests, Allies and Enemies

Having crossed over the First Threshold, the hero is faced with circumstances for which old rules and maps don't apply. There is a need to discover new strategies and rewrite the maps he has been given in order to progress on the journey. Joseph Campbell referred to this new special world as "a dream landscape of curiously fluid, ambiguous forms, where he must survive a succession of trials." The inadequacies and inappropriateness of old myths and rules that previously governed the hero become more apparent as he faces new challenges. People learn from trial and error. Without trials there can't be errors, without errors there is not likely to be true learning. Milton Erickson, M.D. was known to say, "The good thing about falling flat on your face, is at least you know you are heading in the right direction." Campbell says it a little differently: "It is by going down into the abyss that we recover the treasures of life. Where you stumble, there lies your treasure."

"Heroes open themselves up to priceless learning when they recognize what they don't know or admit they have been mistaken.

The confidence that was gained through our mentoring at THREE can quickly turn to feelings of inadequacy and hopelessness. To progress, heroes must see the hopelessness of applying the old rules and strategies of the Ordinary World to the emerging circumstances of the journey. Old self-concepts and belief systems must be seen through so heroes can find out what is true. Heroes often feel like they are going mad, or even becoming suicidal; however, thoughts like, "I can't go on living" are realized to mean, "I can't go on living *like this* anymore," because the old ways of living are no longer adequate and there has got to be a better way. The hero undergoes a metaphoric death, a loss of identity or ego death, as he enters into what Thomas Aquinas called the long dark night of the soul. Hardships and failures can leave the hero wondering why he bothers with the struggle. To find the answers he must search within his soul to connect with his core values and what matters most — a deeper motivation.

At this stage, the hero discovers who his allies and enemies are — learning to discern which inner voices can or can't be trusted. All trust is ultimately related to self-trust and the ability to be honest with oneself. The more honest the hero is with himself and sees through his own deceptions, the easier it becomes to discern who would deceive him from who is there to support him on his journey.

What we experience as an enemy at phase THREE, such as despair, we can realize at phase FOUR is in actuality an ally. In Vajrayana Buddhism this is depicted by the images of wrathful deities, sometimes known as protectors. A protector might show up, like it did in Gautama's life, as a growing dissatisfaction and despair. This served as Gautama's ally in seeking out a more meaningful life and protected him from getting trapped by the seductions of wealth and power.

The essential quality of FOUR is forgiveness. To forgive is to put the past behind and embrace each emerging moment uniquely. Forgiveness is not always instantaneous. Often the hero needs to repeatedly see how reactions based on past experiences perpetuate suffering, before being willing to let go of the past and responding more creatively. Being willing to forgive rather than punish encourages honesty about mistakes. We can see this in the child whose parents treat him like he's doing the best he can and who explore where he went wrong, compared with the child whose parents punish and humiliate him for his mistakes. One child learns to embrace his inadequacies with curiosity, while the other learns to hide his inadequacies to avoid shaming. Being able to honestly face the consequences of our mistakes is all that is needed to be motivated to learn a better way. No one can mold a hero's behavior; he must find what works for himself.

When Siddhartha crossed the boundaries that defined his homeland for the first time in his life, his fearful mind (Mara) tempted him to go back, wooing him with promises of great power and dominion over the whole world. Siddhartha reminded himself that finding enlightenment and bringing freedom to the world, rather than ruling it, is what his heart genuinely longed for. However, this temptation would haunt him whenever confronted with his fears and inadequacies.

After taking the initial steps on the new path, old attachments and weaknesses haunt the hero and test his resolve. Circumstances can arise that seem to promise even an easier and more abundant life back in the Ordinary World. One marijuana smoker reported that immediately following his commitment to leave his habit behind people began offering him large amounts of the finest marijuana at no cost. We've probably all had the experience of resolving to give something up, such as eating sweets, only to be confronted with a situation, such as party, where that very behavior is possible, and even encouraged.

Temptations help the hero clarify what he wishes to honor most. Just because he makes a conscious decision to let go of old attachments, doesn't mean they go away; they will continue to tempt him and these challenges will reveal his weaknesses. At THREE there is a connection to NINE and the social systems to which we belong will often exert their influence to pull heroes back into the Ordinary World prematurely. People are frightened of change, and when one person changes, it destabilizes the lives of the people they have been involved with. The people who are most connected to the hero may try to stop him before he goes beyond the point of no return.

As the story continues, Siddhartha gives his fine jewelry to Chandaka to return to the palace. He then cuts his hair and exchanges his fine garments with those of a deer hunter, whose clothing was similar to the style worn by spiritual seekers. Changing the external image he presents to the world is part of the transition from THREE to FOUR. At THREE people dress to show off their status in the ordinary world. At FOUR the hero will adopt styles of dress or presentation that symbolically represent his deeper values and differentiate these from the values of his Ordinary World.

Siddhartha learned to beg for his food and sleep on the ground with no shelter. He realized that he needed to find a teacher, and shortly there after he was led to one. After learning, with relative ease, the metaphysical teachings and meditative practices of this first teacher, he moved on to a second, who helped deepen his practice. Both teachers offered Siddhartha leadership of their respective spiritual communities, but he declined. In a way, they were inviting him to live like a prince within the spiritual community, simply recreating his ordinary world in a different context. Instead, feeling there was nothing further he could learn from them, he followed his longing with an even deeper commitment to his goal of enlightenment.

Having succeeded in developing certain capabilities, there can be a temptation to use these gifts indulgently to enhance or recreate our ordinary world, rather than using them to continue the journey into the realm of unknown possibilities.

Exploring Your Heroic Journey

Tests, Allies and Enemies — What gets in the way? What do I really want?

1. What difficulties, flaws, inadequacies or insecurities tested your resolve?
2. Who tried to lead you astray?
3. Who or what helped you to remain true to your deeper calling?
4. How did you attend to your weaknesses?
5. What past grievances did you need to forgive or move through?

6. What deeper longings or desires did you become aware of in that difficult time?
7. What dreams helped to propel you forward in spite of the difficulties?
8. What did you envy about other people's lives that helped to remind you of what was most important to you?
9. How did your own unique qualities or creativity aid you?
10. How did your own unique qualities or creativity lead you to greater challenges than you expected?
11. How did your feelings about mundane day-to-day activities change?
12. How did sadness or disappointment help you do the soul searching needed to listen to your deeper calling?

FIVE — Approach to the Inmost Cave

The hero comes at last to the edge of a dangerous place, sometimes deep underground, where the object of the quest is hidden. Often it's the headquarters of the hero's greatest enemy, the most dangerous spot in the special world, the Inmost Cave. When the hero enters that fearful place he will cross the second major threshold. Heroes often pause at the gate to prepare, plan, and outwit the villain's guards.[87] *Christopher Vogler*

The hero may, or may not, be consciously aware that he is approaching the greatest ordeal of his journey. However, it is natural after having been through various tests, and having encountered enemies and made allies, to stop and take stock of what he does and doesn't know — to reflect on where he has come from and where the journey may be taking him. His sense of what lies ahead, along with the knowledge of the Special World he has gained, will help him determine what is needed to survive and succeed in his quest. By stepping back from life, he tries to make sense of his experiences within a broader framework. As the bigger picture comes into focus, the hero encounters the limitations of his old maps. Many of his new experiences just don't make sense within the context of his existing understanding of the world. The more he learns, the more he realizes he doesn't know. This heightens the hero's awareness of less obvious details and how they might fit together with what he has already learned into a predictable pattern. The wisdom found in these patterns prepares the hero for upcoming ordeals.

Illusionary temptations may seduce the hero into staying in this transitory state, promising safety from the challenges that await him. It's like being trained and coached as a swimmer, improving competition by competition, and then, when faced with the championship race that you have always dreamed of winning, saying to yourself, "Who needs to compete in the big race? I know what I need to know. Who needs all that pressure? I may not win anyway." With meditation, people will learn how to relax and be comfortable. Instead of using that platform to open to more profound states and enlightened consciousness, they get seduced by the comfort and pride of knowing that much, or even believing, 'This is as good as it gets.'

As part of the hero's preparation, he may enter into another special world where additional lessons and further preparations for his upcoming ordeal are made. In this period of approach, the smaller challenges he faces help the hero accumulate additional resources and learnings. Even though these smaller challenges might be perceived as a diversion, they nonetheless bring him closer to facing his greatest nemesis or fear. These smaller challenges are not always handled successfully, however heroes learn and become stronger from failure, as well as success. It may even appear that the hero hasn't learned from his mistakes; he's missed his chance and all hope is lost. Luckily, life is patiently forgiving and, short of death, new opportunities do arise to overcome fear and realize one's potential.

In a further attempt to free himself from the attachments that held him in the transient world of birth, old age, sickness and death, Siddhartha followed the yogic tradition of engaging in extreme ascetic practices. He committed himself wholeheartedly to these practices in order to attain enlightenment or die. Having pushed himself to the limit and coming close to death, he had failed to transcend the ordinary human state. Feeling weak and disheartened he enjoyed the special sweet rice dish that was brought to him by a young woman, and began eating one meal a day again. Even looking at a woman, let alone receiving food from a woman, was considered one of the greatest transgressions a spiritual seeker at that time could make. His companions and followers were appalled with him for abandoning the path, renounced him, and went on their way.

At FIVE, the hero explores all that can be learned from others or by known means. However, realization of our true nature and full potential can never be found in formulas or concepts. It can only be found through relinquishing what we know and opening to the unknown. Following others' paths can bring us to the edge of the known, yet there is no path into the unknown. Every hero must open to what is true for him, not what is correct according to any system. In the Inmost Cave, the hero discerns what is necessary to survive and must sort what is essential from what must be abandoned in preparation for the supreme ordeal.

Allies and others who support the hero's journey can only accompany him so far. As with Siddhartha, only the most revered companions can travel with the hero to the threshold of his ordeal, which he must then inevitably face on his own.

Exploring Your Heroic Journey

Approach to the Inmost Cave — Why am I going through this?

1. What mistakes did you make? How did they help you deal with later challenges?
2. What sustained or kept you going through the most difficult times?
3. What did you find you needed to have space from?
4. Where did you retreat in order to digest your experience up to that point?
5. How did detachment help you to put the different elements of your life into perspective?
6. What beliefs kept you going, or helped you to make sense of the difficulties?
7. What helped you realize what was essential and what was expendable in your life?

8. How did you go about gaining the information and skills needed to support the change?
9. Who, or what sort of things, did you emotionally detach yourself from?
10. How did not taking things personally help to put things into perspective?
11. How did you maintain some sense of predictability in that time of flux?
12. What ways did you have of compartmentalizing different aspects of your life that helped you gain objectivity or clarity?
13. What patterns of thinking, feeling and behaving were you able to step back from and examine objectively?

SIX — Ordeal

This is a critical moment in any story, an Ordeal in which the hero must die or appear to die so she can be born again. [88]
Christopher Vogler

At the Supreme Ordeal, the hero often hits rock bottom, as he faces his greatest challenge. Fear-based beliefs and associated habits with must be challenged and overcome. Heroes will say things like, "This isn't me. I don't do things like this." In some circumstances, the hero must face his own mortality, but in most cases it is the ego that must die. In facing his greatest fears, he disproves some of the core beliefs his identity is based upon and discovers that, thankfully, he isn't who he feared he was.

Ambivalence can leave the hero frozen in indecision. However, when the hero can see both sides of a concern equally, fear and judgments can dissolve into deep acceptance of things as they are. Ambivalence is part of the process of dissolving 'either/or ', 'good/bad' thinking. Embracing ambivalence facilitates 'both/and' logic, an understanding that things are both good and bad, and getting better and worse, all the time. It is a delusion to believe that life will continue forever in one direction or conform to our notions of what is right. We will not live forever without dying. No one will be the perfect husband or wife, and we are not going to live happily ever after. Ambivalence leads us to accept that we will live and die, that people have strengths and weaknesses, there will be happiness and sadness, ease and struggle, and so forth. Acknowledging ambivalence has the effect of freeing us from limiting concepts and creates an opening for new ideas or possibilities to come to us.

The ordeal is the major crisis in the story, in contrast with the climax when the characters find some sort of resolution. Webster's dictionary defines crisis as, "The point in the story or drama at which hostile forces are at the tensest state of opposition." It is the turning point, where the hero either moves towards defeat or victory, death or recovery, yet hasn't found what he is seeking, or arrived at his desired destination.

The hero may nearly die, or appear to be defeated, only to discover some deeper strength or courage. Having faced the fear and survived, the fear is no longer the obstacle it was. Many fears are expressions of his Shadow: aspects of the psyche that haven't been accepted or integrated. He must reconcile parts of himself that have been denied or avoided. In Jungian psychology, this is referred to as the integration of opposites. In the attempt to maintain his limited self-image, what is feared or unacceptable is often denied and projected on to others. If we have a generally negative self-image, we will tend to project our good qualities on to someone else, idolizing them and being unable to accept praise. If we have a positive self-image, we will tend to project our own disowned negative qualities onto someone else. We experience our essential wholeness when we accept the positive and negative qualities, the light and the dark, and as a consequence, identification with a self-image becomes less relevant.

Enemies and villains can be looked at as symbolic representations of the hero's Shadow. No matter how alien the enemy's values, in some way, they are the dark reflection of the hero's own desires magnified and distorted — his greatest fears come to life. What we judge others for is often a disowned part of ourselves that we have yet to accept and integrate. The hero needs this acting out of his inner conflict and polarization to clarify the consequences of his perception of the world and himself. If he has been identified with being cowardly and weak, he must accept his courage and strength. Conversely, if he has been identified with being courageous and strong, he must accept his cowardice and weakness. If he has seen himself as the good guy, he must accept the part of him that can do bad things. If he has been identified with being the bad guy, then he must accept his potential for goodness. Only inflated egos suffer the humiliation of failure and defeat. Humiliation teaches the hero humility — the acceptance that there is more to life and oneself, than what can be consciously controlled. Transformation results from having faith in the unknown and embracing the mystery of life.

The ordeals a hero faces bring his self-defeating patterns even more into focus. These conditioned patterns, maintained by guilt and fear, take the form of sloth, anger, pride, deceit, envy, greed, fear, gluttony, or lust — sometimes known as sin, which in its original meaning, derived from archery, translates as 'missing the mark'. The ego's motto is 'seek but do not find', as it tries to keep the hero focused on petty alienating preoccupations, rather than surrendering to the unconditional greatness of his essential wholeness.

Siddhartha sat down under a tree and vowed not to move from that spot until he attained enlightenment or died trying. However, Mara, the fear-driven egoic mind, doesn't give up that easily. In fact, the ego, when it sees we are ready to disinvest in it, tries all the tricks in its repertoire. Siddhartha was assailed with doubts, guilt, worries and insecurities. When Siddhartha remained unmoved, then came all the promises of fulfilling desires for security, romance, sex, pleasure, wealth and power. Unmoved by these temptations, his ego mind assaulted him with icy terror and then burning rage and then utter despair and hopelessness. As Campbell says, "He must put aside his pride, his virtue, beauty and life, and bow or submit to the absolutely intolerable."

When Siddhartha failed to become entranced by any of these, Mara then tried one last trick, asking him, "What have you done to deserve freedom?" At this point, Siddhartha touched the ground and declared the earth as his witness of his right to be there. Symbolically and literally, he was proclaiming that the ground is real, and all the disturbing and distracting fabrications of the ego mind are unreal.

By staying mindfully present and not giving in or acting out our disturbing emotions, nor indulging our tempting desires, all of these things fall away and we settle into the ground of Being. We realize the essential wholeness of our buddha nature, that which has always been free. It is Freedom itself.

Exploring Your Heroic Journey

Ordeal — What do I remain faithful to and what do I need to let go of?

1. What from your old lifestyle was most frightening to face or let go of?
2. What did you come to accept about yourself and the world we live in that helped you to face reality more directly?
3. What were your greatest fears and doubts?
4. What helped you to face your fears and find the courage to follow your heart?
5. How did your worries help you to prepare for upcoming challenges or possible pitfalls?
6. What authorities, institutions, or rules did you find yourself in conflict with or questioning?
7. Which loyalties supported the change and which seemed to hold you back?
8. Who were your allies and who seemed to be your opponents, oppressors or enemies?
9. Whose approval or friendship did you feel you had to risk losing to be true to yourself?
10. What concepts about yourself or the world you lived in did you question or feel confused about?
11. What greater cause, or societal change, did you come to realize your own personal evolution was a part of?
12. Who or what seemed to have less control over you as you found more faith in yourself?

SEVEN — Reward (Seizing the Sword)

Having survived death, the hero takes possession of the treasure he has been seeking. It could be a sword, the Holy Grail, a jewel, a sacred text, a magical healing elixir, a lover's heart, enlightenment, or anything else personally meaningful to the hero. The prize is not always freely given to the hero, even if it has been paid for or earned. Instead, it must be taken. Campbell refers to this process as *elixir theft*.

Having met the challenge of the Ordeal, the hero is often initiated into a higher level of recognition by his peers, his superiors, or even the gods (those forces that guide fate and luck). At SEVEN it is like the hero has died and now is reborn at a higher level of functioning. Sometimes the hero is given or chooses a new name that reflects the newly emerging identity. In some Native American cultures, in the transition from adolescence to adulthood, a mature adolescent must venture into the wilderness on a vision quest. When they have crossed the threshold to adulthood, a name will come to them in a vision that embodies who they envision themselves becoming as a more responsible member of the community. The new name inspires the young person to explore new ways of living, but he has yet to discover whether he can truly live up to it.

Siddhartha effortlessly opened to ever deeper and more profound meditative states. Resting in the vast emptiness of that which is unborn, undying and uncreated, he was liberated from the suffering of birth, old age, sickness and death, and could clearly see the circular nature of suffering and the laws of cause and effect (karma). Seeing through the last traces of ignorance, he realized enlightenment and became Buddha. He contemplated teaching his realizations, but the idea of overcoming the stubbornly delusional nature of people's thinking seemed too difficult.

At SEVEN the rewards of his efforts are now the hero's for the taking. Having broken the bonds of his old identity and corresponding belief system, new experiences and insights come freely and easily, as he savors the elixir of enlightenment. New perceptions may come as epiphanies, such as an enlightening realization of one's true nature, the experience of being at one with the universe or God, or simply the profound experience of being a loving human being. His mind is naturally curious to explore, experiment and entertain new possibilities. The hero is inspired by the freedom of following his bliss and what comes easily. His sense of blessed abundance leads to a natural inclination to pass on the good fortune. He is open to considering various options, but is not yet ready to commit to anything too challenging. However, one of the consequences of having faced the ordeal and gaining the elixir of enlightenment is that the journey will demand more of him before he returns to the Ordinary World.

Exploring Your Heroic Journey

Reward (Seizing the Sword) — What is next? How do I enjoy what I have realized?

1. How did giving yourself permission to act spontaneously or seize an opportunity lead you to new places or open new options?
2. What new possibilities did you become aware of and how did you begin exploring them?
3. What new associations or insights expanded your perception of what was possible?
4. Where did you go or whom did you meet that helped open up new possibilities for you?
5. What did you feel free from, that once you felt stuck in?
6. What sort of options did you consider before committing to a specific path?
7. How did keeping your options open assist you?
8. What sort of plans or fantasies helped you to feel optimistic?
9. What helped you to avoid being pulled back into old habits?
10. How did freeing yourself from responsibilities support you in making new discoveries?
11. What part did luck or grace seem to play in helping you to find what you were looking for?
12. What sorts of things that you previously judged negatively were you able to see in a more positive light?
13. How did feeling you deserved something better influence you?

EIGHT — The Road Back

The demons or enemies the hero has subdued or overcome may come back with a vengeance at this stage. The stakes are usually higher than with the Supreme Ordeal and the hero needs to rededicate himself to change in order to conquer his old nemesis and gain mastery of his new domain. If he fails, he stands to lose the rewards gained previously. The challenge is to gain mastery of what he has learned, discovering how to make use of it and manifest it in the ordinary world he returns to. Heroes don't keep treasure for just themselves, or only use their power for their own selfish gains; they find a way to share the wealth. This process of integrating his new found enlightenment into his life provides challenges that often mirror those faced in the Supreme Ordeal and tests the hero's commitment to his newly realized powers and insights.

Out of compassion, and the recognition that he couldn't really separate himself from the rest of humanity, the Buddha consented and committed himself to passing on what he had realized. At EIGHT we open to Universal Will — our part to play in the Dharma. There is a connection to FIVE, which enables us to see the big picture and where we fit in it. However, seeing the immensity of what life asks of us can be extremely overwhelming, causing us to balk. The inner connection to TWO reminds us of our relatedness to all beings, and that compassionate awareness helps determine what roles we choose to play in making our contribution to the evolution of the Ordinary World (NINE).

The Buddha began teaching the Eightfold Path and the Four Noble Truths. Students asked to be ordained as monks and he began to establish a community of followers in the Deer Park near modern-day Varanasi in India, where he first began teaching. The Buddha, having chosen to dedicate the benefit of his realization to all of humanity, invited those who chose to walk in his footsteps to take the Bodhisattva Vow to do everything in their power to liberate all beings from suffering. The hero realizes the more he shares the elixir of enlightenment, the more he receives the benefits — increasing his abundance and consequently his ability to make a difference, in a self-perpetuating feedback cycle.

Resurrection

The Resurrection stage is a second life-and-death moment, almost a replay of the death and rebirth of the Ordeal. In defeating his old nemesis, the hero establishes himself more firmly in his new identity. He is no longer the kind of person who is at the mercy of those forces that previously controlled or threatened him. He is freer to manifest a greater destiny. The hero's mastery of newly acquired understandings, redefined values, and emerging capabilities enable him to take action towards his evolving ideals, and are incorporated as enduring aspects of his personality into a new social identity.

There is often a catharsis, some sort of purging or declaration of his deepest truth. Emotions that have been denied may come pouring out when he owns up to the truth. In therapy, when people make profound shifts in their beliefs or ways of relating, there is often an outpouring of grief for the suffering of the past and all of the missed opportunities. The hero bows to his deepest truth — God's Will or Dharma. By living his deepest truth, he honors his role in the unfolding of creation. Campbell says, "The goal of life is to make your heartbeat match the beat of the universe, to match your nature with Nature.

"This often requires sacrificing a habit or belief that is contradictory to the person he is becoming. The definition of sacrifice is 'to make sacred'. To make sacred is to honor what is true. By overcoming his reluctance to teach, Siddhartha honored the Dharma and in the process of answering his true calling, realized his role as Buddha.

Another consequence of the truth coming out is that justice will prevail. Those who have honored the truth will be rewarded and those who have dishonored the truth will suffer the consequences. Rather than happening at some far-off Judgment Day, this happens in each and every moment where truth is honored, and those whose fear-driven minds hold onto erroneous views and behaviors intrinsically suffer from misperception, conflict, and other difficulties.

It is important here to distinguish between justice and revenge. Revenge is doing unto others as they have done unto us. Justice is the natural consequence of one's actions. The seeds of our actions determine the conditions of the Ordinary World to which we return. Buddhists teach that when you die, the tendencies of your mind (your views, beliefs and habits) become the theme (your karma) of your next incarnation. This pattern can also be seen in the way a person ends one relationship, particularly the unresolved issues, which often then become the theme for the next one. The end of a relationship is not just the physical separation, as emotional completion usually takes much longer, and that which has not been worked through and put to rest, tends to get reenacted over and over again until it is. Revenge is one of the most common ways people stay stuck in victimization, blaming and trying to play God, rather than learning their lessons and surrendering to the natural consequences of life.

Exploring Your Heroic Journey

The Road Back and Resurrection — What do I want to master or manifest?

1. What new things did you eventually commit yourself to?
2. What did you claim as your own, even if it meant fighting for it?
3. What new rules did you make, and how did you alter them to fit your objectives?
4. How did you decide to make the most of your circumstances?
5. What fueled your determination?
6. How did you have to discipline yourself to accomplish your objectives?
7. What temporal and spatial boundaries did you need to set up to do this?
8. In what way did your self-concept change?
9. How did the way you identify yourself change? What sort of a difference did it make taking on a new title (mother, father, student, job title, husband, wife, adult, spiritual seeker, etc.)?
10. Whose opinions or feelings did you need to dismiss, at least for a period of time, to manifest your dream or desire?
11. What personal needs or weaknesses did you need to over-ride while you were rising to the challenge?
12. How did you go about protecting your gains?

NINE — Return with the Elixir

The hero returns to the Ordinary World, but the journey is meaningless unless she brings back some Elixir, treasure, or lesson from the Special World. The Elixir is a magic potion with the power to heal. It may be a great treasure like the Grail that magically heals the wounded land, or it simply might be knowledge or experience that could be useful to the community someday. [89] *Christopher Vogler*

If the hero returns with nothing for the community, he is not a hero. You can only be a hero in relation to others. To demonstrate final mastery of their problem, heroes, having gained something from their journey ––, realize that the best way to hold on to something is to give it away. Sharing our rewards with others enriches and transforms the world we live in, which is then better able to support us. Teaching others what we know helps us to gain greater mastery of those skills or understandings. Even on a fiscal level, investing our newly acquired wealth into our local economy will make business better for others, while helping our capital to grow, as compared with simply hoarding, and selfishly living off our wealth. This is true for anything we gain for ourselves, especially spiritual development.

Even if the hero is defeated, the community (or in the case of a story, the audience) can gain wisdom from the consequences of the hero's mistakes. The hero and the community may be sadder, but they will be wiser.

At NINE, changes are incorporated into new routines, as part of an evolving Ordinary World. The hero takes what was extraordinary and infuses it into his ordinary world. Consequently, his ordinary world becomes more extraordinary. The hero's personal evolution will change the way he relates to others and call forth in them new ways of relating to him. This may lead to changes in his family system, marriage, friendships, workplace, or whatever larger social systems he participates in. These new relationships will continue to challenge and support him in new ways that his old Ordinary World couldn't. At NINE the changes that have been set in motion gain a momentum of their own, snowballing into richer, more substantial, automatic patterns of living — a new ordinary world.

One of Buddha's most fundamental teachings was that there is no such thing as a self, merely the illusion of self; that ultimately, only the field of infinite potential exists, out of which all perceptions of separate or discrete phenomena arise. The experience of ourselves as no-self, at one with all things, is represented by the whole circle of the Enneagram, yet is most fully realized as we embrace stage NINE in the evolution of consciousness. Sharing the elixir of our enlightenment, directly or indirectly, with our community or family system initiates changes in individual members of those groups. These changes will precipitate a reorganization of the social systems at a higher level of functioning. Social systems don't initiate change; individuals initiate change. People within the systems must reorganize themselves in order to incorporate the changes brought about by the heroes, and make their own heroic journey.

The Buddha returned home to his father's palace and family. Along with the other followers, eventually his father, mother, wife and son, each in their own way, embraced his teachings and their lives changed accordingly. A new sort of Sangha (spiritual community) was organized as the Buddha put his teachings into practice, and one of the world's great spiritual traditions was established.

Exploring Your Heroic Journey

Return with the Elixir — How do I consolidate my efforts and maintain the changes in my life?

1. Who else benefited from your new way of life?
2. Who supported you in this new way of life?
3. What adjustments did they make to support you?
4. What new habits or routines developed as you consolidated your efforts?
5. What became more automatic that initially took more conscious effort?
6. How did your environment change in response to your accomplishments?
7. What adjustments did you make order to fit in with people who were important to you?
8. How did you learn to help things roll along more harmoniously?
9. What conflicts of interest were you able to mediate in order to maintain stability?
10. How did the momentum of your previous choices help you to consolidate your efforts?

Reflecting on the Journey

Having come full circle on the Hero's Journey, we become more familiar with the process of change. We see how the circumstances in one's Ordinary World (NINE) evolve in some way as the hero in us is Called to Adventure (ONE). As we are creatures of habit and stuck in our limiting self -concepts, we usually try to avoid major change or Refuse the Call (TWO). When we eventually take responsibility for our lives by taking the initial steps (THREE), we will have some sort of empowering experience, such as a Meeting with a Mentor, which helps us to overcome our reluctance by preparing us for the Crossing of the First Threshold. Having left the immediate familiarity of our Ordinary World, we are faced with certain Tests, Allies and Enemies (FOUR) that we must contend with and learn from if we are to Approach the Inmost Cave (FIVE) in preparation for the big change we are being called to make. When we eventually attempt the big change we are faced with an Ordeal (SIX) that requires us to find the courage to face our deepest fears in order to reap the Reward (SEVEN) that our dedication to the journey brings us. The consequences of having acted out of character require us to explore new ways of responding to life's demands if we are to successfully find our Road Back to our Ordinary World, Resurrected (EIGHT) as a new person. We finally Return with the Elixir of enlightenment, with all we have learned and gained from our journey. Final mastery is gained by sharing what we have learned with our community or the people who mean the most to us (NINE), enriching the lives of all.

In being able to so clearly understand and articulate this process, we learn to help ourselves and others frame the events of our lives in the context of a Hero's Journey. Demonstrating this knowledge by embracing the trials, tribulations, lessons and teachers, in whatever form they appear in our lives, with more Mindfulness, Compassion, Strength, Forgiveness, Spaciousness, Acceptance, Joy, Willingness, and Peace — begins to makes us authorities on the process of change and the evolution of human consciousness. As authorities, we are able to then participate in the re-authoring of not just our individual lives, but the ecology of consciousness to which all beings belong.

Questions for Guiding your Current Heroic Journey

NINE — *The Ordinary World* — How to maintain stability?

1. Describe your *ordinary world*.
2. What are your routines?
3. What helps you maintain a sense of security and/or stability?
4. How do you try to cope with stress and difficulties?
5. Who and what helps you feel stable and/or comfortable?
6. What do you avoid because it feels too stressful, difficult or unusual for yourself or your family or friends?
7. What do you appreciate?
8. What is working?
9. What don't you want to change yet? Why?
10. What do you want to come back to?

ONE — *The Call to Adventure* — What is not right? What is the ideal?

1. What are signs (calls to adventure) that tell you something needs to change?
2. What is frustrating or unfair about your circumstances?
3. How do you try to cope with those frustrations or injustices?
4. What's not working for you in your life?
5. What do you wish would just go away?
6. What have you done to try to fix things?
7. If a miracle could happen, what would you ideally hope for?
8. How is your life at the time not matching up to how you ideally would like it to be?
9. What are you most critical of about yourself? About others?
10. What problems or mistakes are most difficult for you to admit to yourself?
11. What concerns are important for you to take more seriously?
12. What happens when you try to do the 'right thing'?
13. What do you need to focus on in order to get you out of your rut?
14. Who is it easiest to express your anger, frustration or disappointment to?

TWO — *Refusal of the Call* — *What is needed?*

1. What is Life trying to get you to embrace that you have been trying to avoid?
2. What would help you to deal with your frustrations and begin moving towards your ideals?
3. What self-limiting patterns are you reluctant to change?
4. Who is it easy to ask for help? Who is it hardest?
5. How has pride or fear of embarrassment stopped you from admitting you need help?
6. Whose permission do you think you need before you can do what you want to do with your life?
7. How do you balance what you need in relation to what parents and friends expect of you?
8. Whose problems have you tried to change, rather than your own? Has it been beneficial?
9. How does your dependence on others help or hinder you in taking the necessary steps to making the most of your situation?
10. How does others' dependence on you, help or hinder you taking the necessary steps?
11. What are three reasons why you shouldn't begin attending to the difficulties in your life with more care and effort?
12. Who wants to support you in making the changes you want to make?
13. How would you like to be more independent and what responsibilities come with that?

THREE — *Meeting with the Mentor and Crossing the First Threshold* — *How to begin?*

1. Who are your mentors? What do they help you learn?
2. Who are your tor-mentors? What do they help you learn?
3. If you were guaranteed success what would you do?
4. What is the first step you will take (or have taken) to move toward your goal?

5. How willing are you to let others show you the way, or do you need to figure it out all yourself?
6. What talent or ability of yours would like to have a chance to prove itself?
7. What life experiences remind you that you have the inner strength to make the most of any opportunities or challenges?
8. How would you like to be living in five years time? What is that future self doing? How does he feel about himself? If that future self could talk to you now what advice or encouragement would he have for you now?
9. Who inspires you the most? Why?
10. Who would you like to emulate? In what way?
11. What can you tell yourself to help motivate you out of your comfort zone?
12. Who, if anyone, do you hope would notice and appreciate your efforts?
13. What will you need to ignore or disregard to get the ball rolling?
14. What sort of promises or oaths do you need to make to yourself and/or others?

FOUR — Tests, Allies and Enemies — What gets in the way? What do I really want?

1. What difficulties, flaws, inadequacies or insecurities have, or could, tempt you to give up on your aspirations?
2. What is lacking in your life that if only you had it, then you could follow your deepest desire? What difference would it make to have it?
3. Who tries to lead you astray from what is most important for you to do?
4. Who or what helps you to remain true to your deeper calling?
5. How do you attend to your weaknesses? How could you improve on this?
6. What past grievances haven't you forgiven yourself or others for yet?

7. What deeper longings or desires do you become aware of in difficult times?
8. What dreams help to propel you forward in spite of the difficulties?
9. What do you envy about aspects of other people's lives that remind you of what you value?
10. How are you unique? How does that inspire you to make the most of your life?
11. How are your feelings about mundane day-to-day activities changing?
12. How does feeling sad or disappointed help you do the soul searching needed to tune into your deeper calling?

FIVE — Approach to the Inmost Cave — Why am I going through this? What do I need to learn?

1. What mistakes have you made? What are they teaching you?
2. What keeps you going through difficult times?
3. What is important to have space from in order to put things in perspective?
4. Where can you retreat to when you need time to make sense of things?
5. How would a scientist viewing you from a detached perspective describe this transition you're going through?
6. What do you believe that keeps you going, or helps you make sense of the challenges in your life?
7. What is most essential and what is expendable in your life?
8. What do you need to know more about or know how to do better that would help you face your fears?
9. Who or what is it important to emotionally detach yourself from?
10. How does not taking things personally help to put things into perspective?
11. How can you maintain some sense of predictability in this time of change?
12. How could getting clearer boundaries between the various domains of your life help you feel more organized or in control?
13. When you observe your thoughts rationally, which ones support you and which ones weaken you?

SIX — Ordeal — *What do I remain faithful to and what do I need to let go of?*

1. What from your old lifestyle is most frightening to face or let go of?
2. What is difficult for you to accept about yourself and the world we live?
3. What have been your greatest fears and doubts?
4. What could help you to face your fears or to find the courage to follow your heart?
5. How about listing your worries and then brainstorm ideas for what could help you avoid or prepare for those possible challenges?
6. What authorities, institutions, or rules have you tended to question or be in conflict with?
7. Which of your loyalties support your being true to yourself and which seemed to hold you back?
8. Who do you need to reach out to and who do you need to walk away from at this time?
9. Whose approval or friendship do you feel you might risk losing to be true to yourself?
10. What beliefs are you questioning or feel confused about?
11. Who else is going through similar challenges in their life? How might this be part of some bigger trend?
12. Who is having (or could have) less control over you, as you find more faith in yourself?

SEVEN — Reward (Seizing the Sword) — *What is next? How do I enjoy what I have realized?*

1. Can you give yourself permission to act more spontaneously or seize a promising opportunity?
2. What new possibilities are you becoming are of and how can you begin exploring them?
3. What new ideas and insights are expanding your perception of what was possible for you?

4. Where could you go, who would you like to meet, or what could you read that might help open up more new possibilities for you?
5. What are you ready to free yourself from? So you can be freer to do what?
6. What sort of options are you considering before committing to a new path?
7. How might keeping your options open assist you at this time?
8. What sorts of plans or fantasies boost your optimism?
9. What can help you avoid being pulled back into old habits?
10. What responsibilities could you take a break from to make space for some new discoveries?
11. Are you willing to take a leap of faith and let luck or grace help you follow your bliss?
12. What sorts of things that you previously judged negatively are you seeing in a more positive light?
13. How does feeling you deserve something better influence your choices?

EIGHT — *The Road Back and Resurrection* — *What do I want to master or manifest?*

1. Of all the new things you have been exploring what are you ready to commit yourself to?
2. What are you ready to claim as your own, even if it means fighting for it?
3. What new rules are you making for yourself to reach your objectives?
4. What are you choosing in order to make the most of your life?
5. What in you drives you to really go for it?
6. How will you need to discipline yourself in order to accomplish your objectives?
7. How might you need to guard your time and space in order to get to where you want to go?
8. In what way is your self-concept changing?
9. What sort of person are you beginning to think of yourself as?

10. How is the way you identify yourself changing? What sort of a difference is it making taking on a new title (mother, father, student, job title, husband, wife, adult, spiritual seeker, etc.)?

11. Whose opinions or feelings might you need to dismiss, at least for a period of time, so that you can have a chance at manifesting your dream or desire?

12. How might your willpower and determination help you override some personal needs or weaknesses to rise to the challenge?

13. How will you protect your gains?

NINE — *Return with the Elixir* — *How do I consolidate my efforts and maintain the changes in my life?*

1. Who else will benefit from what you're putting into practice?
2. Who supports you in this new way of life?
3. What adjustments could they make to support you?
4. What new habits or routines are you establishing to consolidate your efforts?
5. What is taking less conscious effort, as it becomes part of your routine?
6. How is your environment changing in response to, or to support this new way of life?
7. What adjustments are you making to fit in with people who are important to you?
8. How do you help things keep rolling along harmoniously?
9. What conflicts of interest do you need to mediate to maintain stability?
10. In what direction is the momentum of what you have started taking you?

CHAPTER NINE

Compulsions of Personality

All suffering comes from the grasping of the self. *Sogyal Rinpoche*

Wholeness is the perceptual content of miracles. They thus correct, or atone, for the faulty perception of lack. *A Course in Miracles*

Understanding the compulsions of personality from a systemic perspective provides a liberating framework for our approach to life. Doing so allows us to more effectively help others do the same. If we place our compulsions of thinking, feeling and acting in the context of a personal ecosystem it's easier to see how resisting our intrinsic nature leads to more suffering. And if we embrace our essential wholeness we support our own healing and evolution and that of the wider society.

With a more limited sense of self, most of us tend to desire experiences that we can label 'good', while trying to avoid experiences labeled bad. The internal 'good' experience is said to be ego-syntonic (they fit our self-concept or idea of 'me'); the 'bad' are said to be ego-dystonic (they don't fit our self-concept or idea of 'me'). The more rigidly we identify with our personality, the more rigidly we cling to a limited collection of 'me' experiences and deny, reject or avert those experiences that we think are 'not me'. Some might say: Happiness is 'me' and sadness is 'not me', success is 'me' and failure is 'not me', or, anger is 'me' forgiveness is 'not me'. Instead of recognizing and embracing ourselves as a full spectrum of complementary qualities and experiences, we become identified with the parts that seem imperative to the survival of who we think we are. We disown or resist anything that threatens our notion of self.

Of course, it's important for survival to have a strong idea of what is good for us; but protecting a self-concept that separates us from our true wholeness is an attempt to keep a make-believe version of reality. Reality is always present, and is what it is. So the battle is never-ending and impossible to win. If we are merely fighting for our survival (a function of the reptilian fight or flight brain) we are not using our creative human potential. Fear is the habitual driver, rather than love. Acting out of fear brings about more of what we fear, reinforcing the need to attack, defend or retreat.

Consider this simple example: Bill feels annoyed about something his wife does. Instead of saying something about it, he just carries on as if nothing has happened because he likes to think of himself as a peaceful easy-going person (type NINE). Part of him is annoyed and tensions build in the back of his neck and head, magnifying his annoyance on a somatic level. The tension has turned into a headache and he takes an aspirin. There is temporary relief, but the tension is not neutralized. He is grumpy and easily annoyed. He is comfortable with tolerating (and medicating) annoyances, rather than talking about conflict, so he does more of the same.

As his wife doesn't know he's annoyed with her behavior, she doesn't even think about modifying it, let alone comforting or empathizing with him. The more he switches off from himself, the more he switches off from her. She feels ignored and either does things to try to get his attention or nags him about little things, which he also tries to ignore. In this way, the pattern is perpetuated and intensified.

Clinging to Your Self-Concept = Suffering

The more we defend our self-concept, the more separate we feel from our essential wholeness. "Thinking of ourselves as separate from the rest of the universe," said Einstein, "is an optical delusion, and it is our task as humans to broaden and deepen our sphere of compassion." Every experience is an opportunity to either remember our true nature by opening our sphere of compassion and identifying with more of creation, or to react in fear — retreating from or attacking what we are perceive as 'not me'. The more separate we feel from something, the more we tend to fear it. On an internal level, the more we demonize aspects of ourselves, the more we feel our demons are out to get us. Projecting this outward, the more we demonize other people, the more we will feel that they are out to get us.

Of course, in the nicest way, the world and our demons *are* out to get us. The whole universe and our whole selves are out to reclaim us. Reality is always impinging on our delusion of being separate, isolated, incomplete egos.

Personality Masks True Nature

The habitual ways we struggle against reality form the compulsions of personality. The word personality, from the Greek 'persona', translates as mask. A mask is used to hide our true self and enable us to play a role. In order to fit into a world where most people are acting as if the masks they wear and the roles they play are all there is, we all learn to adopt a persona. We become so identified with the mask that we lose touch with our true nature.

Being trapped in the compulsions of personality is to be overly identified with the Essential Quality, Developmental Task, Basic Function and PsychoLogical Network of one phase in the process of change. Albert Einstein said, "Insanity is doing the same thing over and over again and expecting different results." The more compulsive we are with our grasping and aversion, the further down the scale of psychological health we digress, and the more psychologically disordered we become. The DSMV categorizes the NINE styles of 'insanity' in terms of various personality disorders and other psychiatric conditions.

Everyone has a personality type, which means we automatically favor qualities associated with one phase of the Enneagram. Like the rest of creation, we flow through all the phases. The more psychologically healthy we are, the more we are allowing of our wholeness and tend to be more internally, and usually externally, well-rounded. As our psychological health slips towards being more disordered, we become increasingly fixated around one point. As the stress of this vicious circle intensifies, there is tendency to slide into the dysfunctional process associated with the stress point (direction of the arrows) on the Enneagram.

At most stages, our ego mind perceives evolution as a threat as it requires the dissolution of (or at least disillusion with) our perceived identity (ego *death*). As outlined in the previous chapters, our lives are ongoing, overlapping cycles of change in which our self-limiting identity regularly dissolves and is reformed in richer, fuller and less deluded ways. The more our ego mind attempts to maintain the perception of a separate solid self, the more disordered or stagnant our lives become. The more we try to cope with escalating external chaos or stagnation in the usual ways, the more we suffer psychological disorders.

Fundamentalism of Personality

The compulsions of personality are inherently fundamentalistic. A compulsion is based on the notion there is one right way of living life and that way is already known and literally defined by a set of beliefs, values, behaviors and ideals that never change or evolve. Family therapist, Lynn Hoffman, wrote, "Problems are stories that people have agreed to tell themselves." Personality is the character we have defined ourselves to be within the stories of our lives. The freer we are from the compulsions of personality, the more freely our lives evolve over time. Although there are aspects of the stories that remain consistent, over time, our character develops, matures and discovers more fully who we are and our place in the universe. The more rigidly we adhere to the fundamental dictates of our personality, the narrower and less life affirming our lives become. Whether on an individual level within families, or on a political level between nations, different fundamentalist identifications arise in reaction to one another.

Fundamentalism labels anything outside of its ideology as crazy, bad and/or sick. Instead of being curious about how we might relate to other ways of living, we try to eliminate them by extermination, incarceration, intimidation, alienation, reprogramming, medication, or some method of social control. Fundamentalism promises salvation (safety and security) through adherence to its doctrine. Rigid adherence to the doctrine, however, leads to an escalation of the problems. As life becomes more chaotic, we can either respond by trying to impose the fundamentalist approach with more force, or threats of force; or open up to how life is trying to evolve through us.

As we have seen, each number on the Enneagram represents a fixed-point attractor, which is part of the systemic process that includes the other eight attractors. Some attractors help free the system from old patterns of relating and some attractors help reorganize it around new patterns.

When our life becomes overly organized around a single attractor, it begins to approximate the type of order found in nonliving systems, like the predictability of planets revolving the sun, on one hand, and the chaos of a tornado, on the other. Living systems, however, thrive between the boundaries of too much chaos and too much order. In general, too much order leads to stagnation and depressive or somatic conditions; whereas too much chaos leads to disorganization, and anxiety, and thought and behavior disorders. It is fluctuating between order and disorganization within the *River of Integration* (Seigel 2010) that allow evolution and growth.

Aristotle said, "We are what we repeatedly do." But it is not that we actually *are* what we repeatedly do; it's just who we think we are. Personality is really a case of mistaken identity. When stuck in the compulsions of personality, we have mistakenly come to believe we are the patterns of thinking, feeling and behaving. Compulsions of personality are habits. Habits are like a comfortable bed: easy to get into, but hard to get out of. What is familiar is comfortable. Frequently, it's not until we have bedsores, or the rest of the house is falling apart from neglect, or our partner gets fed up, that we pull ourselves out of our comfortable bed-like ruts. However, once we are up and making the most of our lives, we are less likely to waste too much time lying around. We get into the miraculous experience of life. When we are stuck in the compulsions of personality it is like we are asleep to our true nature and life can increasingly be a process of just getting by, at best, or a nightmare-like existence, at worst.

Personality Types

In this chapter, I outline the preoccupations and compulsions of the nine personality types the Enneagram describes. Since descriptions of these types are well documented in other publications, I will not go into great detail; however, I do want to highlight how the rigidities of personality arise when we aren't flowing with the natural ever-changing processes of an evolving universe.

I also briefly offer some methods for each type to come back into greater harmony with these natural processes.

Repetitive maladaptive behavior, psychological symptoms and personality disorders can be understood as resulting from how each personality type becomes overly-identified with the Essential Quality of the associated phase of change, performing the Basic Function compulsively to hold onto the achievements of the Developmental Task, in relation to the associated PsychoLogical Network.

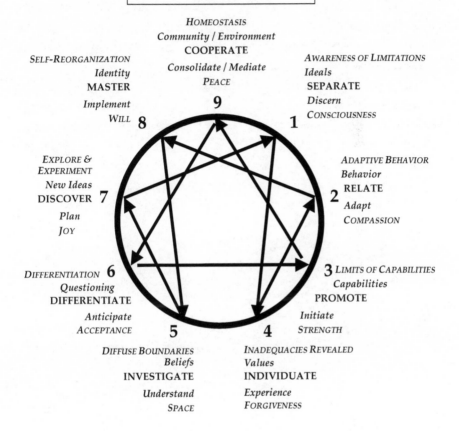

ENNEAGRAM OF
CHANGE CYCLE
PsychoLogical Networks
DEVELOPMENTAL TASKS
Basic Functions
ESSENTIAL QUALITIES

HOMEOSTASIS
Community / Environment
COOPERATE
Consolidate / Mediate
PEACE
9

SELF-REORGANIZATION
Identity
MASTER
Implement
WILL **8**

AWARENESS OF LIMITATIONS
Ideals
SEPARATE
Discern
CONSCIOUSNESS
1

EXPLORE &
EXPERIMENT
New Ideas
DISCOVER **7**
Plan
JOY

ADAPTIVE BEHAVIOR
Behavior
RELATE
Adapt
COMPASSION
2

DIFFERENTIATION **6**
Questioning
DIFFERENTIATE
Anticipate
ACCEPTANCE

3 *LIMITS OF CAPABILITIES*
Capabilities
PROMOTE
Initiate
STRENGTH

5

4

DIFFUSE BOUNDARIES
Beliefs
INVESTIGATE
Understand
SPACE

INADEQUACIES REVEALED
Values
INDIVIDUATE
Experience
FORGIVENESS

Why do we do this? Generally, it's done out of fear of regressing to the previous phase, as well as worrying about what the next phase in the process of change holds for us. The less we trust the process of life, the more we try to cope with life using the strategies and resources we know best. Our personality is genetically predisposed to the strengths and weaknesses of a particular temperament. The more traumatic and less nurturing our

285

early lives (birth to age five), the less trustful we are likely to be. The less trustful of life, the more compelled we are to use what we know best to maintain a sense of stability. Instead of going with the flow of life, we organize our perceptions and actions, to a greater or lesser degree, around a single attractor.

As we become more rigidly identified with one-ninth of our essential wholeness, our lives get more stuck in vicious cycles. As we recreate the experiences we are most familiar with, we reinforce our perception that life is something to be coped with, rather than something to trust and make the most of.

If life is like a journey down a river, to be stuck in rigid coping mechanisms that maintain problems, is like being caught in a whirlpool or eddy. People often come to therapy because they are experiencing the same emotion over and over. I like to draw them a graph of healthy experiencing of primary emotion — it shows a bell curve starting from an emotional baseline. Emotional triggers activate the emotion and it grows in intensity until it peaks. It then starts dissipating until it returns to baseline.

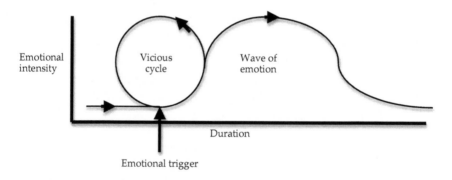

What happens when we create and use coping mechanisms, is that instead of allowing the emotion to move through the system naturally, an avoidance mechanism is activated, which diverts the process. The emotion, having not been accepted and experienced in a compassionate, understanding way, gets put into a 'too hard basket'. The resistance to the primary emotional response creates a secondary emotional response: anxiety (fear of fear) or resentment (resisting vulnerability) or depression (resisting grief). It is these secondary responses that typically bring people to therapy. When a situation, or even a thought, reminds a person of the upsetting event, the emotion is triggered, resulting in a vicious cycle. Post-Traumatic Stress Disorder is an extreme version of this process.

When we open fully to all of life's events with our essential wholeness, we go through expanding spirals of learning, growth and evolution, which transcend previous levels of functioning. When we get caught in the compulsions of ego defenses, at best we get stuck in vicious cycles (eddy), and at worst spiral into greater depths of dysfunction and psychological disorders (whirlpool).

We have seen how identifying too strongly with one quality cuts us off from our essential wholeness; and the more our self-concept is rigidly identified with one essential quality, the more we lose touch with the actual experience of the essence of *that* quality. If we are deeply identified, we get lost in concepts; for example, the concept of compassion is not the experience of compassion. Concepts are not reality. Identifying with a concept is to identify with a constructed reality, as opposed to directly experiencing the flow of life. We end up confusing the map of how we define our lives with the journey through the territory of our lives. The more we try to hold onto how life is supposed to be, the more we invest in a delusion and must deny, avoid and resist reality. We do this without consciously realizing it, yet it is the maintenance of the delusion that perpetuates our suffering.

As we get stuck in the qualities associated with one-ninth of the process of change and our essential wholeness, freeing ourselves from our compulsions begins with being willing to face our fears, and let go of what we are most identified with. Then, by embracing the Essential Quality of the next phase, we are more easily able to perform the Basic Function and accomplish the associated Developmental Task in relationship to the PsychoLogical Network of next the phase of change. How this happens with each personality type will be described in detail.

The Inner Web

The inner web of the Enneagram is made up of two structures: the equilateral triangle connecting THREE, SIX and NINE, and the butterfly shaped figure that connects ONE, FOUR, TWO, EIGHT, FIVE and SEVEN. The lines that connect the points represent relationships between respective qualities of each phase.

In any ecosystems, there are the most obvious cyclical relationships. However, there are also more hidden dimensions, less directly obvious in their interactions, but which serve to maintain overall integrity of the web of life.

Although we always live within our wholeness, albeit dissociated from the direct experience to varying degrees, at each phase in the process of change, we primarily access and utilize the qualities of that phase, and secondly the qualities of the phases connected to that phase by the internal lines. The connected phases in the direction of the arrows have traditionally been called the Stress Point or the Direction of Disintegration, and against the arrows, the Security Point or the Direction of Integration.

It has been observed that when under more stress, there is a tendency for us to manifest the qualities associated with the Stress Point, which leads to further disintegration of normal functioning. When life is smoother and we are feeling more secure, we tend to manifest more of the qualities associated with the Security Point and support further integration of our current lifestyle.

For example, when relaxed and on vacation, the normally quite focused and serious type ONE will utilize a lot of the qualities of SEVEN and entertain a lot of options in a playful way. They may also be inspired to play around with diverse perspectives and find a new way of integrating whatever they have been working on. Whereas, the same Type ONE, when under a lot of stress can become even more aware of their inadequacies and deeper longings and may even try to express themselves through poetry, like a type FOUR. Instead of trying harder to fix things in their life, they may become more despondent and, out of desperation, recognize the need to surrender to the processes of life that are beyond their conscious control.

The Stress and Security Points can be resources for our healing and evolution or they can be pitfalls that take us deeper into vicious cycles of suffering depending on how much we accept the way things are or how much we deny and resist.

Since life is an ongoing process of integration, disintegration and reintegration, at a higher level of organization, integration and disintegration are neither good nor bad; they are just part of the process of life. Moving to our points of integration or disintegration can help us find the resources of our essential wholeness and support either the disintegration of redundant patterns of interaction or support the integration of emergent potentials into our lives.

Uniqueness and Patterns

The following descriptions of personality types are generalizations of how people organize their lives when trapped in the compulsions of personality. There are infinite ways people enact these patterns. Let us remember, however, that people are not their personalities and therefore these generalizations don't include the myriad of ways each one of us uniquely expresses our essential wholeness, even when caught in our compulsions to varying degrees.

Personality Type NINE

Type NINEs identify with the:

- change cycle phase of homeostasis
- essential quality of peace
- basic function of mediation
- developmental task of cooperation
- psychological network of community/environment

Type NINEs tend to resist the:

- change cycle phase of awareness of limitations
- essential quality of consciousness
- basic function of discernment
- developmental task of separation
- psychological network of ideals

NINEs fear slipping back into the ordeals associated with gaining mastery and manifesting their will. They cope by compromising their own agenda to blend with others and maintain peace and stability. They compulsively ask:

- How do I consolidate my growth and development?
- How do I mediate harmony and cooperation?

They avoid asking:

- What's wrong?
- What's the ideal?
- What am I aware of now?

At their worst, NINEs demonstrate the symptoms of dissociative and dependent personality disorders.

When NINEs embody their essential wholeness, they are conscious of the complexities in human interactions. That enables them to get along well with others, form deep lasting relationships, and help others cooperate. They can mediate conflicts and remain true to their ideals and values. Their openness to other's ideas makes them good leaders who purposely include a diversity of opinions in their teams.

Healthy NINEs are appreciative of what they have while still motivated to honor their ideals. NINEs are active members of organizations and social networks, willing to take initiative, and they are good at offering constructive criticism. At their best, NINEs' qualities can be seen in people like: His Holiness, the Dalai Lama, Carl Jung, Abraham Lincoln, Ralph Waldo Emerson, Carl Rogers, George Lucas and Bill Clinton.

Type NINE

HOMEOSTASIS
Community / Environment
COOPERATE
Consolidate / Mediate

SELF-REORGANIZATION   PEACE   AWARENESS OF LIMITATIONS

Identity   **9**   *Ideals*

MASTER   **8**   **1**   SEPARATE

Implement   *Discern*

WILL   CONSCIOUSNESS

7   **2**

6   **3**

5   **4**

Type NINES

Identify with Phase NINE	**Resist Phase ONE**
I am stable (homeostasis).	I resist being aware of the limitations of the system.
I am peaceful.	I resist being mindful.
I am consolidating and mediating.	I resist being discerning or critical.
I am cooperative.	I resist being separate from others.
I am my community and environment.	I resist acknowledging my ideals.

Fear Slipping Back to Phase EIGHT	**Try to cope by trying to do more: Phase NINE**
I fear reorganizing my life.	I cope by trying to maintain homeostasis.
I fear exercising my will.	I cope by trying to be peaceful and compliant.
I fear implementing my agenda.	I cope by trying to compromise my agenda.
I fear mastery and authority.	I cope by trying to cooperate with everyone.
I fear having a strong identity.	I cope by trying to blend into the group or environment.

Identify with Phase NINE / Resist Phase ONE

Type NINEs tend to identify overly with the Essential Quality of Peace. To maintain their self-image of being a peaceful person, they mediate conflicting factors to maintain cooperation within their community (family, organization, etc.).

However, they also avoid becoming more conscious and discerning of the limitations of their circumstances, and distinguishing what separates who they are as individuals from the rest of the community, as well as other members of the community from one another.

Their resistance to being aware of their ideals, means they have no standard for determining a hierarchy of importance to available choices. What is important for personal growth and wellbeing, as well as the growth and wellbeing of the community, is mediated into equal importance with the most trivial of matters. Deciding what color of toothbrush to buy holds equal importance with to how to tell your spouse you almost had an affair.

The more NINEs try to maintain an image of peace, the more their lives, inwardly and outwardly, become filled with conflict and chaos. They switch their consciousness off from anything disturbing, and hope that by ignoring problems and conflicts they will go away. When problems don't go away, and their frustration builds sufficiently, NINEs explode in anger.

The provoking incident often is something trivial — often to the bemusement of those on the receiving end of the anger. When NINEs regains their composure, they often see how irrational and exaggerated their anger was, although they often remain unaware of the underlying issue. Instead of looking into what is fueling their reaction, they vow to not let these little things bother to them so much and thereby perpetuate the cycle of repression.

Type NINEs are aware of how much willpower it takes to manifest systems of organization. They prefer to appreciate what they have, and hope that if they ignore problems, they will go away. They are intrinsically aware of the demands life can make on them when they listen to their call to greatness and follow their dream.

NINEs fear having to go through phase EIGHT again, so they resist doing anything that could highlight unmet needs, aspirations or desires. If they identify themselves as peaceful people (NINE) it seems incompatible with the willful assertiveness associated with EIGHT or the idealistic intensity associated with ONE.

One of the more critical descriptions of NINEs is that they are said to be lazy. Laziness, generally, comes from a lack of motivation. Whilst NINEs are often are very busy, trying to keep everything rolling along, this is because they are very motivated to maintain the status quo. Their laziness is in regard to growth and development. NINEs forget that ideals and problems relative to how things could ideally be are what inspire us to reach beyond the familiarity of the patterns of our day-to-day existence.

NINEs avoid thinking about ideals that would highlight conflict between how things are and how they could be because they fear not feeling peaceful. Their motto is often 'peace at any price,' and that price is personal satisfaction and development. To cope, they become more enmeshed with family or community. Their language is predominantly in terms of 'we' and 'us', and they avoid 'I' statements.

NINEs avoid making decisions, simply going along with what others are doing or seem to expect, as making a decision requires discerning what is best in a situation. Making a decision can create conflict, as different people may have conflicting agendas. If choosing to go along with one family member, for example, puts them in conflict with another, they get frozen in indecision. Although they try desperately not to upset anyone, others can find the NINE's indecision infuriating.

When they are children, NINEs are often forgotten, invisible or low-maintenance. Under stress they blend in with the environment, minimizing needs and wants in the hope of maintaining stability. This pattern continues into adulthood. As they are so consistent in behavior and demeanor, it is easy for others to take them for granted.

'If you don't have something nice to say, don't say anything at all' is a powerful maxim for NINEs. Although NINEs may physically be present and this presence may be acknowledged, their emotional self remains invisible and, often, is not taken into consideration because they tend to be compliant. Not only do others not check in with them, NINEs don't even check in with their own desires, let alone how they feel about other's expectations, demands and wishes, before acquiescing.

NINEs resist moving to ONE where they would naturally become more conscious of who they are separate from and the groups to which they belong. NINEs, more than any other type, are attracted towards a stationary state, as close to equilibrium and as predictable as possible.

As biologist Ilya Prigogine said, a system operating within this range tends to "forget its initial conditions" of growth and evolution. NINEs respond predictably like non-living systems, following the basic laws of physics, such as inertia. When NINEs reach their limit of compliance, rather than saying, "No more!" they often simply refuse to budge in response to initiative.

To maintain the status quo, NINEs compromise personal expectations and ideals, and dissociate from any awareness of things they aren't happy about. NINEs lie by omission, simply leaving out parts of explanations that they perceive as contentious or selfish. People in relationship with NINEs stuck in that compulsion, describe them as generally nice, but boring, helpful but not deeply satisfying, and friendly but not intimate. As their awareness is fixated on the community, environmental context and maintaining the status quo, NINEs rarely initiate activities. Initiation requires knowing what they want and doing something to make it happen. To begin any creative process, they must move from NINE to ONE to discern their preferences and to begin articulating what is right for them.

Fear slipping back to phase EIGHT / Try to cope by doing more phase NINE

NINEs keep their attention on what is comfortable and easy to the exclusion of what is perceived as uncomfortable or challenging. They fear needing to exercise their will and the effort that goes into mastering a skill or area of knowledge. To cope with fear, they pad their lives with simple comforts and things that provide easy distractions from any issues that demand attention. They distract themselves with trivial or uncharged activities or objects as a way of avoiding anything that might disrupt the homeostasis. NINEs fear having a strong identity. More than any other type, they are likely to say, "I'm nobody." People with strong identities stand out in a crowd; people look to them to take charge or help organize things. NINEs fear controversy where their agenda might conflict with someone else's (rock the boat).

NINEs are overly identified with the patterns of relating between different individuals that defines a community. When the limitations of these patterns become apparent, NINEs identify with the limitations and think, "I'm not good enough (inadequate)," rather than, "There is something wrong with the way I (we) have been doing things". NINEs think in global unchanging terms, believing the way things are is as good as they get, and how they act is who they are and how they will always be. NINEs resist taking a stand that potentially separates them from the groups or contexts they are a part of. In phases EIGHT and ONE, we stand apart from the whole to implement or initiate change.

Hero's Journey — The Ordinary World

You got to be careful if you don't know where you're going, because you might not get there. *Yogi Berra*

On the Hero's journey, NINEs try to stay comfortable in their ordinary world. They limit their awareness of problems or opportunities — resist calls to adventure by minimizing the value, importance or urgency of issues — positive and negative. Even when an opportunity for a new job, relationship or anything novel arises, they pass it by in favor of maintaining predictable day-to-day routines.

Aldous Huxley reminded us, "Facts do not cease to exist because they are ignored," yet NINEs, more than any other personality type, believe ignorance is bliss. NINEs are wearing blinkers that block-out anything but the well-worn path, the set routines. They make the same mistakes over and over, even with feedback (consequences or friendly advice) to help them make different choices. As they fear the need to change, they easily forget about problems of the past; each time a problem arises, it is like it is happening for the first time.

Without awareness of their ideals, NINEs fail to set goals for themselves. In relationship counseling, one NINE proudly proclaimed, "I'm not the one who has changed. I'm the same as I have always been!" which, of course, was exactly what their spouse was unhappy about. If our relationship skills haven't improved in fifteen years of marriage, we have missed many opportunities to grow, and probably haven't had any goals other than staying together. The longer we resist change, the more any relationship deteriorates. This leaves the NINE with the perception that life is something merely 'to be gotten through'.

Many NINEs take pride in the ability to endure impoverished, unpleasant and unjust circumstances, even to the point of thinking that we show love by putting up with someone's crap. As a result of this lack of assertiveness, some NINEs never achieve much individuation from parents or significant others. If allowed to, they might never leave home, especially if they are the youngest child, choosing instead to stick around and hold the family together.

A "No" uttered from deepest conviction is better and greater than a "Yes" merely uttered to please, or what is worse, to avoid trouble. *Mahatma Gandhi*

Tales from the Therapy Room: Waking Up

Jane, who came in with her husband Bill for marital therapy, was shocked when her husband announced he was leaving the marriage to live with a woman he'd been having an affair with for some time. Although she had voiced some complaints over the years, mostly she had allowed him to dictate the terms of the relationship. Since he hadn't been very good at asking her for what he wanted, it had been easier for him to meet some of those wants within another relationship. Jane's way of coping with her lack of satisfaction was to get involved with other activities: study, grandchildren, housework, and so on. What I discovered when she did complain, is that she spoke in a monotonous voice, with long roundabout explanations. As she spoke, her husband's eyes would get very heavy, as if he was about to fall asleep. She said there were times he actually did fall asleep.

When I asked her why it was important to be speaking in this monotone, she said she didn't want him to get upset. When I asked Bill what he thought she was trying to communicate to him, he said he wasn't specifically sure, but that this happened quite often. Bill's sleepy, bored, unanimated state confirmed her fear he was bored with her and was going to leave. Her boring monologues confirmed his perception of her as being boring and not interested in a more passionate relationship, leading him to further consider the possibility of leaving. As is the case with all of our compulsions, the way we try to prevent our worst-case scenarios creates the very circumstances we fear most.

As Jane connected with her right to protest and to ask for what she wanted, her voice became more animated, and he came to realize she actually wanted many of the same things he did. Because she actually showed her anger to him about these things, he took it to mean she felt what they had together, was worth fighting for. Her emerging assertiveness led to new sexual and intimate relating and his decision to end the affair. Although it was difficult for her to forgive him for the affair and the lying that surrounded it, she at one point thanked him for waking her out of her complacency and slowly fading into a sort of sexless, selfless sense of early grandparenthood. Over the following months, she became the motivating force in helping both of them realizing their potentials for a more intimate, passionate marriage.

Diagram 9d

The Connections from NINE to THREE and SIX

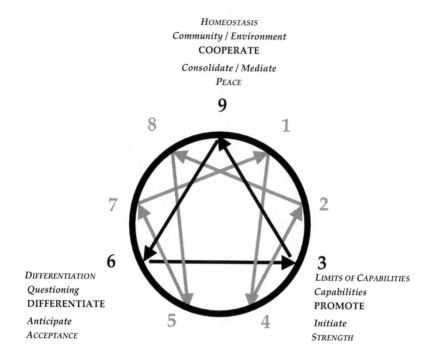

HOMEOSTASIS
Community / Environment
COOPERATE
Consolidate / Mediate
PEACE

DIFFERENTIATION
Questioning
DIFFERENTIATE
Anticipate
ACCEPTANCE

LIMITS OF CAPABILITIES
Capabilities
PROMOTE
Initiate
STRENGTH

Connection to THREE

During periods of integration and stability, type NINEs tend to connect more with the qualities of THREE: exploring limits of capabilities, strength, initiation, promotion and capabilities. To help maintain stability and reinforce their implacable identity, NINEs use their strength to stubbornly refuse to address problems. They go to the limits of their capabilities to maintain the status quo, promoting a false image of success to ward off a growing awareness of the limitations of their circumstances. To keep this image up, they must be increasingly deceitful, especially with themselves, but also others. Bill Clinton demonstrated this in his presidency and marriage; however, like a lot of NINEs, his easygoing nature made him easy, for some, to forgive.

Connecting with essential strength enables NINEs to stand on their own with more autonomy, allowing them to connect more with personal ideals and preferences. From this position of strength, it becomes easier to discern what is working from what isn't. Instead of just reacting and responding to people and demands in their environments and social systems, they are able to initiate actions that promote their needs separate from other's expectations.

Connection to SIX

During periods of disintegration and when approaching chaos, type NINEs tend to connect more with the qualities of SIX: differentiation, acceptance, differentiate, anticipation and questioning. Things often get worse before they get better. Rather than consciously facing the growing instability of their circumstances, NINEs fall deeper into confusion and anxiety. The compulsion of looking for peace outside of themselves extends into looking for acceptance from others. The more they deny their individuality, the more they give others the power to accept or reject them. They may begin to obsess about who is with them and who is against them, descending into paranoia as stress increases. The fear of change gets expressed in anticipating what could go wrong if they were to step out of their routines. They even begin doubting and questioning aspects of themselves they have felt comfortable with in the past. This movement to SIX intensifies the disintegration process, making their flaws and the flaws of social systems more apparent, and the need to become more conscious and discerning even more compelling.

NINE's connection to SIX helps them to accept themselves more unconditionally. Accepting what is not okay, as well as what is, helps them address the limitations of their circumstances. Differentiating their agenda from the collective and questioning the assumptions of the status quo helps them separate enough to begin attending to their agenda and initiate change in their social systems. Once NINEs break out of their homeostatic routines, they can move into a sort of evolutionary momentum that makes them hard to stop.

Understanding how type NINEs tend to resist the natural processes of change and cling to fixed ideas of themselves helps us to meet them where they get stuck and show them the possibility for greater freedom.

Personality Type ONE

Type ONEs identify with the:

- change cycle phase of the awareness of limitations
- essential quality of consciousness
- basic function of discernment
- developmental task of separation
- psychological network of ideals

Type ONES tend to resist the:

- change cycle phase of adaptive behavior
- essential quality of compassion
- basic function of adaptation
- developmental task of relationship
- psychological network of behavior

ONEs fear slipping back into the problematic patterns associated with the homeostatic functioning of systems to which they belong. They cope by being idealistic and hyper-conscious of the limitations of themselves and the world around them. They compulsively ask:

- What's wrong?
- What's the ideal?

They avoid asking:

- How does the problem happen?
- What is needed to improve situation?

At their worst can demonstrate obsessive-compulsive and depressive personality disorders and possibly eating disorders.

When ONEs embody their essential wholeness, they are great teachers, prophets and reformers. They show great integrity and practice what they preach. They tend to lead by example. They are good at seeing and bringing out the best in others, helping those around them become more responsible members of the community. Deeply compassionate about human suffering, they work tirelessly to make the world a better place. They are able to discern the most practical ideas, words and actions to promote the best outcome for the most people over the longest period of time. At their best they manifest qualities seen in people like: Nelson Mandela, Confucius, Anne Frank, Noam Chomsky, Buckminster Fuller, Ralph Nader, Carl Sagan, Ayn Rand and Albert Ellis.

Type ONE

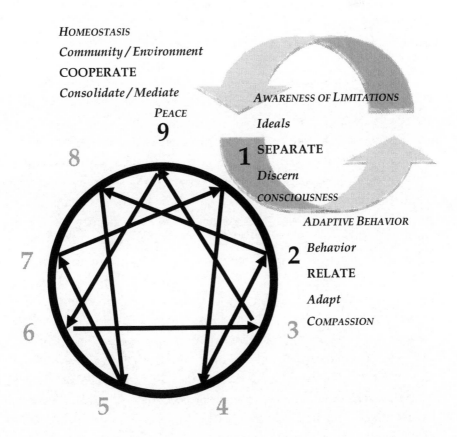

Type ONEs

Identify With Phase ONE	**Resist Phase TWO**
I am my awareness of limitations.	I resist adapting my behavior.
I am conscious.	I resist being compassionate.
I am discerning.	I resist being adaptable.
I am separate.	I resist relating.
I am my ideals.	I resist acknowledging my behavior.

Fear Slipping Back to Phase NINE	**Try to Cope by Doing More Phase ONE**
I fear getting stuck in homeostasis.	I cope by staying aware of limitations.
I fear being at peace.	I cope by being self-conscious.
I fear compromise.	I cope by judging.
I fear having to cooperate.	I cope by separating myself from others.
I fear losing my self in the community.	I cope by holding on to my ideals.

Identify with Phase ONE / Resist Phase TWO

Type ONEs tend to over-identify with the essential quality of mindfulness. They like to think of themselves as being mindful of what they do and why they are doing it. In trying to be in conscious control of everything they do, they become rigid and out of connection with who, or what, they are relating to. They become so identified with their ideals that they disown or conceal any ideas or behaviors that don't fit with these. Conscience is the conscious discernment of the degree of alignment we have with our ideals in any situation. ONEs come to identify with their conscience as the true inner self or the voice of God, which turns it into a formidable superego. They become preoccupied with judging situations and constantly discerning right from wrong. This compulsion gets in the way of their hearts opening to a compassionate relationship with the objects of their judgments. Ideals generate intentions, and ONEs are so identified with their good intentions they fail to correlate their behavior to the less than ideal outcomes to their endeavors. Instead they blame others for things not turning out the way they 'should'. They strive to live up to their ideals, but fail to ask what they need to grow in that direction. ONEs are the ultimate *try-hards*. They have forgotten, more than anyone, the Chinese proverb, 'Tension is who you think you should be. Relaxation is who you are.' The harder they try to get things right, the more uptight they get and the more out of sync with life they become.

The typical defense mechanism of a type ONE personality is referred to as reaction formation, which refers to the tendency to engage in behavior directly opposed to unconscious forbidden desires. For example, attacking other people's sexual orientation, while denying their own sexual desires. Identification with an ideal self-image leads to a denial of their unattended needs. To have needs implies they aren't perfect, so to maintain this self-image of perfection they must avoid any activity that might highlight their needs. They become overly identified with being separate and autonomous, further cutting themselves off from the relationships they need to evolve towards their deepest ideals.

As they aren't giving to themselves what they really need, problems get worse and increasingly beyond conscious control.

The more they try to fix these 'imperfections' in the usual way, the worse things get. The over-identification with consciousness restricts communication with their unconscious minds. Instead of asking their inner self what is needed to deal with a particular symptom, they demand stricter adherence to their perfectionist regime. ONEs often have strict dietary, exercise or spiritual regimes they feel they must adhere to. When difficulties arise, instead of tuning into the needs of their emergent or neglected self, they try to force themselves to be even more obedient and regimented.

The harder they try to keep things under conscious control, the greater the split between conscious and unconscious processes. The more the unconscious parts are repressed or go unattended, the more those parts continue to act out symbolically or simply rebel against the oppressive regime. ONEs can be drawn to alcohol because it helps relax their harsh superego. However, the 'inappropriate behavior' that sneaks out when intoxicated can leave ONEs feeling guilty and vow to try even harder to be good, winding up the self-control even tighter.

The harder ONEs try to conform to self-imposed regimentation, the more resentful they become. They feel, 'No matter how hard I try it isn't good enough.' They feel angry at having to try so hard when life appears so much easier for others. Anger and resentment are not part of their idealized self-concept and therefore must be controlled and hidden from themselves and others. Repressing anger often leads to more physical symptoms and a judgmental demeanor. The anger leaks out in the form of criticism, which gives them more to feel guilty about. To prevent additional 'mistakes' they try to be more conscious of everything they say and do, making them more stiff and awkward. Although they might try to say the 'right' thing, anger leaks out through lecturing and preaching, alienating them even more. When it gets all too hard, ONEs retreat into isolation, where they don't have to worry so much about doing something wrong.

ONEs are constantly trying to prove themselves by 'doing the right thing'. If they think someone might possibly think otherwise, they feel they must justify their actions. They feel like they will be presumed guilty until proven innocent. At the heart of fundamentalist religion is the idea of original sin, the basic idea being that we are born sinful into a sinful world and it is only through strict adherence to the literal translation of the religious text into a set of rules that we will one day be saved. Whether or not ONEs are part of a religious context, they believe they must religiously adhere to a set of principles to control and direct thoughts and actions. The more they do this, however, the more they deny themselves the compassion needed to attend to their wounded, neglected and emergent selves.

Fear slipping back to phase NINE / Try to cope by doing more phase ONE

Idealistic ONEs are very conscious of the flaws in their relationship systems, whether family, company or nation, and get stuck in feeling angry with others and themselves for being lazy, irresponsible and incompetent. ONEs have felt let down by family and society and often feel there is no one to rely on. They feel they must be self-reliant, self-sufficient and self-directed to protect themselves from being dependent and trapped in imperfect social systems. They will spend a lot of time alone, doing what they know they can do the 'right way', or at least where no one else can see they aren't living up to their idealistically high standards.

Although ONEs are trying to help correct the ills, the recipients of their 'helpful' criticism, condemnation and lecturing feel attacked and put down, rejecting what compulsive ONEs have to say. This reinforces the ONE's belief that people don't care about or support them.

ONEs are afraid to make compromises. They fear compromising their separate sense of self and merging with the collective dynamics of family, workplace or larger community. For a ONE, a compromise is doing anything that isn't true to their ideals. Since they feel they *are* their ideals, any compromise of their ideals feels like a compromise of themselves. They cope with this fear of having to compromise their ideals by judging others as not worth their efforts and criticizing them from a distance and/or withdrawing further from relationships.

Gregory Bateson described mind as being immanent rather than transcendent. In Acceptance and Commitment Therapy (ACT) it is the recognition of self as context. In other words, everything happens within consciousness. As quantum physics has shown, consciousness is not separate from what is observed. When we are in rapport with life, this immanent (intuitive) mind guides our thinking, feeling and acting. It is the same sort of knowing that takes over when we are deeply involved in an intimate conversation, lovemaking, playing music: whenever we lose ourselves in an activity and it takes us over.

To the ONE who is overly identified with the conscious mind, the intuitive mind is relegated to the realm of the unconscious mind. Type ONEs don't trust the automatic behaviors of the unconscious mind. Unconscious minds make mistakes and ONEs get stuck in trying to correct and not make mistakes by maintaining conscious control over their every move. The conscious mind however only concentrates on one thing at a time and generally only thinks as quickly as we can talk to ourselves. It is possible, for example, to play only the simplest melody on a piano with this sort of consciousness. To play a complex piece of music, we must be able to let go of conscious control and allow our unconscious skill take over. The conscious mind is then free to fine-tune little details in our style or presentation. So whether it's music, conversation or lovemaking, ONEs often lack style, complexity and feeling, even if they are technically 'right'.

Hero's Journey — The Call to Adventure

ONEs get stuck in the call to adventure phase. They are very aware of the limitations of their Ordinary World and the possibilities for a better life. Instead of even considering the journey, they get stuck in criticizing their ordinary world. They refuse the call, and then resist acknowledging their refusal of the call. Instead, they try to convince themselves they are living the adventure, without taking the actions that would take them into realms of new possibilities.

Because ONEs are identified with their ideal images, to actually go on a quest for healing or enlightenment would be an admission they aren't already healed or enlightened. ONEs resist taking a step toward getting what they need. By refusing to acknowledge their refusal of the call they resist making the necessary adaptations to their challenging circumstances and emerging needs.

Self-defeating Principles

It is easier to fight for one's principles than to live up to them.
Alfred Adler

ONEs get into arguments about principles. People's words and actions become symbolic of what the ONE sees as underlying principles. ONEs sacrifice cooperation and resist feeling compassion, to stand up for the principles and ideals they most identify with. An attack on those principles, or a perceived attack on what they see as a symbolic representation, is provocation for a battle.

Tales from the therapy room

Mike, a seventeen-year old, was strongly identified with the principle of freedom of expression. He felt it was his right to express himself openly no matter what. If he thought his opportunities to express his opinions in any way were going to be compromised, he would protest vehemently, using every form of profanity at his disposal. Defending his right of self-expression was more important than being understood or responded to. Swearing became one of the symbols of his right of self-expression. Fighting for his right to swear, in principle, led him to swear more. The more he swore in his relationships with adults, the less they wanted to listen and the more they would use threats and punitive measures to stop his swearing. Because of his identification with the principle, his battle to defend his right to swear, it felt like a life and death struggle.

ONEs, like Mike, become overly identified with their principles to the neglect of learning how to adapt behavior to best put their principles into practice. Resisting the movement to TWO, ONEs have a hard time putting themselves into another person's perspective, and therefore don't see the effect they are having on who they are relating to.

ONEs sacrifice relationships to hold onto to their interpretation of the principles they are most identified with. ONEs caught in their compulsion would rather be 'right' than happy. This need to be right, and to uphold, defend, and convert others to their principles, gives ONEs a persona of righteousness. Well-rounded ONEs can become great reformers. Mahatma Gandhi, Ralph Nader and Martin Luther were all ONEs whose powers of discernment helped bring about important social changes.

The Connections from ONE to SEVEN and FOUR

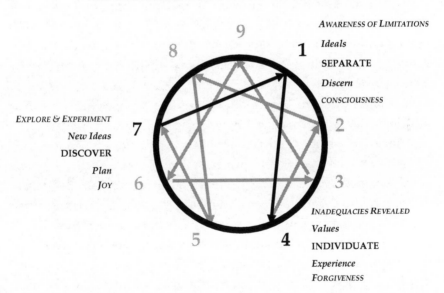

Connection to SEVEN

During periods of integration and stability, type ONEs connect more with the qualities of SEVEN — exploration and experimentation, joy, discovery, planning and new ideas.

Type ONEs fantasize about idealized futures to compensate for the lack of satisfying experiences in the real world. They obsess about what they will do once they find the perfect partner or job. ONEs who feel they must keep up their image of perfection will covertly explore and experiment outside their rigid code of principles. The religious puritan might secretly indulge in pornography or visit prostitutes. The health food fanatic might make midnight runs to McDonalds. Instead of loosening up rigid ideas of how they should live and seeking a way of integrating the needs expressed in these activities into their lives, they feel guilty about their desires and hide them away.

ONEs stress themselves out with overly demanding work schedules, but then play and have fun on vacations. As long as they give themselves these periodic SEVENish breaks, they can maintain the stability of their perfectionist lifestyle. ONE's developmental challenge is to find a way to recognize and compassionately attend to their needs and find a way to integrate them into life: to find a way that is congruent with their principles. Being open to entertaining new ideas and freeing themselves to experiment with and explore new options, over time loosens the restraints on embracing the next cycle of change.

ONEs would do well to take Groucho Marx 's advice: "Before you criticize someone, you should walk a mile in their shoes. That way, when you criticize them, you're a mile away and you have their shoes."

ONEs get stuck in thinking there is one and only one right way of thinking about and doing things. At SEVEN we are able to entertain multiple perspectives simultaneously. Multiple meanings and nonlinear logic is the basis of much humor. The connection to SEVEN allows ONEs to not take life so seriously and get in touch with the sort of crazy wisdom that helps them to embrace the dimensions of life outside of conscious mental frameworks.

Connection to FOUR

During periods of disintegration and when approaching chaos, type ONEs move towards: revealing inadequacies, forgiveness, experience, individuation and values. Type ONEs' inability to live up to their own ideals and their powerlessness to reform others leads them to increasingly feel inadequate and defeated. Hope of making things right turns to hopelessness. In hopeless defeat, ONE's realize the futility of trying to manage their lives with conscious control. Becoming disillusioned with their images of how things should be, and the rigid guidelines of what is supposed to be done to attain them, opens them to experiencing feelings more deeply. They become more affected by their personal woundedness and what has been getting in the way of moving towards their ideals. ONEs caught in their compulsion will then fluctuate between feeling sorry for themselves and berating themselves for being so weak and pathetic. They lecture themselves about how they should be over those hurts by now. This only magnifies the basic pattern of not having their emotional needs attended to, while being pushed to behave as if everything is perfect. This drives them into despair and they give up trying to do the right thing. ONEs can fall into depression or resort to obsessive thinking and compulsive behavior to maintain control over an ever-shrinking domain.

Disintegrating into a greater awareness of their own inadequacies humbles ONEs into forgiving the world and themselves for not being perfect. The intensity of pain and longing leads them to ask what they need in order to attend to neglected parts. At this point, ONEs might finally ask for help, rather than hiding flaws and keeping problems to themselves.

Coming Out of Hiding

Bill, a ONE, is married to Jane, the NINE we met in the previous section. He had some very rigid principles about his roles as a husband and a father. He worked very hard to do the right thing by providing for them. As he had become identified with what he eventually labeled as the benevolent dictator role, there was no room for him to ask for what he wanted or to get help with sorting out his problems. After all, he was the one who solved problems. Since he didn't feel he could ask his wife for the sort of relating he wanted, he ended up sneaking outside his marriage to get it. He was stuck in trying to live up to his ideals of being a man who is good, strong, helpful and in control. He hid the parts of himself he labeled as being bad, weak and needy from his family, friends and work colleagues.

When Bill's wife discovered he was having the affair a second time, after he had already promised to end it, he could no longer uphold his image of the good husband. He finally was able to admit he had problems out of his conscious control and needed help. Over time, he was able to begin integrating the parts of himself he had expressed in the affair into his marriage and family life. To keep his secret feelings and guilt hidden from his wife and kids, he had isolated himself in work-related activities and reading. Once Bill no longer needed to maintain his unblemished image, he found it much easier to engage in conversation. Not only could he ask for help, he was able to be more empathetic and supportive to the people he was closest to.

Understanding how type ONEs tend to resist the natural processes of change and cling to fixed ideas of themselves helps us to meet them where they get stuck and show them the possibility for greater freedom.

Personality Type TWO

Type TWOs identify with the:

- change cycle phase of adaptive behavior
- essential quality of compassion
- basic function of adaptability
- developmental task of relating
- psychological network of behavior

Type TWOS tend to resist the:

- change cycle phase of exploring limits of capabilities
- essential quality of strength
- basic function of initiation
- developmental task of promotion
- psychological network of capabilities.

TWOs fear slipping back into the separation and isolation associated with the judgments and conflicts that arise when consciously being true to their ideals. (ONE). They cope by being overly compassionate and adaptive of their behavior in relationships. They compulsively ask:

- How does the problem happen?
- What is needed to improve situation?

They avoid asking:

- What is the best I can do under these circumstances?
- How else can I get what I need?

At their worst, they can demonstrate symptoms of histrionic personality disorder, hypochondrias, somatization and codependency.

When TWOs embody their essential wholeness, they are beacons of love, charity and nurturance. As they are in touch with the source of love within, they can be the best friend, partner, spouse or colleague, who is there when you need them most. Rather than creating dependency, they help others to trust in their own inner strengths and capabilities, as they have. As they are good at recognizing people's strengths, they are good at networking and helping others to make mutually beneficial connections.

Through their own healing journey they become intuitive healers; and with their loving presence help people surrender guilt, fear and self-doubt. Their greatest gift is the humility of knowing they are servants of spirit, which frees them from taking anything personally. At their best, they manifest qualities seen in people like: Jesus, Desmond Tutu, Leo Buscaglia, Jimmy Carter, Florence Nightingale, Eleanor Roosevelt, Mother Teresa, John Travolta, Lewis Carroll, Liv Ullmann and Luciano Pavarotti.

Type TWO

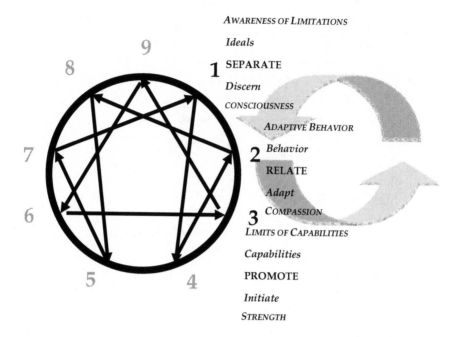

AWARENESS OF LIMITATIONS

Ideals

1 SEPARATE

Discern

CONSCIOUSNESS

ADAPTIVE BEHAVIOR

2 *Behavior*

RELATE

Adapt

3 *COMPASSION*

LIMITS OF CAPABILITIES

Capabilities

PROMOTE

Initiate

STRENGTH

Type TWOs

Identify With Phase TWO

I am my adaptive behavior.

I am compassionate.

I am adaptable to others' needs.

I am my relationships.

I am my behavior.

Resist Phase THREE

I resist going to the limits of my capabilities.

I resist acknowledging my inner strength.

I resist taking the initiative in my own life.

I resist promoting my own agenda.

I resist acknowledging my full capabilities.

Fear Slipping Back to Phase ONE

I fear being aware of limitations.

I fear being conscious of my self.

I fear being judgmental and discerning.

I fear separation.

I fear being idealistic.

Try to Cope by Doing More Phase TWO

I cope by adapting my behavior.

I cope by being more compassionate to others.

I cope by being adaptable.

I cope by being needed in relationships.

I cope by behaving according to others' expectations.

Identify With Phase TWO / Resist Phase THREE

He who is too busy doing good, finds no time to be good.
Rabindranath Tagore

Type TWOs overly identify with the essential quality of compassion. Above all they need to be seen and see themselves as a caring person. They take pride in adapting not only what they do, but also in how they present themselves, as they intuit what significant others need them to be. Their motto is, 'I'll do whatever and be whoever you need me to be.' TWOs resist taking on responsibility for their own needs and instead take on responsibility for the most important others in their lives. They are prone to codependency and enabling — rescuing others from responsibilities and making them feel dependent. They compromise attending to their needs for an image of themselves of being needed. They take pride in being able to adapt themselves to the other person's agenda and expectations. To accomplish this they resist taking the initiative in promoting their own agenda. Although they take great pride in what they do for others, internally they don't feel capable of doing things for themselves. As they don't develop the capabilities needed to successfully promote their own agenda, they end up having regrets about undeveloped potential.

Instead of realizing the self-confidence that comes with developing their potential, they settle for the pride of being 'indispensable' to significant others. TWOs project unmet needs and agendas on others, and then, in some distorted way, try to give that person what they themselves need or would like to achieve. Whereas giving freely is one of the most rewarding activities humans engage in, *giving to get* is not only draining to the giver, it doesn't feel good to the recipient. Although the TWO craves appreciation for their efforts, the more they are stuck in their compulsion, the less the thanks are forthcoming, as what they give isn't really what others want. Others can feel manipulated by the TWO's unspoken agenda, rather than actually assisted. The TWO may complain about the significant other not showing enough appreciation or in the right way, which is when the TWO will say things like, "How could you not do X … after all I have done for you?" They have a sense of entitlement stemming from all the sacrifices they feel they have made, and use spoken or unspoken guilt trips to manipulate others to do what the TWO is not willing to take direct responsibility for.

When they are not connecting with their inner strength, TWOs either cling to someone who they feel has the strength they are lacking, or to someone whom they feel stronger than. Caught in their compulsion, they rarely choose to be in relationship with someone considered an equal. Instead, they end up feeling either one up or one down.

Attending to others' needs and expectations means they are neglecting their own, which leaves them feeling needy. The more needy they feel, the more they feel they have nothing to offer within themselves. The sense of having nothing to offer leads them to try harder to support other people's talents or projects.

We see this in a wife who selflessly supports her husband's career aspirations, while not considering what her own calling might be. Sometimes they can be the *power behind the throne*, like Nancy Regan who dictated many of Ronald's decisions while president. TWOs can take on so much responsibility for the other person's life that the other person can feel that their own life is no longer theirs. They end up feeling controlled, rather than helped.

Fear Slipping Back To Phase ONE / Try to Cope by Doing More of Phase TWO

Type TWOs fear being conscious of their limitations, and cope by overly adapting their behavior to meet the perceived expectations of their significant others. They try to please out of the fear of not being good enough. They try to hide or patch up the problems of significant others to bolster their sense of pride in being needed. They fear the sense of separation that comes with discerning what is right for them. To cope with this fear, they attempt to be even more adaptable and tolerant. They end up putting up with more problematic (needy) behavior from others, settling for even less of what they want.

The more they project their own needs onto other people, the more dissociated they become from themselves. The more they disregard their own emotional needs the more overwhelming their fear of being self-conscious becomes. When they bring their awareness back into their body, they get in touch with the emptiness behind the inflated sense of pride, and discover an overwhelming sense of neediness. This seems to confirm their belief that they are nothing without their significant other. If you feel you're nothing without the other person, then the last thing you want is to be separated from them. To protect themselves from possible separation, they attempt to make themselves more indispensable, which requires ever-increasing self-sacrifice.

They fear and avoid being conscious of their ideals, as this could potentially highlight the inadequacies of their circumstances. Carl Jung explained, "Through pride, we are ever deceiving ourselves. But deep down below the surface of the average conscience a still, small voice says to us, 'Something is out of tune'." Instead of trying to live up to their own ideals, they try to be someone else's ideal parent, spouse, or significant other of some sort.

Hero's Journey — Refusing the Call to Adventure

TWOs get stuck in refusing the call. They make excuses why they shouldn't do what's needed for their developmen, thinking it would be selfish for them to follow their own calling. Although the limitations of the self-repeating patterns of their ordinary world become increasingly apparent, they become so identified with their relationships with significant others that to journey beyond these patterns feels like death. There is no other personality type more aware of how innately interdependent we are on one another, and therefore how vulnerable we are to being hurt or let down by those who we depend on. Instead of responding to the call, they sacrifice even more of their own agenda to try to keep the 'relationship' alive. TWOs can be so good at altering their behavior to improve their position they deny how vulnerable and dependent they are. However, the more they invest in manipulating circumstances, the more weakened they become by their unacknowledged needs. Their inability to accept their need for help means they deny themselves the mentoring needed to help them cross the first threshold.

Promoting their Own Agenda

When you meet someone better than yourself, turn your thoughts to becoming his equal. When you meet someone not as good as you are, look within and examine your own self.
Confucius

Family therapist, Virginia Satir, herself a TWO, describes the importance for the TWO to promote her own agenda and maximize her capabilities by taking the initiative 'to change when the situation calls for it'.

Over the years I have developed a picture of what a human being living humanely is like. She is a person who understands, values and develops her body, finding it beautiful and useful; a person who is real and is willing to take risks, to be creative, to manifest competence, to change when the situation calls for it, and to find ways to accommodate to what is new and different, keeping that part of the old that is still useful and discarding what is not..[90]

The less TWOs develop their capabilities to influence circumstances, the more they need to adapt to their *ordinary world*. Repeated disappointment can lead to greater compromising of hopes and desires. TWOs learn to stop hoping for what they don't think is possible and settle for what they can get. As children our survival depends on our primary caregivers; we continue to adapt ourselves to the way they are until we operate in the best way we can find. However, if our parents are not residing in their essential wholeness, we learn to adapt to their dysfunctional patterns in ways that deny our essential wholeness.

Codependence

The codependent TWO perceives the need for a special someone in their life. If that person has a serious drinking problem, they adapt their ways of coping and behaving to fit in with the drinker in hope of getting more of what they want. TWOs become too preoccupied with making adaptations and lose sight of what the adaptations were for in the first place. The adaptations become the ends instead of the means. Codependent TWOs will make excuses for the alcoholic, cover up their mistakes or even justify their addiction. TWOs believe they *are* their relationship. For the relationship to end feels like death; therefore, they must keep it going, no matter how unfulfilling it becomes. The more they become identified with the relationship, the less connected to their essential inner strength and capabilities they become. Feeling weak and incapable of supporting themselves reinforces the need to have someone to lean on. Their disowned inner strength is projected into their dependent partner and they'll believe that person has an inner strength they lack, in spite of the other's weaknesses. There is often an unspoken agreement of, "I'll be here for you if you'll be here for me and by leaning on one another we'll be able to get through." They try to convince themselves they are the ones who are being leaned on — however, when the dependent person moves away from the relationship, the co-dependent TWO quickly falls into a heap.

To feel compassionate empathy for someone, we extend our awareness into the other's mind-body. We literally *sense* what it's like to be them. Codependent TWOs spend little time in their own mind-body space. The lack of internal references means much of the information they have about themselves is based on how they think others see them, which is usually 'never good enough'. This false intuition leads them to trying even harder to live up to what they 'intuit' to be the others expectations.

Tales from the Therapy Room

Jason spent most of his non-work time trying to give his girlfriend Diane what she needed. Diane felt very wounded and neglected by her parents, and as a young woman felt unable to take care of herself. Jason took it upon himself to give her the kind of parenting he thought she needed. When he wasn't helping her, he would engage in the rescuing of friends. As a teacher, although there were a few needy students he tried to help, mostly he did the minimum of what was expected, so he could get back to where he really felt needed. Jason's career suffered as he neglected developing his capabilities and taking initiative in the workplace. Instead, he put his efforts into helping Diane cope with her problems and pursue her career goals. The more successful Diane became, the better she felt about herself and the less she needed Jason. As Jason's caretaking became less important to her, she began to experience it as demeaning. Diane found herself being attracted to men who were doing more with their lives. Jason tried to hold on to Diane by saying things like, "How can you want to leave me after all I've done for you?" This only made Diane feel more trapped and less desirous of Jason. This pattern escalated and Jason drove her right out of his life. For many TWOs, it's not until their primary relationship fails that they start taking more responsibility for themselves. It was at this point Jason finally sought therapy.

The Connections from TWO to FOUR and EIGHT

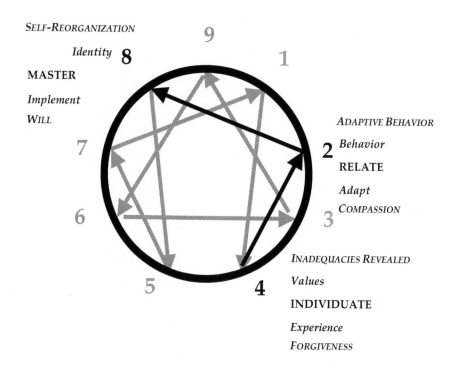

318

Connection to FOUR

During periods of integration and stability, TWOs connect more with the qualities of FOUR: revealing inadequacies, forgiveness, experience, individuation and values. When TWOs feel stable and safe they exhibit a sort of innocence that comes with revealing their inadequacies and needs. This balances the tendency to be the caregiver. Caught in their prideful compulsion, however, this awareness drives them to try even harder to be helpful to compensate for feelings of inadequacy. TWOs' compassionate nature makes it easy for them to be forgiving; however, caught in their image of themselves, they use pseudo-forgiveness to put themselves above people and avoid taking responsibility for their part of the interaction.

The connection to FOUR helps them to direct their sensitivity inward and connect with more of their personal experience. This lessens the tendency to project their agendas onto others. As they connect with neglected wounds and emergent values, they get a stronger sense of what capabilities they need to develop to promote their own agenda.

Connection to EIGHT

During periods of disintegration and when approaching chaos, type TWOs connect more with the qualities of EIGHT: self-reorganization, will, implementation, mastery and identity. The lack of ecological balance between giving and receiving leaves the TWO feeling increasingly resentful. When the indirect manipulation of *giving to get* prove unsatisfactory, TWOs explode with angry threats and intimidation. They try to use their will to force others to do as they expect.

The TWO, who usually has poor personal boundaries, at EIGHT reconnects with their ability to say 'No' and to ask for what they want. In the crisis of realizing their significant other is not going to meet all their needs, they realize the need to implement their own skills. Working towards mastering skills helps them to believe in themselves more. They are able reorganize enough of their life so they can promote their emergent agenda and get back into the flow of life.

Understanding how type TWOs tend to resist the natural processes of change and cling to fixed ideas of themselves helps us to meet them where they get stuck and show them the possibility for greater freedom.

Personality Type THREE

Type THREEs identify with the:

- change cycle phase of exploring limits of capabilities
- essential quality of strength
- basic function of initiation
- developmental task of promotion
- psychological network of capabilities

Type THREEs tend to resist the:

- change cycle phase of revealing inadequacies
- essential quality of forgiveness
- basic function of experience
- developmental task of individuation
- psychological network of values

THREEs fear slipping back into adapting their behavior to meet others needs (TWO). They cope by utilizing strength to maximize the capabilities needed to promote themselves. They compulsively ask:

- What is the best I can do under these circumstances?
- How else can I get what I need?
- How can I promote my agenda?

They avoid asking:

- What is most important?
- What's missing?
- Where am I stuck?

At their worst can demonstrate narcissistic and borderline personality disorders, and the heart disease-prone Type A personality.

When THREEs embody their essential wholeness they succeed by making a valuable contribution to the world. They are very forgiving of mistakes, which, along with their motivation to realize their full potential, helps them learn quickly. They know better than anyone that the best way to enrich your life is to enrich others' lives, which makes them charming and gracious. People look to them as role models of how to succeed in their field of endeavor. At their best they manifest qualities seen in people like: Deepak Chopra, Oprah Winfrey, Anthony Robbins, Sting, Christopher Reeve, Werner Erhard, Will Smith, Paul McCartney, Nora Ephron, Jesse Jackson, F. Scott Fitzgerald and Shirley MacLaine.

Type THREE

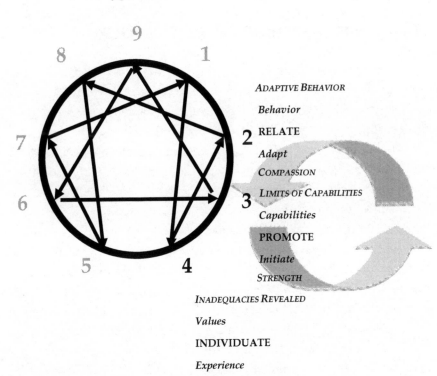

ADAPTIVE BEHAVIOR

Behavior

RELATE

Adapt

COMPASSION

LIMITS OF CAPABILITIES

Capabilities

PROMOTE

Initiate

STRENGTH

INADEQUACIES REVEALED

Values

INDIVIDUATE

Experience

FORGIVENESS

Type THREEs

Identify with Phase THREE	Resist Phase FOUR
I am going to limits of my capabilities.	I resist revealing any inadequacies.
I am strong.	I resist forgiving.
I am an initiator.	I resist feeling my personal experience.
I am my self-promotion.	I resist my unique individuality.
I am capable.	I resist acknowledging my deeper values.

Fear Slipping Back to Phase TWO	Cope by Doing More of Phase THREE
I fear adapting my behavior.	I cope by pushing myself to my limits.
I fear being compassionate.	I cope by being strong.
I fear adapting to meet others' needs.	I cope by taking the initiative.
I fear being needed in relationships.	I cope by promoting my agenda.
I fear needing to do what others need.	I cope by being as capable as possible.

Identify with Phase THREE / Resist Phase FOUR

Type THREEs are overly identified with the essential quality of strength. They want more than anything to be perceived as being strong and capable. To maintain this perception they avoid revealing their inadequacies, not only to others, but also to themselves. The process of not admitting to their mistakes, failures and woundedness denies them access to their forgiving nature and can lead them to be ruthless in their pursuit of their goals. The preoccupation with taking the initiative to successfully promote their agenda keeps them oriented toward the future and away from past hurts and mistakes. Needing to perceive themselves as capable and successful requires resisting experiencing how their agenda fails to express their deeper values. They connect with their heart's true yearnings when they stop promoting their self-concept and connect with their unique experience in each moment. The more they identify with the images of success, the more out of touch with their essential wholeness they become. The emptiness inside the shell of their image is perceived as evidence that they are nobody and to compensate they try even harder to become a self-made man or woman. Caught in their compulsion, no amount of money, prestige or victory is ever enough.

THREEs can forget the reason they decided to work so hard in the first place was to be a good spouse, parent or provider. Polishing the image of success in these roles, rather than connecting with loved ones, means they are out of touch with what is really wanted or needed — which is more of their presence. Their optimism blinds them to the inadequacies of their marriage, often until faced with divorce. It is with the humiliation of failure that they remember what matters most and resurrect their marriages, or do better next time around. There are THREEish men that remarry and start a new family in order to experience what they missed out on the first time around while they were being workaholics.

A THREE's commitment to succeed is often an attempt to correct a perceived failing of a parent. Little boys who see their mothers let down by their fathers will strive from a young age to be the man their fathers never were. This original motivation is often forgotten, but continues to drive their behavior unconsciously; anger and/or guilt continue to drive them. Due to their tendency to resist awareness of past inadequacies or what is unhealed, they deny themselves the opportunity to forgive the past. Without forgiveness, they condemn themselves to repeat the problematic themes.

Tales from the Therapy Room

One middle age man in therapy blamed not only his father for abandoning his mother, but also himself for not adequately filling the gap of his father's absence. He perceived this as the cause of his mother's depression. At FOUR we recognize not only our own inadequacies but also others'. By doing so, we are able to begin seeing how we're all doing the best we can, given what we know or what we are capable of at the time — this is the basis of forgiveness. He had never forgiven himself or his father for his mother's unhappiness. At a young age he had made a promise to himself he would never be like his father and he would always look after his mother, and his future wife and kids. As a middle age man, he had kept his commitment; he was still supporting his mother, who never remarried, or made much of her life. He was a very good provider for his family, but hardly ever saw them. He worked very long hours under

---

the motto of giving his kids the things he never had. His wife initiated marital therapy with the complaint that she felt he had neglected her and the kids in favor of his career. This came as a great shock to him and he argued vehemently that everything he did was for them. When I was eventually able to help him acknowledge how little love and intimacy he was settling for and the loneliness of working such long hours, it unleashed a great well of grief from his own childhood. He realized how, in his attempt to be strong and help his mother cope with her separation from his father, he had never felt his own grief and his own unmet longings. His rigid adherence to his naive commitment to be strong, not weak like his father, had blocked him from getting in touch with the very feelings and sensitivities needed to form meaningful connections with his wife and children.

Fear Slipping Back to Phase TWO / Cope by Doing More of Phase THREE

Type THREEs fear feeling dependent or being depended upon and needing to adapt what they do to meet others' expectations. However, since what you resist persists, compulsive THREEs push themselves to the limits of their capabilities to succeed in the eyes of significant others (often a parent, even if deceased). THREEs fear empathizing with others for two reasons. First, since they ruthlessly do whatever the feel they must do to succeed, no matter what effect it may have on others, to actually acknowledge their effect on others, would force them to question their agenda. Second, feeling others' pain requires us to be in touch with our own emotional vulnerability, which threatens THREEs' strong and capable self-image. They cope with the fear of emotional weakness, by being strong and soldiering on. This can mean that people in their path may unwittingly get trampled. The more people they hurt or disappoint, the more obvious the need to adapt what they are doing to meet other's needs or to behave according to their expectations.

THREEs live according to images that their culture, including their family, deems worthwhile, yet avoid feeling the pain and emptiness of these pursuits. THREEish children can feel overwhelmed by a parent's pain and what it means to have such a wounded parent. To cope with the despair of their family situation, they commit themselves to making the status quo function, or at least appear to. Without the emotional maturity to know what is really needed, they do their best by drawing on external images of what a 'successful' family looks like and try their best to replicate it in their immature way. To feel deeply into either their parent's pain or their own would leave them as incapacitated as their parents, so they dissociate from the present and live in the image of a desirable future.

Lacking connection to many internal as well as external resources, they limit themselves to achieving in those arenas they feel capable of succeeding in, which naturally neglects those dimensions of their lives that are most lacking. For this reason, they fear acknowledging dependency in relationships, and grow up taking pride in thinking of themselves as 'self-made' men and women. Having deep compassion for themselves would reveal the emptiness of this self-made image and therefore this must be avoided at all costs. Continuing this pattern into adulthood translates into keeping up appearances, but not developing the skills needed to relate in more mature and meaningful ways.

Phillip came to counseling because he was willing to do everything it took to make his relationship with Leanne work. The presenting problem was frequent misunderstandings and arguments. Leanne felt uncomfortable with his sarcasm and aggravated voice tone, which would burst into conversations whenever she started to ask too many questions or express her doubts about their relationship. He labeled her doubts and questions as merely her neurosis. He believed he was fulfilling his role as her boyfriend and any critique of his behavior was an attack on him. When asked, he said he regularly operated at a stress level of seven out of ten. Concurrently, he said he was happy most of the time, except when she 'made' him feel bad. In trying to remedy the misunderstandings, he had tried to 'listen' better and succeed in behaving in the ways she wanted him to, while ignoring the emotions and stress that caused him to react aggressively. The more he tried to present himself as the caring and understanding guy he thought he was supposed to be, the less she trusted his genuineness. How could he be sensitive and understanding of her feelings when he constantly ignored and overrode his own internal signals? He couldn't understand how she could be concerned about all these 'unimportant' issues when they had everything going for them. His usual remedy for her was she just needed to be more confident like him. It wasn't until Leanne left him that he finally realized he needed to care for his emotional self.

Hero's Journey — Meeting the Mentor and Crossing the First Threshold

The THREEish person gets stuck in the Meeting with the Mentor and at the Crossing of the First Threshold. THREEs commit themselves to change, but get stuck in simply trying to improve the status quo. They are good at empowering themselves with the maps and capabilities needed to follow their calling, but resist crossing the threshold from their ordinary world into unknown realms where they are less assured of success in the short term. Many modern businesses operate in this model of maximizing short-term profits, while ignoring the inadequacies of the system that need to be addressed for long-term financial and ecological sustainability. THREEs are very good at modeling mentors. To model a mentor they go into what in hypnosis is called deep-trance-identification. This can be a useful way of learning from others' experience, but THREEs get stuck in role-playing the other person and lose connection to their inner self. To prop up their image further, THREEs collect status symbols for themselves, as well as give them as gifts. Status symbols are symbolic representations (proof) of success within the status quo. They buy the type of car, jewelry or articles of clothing that polishes their image of success. This is contrasted with the type FOUR's tendency to collect possessions that reflect an image of uniqueness, or SEVENs who want whatever is the latest fashion.

There is a sense of power and safety in modeling a powerful person, but in order to grow and discover our potential, we must connect with our unique individuality.

One type THREE man I worked with had modeled himself on a sophisticated television detective. This character became the blueprint for operating in the world. He even wore the same style of clothes and drove the same model of car. He said it gave him confidence in the world of sales and superficial interaction, but he was at a loss of knowing how to get close to people. It wasn't until his wife of many years left him that he began to get to know his neglected inner self. As THREEs can be so confident in the world, it is their partner's unhappiness that brings them to therapy, rather than their own sense of inadequacy.

THREEs keep themselves so busy improving their ordinary world, they don't have time to acknowledge the inadequacies of that existence or longings for something else. The lack of connection to emergent values lends a growing sense of meaninglessness to their actions and they attempt to compensate by cramming in even more goal-oriented activity. One THREE asked me to hypnotize him into needing less sleep so he could work longer hours, then revealed that he was only sleeping about four hours per night already.

Philosopher Bertrand Russell warned, "One of the symptoms of an approaching nervous breakdown is the belief that one's work is terribly important." Type THREEs' identification with being strong and capable blinds them to the reality that successfully promoting their agenda eventually brings them to the limits of their ordinary world. The better they do, the more pronounced the inadequacies of that way of living become. In trying to maintain their successful self-image they keep doing more of what they are already good at, which only highlights the problems even more.

THREEs tend to seek out mentors to help them do what they are already doing better, like the man who wanted to sleep less. A true mentor will help them explore what has been neglected. Often they get dragged over the first threshold and into the FOURish 'long dark night of the soul' with things like illness, death of a loved one, or a relationship breakdown. These issues, which can't be managed with the usual methods, force them to go on a journey into the unknown to find what has been missing or neglected.

Embracing Inadequacies and Deeper Values

Try not to become a man of success, but rather try to become a man of value.
Albert Einstein

Your task is not to seek for love, but merely to seek and find all the barriers within yourself that you have built against it. *Rumi*

Embracing their inadequacies, rather than avoiding them in their usual ways, leads the THREE to an awareness of deeper values and eventually

327

a new identity. A therapist I was supervising was working with a gambler. She, along with her client, was feeling very helpless about the $150,000 debt he had. He was doing his best to convince her to lend him $700 to pay back some of the money he owed his girlfriend. He was very capable at convincing people to lend him money; in fact, the therapist almost gave it to him. She resisted the temptation, embraced her own helplessness about the situation and in the process her client was forced to face his helplessness. His failure to handle the situation in his usual way, forced him to find another solution. With the help of a financial adviser he drew up long-term contracts to pay back the money. He reported for the first time in as long as he could remember that he felt a sense of respect for himself. In his failure to do things in his usual way, he had the opportunity to connect with some of his deeper values of honesty, patience and responsibility. As he incorporated these new values into his life, it became inconceivable for him to try keep up his affluent image of success through gambling and deceit.

America — Type THREE

One reason so many people may be suffering from depression in American society (predominantly a THREEish culture) is the unacknowledged disillusionment with the cultural myths (especially materialism) we have been living by. Many people have believed if they work hard, earn money and are able to buy the things they want, they will find fulfillment. Instead of experiencing the emptiness of the pursuit, they keep trying even harder. For these people the cure for unhappiness is to keep busy. Type THREEs often use mechanical metaphors when speaking of themselves, such as, "I'm a success machine" or, "I'm really powering now." Operating mechanically, they lose the opportunity to allow their deeper values to evolve, and hence to seek fulfillment in other ways.

The more stuck a type THREE becomes, the more prone they are to deceiving others, and more importantly themselves. Their lies are both of omission and commission. American media and government sources, for example, usually like to present America in the best light. However, to do this there has been a tendency to withhold much of what really goes on, and in certain cases, for example, the Vietnam War, there were lies told about US ships being attacked in the Gulf of Tonkin to justify America's attack. Lies were also told at the beginning of the Persian Gulf War regarding Iraqis removing Kuwaiti incubators from hospitals.

America's history is dotted with examples of its tendency to want to been seen as the upholder of democracy and justice, yet rather than openly admitting to many of their inadequacies so we can continue to evolve as a society, there have often been cover-ups and lies. THREEs develop amnesia for past mistakes and continue to live their lies as if they were true. Some of America's greatest moments, as with any type THREE, are often when the administration and population owns up to our failings and courageously begins taking the steps to address the failures and injustices, and strives towards upholding our most profound democratic ideals. The more people spend time with a fixated THREE, the more they mistrust the 'too-good-to-be-true presentation'. THREEs are surprised to find that when they reveal their inadequacies, people tend to paradoxically trust and respect them *more*.

The Connections from THREE to SIX and NINE

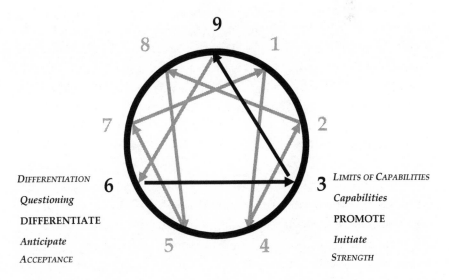

HOMEOSTASIS
Community / Environment
COOPERATE
Consolidate / Mediate
PEACE

9

8   1

7   2

DIFFERENTIATION **6**
Questioning
DIFFERENTIATE
Anticipate
ACCEPTANCE

3 LIMITS OF CAPABILITIES
Capabilities
PROMOTE
Initiate
STRENGTH

5   4

Connection to SIX

During periods of integration and stability type THREEs connect more with the qualities of SIX: differentiation, acceptance, anticipation and questioning. Type THREEs' connection to SIX helps them to anticipate problems before they occur, supporting their ability to succeed within an area of interest. It helps them to avoid those situations outside their realm of expertise and therefore any sense of inadequacy. Their connection to SIX helps them to differentiate what works best without looking beyond recognized models. They use their ability to not react to other people's reactivity to stay on track with their objectives. However, they do it in conjunction with avoiding connection to emergent or neglected selves; rather than connecting with unconditional acceptance within, THREEs caught in their compulsion almost continuously seek out acceptance (approval) from others. As they resist connecting with core values, they look toward authority figures within the status quo to help them differentiate what they should believe or not believe in. This dependence on outer authority further weakens their ability to connect with their individual uniqueness. Instead of questioning the values and beliefs that limit choices, THREEs question their ability and whether they deserve appreciation and love.

The connection to SIX leads the overly confident THREE to question the successful self-image they promote. The more safe and secure their life seems, the easier it is for them to allow themselves to feel vulnerable. They begin to question if all the striving for status is worth it. This doubtful reflection allows for deeper values to be acknowledged and the inadequacies of their current way of functioning to be revealed.

Connection to NINE

During periods of disintegration and when approaching chaos, type THREEs connect more with the qualities of NINE: homeostasis, peace, mediation, cooperation and community /environment. Under stress, type THREEs try to cope by lowering expectations, in an attempt to regain homeostasis. Instead of needing to be seen as strong and capable, they retreat into blending into the community or environment. They try to smooth over or mediate the conflicts of interest they have created while in pursuit of their aims. As the THREEs' ordinary world breaks down, they remember how important family, community and organization are, and work to re-establish cooperative relationships with the people they care about. If they are really stuck in their compulsion, however, this could mean repressing their emergent agenda to keep the peace, rather than gathering support to cross the first threshold of their hero's journey. It's like they take themselves to the very brink of making a life-transforming shift, but at the last moment retreat back to the safety of known territory. Trying to regain stability by retreating from life, rather than engaging more deeply, takes the form of apathy and resignation, known in ACT as experiential avoidance. As they regain confidence, they might make this approach several times before they find the courage to push over the attractor basin of their current belief system.

When forced to slow down through sickness or failure, THREEs can at times give up trying to prove themselves, and connect instead with a sense of inner peace. Rather than trying to impress family and community, they feel their connection with them. The opening of the boundaries between outer presentation and emotional self helps them to connect more intimately with their inner-selves.

Understanding how type THREEs tend to resist the natural processes of change and cling to fixed ideas of themselves helps us to meet them where they get stuck and show them the possibility for greater freedom.

Personality Type FOUR

Type FOUR identifies with the:

- change cycle phase of revealing inadequacies
- essential quality of forgiveness
- basic function of experience
- developmental task of individuation
- psychological network of values

Type FOUR tends to resist the:

- change cycle phase of diffuse boundaries
- essential quality of space
- basic function of understanding
- developmental task of investigation
- psychological network of beliefs

Type FOURs fear slipping back into having to initiate their own agenda only to discover the limits of their capabilities. They cope by clinging to personal experiences that demonstrate their uniqueness or sense of inadequacy, while longing for what is unavailable. They compulsively ask:

- What is most important?
- What's missing?
- Where am I stuck?

They avoid asking:

- Why is this happening?
- What is the pattern?
- What is, and is not, essential?
- What do I need to know to get through this?

At their worst, they can demonstrate depressive, avoidant and narcissistic personality traits.

When FOURs embody their essential wholeness, they bring unique insights to the human condition, which they usually find some creative or symbolic way of expressing. They can relate to experience personally, impersonally and transpersonally — they are aware of the big picture, as well as the fine details. This helps them bring a deep playful intimacy to all their relationships, not just romantic partners. They have a rich appreciation for beauty and if there is isn't any beauty, they will find a way to turn what others see as rubbish into art. At their best, they manifest qualities seen in people like: Rumi, Walt Whitman, Gangaji, Pema Chodron, Stephen Gilligan, Dylan Thomas, Leonard Cohen, Ingmar Bergman, Thomas

Merton, Isabelle Allende, Allen Ginsburg, Joni Mitchell, Michelangelo, T. H. Lawrence, Alan Watts and Rudolf Nureyev.

Type FOUR

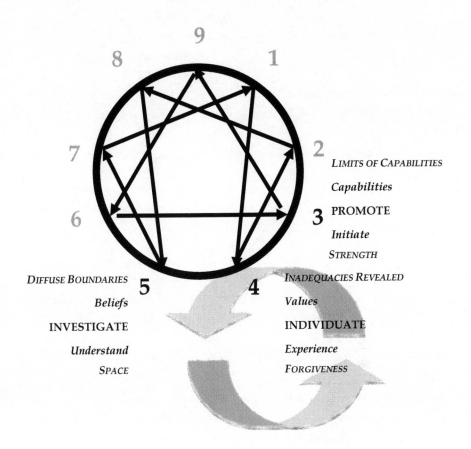

LIMITS OF CAPABILITIES

Capabilities

PROMOTE

Initiate

STRENGTH

DIFFUSE BOUNDARIES

INADEQUACIES REVEALED

Beliefs

Values

INVESTIGATE

INDIVIDUATE

Understand

Experience

SPACE

FORGIVENESS

Type FOURs

Identify with Phase FOUR	**Resist Phase FIVE**
I am my inadequacies.	I resist opening to new information.
I am forgiving.	I resist allowing myself the space to be.
I am my personal experience.	I resist understanding myself.
I am a unique individual.	I resist investigating my circumstances.
I am my values.	I resist becoming aware of my beliefs.

Fear Slipping Back to Phase THREE	**Cope by Doing More of Phase FOUR**
I fear going to the limits of my capabilities.	I cope by revealing my inadequacies.
I fear my strength.	I cope by telling myself I'm doing the best I can.
I fear taking the initiative.	I cope by clinging to personal experiences.
I fear promoting myself.	I cope by cherishing my uniqueness.
I fear being capable.	I cope by inflating the importance of my values.

Identify With Phase FOUR / Resist Phase FIVE

Type FOURs are overly identified with the essential quality of forgiveness. FOURs tend to be very tolerant of other's flaws and foibles. Caught in their compulsion, they take a sort of perverse pride in their own inadequacies; desperate to prove their wounds are more tragic than anyone else's. Identifying with forgiveness, rather than being forgiving, leads them to take the pseudo-forgiving attitude — "I know that person who let me down was doing the best they could," but also thinking, "The reason *they* aren't more loving is because there is something wrong with *me*." Pseudo-forgiveness can also take the form of, "Even though you scarred me for life, I forgive you." The result of this unresolved anger turned inwards is that the FOUR withdraws from people and leaves others at the receiving end of their icy rejection. Real forgiveness is always self-forgiveness. It involves recognizing that it was our misinterpretation of the situation that caused us to suffer well after the event itself had passed. It is this self-centered misinterpretation that FOURs often have difficulty giving up.

Forgiveness releases regret, resentment and guilt. These emotions are in reference to past events. By limiting awareness to the past, FOURs don't give themselves the space to experience the present free from past pain.

They compare life to how it was or could have been, if only they hadn't ruined it for themselves. They maintain identification with inadequacies by resisting any information that would contradict this perception, while identifying with emotional memories that reinforce this self-perception. It's difficult to share these feelings, because they don't feel anyone could possibly understand them. Stuck in their subjective perspective, they don't gain objective understanding of themselves, and by not sharing them they close themselves off from perspectives that might lead to new understandings. To see things more objectively is frightening, as their identity is dependent on their sense of tragedy; if they were to lose this, they would feel like nothing.

A fearful mind will tend to misperceive the essential quality of space as deficient emptiness, a sense of hollowness or lack of substance. To compensate for this the feeling of emptiness, they cling to the idea they are uniquely special — alone in a world where no one can understand or relate to them. This specialness comes across often as a haughty contempt. They will judge people for being superficial and out of touch with the painful reality of life. This attitude distances them further, as they don't even give anyone a chance to understand them or to discover what suffering people share in common with them. FOURs forget the simple truths that everyone is unique, living in an imperfect world, with no escape from disappointments. No one gets all the love they feel they need. We all learn to live with the imperfections and inadequacies of planet Earth to varying degrees, not only FOURs.

On one level, what gives something value is its specialness. We consider gold or diamonds to be special, therefore they hold greater value than other substances. Air and water are not generally thought of as valuable substances, until they are in short supply. If air and water were in short supply, then gold and diamonds pale into insignificance, and we would trade our treasures to get the air and water we need to survive. FOURs identify with what they value as special and lose appreciation for the simple essentials of life. They forget that they are loveable and worthwhile simply because they are one of us — another strand in the web of life.

Fear Slipping Back to Phase THREE / Cope by Doing More of Phase FOUR

Type FOURs fear testing the limits of their capabilities. To cope with failed attempts — or failure to even make the attempt — they remind themselves and others of their inadequacies. FOURs intuitively know that success in the status quo eventually leads to the realization of the inadequacies of that pursuit, so why bother putting in the effort in the first place. This frequently happens in the realm of personal relationships, earning them the tag of 'Hopeless Romantics'. Instead of viewing the relationship breakdown as an opportunity to let go of the old ways of relating in order to develop new ones, they simply take it as evidence for their inadequacy and/or the inadequacy of others.

FOURs are prone to a sense of learned helpless that leads to feeling hopeless. The more identified they are with their sense of inadequacy, the more threatening their inner strength is to their constructed identity. They cope with this fear of their strength with more pseudo-forgiveness, in which they tell themselves they are doing their best given who they are. With this sense of helplessness, they fear taking the initiative to promote any agenda and instead cling to painful touchstone memories. Rather than promoting their emergent self, they cling to their sense of unique inadequacy. Afraid of developing their capabilities, they cope by clinging to their high standards. For example, rather than developing musical capabilities, they inflate the importance of their musical taste, assessing it as much more sophisticated than other people's. Since they overly identify with their values (tastes), it leads them to the haughty attitude of feeling alone in a superficial world.

Hero's Journey — Tests, Allies and Enemies

On the Hero's journey, FOURs get stuck in the phase of being tested in their resolve. They haven't yet made up their mind if they are committed to find the way through the long dark night of the soul. It's like they sit down in the middle of the long dark tunnel with no light shining from either end, and feel lost and hopeless. Instead of taking Winston Churchill's advice, "If you're going through hell, keep going", type FOURs will ruminate about all that has gone wrong and the evidence that condemns them to their personal purgatory or hell. They fail to recognize allies trying to assist them on their journey, while clinging to people or things detrimental to them. Instead of seeing falling flat on their face as a sign they are moving in the right direction, they take as proof to their destiny to fail. Being stuck in the feeling of failure gets expressed with the attitude of, "What difference does it make what I do, anyway?" When old maps of their ordinary world fail them in the dreamy landscape of the transitional world, they can resign themselves to the suicidal attitude of, 'I can't go on living anymore', instead of simply noting, 'I can't go on living *in this way* any more'.

Making alliances with enemies and not joining with true allies exacerbates this self-destructive cycle that can end in suicide, whether intentional or accidental. A man in his mid-fifties wrote a letter to his psychiatrist outlining his suicidal feelings, and a short while later died in a motorcycle accident trying to keep up with his young lover. One of the words to describe FOURS is dauntless, which can make them seem to have a death wish.

Trapped within melancholic, lonely helplessness, they look upon those enjoying satisfying relationships with envy. Instead of motivating them to follow the example of others, the FOURish person thinks, "What's wrong with me? No one is ever going to love me like that."

Comedy and Tragedy

> The images of the unconscious place a great responsibility upon a man. Failure to understand them, or a shirking of ethical responsibility, deprives him of his wholeness and imposes a painful fragmentariness on his life. *Carl Jung*

The difference between a comedy and tragedy is where the story is punctuated. As great comedians show us, the most tragic events of life can make the funniest stories — once we have gained enough distance from them to understand the errors of our actions and perceptions, free of guilt and shame. Humor is a sign we have been able to forgive the past and come to a greater sense of acceptance. FOURs evolve by embracing a spacious mind that helps them view their memories more objectively, like a movie on a screen. Then, like a Woody Allen classic, they unpretentiously see the humor in their tragic romanticism.

Myth of Romantic Love

More than other types, FOURs imagine salvation comes from a special person who will make them feel loved. They dissociate from their essential loving nature and project it into an unattainable lover. Feeling empty without the other, they feel undeserving and incapable of love. Consequently, they don't reach out or respond to the opportunities for relating. If they manage to give someone a chance, they place such high expectations on the other person, that when this person doesn't bring salvation, FOURs think it must not be the right person.

After several failed romances, FOURs can resign themselves to the perception there is no one in the world suited for them — or they are the ones not suited to this world. They avoid examining the beliefs underlying their perceptions, remaining blindly submerged in unconscious personal and cultural myths. To grow, they need to be able to step outside themselves and begin to see the patterns that have captured them and the underlying beliefs that have shaped their perceptions and choices.

Embracing Emptiness

> Who are we? We find that we live on an insignificant planet of a humdrum star lost in a galaxy tucked away in some forgotten corner of a universe in which there are far more galaxies than people. *Carl Sagan*

FOURs evolve when they face their fear of going to the limits of their capabilities and take responsibility for attending to inadequacies. They open to a more spacious sense of themselves, in which problems are just part of their personal experience. When FOURs remember they're unique, just like everyone else, they stop taking everything so personally. They realize they are merely a part of an unfolding human drama. Instead of merely re-experiencing recycled emotions, they begin to investigate why they feel that way, and what they have done to perpetuate their problems.

By stepping back from their habitual wants and desires, they can examine more closely what they were hoping those desires would do for them. Following this inquiry deep enough leads them back to the unconditioned qualities of their essential wholeness. Instead of looking for love in all the wrong places, they tap into their loving nature and discover how to express that in the world. Irish play-write Brendan Francis points out, "At the innermost core of all loneliness is a deep and powerful yearning for union with one's lost self."

Tales from the Therapy Room

I asked Judith, who complained of feeling lonely and depressed: What is your 'inner longing' hoping to experience once you have that perfect lover?

Judith: Being wanted.

Therapist (deepening Judith's experience with hypnotic principles): And once you deeply knew you were wanted, what would that enable you to experience?

Judith: Feeling appreciated.

Therapist: And once you knew you were appreciated, what would that enable you to experience?

Judith: Feeling loved.

Therapist: And once you're totally feeling loved in just the way you imagine it, what does that enable you to experience?

Judith: I am loveable.

Therapist: As you imagine experiencing yourself as loveable, what does that enable you to experience on an even deeper level?

Judith: It's okay to be me.

Therapist: And now that you are imagining it is okay to be you, what does that open you to experience?

Judith: Nothing.

Therapist: What do you mean?

Judith: I just feel neutral, it's like I don't have to feel anything.

Therapist: Notice what happens when you open to that neutral sense of not having to feel anything.

Judith: I am just letting myself be.

Therapist: How does that feel?

Judith: Peaceful.

Therapist: Notice what happens when you let yourself disappear into that experience of peacefulness.

Judith: I feel full of love and gratitude.

Therapist: What does that sense of love and gratitude want to communicate to the part of you that has felt so lonely and depressed?

Judith: Relax and trust in your good heart, you have so much love to offer.

Unlike a type THREE, a FOUR's greatest pretenses are built up not to hide evil and the ugliness in themselves, but emptiness. In fact, the person caught in the compulsions of phase FOUR would rather cling to self-perceived ugliness than fall into empty spaciousness. Once they do, however, they have a chance to let go of their identity of inadequacy and begin to connect more fully with their essential nature. It is out of the humiliation of failing to succeed within the status quo, that we learn humility. Whereas type THREEs resist humiliation, FOURs hold on to feeling shame and humiliation, resisting the humility that comes with realizing they are simply a part of an unfolding process that is much bigger than their personal drama.

The Connections from FOUR to ONE and TWO

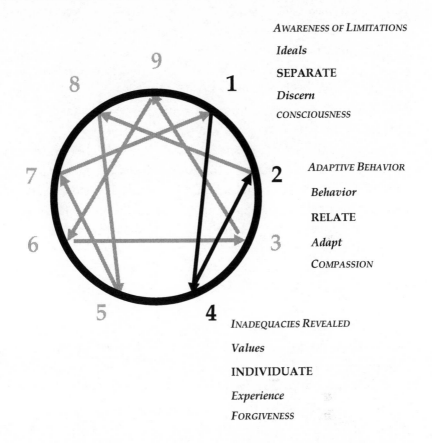

AWARENESS OF LIMITATIONS

Ideals

SEPARATE

Discern

CONSCIOUSNESS

ADAPTIVE BEHAVIOR

Behavior

RELATE

Adapt

COMPASSION

INADEQUACIES REVEALED

Values

INDIVIDUATE

Experience

FORGIVENESS

Connection to ONE

During periods of integration and stability, type FOURs connect more with the qualities of ONE: awareness of limitations, consciousness, discernment, separation and ideals. Caught in their compulsion, FOURs become very judgmental, seeing what is wrong not only in them, but in the world. This makes getting what they want seem even more impossible. To cope, they become even more obsessed with images of their ideal romance, job, or whatever they see as the salvation from despair. Compared to these brilliant fantasies, the world around them takes on a bland grayish tone, depressing them more. Projecting these idealized fantasies onto others leads them to feel envious and resentful of the unfairness of life. These perceptions magnify the sense of isolation and separation, which only reinforces the need to cling to their sense of specialness.

They put effort into doing the 'right thing', but expect to be rewarded, rather than experiencing the satisfaction of acting with integrity. When they aren't rewarded in the way they think they should, they take it as evidence that there must be something wrong with them, and that obviously no one wants to give them what they need.

However when FOURs remember that ideals are something to inspire them, not necessarily to attain, they use their discerning mind to begin making principled choices, rather than acting out their emotionality. The lack of drama helps them experience the spaciousness needed to observe the workings of their minds and their patterns of interaction, from which new understandings can arise.

Connection to TWO

During periods of disintegration and when approaching chaos, type FOURs connect with the qualities of TWO: adaptive behavior, compassion, adaptability, relating and behavior. In isolation, FOURs need for relationships gets even more desperate. They may try to prove themselves to important others by being overly helpful, too adaptable to other's expectations and too caring, like a compulsive TWO. They might try to adapt their image to meet the expectations of a prospective lover or significant other, or go through the motions of acting the way they think will be appreciated. However, they may not be aware how the sense of inadequacy translates into a feeling of desperation that keeps others at a distance.

To get someone's support, they might remind them of how they need the FOUR's uniqueness to enrich their existence the implication being that the other person's life would be boring without them. People generally take this as a putdown and distance themselves further from the FOUR. The harder they try to make the relationship work while trapped in their uniquely inadequate identity, the more they verify how unlovable they are. In their misery, FOURs resort to guilt trips like, "Look what you have done to me. You owe it to me to give me what I need," with a subtext of, "even though I know I don't deserve it."

Feeling more compassionate helps them to feel others' pain, and in doing so realize they are not alone; others suffer as they do. They also begin to relate more intimately with their wounded self. Instead of being stuck in a habitual way of feeling wounded or inadequate, they ask their wounded self how can they help. It's like the adult part of them taking care of the wounded child part. FOURs realize there are things they can do for themselves to feel better. This can lead to spontaneous insights about the repetition the childhood relationship patterns, internalized attitudes and interactions with their parents. These types of insights lead them to investigate their circumstances more fully in search of understanding, acceptance and freedom.

Understanding how type FOURs tend to resist the natural processes of change and cling to fixed ideas of themselves helps us to meet them where they get stuck and show them the possibility for greater freedom.

Personality Type FIVE

Type FIVE identifies with the:

- change cycle phase of diffuse boundaries
- essential quality of space
- basic function of understanding
- developmental task of investigation
- psychological network of beliefs

Type FIVE tends to resist the:

- change cycle phase of differentiation
- essential quality of acceptance
- basic function of differentiate
- developmental task of anticipation
- psychological network of questioning

Type FIVES fear slipping back into the experience of having their inadequacies revealed (FOUR). They cope by maintaining diffuse boundaries, which enable them to investigate their circumstances without investing too much time or energy. They compulsively ask:

- Why is this happening?
- What is the pattern?
- What is, and is not, essential?
- What do I need to know to get through this?

They avoid asking:

- What will I remain faithful to?
- What have I lost faith in?
- What is worth sacrificing for?

At their worst FIVEs demonstrate schizoid, schizotypal and avoidant personality traits.

When FIVEs embody their essential wholeness they realize the more they learn, the less they know. This allows them to hold their beliefs and theories lightly while they investigate further into their areas of interest. Through being able to understand all sides of a question, they can demonstrate true objectivity. The greater their insights, the greater their foresight into anticipating where different choices will lead. Their passion for learning doesn't just bring understanding; FIVEs can attain mastery of whatever skills they become fascinated by. At their best they manifest qualities seen in people like: Buddha, Ramana Maharshi, Albert Einstein, Ken Wilbur, Eckhart, Tolle, St. Thomas Aquinas, Gregory Bateson, Hannah Nydahl, Ernest Rossi, Samuel Beckett, Anton Chekhov, T. S. Eliot, Herman Hesse, Russ Hudson, Ludwig Wittgenstein, Oliver Sacks, B. F. Skinner and Daniel Day Lewis.

Type FIVE

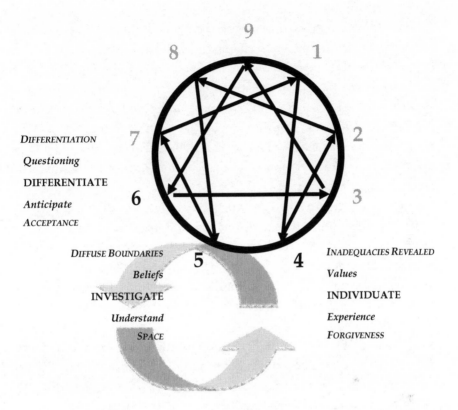

Identify with Phase FIVE
I am unboundaried (diffuse).
I am my space.
I am my understanding.
I am what I investigate.
I am my beliefs.

Resist Phase SIX
I resist differentiation.
I resist acceptance.
I resist differentiating between fact and assumption.
I resist anticipating my next step.
I resist questioning my beliefs.

Fear Slipping Back to Phase FOUR
I fear revealing my inadequacies.
I fear forgiveness.
I fear personal experience.
I fear my uniqueness.
I fear honoring my deeper values.

Cope by Doing More of Phase FIVE
I cope by remaining diffuse and undecided.
I cope by protecting my space.
I cope by clinging to what I understand.
I cope by investigating other things.
I survive by maintaining my existing beliefs.

Identify with Phase FIVE / Resist Phase SIX

Type FIVEs overly identify with the essential quality of space. This mutates into identifying with needing personal space. This, coupled with diffuse personal boundaries, leaves them vulnerable to feeling invaded or overwhelmed by people's expectations, opinions and presence. They resist the essential quality of Acceptance. Spaciousness without Acceptance is experienced as deficient emptiness, or as, 'I'm nothing, or nobody.' FIVEs try to get as much space from life as possible. However, the more they seek the space outside themselves, the less they open into the inherent spaciousness of their being.

FIVEs try to remain emotionally detached in circumstances in which they may not feel accepted or could be required to commit to a specified role. In the process of maintaining detachment and space from others, they create a lifestyle void of human contact and warmth. The insubstantial nature of their relationships magnifies the sense of deficient emptiness, making it more difficult to engage without feeling disrespected or overwhelmed.

Resisting differentiation denies them the opportunity to make distinctions regarding how much time and energy to invest in others, and who they want to be in relation to others. There is a sense of needing to fill the emptiness to be somebody. Their identification with understanding leads them to compulsively fill their minds with information that validates what they understand and believe to be true. They compensate for the lack acceptance by investigating the nature of things from a dissociated objective observer position. FIVEs would rather research or observe than actually get involved. They are protective of their solitary study, not wanting to be intruded upon while pursing their area of interest. They keep observations, understandings and beliefs to themselves, as sharing them leaves them open to questions and doubts.

For FIVEs, who tend to identify completely with their beliefs and understandings, having a belief proven false can feel like a mortal blow. This FIVEish pattern is observed in some so-called 'scientific research' in which the investigators ignore or label results as aberrant and therefore invalid, if they don't coincide with the theory they are seeking to prove. FIVEs resist acknowledging information that would lead them to question beliefs and force them to generate new hypotheses. Their identification with being knowledgeable gets in the way of making new discoveries and truly becoming wise.

If they must share their thoughts, they do it in an impersonal way. They might quote what they have read, or what the experts on a subject might say. Instead of saying, "I think or feel _____", they start sentences with something like, "One might say ___" so if questioned or challenged, they haven't directly connected themselves to the statement.

Putting Others to the Test

My friend George would tell me about what he had read, or what someone else had told him. In hindsight, I realized he was indirectly conveying ideas to me he felt very identified with. Like most FIVEs, however, he communicated what he felt strongly about from a dissociated third person's perspective.

As a ONE (opinionated and not always empathetic), I offered my contrasting opinion on the topics. I didn't realize at the time that he, most likely unconsciously, was testing me to see if I would be accepting of his ideas and, therefore, of him. When I finally was able to inquire as to why he was avoiding me, he informed me of his perception of me as being judgmental of him. As a ONE, I know I can come across in this way. In actuality, I liked really liked and respected George. Needless to say, I failed his test, along with most people who try to get close.

FIVEs don't feel accepted by others until they themselves stop resisting the essential quality of Acceptance within. FIVEs project their lack of acceptance onto others and then isolate themselves to prevent feeling rejected. George believed people are basically unaccepting and out to invalidate him. FIVEs maintain beliefs about the untrustworthiness of people by testing them, often unconsciously doing so in ways bound to prove their suspicions. Any attempts to spend more time getting to know him better (I heard through a mutual friend) felt like an invasion of George's personal space. Years later he apologized, explaining how his most recent wife, by refusing to be chased away by his usual tactics, helped him to learn how to be comfortable in the close proximity to someone he cared about.

Similar to FOURs, FIVEs can get stuck in the long dark night of the soul's journey. Instead of anticipating what the next step might be, they continue gathering more information about their situation. Overwhelming themselves with information makes it even harder to differentiate what is best for them. Feeling lost and uncertain leads them further into thinking if they just had more information, they could consider a plan of action. FIVEs forget that people learn best from experience and that even if they make a poor decision, they can always choose again.

FIVEs get stuck in this observing and analyzing mode, reluctant to commit themselves to anything. In groups, FIVEs position themselves where they can observe without being observed and can exit with ease. Even when unable to gain this position physically, they are positioned this way mentally to avoid feeling emotionally trapped. As a consequence they come across as aloof and unreachable. They can feel overwhelmed by emotion when they are alone and let their guard down. Rather than trusting people, or their own emotions, compulsive FIVEs believe thinking is the only aspect of reality that can be trusted.

FIVEs caught in their compulsion can turn their lives into a social experiment or anthropological study. They keep the different aspects of their lives discretely compartmentalized. Workplace associates may never meet childhood acquaintances, which in turn may never meet friends from the photography club, and so forth. With scientific-like rigor they regulate the variables of different contexts to keep things as predictable and safe as possible.

Fear Slipping Back to Phase FOUR / Cope by Doing More of Phase FIVE

FIVEs can feel so empty and like nobodies, that to tune into inadequacies feels overwhelming. They often feel it takes all their internal resources just to survive and therefore try to minimize any expenditure of time or energy on anything but the bare essentials. To the person in a relationship with a FIVE, they appear to be withholding emotions and emotional needs, yet to share feelings a FIVE must first get in touch with what they feel. To cope with the fear of their unspecified sense of inadequacy, FIVEs keep busy taking in information without any specific outcome they want to achieve. They rationalize this preoccupation with the idea that it might be useful to their survival one day.

FIVEs intuitively know the powerful undertow archetypal experiences such as dreams and fantasies can exert on them. They try to cope by dismissing them as being irrational, using their powerful intellect to dissociate from their inner emotional life. In extreme cases denied memories, dreams and fantasies associated with phase FOUR, can eventually break through into consciousness in the form of hallucinations, visual and/or auditory. As the compulsive FIVE thinks of those internal phenomena as 'not me', their consciousness objectifies them as external phenomenon, or entities that possess them. As a result of this, FIVEs can have difficulty falling asleep. As their 'rational' control relaxes, unconscious images and impulses denied throughout the day stream into awareness. The conscious vigilance needed to control these prevents them from surrendering to the unconscious process of sleep.

FIVEs get stuck between a rock and a hard place in the cycle of change. At FOUR we feel the depths of our suffering. At SIX we must face our deepest fears and make decisions as to what we remain faithful to; we often let go of things we have clung to out of fear. FIVES get stuck in analyzing events, trying to make sense of them, but fear actually opening their hearts to forgiveness. They are afraid if they forgive themselves or the other person, they might forget the past and inadvertently place themselves in harm's way. Consequently, they vigilantly guard their personal space to prevent people from getting close enough to push unhealed emotional buttons.

To be unique can make a person more visible and people who stand out are more likely to come under attack. FIVEs fear their uniqueness and cope by investigating universal patterns and how they fit into the pattern. When asked for their opinions they often quote research or speak in general or abstract terms. When FIVEs fear their personal experience and resist testing their theories, they don't have much experience to ground their ideas in. Sensing the unsubstantiated nature of their beliefs, they invest more time in gathering information that validates their position.

Many FIVEs are minimalists and tend to be frugal. Even when they are well off, financially they are often conservative in the way they spend money. Without a connection to deeper values, they often don't know what to spend money, time or energy on. Because they have so little sense of belonging, they don't trust that life will support them, which they cope with by hoarding whatever might be important to their survival one day.

Hero's Journey — Approach to the Inmost Cave

It is extreme misfortune when theory outstrips performance. *Leonardo DaVinci*

Everything has been figured out, except how to live. *Jean-Paul Sartre*

Above all, type FIVEs want to feel prepared. Their anticipation of the possible ordeals that lie before them causes them to get stuck in preparation mode. As an analogy, if a FIVE were an actor, he would be studying his script, researching his character, rehearsing his part, he might even do a dress rehearsal, but somehow never feel ready to perform. They justify not putting themselves to the test with rationalizations, such as, "I know all there is to know about this role, what's the point in performing it?" FIVEs are susceptible to getting stuck in an ivory tower of knowledge, far removed from the joys and sorrows, successes and failures of real life. FIVEs forget that no amount of preparation substitutes for the wisdom gained from taking on real-life challenges.,

FIVEs are very susceptible to being seduced by the illusory temptations that promise them safety from life's challenges, and yet the place they get stuck (the Inmost Cave) is the most dangerous spot in the special world. Although FIVEs caught in their compulsion try to protect themselves by gathering information or isolating themselves from life, they live in fear. Going back to the life they knew or venturing forward into a life yet to be discovered, seem equally impossible. They avoid the specific challenges life presents them with by thinking in generalities. As a consequence, fear is converted to generalized anxiety, rather than associated to a specific threat or challenge. Caught in their compulsion, they forget what they were preparing for in the first place.

FIVEs are the personality type most likely to become hermits who dig a bomb shelter and store nonperishable food in preparation for apocalyptic disasters. There may be genuine reasons to do this, but the way to survive would be to address the spiritual, psychological and social ills that could drive humanity into those scenarios. Generally, the more we prepare to survive what we fear, the more likely it is what we fear will eventuate. The challenge for FIVEs is to stop avoiding what might hurt them and start facing the challenges that help create a more meaningfully enriching and sustainable future.

The Connections from FIVE to EIGHT and SEVEN

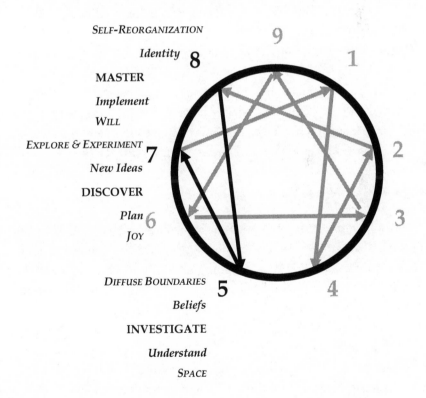

Connection to EIGHT

During periods of integration and stability, type FIVEs connect more with the qualities of EIGHT: self-reorganization, will, implementation, mastery and identity. When caught in their compulsion, FIVEs use willpower to implement their understandings to create a safer 'inner-most cave' to hole up in. Howard Hughes is an example of a FIVE who used his intelligence and power so he could more comfortably live in isolation from life, choosing to run his corporate empire from his penthouse suite. FIVEs often show a high level of mastery within a rarified field of expertise that enables them to conduct research in settings they organize and control. This reinforces beliefs about the world and who they perceive themselves to be. If their way of doing things is challenged they respond with, "I can't help it, it's just who I am."

Connecting with essential will reminds them they have something to contribute; they have a role to play in society. FIVEs begin to feel the impulses to implement their understanding and begin gaining some mastery of their field of interest. The connection to EIGHT helps them to have a more powerful sense of themselves, which enables them to question ideas that have held them back and find the courage to face their fears.

Connection to SEVEN

During periods of disintegration and when approaching chaos, type FIVEs connect more with the qualities of SEVEN: exploration and experimentation, joy, discovery, planning and new ideas. Under stress, FIVEs become less focused in the quest for information. Escalating anxiety causes them to jump from one area of interest to another. They might read ten books at once, or simply collect random ideas from random sources for no particular reason, yet rationalize that they are on the verge of making a great discovery. They engage in a manic planning of ways to escape the narrow confines of their lives. The frantic mental activity and dissociation from their bodies increases difficulty with sleeping. Absent mindedly, they might not even realize they haven't eaten or slept much in days. Sleep deprivation makes them more prone to psychotic phenomena, as the unconscious mind begins vividly dreaming while they are awake.

Eventually, repressed impulses break out, with the FIVE secretly engaging in things like anonymous sex or illicit drug use. Their preferred choices of drugs are narcotics or anything that numbs feelings and/or stimulates thinking.

One FIVEish doctor sought therapy after getting caught using prescription narcotics. He felt uncomfortable at home with his TWOish wife who always wanted more interaction. He would say he was going to a café get some space and read. Late one night she went looking for him and found him passed out in his medical clinic with a needle in his arm. Although he rarely felt sexual desire for his attractive wife whom he loved, he secretly engaged in casual sexual encounters and kept a secret cache of pornography, in effect compartmentalizing love and sex.

Connecting with essential joy, FIVEs feel freer to enjoy life. They play with new ideas instead of being so attached to their precious theories. Entertaining different perspectives leads them to question the views they have been identified with. Their investigations evolve into experiments and explorations that take them out of their 'inner-most cave' and into life, where they differentiate what is useful from what isn't.

Understanding how type FIVEs tend to resist the natural processes of change and cling to fixed ideas of themselves helps us to meet them where they get stuck and show them the possibility for greater freedom.

Personality Type SIX

Type SIX identifies with the:

- change cycle phase of differentiation
- essential quality of acceptance
- basic function of differentiate
- developmental task of anticipation
- psychological network of questioning

Type SIX tends to resist the:

- change cycle phase of exploration & experimentation
- essential quality of joy

- basic function of discovery
- developmental task of planning
- psychological network of new ideas

Type SIXes fear slipping back into the vulnerable space of diffuse boundaries and the need to gain understanding through investigation (FIVE). They cope by seeking others' acceptance that they hope will protect them from anticipated worst-case scenarios.

They compulsively ask:

- What will I remain faithful to?
- What have I lost faith in?
- What is worth sacrificing for?
- What do I need to be prepared for?

They avoid asking:

- What's new or next?
- What's attractive?
- What else is there?

At their worst, SIXes demonstrate paranoid, dependent, dissociative and borderline personality disorders.

When SIXes embody their essential wholeness they are courageous people who are willing to feel their fear and do what is needed to further a worthy cause. They are responsible team players that hold organizations together with charm and playfulness. They can come up with new ideas to troubleshoot foreseeable difficulties. They can respectfully, and often humorously, challenge colleagues, partners and authorities, while remaining loyal and friendly. At their best they manifest qualities seen in people like: J. Krishnamurti, David Schnarch, Julian Assange, Helen Palmer, George Carlin, Byron Katie, Tom Condon, Spike Lee, Robert Redford, Phil Donahue, Ellen DeGeneres and Malcolm X.

Type SIX

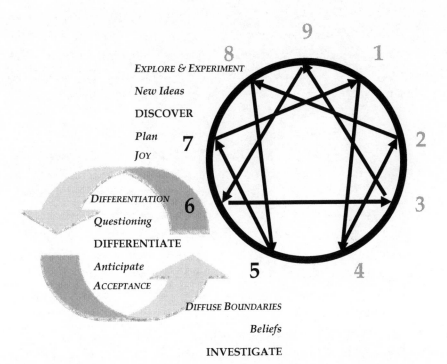

EXPLORE & EXPERIMENT

New Ideas

DISCOVER

Plan

JOY

DIFFERENTIATION

Questioning

DIFFERENTIATE

Anticipate

ACCEPTANCE

DIFFUSE BOUNDARIES

Beliefs

INVESTIGATE

Understand

SPACE

Type SIXes

Identify with Phase SIX

I am differentiating.

I am accepting.

I am in need of making a choice.

I am an anticipator.

I am questioning.

Resist Phase SEVEN

I resist exploring or experimenting.

I resist joy.

I resist discovering or innovating.

I resist planning.

I resist new ideas.

Fear Slipping Back to Phase FIVE

I fear having diffuse boundaries.

I fear space.

I fear investigating things for myself.

I fear my understanding.

I fear articulating my beliefs.

Cope by Doing More of Phase SIX

I cope by holding on to choices.

I cope by seeking acceptance.

I cope by anticipating the worst.

I cope by choosing not to understand.

I cope by questioning my beliefs.

Identify with Phase SIX / Resist Phase SEVEN

Type SIXes become overly identified with the essential quality of acceptance. They like to think of themselves as being both acceptable and accepting. To be accepted by others, they compromise their agenda to gain approval. Acceptance, however, becomes conditional upon living up to others' expectations.

In wanting to be identified as accepting, SIXes outwardly act as if they are in agreement, yet inwardly they will be skeptical. At other times, they might try to prove they don't need acceptance by outwardly being skeptical, but inwardly feel dependent on the other person's approval. Essential acceptance is all-inclusive. Although we differentiate between what is good for us and what isn't, when resting in Essential Acceptance we accept the world and ourselves exactly as we are. By making approval from others a condition of their self-worth, SIXes worry a lot about what they are supposed to do to avoid disapproval. This puts them in opposition to the joy that comes with surrendering to the field of infinite possibilities. Essential acceptance, which recognizes the ever-changing nature of the universe, can turn to resignation. Once resigned, they deny themselves the opportunity to discover what else life has to offer and the joy of entertaining the new possibilities. To compensate, they will either place faith in established authorities and conventions, or take the opposite tack and develop a paranoid skepticism about everything.

SIXes can be full of contradictions. Phase SIX is where apparent contradictions are resolved by opening our minds to what Jung called the union of opposites. SIXes get stuck in differentiating the opposites, yet resist entertaining new ideas that could create a framework that accepts both ends of the spectrum. SIXes organize their psyches in two seemingly opposite and contradictory ways: phobic and counter-phobic. Phobic SIXes externally seek approval (especially authority figures), and play life safe by staying within the bounds of social convention and the dictates of authority.

However, they internally remain skeptical and questioning of those they give their power to. They constantly react to others perceived expectations while inwardly resenting feeling manipulated. As a result of emotional distress, they distrust their own judgment and constantly look for ways to avoid the emotional challenges that are part of growth. Counter-phobic

SIXes externally are rebellious toward authority and defy social convention, taking unnecessary risks trying to prove they won't be controlled by fear. Internally, what they do is still defined by what they think is expected of them; they simply do the opposite. They react to the perceived reactions of others, while inwardly resenting feeling manipulated.

Compulsive SIXes will project their good qualities onto to others and, consequently, feel lacking and bad within themselves, or they will project their bad qualities onto others and feel like the innocent victim. This causes them to fluctuate between fear and anger, aggression and surrender, and victim and persecutor. This polarization keeps them from the experience of essential wholeness, which would allow them to accept themselves, others and everything else the way it is. Instead, they live in a chronic state of self-doubting. Rather than trusting their own perception, they judge everything through their conditioned beliefs, confirming their fears and justifying their anger.

Tales from the Therapy Room

Barry came to therapy because of his failing health and depression. He had been in the military and didn't shy away from violence. However, with a significant loss of muscle mass due to illness, he couldn't dominate others in physical fights as well as he used to. When I asked him how he managed to get into fights so often, he told me about the kind of bars he frequented that were actually known as places where fights happened. Exploring further, he told me how when he entered the bar he would look around to see who could be a threat. If he saw someone looking at him the 'wrong' way, he would confront him. If the other guy didn't back down, this would often lead to a fight. When I asked why he didn't just leave or stay away from those kind of guys, he said he was tired of being a victim and no one was going to stop him from going where he wanted to go. After exploring the victimization he went through in his youth, we discovered that he had come to believe when he was quite young that he must have a 'punch me face' that no one could ever like. Having previously been unaware of this, he projected that onto others, and if someone looked at him in the wrong way it was an excuse to punch *his* face. Barry regained a sense of his essential wholeness when he learned to allow what was strong, accepting and loving in him to look after what felt weak, unwanted and hurt, in a union of opposites. Instead of dissipating his anger and fear, by accepting it, he was able to begin the healing process.

Both types of SIXes resist the movement to SEVEN where they could discover what is right for them personally at any given time. They get stuck in thinking how they differ with authority, but resist exploring and experimenting outside the parameters of the status quo. When free from their compulsions, both types of SIXes grow towards each other: phobic types become more courageous and decisive, and counterphobics become more cautious and conscientious.

SIXes anticipate what could go wrong if they were to venture beyond the boundaries of their ordinary world. They resist any new ideas that would help them devise a plan to deal with the anticipated dangers. SIXes' greatest fear is not the actual failing, but rather losing the approval of others. To cope with fear, they seek the company of people who share the same fears and adherence to the status quo. Giving their power of acceptance away to others, SIXes not only lose the respect of others, but more importantly stop respecting themselves. This leaves them feeling even more in danger of being disrespected and rejected. To cope, they try even harder to not be disagreeable.

Theologian Paul Tillich said, "Doubt isn't the opposite of faith; it is an element of faith." SIXes get stuck in questioning and resist listening to their own answers. They become identified with doubt, which they experience as self-doubt. They get stuck at the place in the change cycle where their old identity must die. The more they experience the internal dissolution of what they held to be true, the more they look for an external authority (a person or a text) they can hold on to.

The more SIXes put faith in the status quo, the less they are able to have faith in the ever-changing web of life. SIXes fear there isn't a place for their emergent self in the world, and survival depends on living up to other's expectations. Resisting the new possibilities that challenge the status quo, they deny themselves the opportunity to more clearly differentiate what greater part they could play in an evolving world. SIXes feel damned if they do and damned if they don't. If they do what is right for themselves they will be abandoned (punishment for not conforming), or else they compromise individuality for an unguaranteed promise of safety from authority figures or a larger social group.

Fear Slipping Back to Phase FIVE / Cope by Doing More of Phase SIX

SIXes fear the uncertainty that comes with having diffuse personal boundaries. As personal boundaries break down further, SIXes cope by holding onto the right to choose, but without really making a choice. They are like deer stuck fixated on the headlights of an oncoming car, unable to choose which way to run. Stuck in their compulsion, they don't commit to anything other than trying to be safe from change. SIXes fear Space, which gets projected into a fear of having too much space from the group and/or authority figure they identify with. SIXes may not trust authority figures, who they see as bullies, yet they tend to gravitate toward them, like Barry going to rough-neck bars. Although they fear it, the sense of spacious emptiness is pronounced. As they fear it, they avoid connecting with the spaciousness of their Being, which maintains the feeling of nothingness inside. They try to feel *like* someone through their associations with them. To maintain dependence on a group or authority figure requires suppressing the qualities of their emergent self that would more clearly differentiate them from others.

The notion that knowledge is dangerous captures SIXes. They fear investigating life deeply. The more you learn, the more you realize what you don't know and to the SIX, what is unknown is frightening and not to be trusted. The more you learn, the more you realize the limits of the beliefs that have been the basis of your own identity. SIXes try to hold onto their narrow-minded sense of self at the expense of objectivity and novelty.

SIXes get confused by choruses of both internal and external voices, each offering opinions of what should be done. To go with one voice over another risks disapproval, leaving them stuck in indecision. Confusion shows us that the frameworks by which we make sense of the world are inadequate to explain seemingly contradictory experiences. Instead of embracing 'not knowing', SIXes try to dispel it by putting (renewing) faith in established belief systems, leaders or group causes. Out of fear of coming to the wrong conclusions and making the wrong choice, they follow along, attempting to find safety in numbers. Fear of disapproval, however, doesn't stop them from acting courageously, even self-sacrificing, on behalf of the group or cause. The real challenge for SIXes is to let go of certainty and develop faith in discovering themselves and their place in the whole of creation. As Krishnamurti said,

> Truth is a pathless land, and you cannot approach it by any path whatsoever, by any religion, by any sect. Truth, being limitless, unconditional, unapproachable, cannot be organized; nor should any organization be formed to lead or to coerce people along any particular path.

Hero's journey — Ordeal

There appear to be more people with type SIX temperament in the world than any other personality type. This is not surprising considering phase SIX is when we face the fear-based beliefs at the foundation of our ego identity. Recall that the compulsions of personality are mechanisms by which we try to cope with what is overwhelming and unfathomable. To cope with trauma, we learn how to shrink our awareness of thoughts, perceptions and emotions to a manageable size.

To personally evolve, all fear-based beliefs and associated behavioral habits the hero has identified with must be challenged and overcome. At times, the heroic SIX must face an ego death. Most of us experience some mistrust of the web of life at this phase, and type SIXes become identified with their mistrust of life. Instead of accepting life on its own terms and questioning their belief systems, they remain loyal to limiting beliefs and mistrust life.

SIXes can be both the most fearful and the most courageous of the personality types. Courage arises when we face our fears. SIXes are often best in an obvious crisis. SIXes can act instinctively and even heroically to whisk a child from in front of an oncoming car or defend a friend under attack.

Difficulties arise when the critical dilemmas that SIXes face are ambiguous and require them to defy convention and risk disapproval. When dealing with issues with their parents, SIXes benefit from the idea that while a parent's responsibility is to provide stability and safety for their children, a child's innate duty is to help parents discover they are more capable than they ever imagined: functioning on less sleep, supporting a family, loving more deeply, and so on. Rather than merely being a good child or a rebel, it is their job, by merely being true to themselves, to help their parents to grow.

When SIXes accept themselves more deeply and face their fears, they re-own the power they have projected onto others. They then realize, and are able to exercise what differentiation implies: the ability to maintain their sense of individuality in close proximity to people they care about, not react to people's reactivity, and self-regulate emotionality so discernment can be used to tolerate pain for growth. If they don't, they run the risk of either tolerating a bad situation or running away and merely transferring their dependence to someone else.

Sexual Ordeal

> Be patient toward all that is unsolved in your heart and try to love the questions themselves. Live the questions now. Perhaps you will find them gradually, without noticing it, live along some distant day into the answer. *Rainer Marie Rilke*

David had difficulty establishing and maintaining intimate relationships. He described his mother as a domineering woman who demanded his unconditional obedience. She had been physically punishing and sexually abusive towards him when he was young. His father was less involved, but was highly critical, expecting him to follow in his footsteps, which David had done with his career.

When David (aged 32) began therapy, he told me he visited his parents at least twice a week. On these visits, they routinely questioned him about why he wasn't married yet. He would reply he was trying, but couldn't find the right woman. David did meet women, but he'd fall into patterns of trying to get approval. At first he would do this by guessing what he thought they expected from him, but as time went on he would just wait for them to tell him what to do. The two basic inhibiting beliefs that controlled him were, 'What I want is not acceptable' and 'I don't have the right to say no'. Attempts at relationships would end either because he was tired of being controlled or because the woman lost interest due to his lack of initiative. He disowned his right to make decisions and projected the power to accept or reject onto his partners.

After several frustrated attempts to develop a lasting intimate relationship with a woman, David expressed to me his concerns that maybe he was gay. Asking him what gave him this impression, he replied he really wasn't sure he was sexually attracted to women. With further inquiry, he discussed how he asked women out because that was what he was supposed to do in order to find someone to marry that his parents would approve of. "Isn't that what everyone does?" he queried. I mentioned to him the findings of the Kinsey report and how men's sexual preferences, when polled, fell on a continuum with many men having a mixture of sexual feelings, thoughts or behaviors towards men and women. I wanted to convey the idea there wasn't one right way to be, and that people expressed a myriad of individual preferences.

Since his conscious mind was confused, I asked if he would like to go into trance to discover if his unconscious mind could help resolve the dilemma.

In hypnosis, his confusion expanded into FIVEish spaciousness, which allowed him to simply notice and accept whatever came to mind. Using ideomotor signals I asked if his unconscious mind could assist him to explore the possibilities of what he wanted sexually over the next week. The *yes* finger unconsciously lifted.

When he returned the following week, he related a story of how one evening he decided he'd had enough of ambivalence and feeling scared of homosexuality. If he really was gay, he wanted to know. He called up a gay man he knew who previously had appeared to come on to him and asked if he was interested in going out. The man declined, saying he was busy. David, still determined to solve this dilemma, went to a gay bar. He sat at the bar all night hoping someone would approach him, but not much happened. Not to be defeated, after the bar closed he went to a gay nightclub, but still nothing happened. Feeling frustrated but determined, he went to the twenty-four hour sex shop. He bought three videos, one with straight heterosexuals, one with gay men, and one with a bondage and domination theme (submissive man and a dominant woman).

Whilst I was wondering where all this was leading, I listened with calm acceptance. After watching the three videos, he said he felt most turned on by the bondage and domination. A day or two later, he phoned and booked an appointment with a professional bondage and domination mistress. He went along and subjugated himself to humiliating, yet to him, sexually arousing activities. At this point I was starting to get a bit nervous, but relaxed into a greater sense of acceptance and was able to ask him more about his experience. At a particular point in time, restrained by a dog collar and leash around his neck and having his backside whipped, he had the sudden realization that, "Since I can come and do this anytime I want, I don't need to continue subjugating myself to women in my ordinary world.".

A few weeks later, David met a woman to whom he was attracted. Out of his usual pattern, he openly showed his interest, initiated contact and even encouraged her to try things outside her comfort zone. David was experiencing a greater sense of unconditional self-acceptance, which led him to explore and experiment with what felt best to him.

The Connections from SIX to NINE and THREE

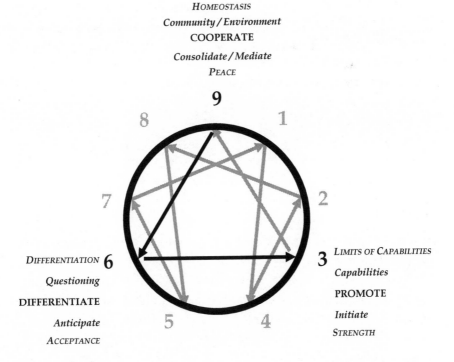

HOMEOSTASIS
Community / Environment
COOPERATE
Consolidate / Mediate
PEACE

DIFFERENTIATION **6**
Questioning
DIFFERENTIATE
Anticipate
ACCEPTANCE

3 LIMITS OF CAPABILITIES
Capabilities
PROMOTE
Initiate
STRENGTH

Connection to *NINE*

During periods of integration and stability, type SIXes connect more with the qualities of NINE: homeostasis, peace, mediation, cooperation and community/environment. Caught in their compulsion, SIXes are good at mediating conflict that might lead to systemic upheaval. They work cooperatively for the benefit of family, community or organization. They find ways to maintain a dysfunctional homeostasis that requires increasing compromises of their agenda and self-awareness. Instead of surrendering to ego-death, they surrender to the self-concept of being nothing without the people they are identified with. In the example of David, the more unfulfilled he was in his personal relationships, the more time he would spend with his parents. Besides denying himself the opportunity to get his life together, he distracted his parents from the unresolved problems and conflicts in their marriage.

In periods of relative stability, SIXes relax into a sense of community and belonging. Trusting in the sense of belonging helps them to feel more peaceful and accepted. They remember there are some aspects of their lives working adequately, so while they are letting go of one aspect of their old way of functioning, not everything needs to change. This sense of stability helps them to venture out and experiment and explore new ways of thinking about and relating to life.

Connection to *THREE*

During periods of disintegration and when approaching chaos, type SIXes connect more with the qualities of THREE: exploring limits of capabilities, strength, initiation, promotion and capabilities. As life becomes increasingly unstable, THREEs push themselves to the limits of their capabilities to regain some sense of security. They can show almost superhuman strength in defending the status quo and their position in it. To maintain approval and avoid rejection they become increasing false in the self-image they promote. This naturally arouses people's suspicions, and in their compulsion, SIXes try even harder to present an image of what seems expected. This vicious cycle leads to further disintegration. Counterphobic tendencies emerge more strongly in an attempt to bluff their way out of frightening situations. They fluctuate between, "I can't live without you" and, "You can all f**k yourselves!" Both of these attitudes are increasingly unacceptable to others, making it inevitable the SIX will need to learn to be independent, whether they want to or not.

As the false idols and authority figures they have projected their power onto start to fail them, SIXes reconnect with inner strength and capabilities. They recover confidence in themselves, as they remember how they have exercised capabilities in the past to promote their own agenda. This helps them initiate explorations into new territory so they can make up their own minds what suits them best.

Understanding how type SIXes tend to resist the natural processes of change and cling to fixed ideas of themselves helps us to meet them where they get stuck and show them the possibility for greater freedom.

Personality Type SEVEN

Type SEVEN identifies with the:

- change cycle phase of exploration and experimentation
- essential quality of joy
- basic function of discovery
- developmental task of planning
- psychological network of new ideas

Type SEVEN tends to resist the:

- change cycle phase of self-reorganization
- essential quality of will
- basic function of implementation
- developmental task of mastery
- psychological network of identity

Type SEVENS fear slipping back into questioning their beliefs, anticipating what could go wrong and making choices accordingly (SIX). They cope by constantly entertaining options, and making plans about what would bring them the most joy.

They compulsively ask:

- What's new or next?
- What's attractive?
- What else is there?

They resist asking:

- What am I mastering or manifesting?
- How can I take control and implement my ideas?
- Who am I?
- What is my contribution?

At their worst, they can demonstrate bipolar and borderline personality disorders, and have a propensity for substance abuse.

When SEVENs embody their essential wholeness, they trust that where they are is where they are meant to be, allowing them to more fully commit to gaining mastery and depth in their areas of interest. They tend to organize their multiple interests and talents in such a way that cross-pollinate and support learning and growth. They often slowdown and enjoy the simple things and the inherent goodness of life. They bring their joyful enthusiasm to situations and often inspire others to be more motivated in the endeavor. At their best, they manifest qualities seen in people like: Joseph Campbell, Leonardo Da Vinci, Marianne Williamson, Gerald Jampolsky, Thomas Jefferson, Ram Dass, Joseph Chilton Pearce, Bernie Siegel, Osho, Wayne Dyer, Stephen Spielberg, Charles Tart, Steve Irwin and Rick Hanson, PhD.

Type SEVEN

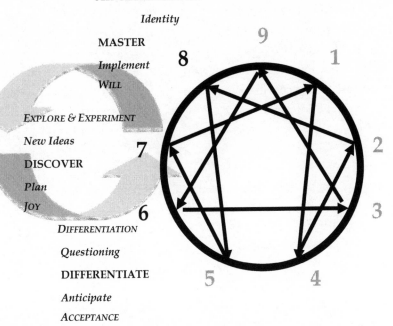

SELF-REORGANIZATION

Identity

MASTER

Implement

WILL

EXPLORE & EXPERIMENT

New Ideas

DISCOVER

Plan

JOY

DIFFERENTIATION

Questioning

DIFFERENTIATE

Anticipate

ACCEPTANCE

Type SEVENs

Identify with Phase SEVEN

I am an explorer and experimenter.
I am joyful.
I am a planner.
I am making discoveries.
I am full of new ideas.

Resist Phase EIGHT

I resist reorganizing my life.
I resist exercising my willpower.
I resist implementing my plans.
I resist making something of my discoveries.
I resist identifying with anything or anyone.

Fear Slipping back to Phase SIX

I fear making choices.
I fear accepting life as it is.
I fear anticipating problems.
I fear differentiating fear and facts.
I fear questioning my beliefs.

Cope by Doing More of Phase SEVEN

I cope by exploring new options.
I cope by seeking joy.
I cope by making plans.
I cope by discovering opportunities.
I cope by entertaining new ideas.

Identify with Phase SEVEN / Resist Phase EIGHT

Type SEVENs identify with the essential quality of joy. They keep options open to do whatever they think will bring them the most joy. They spend a lot of time entertaining ideas about what is the next fun thing to do and they like discovering new things to experiment with. Holding onto their freedom to consider options and go with whatever captures their fancy requires them to avoid organizing their lives by making commitments. Being overly identified with joy means they try to avoid what they perceive to be unpleasant.

Things that require exercising their will to work hard and discipline themselves are not seen as enjoyable. SEVENs are so committed to planning they keep making new plans that override existing plans. Many SEVENS say one of their favorite activities is planning. Fantasizing about the future is fun for them, whereas implementing the plans is unpleasant hard work. For SEVENs, committing their plans to action can lead to feeling trapped in that choice to the exclusion of other options.

Always keeping options open, SEVENs deny themselves the deeper satisfaction that comes from learning to do something really well. SEVENs often have a lot of innate talent, but squander it by not investing time and energy to gain mastery of their skill. As they jump from one enterprise to another, they become the Jacks of all trades, masters of none.

A SEVEN I knew at university was in his sixth year and his third field of study. He really enjoyed university life: the social life, the interesting ideas, and so on, yet when it came time to get into the more advanced courses in his major and work towards graduation and a career, he would switch subjects. When I graduated with my Masters degree, he still hadn't completed a Bachelors degree.

In relationships, compulsive SEVENs get stuck in flirting with possibilities, yet resist making a commitment to something deeper. Not committing to a relationship or field of endeavor means they avoid identifying with another person, area of interest, or even a particular group of people. Constantly entertaining new ideas without implementation means they don't reorganize their lives or personal identities in a way that incorporates their discoveries. They cope with the lack of fulfillment from a more evolved identity by entertaining more options in search of fun. They forget, as conservationist Gifford Pinchot suggests, "The vast possibilities of our great future will become realities only if we make ourselves responsible for that future." Many SEVENs pride themselves on staying young at heart by avoiding the sort of responsibilities that tie people down.

Fear Slipping Back to Phase SIX / Cope by Doing More of Phase SEVEN

Psychiatrist Frank Lake recalled a therapy client's re-experiencing of his birth as an experience of moving from phase SIX to SEVEN. The crowning of the head is occasionally re-lived with an agonizing cry, and a final struggle. Suddenly, all goes flaccid with a sense of relief: 'I feel such relief. I've been squeezed out at last. Press harder and harder, at last I'm through. I'm quite free. Free all round. Lovely. I was born. I feel I've come out of the bowels of the earth. I don't want to sink back again.'

SEVENs get stuck in this desire of not wanting to sink back into the pain and struggle of freeing themselves from the restrictive structures of their previous way of life. As they intuitively understand how painful it can be to let go of those things we become identified with, they resist committing themselves to anything else they intuitively know they will inevitably outgrow. Of course, if we take a longer view of evolution, it becomes clear that we will eventually outgrow *everything*.

SEVENs fear accepting their inner experience. They associate acceptance with acquiescence, complacency and defeat. They fail to perceive the inherent impermanence of all inner and outer phenomena and fear that accepting life as it is in each moment, means accepting what is happening as permanent and unchanging. Both acceptance and commitment feel like a life-sentence without parole. SEVENs are afraid of making choices for fear of being locked into that decision and because they could be held responsible. They cope with this fear by continuing to explore more options.

SEVENS fear anticipating any problems that could arise out of past actions, and cope by looking forward and planning other enjoyable activities. When caught in their compulsion, they feel they are like skating on thin ice, not wanting to slow down to consider the effects of their choices for fear of falling to their doom. Instead they move quickly onto the next adventure, hopefully skating over any possible dangers or concerns.

SEVENs fear differentiating fact from fiction. They live so much in pleasure-seeking imagination that to slow down long enough to realize the superficiality and emptiness of their lifestyle is terrifying to them. To avoid sorting their lives out, they simply discover what else there is to play around with. Out of fear of having their beliefs questioned, they resist organizing their ideas into any sort of belief system and instead keep entertaining themselves with new ideas.

Trying to have a serious conversation with SEVENs can be frustrating, as before you can differentiate fact from fiction about a particular issue, they have switched to another topic or moved onto another activity altogether. Rather than admitting they were mistaken when proven wrong, they quickly move onto to something else, claiming they didn't really care about the issue in the first place. In doing so, they rob themselves of opportunities to put their inventive minds to use in reformulating old beliefs and new ideas into more useful and meaningful ways of reorganizing their lives.

Hero's Journey — Reward (Seizing the Sword)

SEVENs can seem to live a charmed life. As they tend to be good at things they try, they are rewarded with many opportunities. They benefit from the beginner's luck that sometimes accompanies venturing into new worlds. SEVENs hold onto the epiphanies that inspire explorations, but resist taking responsibility for their gifts and developing their potential. They are often inspired, which is inspiring to others; however, when the going gets tough, they get inspired to move onto to something else. They often identify themselves as the 'ideas person', preferring to come up with ideas and let others do the work of implementing them. Instead of facing the demons that get in the way of doing something great, compulsive SEVENs start yet another quest.

Although they are adroit at avoiding old nemeses, their lives are actually controlled and limited by fears and unresolved issues. After having jumped from one path to another repeatedly, the Heroic SEVENs realize although the scenery may be different, they have only been going around in circles. To truly make new discoveries, they must eventually commit themselves to a path and face the challenges that beset them.

Tales from the Therapy Room

Robert always found a way to put a positive frame around whatever problems he was having. He had read a lot of self-help and spirituality books. He knew how to maintain a positive attitude. He was very good at holding on to the concepts he had read, and used these ideas to positively reframe anything that would bring him down. He avoided any situation he couldn't fix with positive thinking. Once he had children, he couldn't move on from his negative wife without letting his children down, which brought him into therapy. He had a big breakthrough when he realized his need for her to be positive got in the way of deeper and more tender ways of relating where it was okay to show vulnerability, previously labeled negativity, and ask for help.

Robert came from divorced parents where he rarely saw his mother, and the way he decided he could support his overworked and emotionally shutdown father was to be happy and just make his own fun. He realized how his attempts to make his wife just 'choose to be happy', rather learning to relate in more meaningful ways, recreated his own upbringing.

In effect, he was asking her to create a home like the one he grew up in, where people couldn't rely on one another and everyone had to act happy, even when they weren't. Robert began to embrace his essential wholeness and his life began to evolve when he invested his optimism in trusting there was a way through challenging circumstances to something more fulfilling.

Enthusiastic Consumers

SEVENs are the ultimate consumers. They follow the philosophy of when the going gets tough, go shopping. SEVENs have a hard time resisting the latest fashion, newly released movie or best-selling novel. SEVENs who take the time to reflect often describe a lack of connection with a nurturing parent. From an early age, they resolved to take care of themselves. Lacking a nurturing connection with one's mother can lead a child to transfer attachment to transitional objects like dolls, blankets, toys or other objects as a way of coping. With emotionally wounded SEVENs, the replacing of genuine emotional connections with material objects continues into adulthood.

The linguistic root for *mater*ialistic is *mater*, Latin for mother. As adults, SEVENs find it difficult to connect with Mother Nature, let alone their own nature; instead, they become the consummate consumers of: things, ideas, intoxicants, and/or pleasurable activities. Much of the time, they are mentally living slightly in the future they dream of. They are rarely fully present in the here-and-now to experience the fruits of their previous planning and efforts, as they can't stop fantasizing about and planning their next enterprise. They are so busy pursuing happiness, they rarely experience the profound joy that comes with surrendering to the present moment.

SEVENs are the most enthusiastic of the personality types. Their relationship to enthusiasm follows the change in meaning the word has gone through over time. The source of the word 'enthusiasm' is the Greek *enthousiasmos*, which ultimately comes from the adjective *entheos*, 'having the god within'. Over time, the meaning of *enthusiasm* became extended to 'rapturous inspiration like that caused by a god', then to 'an overly confident or delusory belief that one is inspired by God', and eventually to the familiar sense of 'craze, excitement, or strong liking for something.'[91]

Nowadays, people can have enthusiasm for almost anything, from water skiing to fast food, without spirituality entering into it at all. When clung to, Essential Joy (enthusiasm) mutates into an egotistical self-righteous belief that one can do no wrong. The SEVENish person doesn't feel accountable to the same ethics and morals as the rest of us mere mortals. Grasping after fleeting pleasures in pursuit of happiness, instead of being spiritually enriched, leads to a fast food approach to life, wanting immediate gratification without much energy or time invested.

Making a Commitment

One SEVENish client I saw on and off for years came in for a single session maybe twice a year. After he told me about some of his fun times, I asked what brought him in. Eventually he articulated the need to sort out his relationship problems. He was married to Elaine, but had been separated for ten years while living with another woman, Louise. He said he loved his wife, not his lover, but wasn't sexually attracted to his wife any more. Louise periodically pressured him for more commitment, which is when he would show up in my office. Although he appeared to find the session useful and left each with a series of new ideas, claiming he would call soon to make another appointment to work on these things, often months would go by before he would call again.

Eventually, I was able to present him with the differentiating choice between being true to his wish of not causing due suffering for others and his compulsive avoidance of making uncomfortable decisions and commitments. Once he realized his avoidance of making choices caused others problems, he finally got a divorce. Once divorced, he realized his relationship with Louise was never going to be more to him than an extended affair and he ended it. About a year later, he met a woman with whom he slowly developed a deeper and more satisfying relationship. SEVENs evolve when they explore the options of depth and longevity over shallow variety.

The Connections from SEVEN to FIVE and ONE

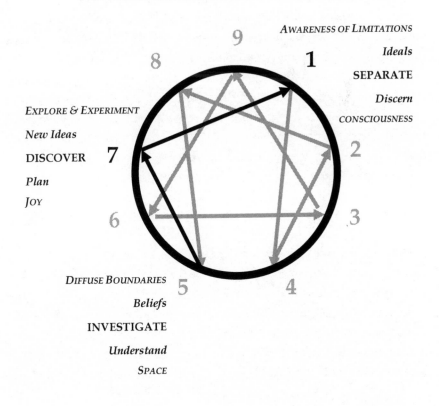

AWARENESS OF LIMITATIONS

Ideals

SEPARATE

Discern

CONSCIOUSNESS

EXPLORE & EXPERIMENT

New Ideas

DISCOVER   7

Plan

JOY

DIFFUSE BOUNDARIES

Beliefs

INVESTIGATE

Understand

SPACE

Connection to FIVE

During periods of integration and stability, SEVENs connect more with the qualities of FIVE: diffuse boundaries, space, understanding, investigation and beliefs. Caught in their compulsion, SEVENs become so diffuse in focus that they get really spaced out. They can become so ungrounded in the exploration and investigation of far-out ideas, as they have no concrete purpose for what they are doing.

One week they are investigating quantum physics, the next it's UFO conspiracies, and then nutritional supplements for increasing longevity. They have a compulsive desire to *get* understanding, but have little, if any, discipline to test the usefulness and validity of the information and theories they collect. Information is consumed as long as it is the flavor of the month, without being digested through reflection, application and experience. Rather than connecting with essential Space, SEVENs work hard to keep space open in their schedules to keep their options open in case something better comes along. They keep space between meetings with particular people, preferring to spread time between different people, so they don't get overly involved with anyone. SEVENs essentially teach people through their lack of commitment not to rely on them as consistent (committed) parts of their lives.

SEVENs support their growth when they step back from life and give themselves a chance to digest the vast array of experiences they have consumed. When they give themselves some space, they are able to learn from the past. Connecting with FIVE, they determine what is essential and what isn't. In categorizing ideas and experiences, patterns emerge that can be implemented in the reorganization their lives.

Connection to ONE

During periods of disintegration and when approaching chaos, type SEVENs connect more with the qualities of ONE: awareness of limitations, consciousness, discernment, separation and ideals. As the SEVEN's life disintegrates further towards chaos, they cling to ideal images of fun and excitement, which increases their appetite for consuming more experiences. Since they often can't achieve their ideal without significant effort, they buy themselves off with quick fixes. Despite increased awareness of the limitations of this way of functioning, they focus on others' faults instead, as they fear looking inward. Their quick minds discern what others should be doing or not doing, but have little or no consciousness of their own poor judgment. Critical preaching may alienate people in their social circle on whom the SEVEN relies on for entertainment and distraction. With fewer people available to play with, in solitude SEVENs may either seek more self-destructive escapes or finally start becoming more conscious of the limitations of their way of life. If cornered by someone pointing out their mistakes, their good-natured charm can evaporate into temper tantrums.

The connection to ONE helps SEVENs become more conscious of the effects of their actions. This self-consciousness can stop them in their tracks long enough to remember the higher ideals that inspire them to commit to something worthwhile. SEVENs begin to see the limitations of a frivolous life. They use the power of discernment to decide what best suits them and what talents are worth mastering.

Understanding how type SEVENs tend to resist the natural processes of change and cling to fixed ideas of themselves helps us to meet them where they get stuck and show them the possibility for greater freedom.

Personality Type EIGHT

Type EIGHT identifies with the:

- change cycle phase of self-reorganization
- essential quality of will
- basic function of implementation
- developmental task of mastery
- psychological network of identity

Type EIGHT tends to resist the:

- change cycle phase of homeostasis
- essential quality of peace
- basic function of mediation
- developmental task of cooperation
- psychological network of community/environment

375

Type EIGHTs fear slipping back into entertaining options, joy, planning and being unstructured (SEVEN). They cope by exercising their will to implement their agenda and organize things under their control. They compulsively ask:

- What am I mastering or manifesting?
- How can I take control and implement my ideas?
- Who am I?
- What is my contribution?

They avoid asking:

- How do I consolidate my growth and development?
- How do I mediate harmony and cooperation?

At their worst, they can demonstrate antisocial personality traits, and are prone to substance abuse.

When EIGHTs embody their essential wholeness they are natural leaders in service of their community, organization, and usually some sort of higher purpose. They help create safe and supportive environments for themselves and others to thrive in. They become true masters of their area of expertise and use that mastery to contribute to the world around them.

EIGHTs will use their power to promote justice and equality, and often are most interested in helping the downtrodden and underdogs of the world. Because of their trust in wholeness, they can drop all hubris and senses of hierarchy and relate to others with humility and an unguarded innocence. At their best, they manifest qualities seen in people like: Nisagadatta Maharaj, Papaji, Eli Jaxon-Bear, Lama Ole Nydahl, David Attenborough, George Gurdjieff, Fritz Perls, Sean Penn, Milton Erickson and Martin Luther King, Jr.

Type EIGHT

HOMEOSTASIS

Community / Environment

COOPERATE

Consolidate / Mediate

9

SELF-REORGANIZATION

Identity

MASTER **8**

Implement

WILL

EXPLORE & EXPERIMENT

New Ideas

7

DISCOVER

Plan

JOY

1

2

6

3

5 **4**

Type EIGHT

Identify with Phase EIGHT

I am an (re)organizer.

I am willful.

I am implementing my ideas.

I am the master.

I am my identity (who I think I am).

Resist Phase NINE

I resist maintaining the status quo.

I resist peace.

I resist consolidating progress.

I resist cooperation.

I resist being part of the community/environment.

Fear Slipping back to Phase SEVEN

I fear experimentation and exploration.

I fear joy.

I fear planning.

I fear discovery.

Cope by Doing More of Phase EIGHT

I cope by organization and control.

I cope by exercising my will.

I cope by implementing my agenda.

I cope by mastering what I know.

Identify with Phase EIGHT / Resist Phase NINE

Type EIGHTS overly identify with the essential quality of will, while resisting peace. Surrendering to the will of God distorts into demanding that other people surrender to the will of the EIGHT. EIGHTs are often blessed by a sense of destiny to implement their agenda, yet they become identified with being the one who is in charge of making things happen and have a hard time delegating authority to consolidate accomplishments. Rather than mediating harmonious cooperation, EIGHTs stir up conflicts and problems in an organization to justify exerting authority. They resist allowing self-maintainin patterns to develop and instead they regularly create disruptions in social systems to reorganize interactions to suit themselves.

Without adequate self-maintaining systems, problems regularly occur that justify the EIGHT's need to take control and tell people what to do and how to do it. Rather than helping to build a more robust organization, community or family system by delegating authority, compulsive EIGHTs undermine other's self-confidence while simultaneously demanding loyalty and subservience. They get caught in a vicious cycle of using the chaos they have helped to create to justify their need to take control, and the more they try to control things, the more out of control things become.

EIGHTs frequently achieve a high level of mastery in some endeavor. The charisma that comes with being so committed draws people to EIGHTs. People sense the greatness of their vision and want to be a part of it. In this way EIGHTs lead by example and command the authority to inspire people to join their cause. With mastery comes control; however, rather than asking how their mastery can benefit the community to which they belong., EIGHTs become identified with being the master that controls others. Knowledge is power, so compulsive EIGHTS in charge only disseminate just enough information for people to carry out their will. People are kept in the dark and only given information on a need-to-know basis.

To maintain their arrogant identity, EIGHTs hide their vulnerability and isolate themselves. The more isolated they become, the less sense of belonging they have and the greater mistrust of others. EIGHTs try to compensate for the lack of belonging and safety by trying to prove how important they are. Inflating self-importance only alienates others further and EIGHTs resign themselves to controlling and manipulating other, ostensibly for their own benefit or protection rather than connecting and sharing. Think of a protective Mafia Godfather.

The more isolated in their compulsion they become, the more they communicate concerns in terms of threats or ultimatums like, "You're either with me or against me; and you don't want to make me mad!"

EIGHTs, at their worst, confuse their will to survive with the will (wrath) of God and feel it is their right and duty to punish those who don't bend to their will. EIGHTs don't trust their community or organization will respond to their needs. They believe if they don't force others to do what they are told, nothing will get done. The EIGHTish boss, for example, doesn't trust their employees to take the initiative. Rather than delegating responsibility and allowing various individuals to collectively find ways to solve problems or implement agendas, they undermine autonomy, telling their employees to do it their way or not at all. Employees, fearing retribution, become increasingly passive, waiting for instructions rather than taking the initiative.

People often feel resentful when their opinions are not valued. This can be expressed passive-aggressively by not working to their full potential, or by leaving the workplace. Whether at home or in the workplace, people's passive-aggressive resistance reinforces in the compulsive EIGHT's mind the need for controlling every facet of operations.

EIGHTs in subordinate positions push boundaries until they get a reaction. This is their way of proving that no one can control them. After all, they are the ones who make the rules.

Fear Slipping Back to Phase SEVEN / Cope by Doing More of Phase EIGHT

Type EIGHTs fear the uncertainty of entertaining new possibilities. Experimentation and exploration put them at the mercy of factors outside their immediate control. They cope with the factors of life that may cause uncertainty by organizing as many things under their control as possible. They fear the innocence of essential joy. To really relax and enjoy themselves is to let down your guard and be open to life. EIGHTs fear they could be taken advantage of if they let their guard down. Even EIGHTs who are caught in their compulsion have a passionate lust for life, yet get caught in trying to possess the object of their desire. This makes EIGHTs very prone to jealousy; feeling like their lover (and their sexuality) belongs exclusively to them.

Caught in their compulsion, EIGHTs don't feel safe unless they are in control. Getting what they want from people isn't the same as simply relaxing into a playful enjoyment of one another (SEVEN) or merging into a more connected union (NINE). As they aren't really connecting, they feel people are out to get them. This fear is often based on past experiences of having their trust abused by someone they depended on. As a consequence, they can misperceive people trying to get closer as attempts to control them.

Life is always reminding us of our connection to humanity and the rest of creation. The EIGHT, who is trying to hold onto the idea that their ego mind is the master of their destiny, constantly fights off evidence to the contrary. The more an EIGHT is confronted with ideas that challenge their view of the world, the more definite they become about who they are, and then compulsively struggle to improve what they are already doing. When threatened by new ideas, they react by thinking things like, "It's not me. I'm not the kind of person that thinks that way" or, "You're expecting me to be someone I'm not."

Unless they feel compelled for some reason, EIGHTs wouldn't necessarily share these thoughts. They just get firmer in the stance of, "If you don't like the way I am, that's your problem." EIGHTs fear plannin: plans contain many unknowns and interactions between different variables. Instead, EIGHTs like to simply deal with things as they arise. When indequate planning is put into maintaining the stability of the system, the more chaotic organizations, families or communities can become. EIGHTS cope with the chaos by taking control and implementing their immediate agenda. The more compulsive they become, the less important achieving goals becomes, while exercising their will and being in control becomes ever more important.

A Course In Miracles says, "In my defenselessness my safety lies," and, "The truth needs no defending." The more EIGHTs try to hide and defend their personal identity, the more they deny their true nature and its wider relationship with the whole of nature (society, humanity, and ecology). Clinging to one's personal identity is like a wave in the ocean fighting to maintain its separate identity from the rest of the ocean. As the forces of nature (divine will) flow through the ocean, different individual waves surface. Some of these waves crash on the shore with great force, yet it is the nature of waves to always return to the wholeness of the sea.

Without the ocean, the wave is nothing; it does not exist. What the EIGHTish person perceives as weakness is his natural interdependence on the rest of creation and the loss of the sense of personal identity that comes when we relax into a larger sense of who we are within the wholeness of creation. The longer they try to hold themselves above and apart from the whole, the more the EIGHT finds themselves in a doomed battle with the Will of the Universe for them to live in harmony (NINE) with the rest of creation.

Hero's Journey — *The Road Back / Resurrection / Return with the Elixir*

Ancient Romans knew the importance of helping soldiers return to ordinary society. Upon their return from battle, the soldiers were ceremoniously helped to remove armor and surrender weapons. They spent time in quarantine, so they could let go of the special identity of the warrior and remember their place in the community and how to reintegrate into society.

We can think of type EIGHTs as heroes that have returned from battle; they have been functioning in warrior mode for such a long time they have a hard time telling friend from foe. To complete their journey, they must be able recover from their wounds, discover how to resurrect their life in the ordinary world and share the elixir of enlightening discoveries from their journeys with the community they return to.

In the US, and in other countries that sent soldiers to the Vietnam War, there were similar occasions that needed this approach, yet didn't achieve it. Soldiers returning from Vietnam initially were not assisted in making this reentry into society. As a result of this lack of support and reintegration, many of them suffered from PTSD and experienced recurrent flashbacks of the war. They were no longer in the war, yet the war was still in them.

For EIGHTS caught in their compulsion, no matter how welcoming the community might be, it is hard for them to fit in as long as internally they feel like they are still on the battlefield. Modern EIGHTish heroes needs to dedicate themselves to bringing the battle to an end and mastering the new domain of the ordinary world they return to. EIGHTs need to remember they are one of us. After defeating their old demons, they more firmly establish themself in their new identity as the kind of person who no longer is at the mercy of those forces that previously controlled or threatened them. They are freer to then manifest their greater destiny in society.

Stuck in the warrior identity of seeking challenges and opponents to overcome, they start fights just so they can feel like there is a place for them. For a warrior on the battlefield, there is no opportunity to care for their wounds; they just keep fighting off their attackers and avenging their losses.

By returning to wholeness (NINE), a hero's healing journey is completed. Type EIGHTs get 8/9ths of the way but then, rather than letting go of the past and discovering how they can resurrect their lives, they get stuck in thinking of themselves as the warrior who survives all attacks and defeats all enemies. EIGHTs deny themselves the essential quality of peace that lays hurts to rest.

Behind the Bully

Many years ago in Fiji, after a day of scuba diving, I was having a beer with my diving buddy in the lobby of a budget hotel. I eventually discovered that one wing of the hotel was a brothel. A dark shadow seemed to be cast across the room from off to my left and I heard this large presence say in an aggressive voice, "What's your fucking problem, Yank?"

Not thinking it could have anything to do with me, I ignored the question. The shadow loomed closer, repeating the question. I turned to see a big barrel-chested guy, about six-foot-four with biceps about the size of my thighs. I was a bit taken aback, not knowing what to say, and he repeated the question in an even more demanding and intimidating manner.

For whatever reason, I remained very calm, although I was acutely aware of the exit behind me. He bent over and said, "I'm talking to you asshole. What's your problem?" to which I replied, "I don't know." He said, "Don't give me that shit." I looked him in the eye, strangely without any fear and said I really didn't know, adding, "Why don't you tell me?"

Strangely enough, he relaxed slightly, sat down and, within a matter of a few minutes, began to tell me his life story.

As a young man in the 1960s, he had illegally migrated to the U.S. from Honduras. He was arrested on some minor charge and the judge told him could either go to jail and be sent back to whatever hell-hole he came from, or he could join the U.S. Army. He chose the army and went to the war in Vietnam.

He told me of the atrocities he had committed trying to gain some sort of control over the insane circumstances he found there. He welled up with grief over losing his buddies and the men he was in charge of. He told of returning to the U.S. after the war, only to be shunned. He said he'd been hiding out in Fiji ever since. Over the next couple of days, we talked a few more times and I was able to convince him to get in touch with Veteran Affairs and get some support for himself from the Vietnam Veterans Association in the U.S.

Behind EIGHTs' domineering exterior are vulnerable feelings they are unable to trust anyone with. When someone is strong enough to not react to them and not run away, EIGHTs can feel safe enough to open up and return to being part of the human community, rather than standing apart or trying to dominate others.

The Connections from EIGHT to TWO and FIVE

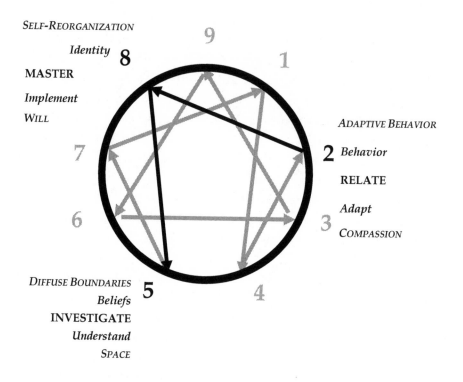

Connection to TWO

Where love rules, there is no will to power; and where power predominates, there love is lacking. The one is the shadow of the other. *Carl Jung*

During periods of integration and stability, type EIGHTs connect more with the qualities of TWO: adaptive behavior, compassion, adaptability, relating and behavior. To help maintain stability, EIGHTs often take pride in doing anything in their power for the few they care about. They like to think of themselves as the one others depend on, the solid rock when everyone and everything else is falling apart. Having people depend on them reinforces the EIGHT's control over them.

When Iraq was under international economic sanctions, instead of weakening Saddam Hussein (an EIGHT), his dictatorship grew more powerful by running an efficient, centralized food distribution service. The population was then dependent on him for nearly all sustenance.

However, while EIGHTs can show great compassion for victims and underdogs, often rescuing or protecting them becomes a thinly veiled excuse for exercising control over their lives. Most despotic rulers claim they must take citizens' rights away so they can provide better protection against possible threats. The EIGHT helps to create and maintain a perception of threatening enemies at the gates by refusing to join and work cooperatively with the larger community. Many people (especially phobic SIXes) naturally turn to a powerful leader in a crisis — a role the 'compassionate' EIGHT is happy to fulfill.

To maintain a sense of control, EIGHTs can be quite adaptable in their behavior. Just when people start settling into routines, EIGHTs do something different, forcing others to adapt. As they have a good sense of what people need and how they will emotionally respond, they are good at using strategies like emotional blackmail to get their way.

By opening their hearts to compassion, EIGHTS remember their connection to others. They feel how their actions affect others. Having power over others evolves into the power to help. EIGHTs learn to adapt organizational skills to meet the needs of the communities to which they belong. Building interdependent relationships consolidates their achievements into self-maintaining systems.

Connection to FIVE

During periods of disintegration and when approaching chaos, type EIGHTs connect more with the qualities of FIVE: diffuse boundaries, space, understanding, investigation and beliefs. As their life falls apart and normally ironclad boundaries weaken, EIGHTs withdraw and guard their personal space. It's hard to contact an EIGHT if they don't want to be reached. If they can't escape, EIGHTs hide vulnerability behind acts of intimidation or by excessively indulging themselves with things like drug and alcoholic binges or sexual promiscuity. It's like they are out to prove they are immune to the dangers that threaten others.

EIGHTs withdraw to gain understanding of how they lost control and what they need to do get it back. If an EIGHT has an argument with someone and they feel they are losing, instead of taking space to examine misperceptions, they merely try to gather or recollect information they can use as ammunition to shoot holes in the other person's argument or reputation. EIGHTs approaching chaos will go to the extent of conducting ruthless investigations to find out who is to blame for their ill fortune. Rather than relying on appropriate institutions, EIGHTs become judge, jury and executioner. Under stress they can become icy-cold, devoid of emotion, and can 'rationally' construct explanations to justify their position and methods of getting justice. Instead of allowing themselves to recognize their intrinsic innocence or the innocence of others, they feel compelled to defend their honor, and exercise their right to be arrogantly superior. Paradoxically, the more they defend their honor at others' expense, the more alienated they become from a sense of community in which they could feel safe.

When EIGHTS embrace spaciousness instead of controlling the space around them, they remember the inherent emptiness of self. They can see the way they have constructed and maintained their identity at the expense of their connection to the rest of humanity. This leads to a softening of personal boundaries, and feeling how inter-connected we all really are.

They remember that they may be an important strand, yet nonetheless, merely a strand in the web of life. In the end, it will not be their will, but *divine will* that enables them to find contentment and inner peace. The connection to FIVE enables them to step back and see the big picture and where they fit in, and reap the benefits of the contributions they have made.

Understanding how type EIGHTs tend to resist the natural processes of change and cling to fixed ideas of themselves helps us to meet them where they get stuck and show them the possibility for greater freedom.

Awakening from the Trance of Personality

The world we see merely reflects our own internal frame of reference — the dominant ideas, wishes and emotions in our minds. "Projection makes perception". We look inside first, decide the kind of world we want to see and then project that world outside, making it the truth as we see it. We make it true by our interpretations of what it is that we are seeing. If we are using perception to justify our own mistakes — our anger, our impulses to attack, our lack of love in whatever form it may take — we will see a world of evil, destruction, malice, envy and despair. All this we must learn to forgive, not because we are being "good" and "charitable", but because what we are seeing is not true. We have distorted the world by our twisted defenses, and are therefore seeing what is not there. As we learn to recognize our perceptual errors, we also learn to look past them or 'forgive' them. At the same time we are forgiving ourselves, looking past our distorted self-concepts to the Self that God created in us and as us. *A Course in Miracles*

No matter what phase of the Enneagram our personality identifies with, that identification eventually causes us to suffer. Instead of merely coping in our habitual ways, every time we become aware of suffering we have the opportunity to free ourselves from limiting habits and embrace the essential wholeness of our evolving nature.

The more people trust their essential wholeness, the more easily they flow through the phases of change. Through accessing the full spectrum of human qualities, their personality type becomes less and less obvious. At the same time, however, everyone has resources associated with their Enneagram type and a role to play within the larger ecology of the communities and organizations suited to their particular strengths.

NINEs will help maintain systems and mediate conflict. ONEs will raise awareness of the need for reforms. TWOs will support those in power to try to address the needs of those in need. THREEs will work hard to optimize the success of the organization. FOURs will see in inadequacies of the existing structure and find creative ways of addressing deeper values. FIVEs will be good at developing a deeper understanding of how things work, and what is and isn't essential. SIXes will be loyal participants who can also trouble shoot possible pitfalls and question old paradigms. SEVENs will tend to be the new ideas people who can help by experimenting with new possibilities. EIGHTs will tend to fall into leadership roles and help make things happen. In this way, essential wholeness is found in us individually and collectively.

We are not our compulsions of personality; we are spiritual beings experiencing the ever-changing nature of creation. The more we open to our true nature, the more we utilize and demonstrate the full spectrum of qualities represented by the Enneagram.

REFERENCES

1   Hayes, Steven C., Kirk D. Strosahl & Kelly G. Wilson (2003). *Acceptance and Commitment Therapy: An Experiential Approach to Behavior Change.* New York: The Guilford Press.

2   Miller, S. D., Duncan, B. L., & Hubble, M. A. (2005*). Outcome-informed clinical work. In J. C. Norcross, & M. R. Goldfried (Eds.), Handbook of psychotherapy integration* (2nd ed., pp. 84-102). New York: Oxford.

3   Norcross, J. C., & Goldfried, M. R. (Eds.). (2005). *Handbook of psychotherapy integration (2nd ed.)* p. 8. New York: Oxford.

4   Norcross, J. C., & Goldfried, M. R. (Eds.). (2005) *Handbook of psychotherapy integration (2nd ed.).* New York: Oxford.

5   Messer, S. B. (1992). *A critical examination of belief structures in integrative and eclectic psychotherapy. In J. C. Norcross, & M. R. Goldfried, (Eds.), Handbook of psychotherapy integration (pp. 130–165).* New York: Basic Books

6   Wilber, Ken, (2000) *Collected Works of Ken Wilber Vol VIII (Introduction).* Boston: Shambhala Publications

7   Lama Ole Nydahl: Mahamudra: Boundless Joy and Freedom. (1991) Nevada City: Blue Dolphin Publishing

8   Rinpoche, Sogyal, (1992) *Tibetan Book of Living and Dying.* San Francisco: Harper Collins

9   Bays, Brandon, (2001). *The Journey: A Road Map to the Soul.* New York: Simon and Schuster

10 Hall, L. Michael, (2001) *Meta-Masters, NS-NLP Mater Practitioner, The Master Prac. Course.* Clifton, Colorado: Neuro-Semantics Publications

11 Almaas, A.H., (2000) *The Void: Inner Spaciousness and Ego Structure (2nd Ed.)* Boston: Shambhala Publications

12 Andreas, Connie Rae, & Andreas, Tamara (1994) *Core Transformation: Reaching the Wellspring Within.* Moab, Utah: Real People Press

13 Bateson, Gregory, (1988) *Mind and Nature, A Necessary Unity.* New York: Bantam Books

14 Luoma, Jason, Hayes, Steven & Walser, Robyn, (2007) *Learning ACT, An Acceptance & Commitment Therapy Skills- Training Manual for Therapists.* Oakland: New Harbinger

15 Siegel, Daniel J., (2010) *The Mindful Therapist, A Clinician's Guide to Mindsight and Neural Integration,* New York: W. W. Norton & Co

16 Siegel, Daniel J., (2010) *The Mindful Therapist, A Clinician's Guide to Mindsight and Neural Integration,* W. W. Norton & Co, New York kindle (p. 2586)

17 Siegel, Daniel J., (2010) *The Mindful Therapist, A Clinician's Guide to Mindsight and Neural Integration,* New York: W. W. Norton & Co kindle (pp. 2671 -72)

18 Almaas, A.H., (1990) *A Pearl Beyond Price, Integration of personality into Being: an Object Relations Approach,* Berkeley, Diamond Books

19 Schucman, Helen, (1985) *A Course in Miracles,* New York: Viking, Foundation for Inner Peace (p. 54)

20 Dhammika, Bhante Dhammavadaka http://www.dhammawiki.com/index.php?title=Dhammavadaka

21 http://www.spiraldynamics.org/aboutsd_overview.htm

22 *Introduction to the Enneagram,* Copyright: The Enneagram Institute 1998-2013. http://www.enneagraminstitute.com/intro.asp#levels

23 Kauffman, Stuart, (1995) *At Home in the Universe, The Search for Laws of Self-Organization and Complexity.* New York: Oxford University Press, (p. 208)

24 Margulis, Lynn (1998) *Symbiotic Planet: A New Look at Evolution,* New York: Basic Books, (p. 85)

25 Capra, Fritjof, (1996) *The Web of Life, A New Synthesis of Mind and Matter.* London: HarperCollins (p. 5)

26 Suzuki, David & McConnell, Amanda (1997) *The Sacred Balance, Rediscovering our Place in Nature.* Vancouver: Allen Unwin (p. 26)

27 Wilber, Ken, (1997) *The Eye of Spirit, An Integral Vision for a World Gone Slightly Mad.* Boston: Shambhala Publications (p. 1)

28 Johnson, George (1995) Fire *in the Mind: Science, Faith, and the Search for Order.* New York: Knopf, Vintage Paperback (pp. 251–2)

29 Kauffman, Stuart, (1995) *At Home in the Universe; The Search for Laws of Self-Organization and Complexity.* New York: Oxford University Press (p. 112)

30 Margulis, Lynn (1998) *Symbiotic Planet: A New Look at Evolution.* New York: Basic Books (p. 111)

31 Maturana, Humberto R. (1970) *Biology of Cognition.* Biological Computer Laboratory Research Report BCL 9.0. Urbana IL: University of Illinois, 1970. As Reprinted in: *Autopoiesis and Cognition: The Realization of the Living* Dordecht: D. Reidel Publishing Co., 1980, (p. 5)

32 Kauffman, Stuart, (1995) *At Home in the Universe; The Search for Laws of Self-Organization and Complexity.* New York: Oxford University Press, (p. 200)

33 Rossi, Ernest edited by Rossi Kathryn Lane (1996) *The Symptom Path to Enlightenment, The New Dynamics of Self-Organization in Hypnotherapy: An Advanced Manual for Beginners.* Pacific Palisades, California: Palisades Gateway (p. 43)

34 Emerson, William: *The Vulnerable Prenate* reprinted from: *Int. J. Prenatal and Perinatal Psychology and Medicine,* Vol. 7, No. 3, (pgs. 271–284).

35 Hamzelou, Jessica, *If mum is happy and you know it, wave your fetal arms* New *Scientist* 16 March 2010, issue 2751.

36 Luoma, Jason, Hayes, Steven & Walser, Robyn, (2007) *Learning ACT, An Acceptance & Commitment Therapy Skills- Training Manual for Therapists.* Oakland: New Harbinger

37 Kauffman, Stuart, (1995) *At Home in the Universe; The Search for Laws of Self-Organization and Complexity.* New York: Oxford University Press,

38 Webster's Revised Unabridged Dictionary (1913) (web1913)

39 Adyashanti, http://www.adyashanti.org/cafedharma/

40 Capra, Fritjof, (1996) *The Web of Life, A New Synthesis of Mind and Matter.* London: HarperCollins

41 Kauffman, Stuart, (1995) *At Home in the Universe; The Search for Laws of Self-Organization and Complexity.* New York: Oxford University Press, (p. 204)

42 Gary Chapman (2004). *The Five Love Languages: How to Express Heartfelt Commitment to Your Mate (new edition).* Birmingham: Northfield Press.

43 Webster's Revised Unabridged Dictionary (1913) (web1913) www.websters-online-**dictionary**.org/

44 Webster's Revised Unabridged Dictionary (1913) (web1913) www.websters-online-**dictionary**.org/

45 American Heritage Dictionary, ah**dictionary**.com/

46 Green, Brian, (1999) The Elegant Universe, *Superstrings, Hidden Dimensions, and the Quest for the Ultimate Theory.* New York: Vintage Books (p.50–51)

47 Capra, Fritjof (1996) *The Web of Life, A New Synthesis of Mind and Matter.* London: HarperCollins (p.261)

48 Andreas, Connie Rae, & Andreas, Tamara (1994) *Core Transformation: Reaching the Wellspring Within.* Moab, Utah: Real People Press

49 Yeshe, Lama Thupten The Bliss of Inner Fire, Heart Practice of the Six Yogas of Naropa. Boston: Wisdom Publications (p. 77)

50 Yeshe, Lama Thupten The Bliss of Inner Fire, Heart Practice of the Six Yogas of Naropa. Boston: Wisdom Publications (p. 79)

51 Rinpoche, Sogyal, (1992) *The Tibetan Book of Living and Dying,* San Francisco: Harper San Francisco (pp. 57–58)

52 Rinpoche, Sogyal, (1992) *The Tibetan Book of Living and Dying,* San Francisco: Harper San Francisco (p. 61)

53 Nydahl, Ole & Nydahl, Hanna, (2007), *16th Karmapa Meditation booklet*, Darmstag: Buddhismus Stiftung Damantweg

54 Friedman, S. Morgan *Albert Einstein Online www.einstein-online.info/*

55 Rinpoche, Sogyal, (1992) *The Tibetan Book of Living and Dying*, San Francisco: Harper San Francisco (p. 64)

56 Rinpoche, Sogyal, (1992) *The Tibetan Book of Living and Dying*, San Francisco: Harper San Francisco (p. 67)

57 Seng'Ts' An, translated by Newton, Steven (2014) *Affirming Faith in Mind*, (www.zentexts.org/faithmnd.html)

58 Seng'Ts' An, translated by Watson, Burton, from Edited by Bercholz, Samuel and Kohn, Sherab Chodzin (1993) *Entering the Stream, An Introduction to the Buddha and His Teachings*. Boston: Shambhala (pp. 148–9)

59 Glossary *Entering the Stream, An Introduction to the Buddha and His Teachings*. Boston: Shambhala (p.323)

60 Rinpoche, Sogyal, (1992) *The Tibetan Book of Living and Dying*, San Francsco: Harper San Francisco (p.67)

61 Nydahl, Ole & Nydahl, Hanna, (2007), The *16th Karmapa Meditation booklet*, Darmstag: Buddhismus Stiftung Damantweg

62 Rinpoche, Sogyal, (1992) *The Tibetan Book of Living and Dying*, San Francisco: Harper San Francisco (p. 69)

63 Castaneda, Carlos (1998) *The Active Side of Infinity*, London: Thomsons of HarperCollins (pp. 72–3)

64 Rinpoche, Sogyal, (1992) *The Tibetan Book of Living and Dying*, San Francisco: Harper San Francisco (p. 72)

65 Seng'Ts'An, translated by Dunn, Philip & Jourdan, Peter (2002) from *The Book of Nothing*. Kansas City: Andrews McMeel (http://terebess.hu/english/hsin.html)

66 Seng'Ts' An, translated by Mater Sheng-yen (1987) Faith in Mind, With a Guide to Ch'an Practice. Dharma Drum Publicatons, DharmaNet Edition (1994) (http://www.angelfire.com/nc/prann/faithinmind.html)

67 Rumi, Jelaluddin, edited by Stephen Mitchell (1989) *The Enlightened Heart, An Anthology of Sacred Poetry*. New York: HarperCollins (p. 59)

68 Moore, Thomas (1994) *Care of the Soul: a guide for cultivating depth and sacredness in everyday life*. New York: HarperPerennial (p. 87)

69 Bateson, Gregory (1973) *Steps to an Ecology of Mind*. Bungay, Great Britain: Paladin (p. 315).

70 Capra, Fritjof (1996) *The Web of Life, A New Synthesis of Mind and Matter*. London: HarperCollins (p. 89)

71 Rossi, Ernest edited by Rossi, Kathryn Lane (1996) *The Symptom Path to Enlightenment, The New Dynamics of Self-Organization in Hypnotherapy: An Advanced Manual for Beginners*. Pacific Palisades, California: Palisades Gateway

72   Jung, Carl, from Rossi, Ernest edited by Rossi Kathryn Lane (1996) *The Symptom Path to Enlightenment, The New Dynamics of Self-Organization in Hypnotherapy: An Advanced Manual for Beginners.* Pacific Palisades, California: Palisades Gateway (p. 173)

73   Whyte, David (2001) *Crossing the Unknown Sea Work as a Pilgrimage of Identity* New York: Riverhead (p. 80)

74   Schnarch, David, M. (1991) *Constructing the Sexual Crucible, An Integration of Sexual and Marital Therapy.* New York: W.W. Norton & Co (p. 114) (originally from Friedman, 1990)

75   Capra, Fritjof (1996) *The Web of Life, A New Synthesis of Mind and Matter.* London: HarperCollins (p. 177)

77   Capra, Fritjof (1996) *The Web of Life, A New Synthesis of Mind and Matter.* London: HarperCollins (p. 226)

78   Campbell, Joseph *The Power of Myth*

79   ² Kelly, G.A. (1969) *The Psychology of Personal Constructs: The selected papers of George Kelly* (B. Maher, Ed). New York: Wiley (p. 19)

80   White, Michael (2005) Workshop Notes Published on www.dulwichcentre.com.au September 21st 2005

81   Vogler, Christopher (1998) *The Writers Journey, Mythic Structure for Storytellers and Screenwriters.* London: Pan Books

82   Vogler, Christopher (1998) *The Writers Journey, Mythic Structure for Storytellers and Screenwriters.* London: Pan Books (p. 88)

83   Vogler, Christopher (1998) *The Writers Journey, Mythic Structure for Storytellers and Screenwriters.* London: Pan Books (p. 15)

84   Edited by Bercholz, Samuel and Kohn, Sherab Chodzin (1993) *Entering the Stream, An Introduction to the Buddha and His Teachings.* Boston: Shambhala (p. 7)

85   Vogler, Christopher (1998) *The Writers Journey, Mythic Structure for Storytellers and Screenwriters.* London: Pan Books (p. 121)

86   Vogler, Christopher (1998) *The Writers Journey, Mythic Structure for Storytellers and Screenwriters.* London: Pan Books (p. 20)

87   Vogler, Christopher (1998) *The Writers Journey, Mythic Structure for Storytellers and Screenwriters.* London: Pan Books (p. 22)

88   Vogler, Christopher (1998) *The Writers Journey, Mythic Structure for Storytellers and Screenwriters.* London: Pan Books (p. 25)

89   Satir, Virginina; http://thinkexist.com/quotation/over_the_years_i_have_developed_a_picture_of_what/339322.html

90   http://www.encyclopedia.com/topic/Enthusiasm.aspx

Eric definitively captures the essence of integration in this treatise on psychotherapy and spirituality. This impressive work well demonstrates the many layers of understanding and experience that are necessary for psychotherapists attempting to navigate the challenges inherent in working wholistically. Eric expresses the deep appreciation of the human condition that can only come from many years of self-reflection, learning and practice as a therapist. Anyone fortunate enough to encounter Eric, either as a reader of this enthralling work or as his clients in psychotherapy will undoubtedly benefit in significant ways.

—Lionel Davis, psychologist, educator and
founder of the Australian College of Applied Psychology

Fascinating reading for anyone interested in the evolution of human consciousness, fractals and their spiraling reflection in the Enneagram. Anyone wanting to gain a deeper understanding where this entropic chaos is going to lead us in the 21st century will love it. This book will become a classic, as did Ken Wilber's Atman Project in the 1980s.

—Horst Peinecke,
Hons Psychology (Hamburg University)

I had used the Enneagram off and on over the past 20 years, but you assisted me to be "enlightened" about it again and see more potential than previously.

—Karel Wearne, Psychologist,
Career Consultant and Executive Coach

I have never been a fan of the Enneagram, and when I revisited it the other day after seeing your presentation, I could see why. You have made it much more interesting, genuinely useable and palatable. The way in which you have woven the elements of the Enneagram into the Buddha's journey to enlightenment is very interesting, and I can see could be a very beneficial framework to use with clients. I will very much look forward to getting a copy of your book.

—Barbara Jones, Psychotherapist and
Director Executive Mandala Coaching